Selected Poems
of Herman Melville

SELECTED POEMS OF
HERMAN MELVILLE

A Reader's Edition

EDITED, WITH AN INTRODUCTION,

BY *Robert Penn Warren*

FRONTISPIECE BY

Barry Moser

A Nonpareil Book

DAVID R. GODINE · *Publisher* · *Boston*

This is a *Nonpareil Book*
Published in 2004 by
David R. Godine, Publisher
Post Office Box 450
Jaffrey, New Hampshire 03452
www.godine.com

First published in the United States of America
by Random House, New York, in 1970

First Nonpareil edition published 2004

The Introduction first appeared, in a different form,
in *The Southern Review*

LCCN 2004105559

ISBN 1-56792-269-4

First Printing
PRINTED IN THE UNITED STATES OF AMERICA

To

John & Anne

Hollander

A Note on This Book

I have called this book *A Reader's Edition*, and the reader I refer to is myself. The book may be regarded as a log of my long reading of Melville's poetry—of my preferences and prejudices, my impressions and speculations, my curiosities and investigations. To some eyes, the book will appear, no doubt, as whimsical and badly proportioned, even eccentric. But I have dared to hope that, in the end, a true account of my experience with the poetry might be as useful as an edition designed for some idealized norm of "the reader." And if some real reader finds a comment not to his taste, or some line of investigation not to his need, he can always go back to the poetry—which is where he ought to be in the end, anyway.

As for the value of that poetry, there is no unanimity of opinion. Randall Jarrell, in "Some Lines from Whitman," says: "Whitman, Dickinson, and Melville seem to me the best poets of the nineteenth century in America." I should agree with him (with perhaps Whittier and Poe to limpingly fight it out for fourth place). But I should record the long pause and sober re-appraisal of the poetry and of my feelings which were forced on me by Edmund Wilson, who, in *Patriotic Gore*, calls *Battle-Pieces* "versified journalism: a chronicle of the patriotic feelings of an anxious middle-aged non-combatant as, day by day, he reads the bulletins from the front";* and by Allen Tate, who, in a letter, dismisses Melville's poetry as of little more than "historical interest."

General acceptance of a more or less rigidly articulated

* For the chronology of the writing of the poems see Introduction, pp. 10–11.

estimate of any poet's work is likely to indicate, not so much the happy discovery of truth, as a widespread atrophy of the critical sense. The work of any good poet invites constant re-interpretation and re-evaluation, and the vitality of that process is an index to the vitality of the work. Certainly, Melville's work is inviting more and more of this sort of attention; and certainly, I do not offer *A Reader's Edition* as more than (and I hope not less than) a seriously meditated remark in what is bound to be a continuing and widening conversation. If this reader has learned anything from the reading of Melville, it is the depth, complexity, and shadowy interfusion of values in poetry; "poetic value" is not a simple thing, but always a resultant of forces, a compound of elements.

"Poetic value" has not been, however, the only consideration in choosing the poems presented here. I have included the poems that I admire most, but I have also included those—and there are many of them—that exhibit only by fits and starts the poet's power. And I have included certain pieces that in themselves offer little poetic attraction, but instruct us about what Melville was struggling toward or about the ideas and attitudes that fueled the poetry.

For all but three of the poems included here we have a printed text which Melville saw through the press, and, in some instances, revised in the margin of his books. For all of these poems, I have followed, except for typographical errors, the text as printed, reporting in the notes Melville's revisions (or possible revisions, for he did not always make a firm decision). For the pieces not published in Melville's lifetime, I have used the manuscript in the Houghton Library.

I have, as a matter of fact, consulted the manuscripts of all poems for which they are available. Even for poems which Melville saw through the press, the manuscript can, when we face the problem generated by a page ending, often establish the break between sections or stanzas, and sometimes, as with "After the Pleasure Party," resolve a deeper problem of structure. Furthermore, the manuscripts and proofs sometimes give considerable insight into Melville's method of composition; and I have recorded in the notes what I regard as the more instructive examples.

In notes on matters other than textual, I have tried, according to the occasion, to do several things. I have tried, in *Battle-Pieces* for example, to see what caught the imagination of Melville in a particular engagement—sometimes an engagement that for us has lost all significance; and when his poem has relation to the *Rebellion Record*, to point out what background may be found there. For his work in general, often including the prose, I have tried to indicate something of the repetition, development, and inter-relation of themes, and thus to outline, to some extent, the growth of his thought and feeling. For particular poems, there are, as usual, questions of interpretation, and many of these I have treated in the notes. Throughout, I have tried to deal with the usual problems of annotation.

I should, perhaps, make special reference to "Billy in the Darbies," which—this time not in the notes but in the Introduction—may seem to be treated at inordinate length; here I was, as usual, keeping a log of my interests, but here the interest can, I think, be amply justified on impersonal grounds. The meaning of the poem cannot be fruitfully discussed without discussing the novel of which it is a part, and the novel cannot be discussed without reference to its history and its relation to Melville's personal life.

It is natural that I should have many debts to acknowledge, and I take pleasure in doing so. I have drawn freely on the work of previous editors and critics, and have gratefully recorded, I hope, all such instances. But I owe special thanks to Robert Ryan and Merton M. Sealts, Jr., for direct and courteous help on a special point; and to Willard Thorp, Charles Feidelson, Jr., R. W. B. Lewis, Cleanth Brooks, Dr. Albert Rothenberg, Dr. Henry A. Murray, John Hollander, Allen Tate, René Wellek, and Albert Erskine, who have read the work at one stage or another, and have done what they could to pull my chestnuts out of the fire. I hope that I have not thrown too many of those chestnuts back in.

I wish to thank, too, Donald Gallup, of the Beinecke Library at Yale, and William H. Bond and the staff of the Houghton Library at Harvard, for kindnesses well beyond the call of duty. And I should thank the Houghton Library for permission to reprint the manuscript material found here.

R. P. W.
West Wardsboro, Vermont
February 15, 1970

Contents

A Note on This Book *vii*
Introduction *3*

FROM *Battle-Pieces and Aspects of the War*

The Portent 91
Misgivings 92
The Conflict of Convictions 93
The March into Virginia 96
Ball's Bluff 98
Dupont's Round Fight 99
The Stone Fleet 100
Donelson 102
The Temeraire 117
A Utilitarian View of the Monitor's Fight 120
Shiloh 122
Malvern Hill 123
Battle of Stone River, Tennessee 125
The House-top 127
The Armies of the Wilderness 128
On the Photograph of a Corps Commander 136
The Swamp Angel 137
The College Colonel 139
"The Coming Storm" 141
"Formerly a Slave" 142
On the Slain Collegians 143

America 145
The Fortitude of the North 147
Inscription 148
An Uninscribed Monument 149
A Requiem 150
On a Natural Monument 151
Commemorative of a Naval Victory 152
The Scout toward Aldie 153
Lee in the Capitol 180
A Meditation 187
SUPPLEMENT 190

FROM *Clarel*

FROM PART I: JERUSALEM

I : *The Hostel* 203
IV : *Of the Crusaders* 208
XVII : *Nathan* 209

FROM PART II: TH EWILDERNESS

IV : *Of Mortmain* 219
XXII : *Concerning Hebrews* 223
XXVII : *Vine and Clarel* 228
XXII : *The Inscription* 232
XXXIV : *Mortmain Reappears* 235
XXXVI : *Sodom* 237
XXXIX : *Obsequies* 241

FROM PART III: MAR SABA

V : *The High Desert* 246

FROM PART IV: BETHLEHEM

XX : *Derwent and Ungar* 251
XXI : *Ungar and Rolfe* 255
XXX : *The Valley of Decision* 259

XXXI : *Dirge* 264
XXXII : *Passion Week* 265
XXXIII : *Easter* 268
XXXIV : *Via Crucis* 270
XXV : *Epilogue* 272

FROM *John Marr and Other Stories with Some Sea-Pieces*

John Marr 277
Bridegroom Dick 285
Tom Deadlight 302
Jack Roy 305
The Haglets 307
The Man-of-War Hawk 315
Old Counsel 316
The Tuft of Kelp 317
The Maldive Shark 318
To Ned 319
Crossing the Tropics 321
The Berg 322
FROM *Pebbles* 324

FROM *Timoleon, Etc.*

After the Pleasure Party 327
The Ravaged Villa 333
Monody 334
Art 335
Venice 336
In a Bye-Canal 337
In a Church of Padua 339
FROM *The Parthenon* 340

FROM *Uncollected Poems*

Immolated 343
Pontoosuce 344

Jonah's Song (FROM *Moby Dick*) 348
Billy in the Darbies (FROM *Billy Budd*) 349

Chronology 453
Index of Titles and First Lines 455
General Index 458

Selected Poems *of* Herman Melville

Introduction

In the fall of 1851, *Moby Dick* appeared, first in England, and shortly thereafter in the United States. Herman Melville was now thirty-two years old, with glamorous adventures and five books behind him. He was already famous, was a success, and now could reasonably expect greater fame and success. At this moment it could matter little that, upon beginning *Moby Dick*, Melville had been in debt to his publishers, and after finishing the novel, was drained by the prodigious effort (he wrote the book in fifteen months); but debt and exhaustion must have meant nothing in the face of his hope, confirmed by Hawthorne's letter of comprehending praise, that he had produced his masterpiece.

But *Moby Dick*, in spite of a few favorable reviews, was a public failure. Almost immediately, not allowing himself to recuperate from the effort of *Moby Dick*, Melville plunged into the composition of *Pierre; or, the Ambiguities*—a work which seemed designed in arrogant perversity to compound the failure of *Moby Dick*. With a stubborn angry energy, streaked, no doubt, by desperation, Melville produced in the next five years two novels, *Israel Potter* and *The Confidence Man*, as well as such shorter pieces as "Bartleby the Scrivener," "The Encantadas," and "Benito Cereno." It was all useless. The world had had enough of Herman Melville; the name was dead some forty years before the man, and if people came to the lectures which, in financial desperation, he undertook for three lecture seasons, they came not to hear the author of *Moby Dick* but to gawk at the adventurer who had sported with pagan beauties and lived among cannibals.

Melville was to write no more fiction until the very end of his life, when, in a kind of Indian summer, he produced *Billy Budd.*

If we are completely to understand Melville's poetry, we must see it against the backdrop of his defeat as a writer, from which he suffered not only the pangs of disappointment and rejection, but the associated distress of ill health, disturbance of vision, and undoubtedly, since his father, after failure, had died mad, the fear of madness. He had reached the hour which he had described in *Pierre,* the time when a man "learns that in his obscurity and indigence humanity holds him a dog and no man," and even the harder hour "when he learns that in his infinite comparative minuteness and abjectness, the gods do likewise despise him." We must see Melville's poetry, too, against the backdrop of grim fortitude and sporadic gaiety, perhaps even grimmer, with which he met the failure; for he clung to the thought, again expressed in *Pierre,* that only after man has passed the hour of total rejection may his soul be "born from the world-husk" and learn to "stand independent."

While running before the spanking breeze of his great creative period, Melville, in *White-Jacket,* had written: "Sailor or landsman, there is some sort of Cape Horn for all. Boys! beware of it; prepare for it in time. Graybeards! thank God it is passed." And among the late poems there is this short but significant one:

Old Counsel of the Young Master
of a Wrecked California Clipper

Come out of the Golden Gate,
Go round the Horn with streamers,
Carry royals early and late;
But, brother, be not over-elate—
All hands save ship! has startled dreamers.

Melville's poetry belongs to that second half of his life after he had rounded his Horn and was trying to beat north to a latitude where peace might, at last, be possible. The theme was to be with him to the end.

Meanwhile, part of the effort Melville made to master his fate, and himself, was a trip, in 1856, on the charity of his father-in-law, to Europe and the Holy Land. The family presumably saw travel merely as a distraction from overwork and self-absorbed brooding, and the trip most likely did benefit Melville in such obvious commonsensical ways. In his ill-starred venture on the lecture platform two of his offerings were to be "Roman Statuary" and "Traveling, Its Pleasures, Pains, and Profits." But Melville sought more than subjects for lectures; in the journey to the Holy Land Melville saw, or came to see, a symbolic import. He was a seeker of ultimates, a hater of illusion. On his way to the Holy Land, Melville had his last encounter with the admired Hawthorne, who, according to Melville, had had the courage to repudiate all easy solutions to the tragic problem of life. Now on the dunes of Southport, a watering place near Liverpool, where Hawthorne was consul, they talked of the great questions. In his journal Hawthorne reports the occasion:

> Melville, as he always does, began to reason of Providence and futurity, and of everything that lies beyond human ken, and informed me that he had "pretty much made up his mind to be annihilated"; but still he does not seem to rest in the anticipation; and I think, will never rest until he gets hold of a definite belief.

Melville had touched bottom, and he was now seeking a belief by which life could be considered and his own life rebuilt; and his poetry, in one dimension, may be read as a record of that search.

In his youth Melville had fled from the Western World

into a land of savage and innocent beauty, an Eden lost in the misty time before civilization. But now, after his Cape Horn, he was going back to touch base at the spot which had been the seedbed of the spiritual life of that Western World. As the Pacific Eden had given him a vision of "natural" joy, out of time, in contrast to the world of modern civilization, so his journey to the Holy Land gave him the vision of man's effort to reach, out of time, the joy of supernatural certainties, in contrast again with the dubieties and flickering aims of modernity. The two adventures gave him the poles of his thought and art in "nature" and "spirit." What meaning or reconciliation could men find in nature? What in the spirit?

The experience of that journey to the Holy Land underlies the epic poem *Clarel*, but the poem itself, however early it may have been meditated, or even begun,[1] did not appear until 1876. Meanwhile, perhaps even during the journey, but certainly in the period just after, Melville turned to writing a group of short poems which, though less explicitly than *Clarel*, are concerned with the past of Western civilization. When, in 1860, he went on a voyage to San Francisco on the Boston Clipper *Meteor*, commanded by his younger brother Thomas, he left a manuscript in his wife's hands with the charge that she find a publisher. Elizabeth Melville failed. It was not until *Timoleon* (1891) that these pieces appeared under the heading "Fruit of Travel Long Ago."

But Melville had, as a matter of fact, written poems long before those belatedly gathered for *Timoleon*, for scattered in *Mardi* are twenty-two poems. Among them, however, there is only one flash of poetry. In "Like the Fish" occurs the line "Like the fish of the bright and twittering fin," and the word *twittering* converts the line into poetry. But one bright phrase would seem a frail promise for a career as a poet.

By the time of *Moby Dick* Melville had indeed become a poet, not only in the powerful conceptions but also in the thousands of vivid images and rhythms; the images and rhythms, however, were absorbed into the texture of his prose, and not offered with the concentration and focus of verse. Even the one exception, now known as "Jonah's Song," which opens with the wonderful rhetoric of "The ribs and terrors of the whale," and which gives a germinal statement of one of Melville's recurring themes, indicates nothing of the direction Melville would follow in the development of his poetry-in-verse.

The same is generally true of "Fruit of Travel Long Ago." If Melville did revise these pieces in later life, they remain the work of a beginner, a poetry of fits and starts, conventional and often inept. But there are flashes. For instance, these lines, reminiscent of Landor, in the middle of a dull group of little poems on "The Parthenon":

> Your beauty charmed enhancement takes
> In Art's long after-shine.

There are other flashes: Venice "rose in reefs of palaces," and on the Cathedral of Milan

> . . . saints over saints ascend
> Like multitudinous forks of fire.

"In a Church of Padua" presents the "low-sieved voice" coming through the perforated panel of the confessional, and in the last stanza the complex rhythm of its first line uncoils to complete the brilliant image of the confession box, an image which embodies one of Melville's characteristic themes:

> Dread diving bell! In thee inurned
> What hollows the priest must sound,
> Descending into consciences
> Where more is hid than found.

But "In a Bye-Canal" shows us most clearly how Melville was, after all, fumbling toward a style of his own. The first section, some fourteen lines, is purely descriptive—the "swoon of noon" on the canal, the clink of the gondolier's oar against a "palace hoar"; then behind the slats of a window,

> What loveliest eyes of scintillation,
> What basilisk glance of conjuration!

Against the patter of the verse, the playful (or is it merely inept?) rhyme of the last couplet, and the triviality of the scene, is thrust the second section, with its charged rhythm and violent imagery, the plunge into a depth:

> Fronted I have, part taken the span
> Of portents in nature and peril in man.
> I have swum—I have been
> Twixt the whale's black flukes and the white shark's fin,
> The enemy's desert have wandered in . . . .

But there comes another shift. From this seriousness and the driving rhythms the poem returns to the easy and conversational tone of the first section, and ends by presenting, with the wit of *vers de société*, a version of the Petrarchan theme of the "cruel fair."

What Melville is aiming to achieve in this poem is the dramatic variation of tone we find magnificently realized in Marvell's "To His Coy Mistress." [2] Melville fails; there are all kinds of clumsiness, for instance, inversions and inert fillers-out of meter. But the style toward which Melville is here groping in his imitation of seventeenth-century metaphysical poetry, gave him the base for the achievement of his next phase.

*

The first volume of poems which Melville published was *Battle-Pieces and Aspects of the War*, which appeared in 1866. It is, in many ways, a very remarkable document in the history of American poetry, and a remarkable commentary on the moment in American history. It is also to be remarked in the personal history of the author. War, despite suffering and horror, fulfills certain deep-seated needs in men, affords certain releases, offers certain compensations. Men yearn for significance in life, for the thrill of meaning in action, for communion in a common cause, for the test of their fiber, paradoxically for both the affirmation of, and the death of, the self. Even Hawthorne, despite a premature sense of age, a bleak awareness of the loss of his life-sense and of his creative force, and a peculiarly detached and ironical view of the conflict, could say that the Civil War had a "beneficial effect upon my spirits," and that "it was delightful to share in the heroic sentiment of the time, and to feel that I had a country—a consciousness which seemed to make me young again."

The same sense of rejuvenation and the tapping of old, nigh-forgotten energies was what the war brought to Melville. For one thing, his personal failure, with the stultifying effects of self-pity and self-absorption, could be sublimated in the national tragedy, and his own distress, in contrast, could be shrunk to a manageable scale. For a second, but related, thing, the deep divisions of Melville's inner life, from the struggle between his natural skepticism and his yearning for religious certitude, to his sexual tensions, which had found expression in previous work, now found, we may hazard, in the fact of a *civil* war an appropriate image which might, in some degree, absorb and purge their pains. It might even be hazarded that these self-divisions provide a secret grounding for one of the themes that runs through *Battle-Pieces*—the theme of the ironical split between concern with the human being and concern with the idea, between the individual and ideology—and that in the objectification of that theme the self-divisions themselves were reduced and energy released for creative effort.

In 1861 Melville was forty-two and not in good health.

Active service was not for him. But as Sidney Kaplan has persuasively suggested in his edition of *Battle-Pieces,* Melville was probably nursing the hope of making himself the poet of the war; he was immersing himself in a systematic study of poetry and poetic theory and was, at the same time, following the war with intense concern. There were the newspapers and bulletins, the hodgepodge compilation of the *Rebellion Record,*[3] visits to Fort Hamilton and the Brooklyn Navy Yard, where he heard a lecture on the Dahlgren gun, and the sight of returning soldiers —including William P. Bartlett, who, at the time when Melville was still trying to make a living from his farm Arrowhead in Western Massachusetts, appeared at the head of his troops in Pittsfield, with a leg shot away and an arm in bandages, to provide the inspiration for one of Melville's most powerful poems, "The College Colonel." In 1864, before the Battle of the Wilderness and that summer of great slaughters, Melville managed, through the good offices of Senator Charles Sumner, to get a pass to the Virginia front, where, as Elizabeth Melville reports, he saw "various battlefields and called on Gen. Grant," and where he went on a "scout" which was to give background for "The Scout toward Aldie."

Despite Melville's intense concern with the progress of the war, and despite the fact that *Battle-Pieces* reads like a log of the conflict, running in chronological order from the execution of John Brown to the Reconstruction, very few of the poems were composed before the end of the war. As Melville puts it in a prefatory note, "With a few exceptions, the Pieces in this volume originated in an impulse imparted by the fall of Richmond,"[4] and even then, the actual composition of the poems took place without reference to the chronology of events. Melville goes on to say that the poems are "as manifold as are the moods of involuntary meditation—moods variable and at times widely in variance." And he adds: "I seem, in most of these verses, to have but placed a harp in a window and noted the contrasted airs which vagrant winds have played upon the strings."

All this might be taken to imply that the book is random and inconsequential. But Melville says, "I seem . . . to have but placed"—not "I have . . . but placed"; and his statement is, finally, an affirmation of the inner unity of the book. The "vagrant winds" that touch the harp all blow from Melville's soul, and the "contrasted airs" that play upon the strings constitute a dialectic. The book is not only a log of the war, but a log of Melville's attempt to make sense of his feelings about the war—and about life.

In a very profound way it can be said that the Civil War made Melville a poet. It gave him the right "subject"; and for him the right subject, in prose or poetry, was absolutely essential. For all Melville's metaphysical passion and thirst for ultimates, his creative mind could work only from the stimulation of the concrete, the specific. I do not mean this merely in the sense that all poets, to be poets at all, must be concerned with the physicality of the world. Melville had, in a very special way, a mind that could be truly stirred, be fully engaged, only by what was urgently human, and such a subject had to be come upon in life, had to be torn from actual life, with the raw validation of life.

The Civil War gave Melville the kind of big, athletic, overmastering subject which he always needed for his best work, and it was bloodily certified by actuality. But there was a paradox in Melville's appetite for the violent subject; such a subject would serve his need only if the centrifugal whirl toward violent action was perfectly balanced by the centripetal pull toward an inwardness of apparently unresolvable mystery, or tormenting ambiguity. Of such inward issues, this outwardly and violently overmastering subject of the Civil War offered God's—and the devil's—plenty.

This complexity in the subject itself—or, rather, the complexity that Melville saw in the subject—had a deep psychological consistency with the kind of style toward which he had been groping in the recent poems. Now, in *Battle-Pieces,* he achieves his best things not by directly imitating the English Metaphysical poets, but by aiming, however uncertainly, at what we may think of as a metaphysical style of his own, which, though vastly different in effect from that of the English poets of the seventeenth century, shared with their style certain assumptions, and even certain methods. He was aiming at a style rich and yet shot through with realism and prosaism, sometimes casual and open and sometimes dense and intellectually weighted, fluid and various because following the contours of his subject, or rather the contours of his complex feelings about his subject.

For instance, in "The March into Virginia," each section has its own characteristic rhythm, weight of line, syntax, and tone. In the first section, where the subject is generalized and philosophized, we find the passage built up line by line, each line a sort of apothegm. In the second section, presenting the gay march, the characteristic rhythm, based on tetrameter, which had been heavy and clogged before, is brisk and light:

> The banners play, the bugles call,
> The air is blue and prodigal.

Or:

> So they gayly go to fight,
> Chatting left and laughing right.

But set immediately against this is the movement of the last section:

But some who this blithe mood present,
    As on in lightsome files they fare,
Shall die experienced ere three days are spent—
    Perish, enlightened by the vollied glare;
Or shame survive, and, like to adamant,
    The throe of Second Manassas share.

In this section, with the first line we have the heavy succession of monosyllables, with retarded, scarcely resolved accentuation, and then the slow uncoiling of the complex rhythm of the entire passage. But even with this general uncoiling, let us notice that the second line, referring again to the uninstructed gaiety of the march, repeats, as a kind of ironic contrast, the characteristic movement of the second section: "As on in lightsome files they fare." With the next line the meter shifts from tetrameter to pentameter, and then the last three lines go increasingly heavy and retarded, an effect based primarily on a dramatic handling of forced pauses, vowel weighting, and unresolved accentuation.[5]

If we set "The March into Virginia" beside "In a Bye-Canal," we may see a relationship, something of the same anecdotal base for a poem, and of the same structure by divisions on contrasted tone to make stages of development of the subject. But "The March into Virginia" is deeply coherent, dramatically and intellectually. It is ordered, as we have said of "In a Bye-Canal," by a series of contrasts in detail as well as in sections, but how much more weight and subtlety of implication are now involved! The "picnic party" is a march to death. The ignorance and innocence of youth are all that makes war possible (and there is the echo of the Melvillian irony: is it all that makes life possible?); but only in "experience," in knowledge, can the true "adamant" of life be forged. Yet the cost of experience may be death. To take another set of paradoxes, the transitory "rapture" of youthful action is always about to enter "story," to become legend or history, dying, as it were, into significance or glory.[6] The intellectual coherence involving such a set of contrasts is fully accounted for in the dramatic situation.

Furthermore, the phrasing has the same density of references. How brilliant are the lines:

> In Bacchic glee they file toward Fate,
> Moloch's uninitiate.

Significantly, no line could be simpler than: "No berrying party, pleasure-wooed," but "berrying party," with its atmosphere of rural gaiety and innocent sunburned youthfulness, is really a secret, and grim, pun: *burying party*, the echo of the military phrase. Or to turn to another detail, the pleasure that woos the innocent picnickers—the "rapture sharp, though transitory"—is a complex one: vanity, dreams of glory, a dramatic sense of duty, a sense of adventure, the need to test the self, a "glad surmise of battle's unknown mysteries," mysteries which involve death and the "pleasure" of death, with all the overtones of that notion.

Or let us look at the word *enlightened* in the line: "Perish, enlightened by the vollied glare." To perish in the moment of enlightenment, of knowledge—to perish of knowledge, by knowledge, in knowledge, in a blaze of knowledge which, for all its deadliness, is, somehow, a blaze of glory, a glare of glory, with both the benign and inimical implications of the word *glare*.

But what of the last two lines?

We may move toward an answer by remembering a line in "Shiloh" which is to be associated with the "vollied glare": "What like a bullet can undeceive?" The "vollied glare," like the bullet, undeceives the romantic young soldier by the shock of death. This is the end of illusion, for those who survive as well as for those who die of the undeceiving bullet. But those who live through the shock of battle have to live with the shame of a human fear that romantic illusion can never again conquer. The "enlightenment"—one aspect of it at least—is this self-knowledge. But such self-knowledge, if survived literally and morally, is necessary to the forging of the "adamant." Once the nature of the self and the terms of life are clear, one can bear the "throe." So here the theme of the poem goes back to Melville's old obsessive theme. First Manassas is like the Horn that must be rounded if man is to be fully man. And here we may remember that the Second Manassas, like the First, was a defeat. But it was a defeat that did not end in a rout.[7]

Few of Melville's poems are as good, as deeply coherent, as "The March into Virginia," but some of the principles of its style do appear rather generally. For example, the use of precise, realistic detail, which was outside the prevailing practice. But not merely the fact of such detail deserves comment; what merits more emphasis is the way in which such prosaic materials are played against the more conventional poetic elements. This contrast occurs at the level of mere vocabulary, for Melville, as Newton Arvin has pointed out in his biography, was given to poeticisms like *fain, deem,* and *wight;* technical terms like *caloric, integral, fraction, escheat, foreclosure;* and coined words like *rugged* (covered as with a rug), *vowelled, sliddery* (as in the sliddery ledges of ice in "The Berg").

Vocabulary is, however, only a starting point for such contrasts. For instance, take the first stanza of "Malvern Hill":

> Ye elms that wave on Malvern Hill
>   In prime of morn and May,
> Recall ye how McClellan's men
>   Here stood at bay?
> While deep within yon forest dim
>   Our rigid comrades lay—
> Some with the cartridge in their mouth,

Others with fixed arms lifted South—
Invoking so
The cypress glades? Ah wilds of woe!

The cartridge clenched in the teeth of a dead man, held there as he prepared for loading, suddenly vivifies the stanza. And we may note, too, how the flattened rhythm of the line strikes across the lyricism of the rest.

The whole of "The Armies of the Wilderness" is based on a system of counterpointing; and one of the elements counterpointed is the sort of realism indicated above. The Federal soldiers look across with a telescope to see a "base-ball bounding sent," and would like to join the game. Or:

By the bubbling spring lies the rusted canteen,
And the drum which the drummer-boy dying let go.

Or:

The wagon mired and cannon dragged
Have trenched their scar. . . .

Long sections of realistic dialogue mark the poem; for instance, these lines spoken by a Confederate prisoner being interrogated by his captors as they overlook the Confederate camp:

". . . on the crest,
The Carolinians; lower, past the glen,
Virginians—Alabamians—Mississippians—Kentuckians
(Follow my finger)—Tennesseans; and the ten
Camps *there*—ask your grave-pits; they'll tell.
Halloa! I see the picket-hut, the den
Where I last night lay."

Over against such passages we find a lyricism like:

Where are the birds and boys?
Who shall go chestnutting when
October returns? The nuts—
O, long ere they grow again.

Such stylistic contrasts are most obvious, of course, when occurring within a single poem, but the principle sometimes appears in the juxtaposition of separate pieces. There are poems like the elaborately lyrical "Shiloh" and poems as scrupulously prosaic, except for rhyme, as "Running the Batteries." The most clearly marked instance of stylistic contrast among poems themselves is in the pairing of two poems suggested by the fight between the *Monitor* and the *Merrimac*—the requiem for the "fighting Temeraire," supposed to be spoken by "an Englishman of the old order," and "A Utilitarian View of the Monitor's Fight." The first poem ends:

> But Fame has nailed your battle-flags—
>   Your ghost it sails before:
> O, the navies old and oaken,
>   O, the Temeraire no more!

The second poem begins, "Plain be the phrase," and the plainness of phrase is part, as it were, of the subject matter of the poem—of "The clangor of that blacksmiths' fray," in which

> . . . all went on by crank,
>   Pivot, and screw,
> And calculations of caloric.

The poem ends with a brilliant metaphor which snatches the poem from the jaws of prose:

> War shall yet be, and to the end;
>   But war-paint shows the streaks of weather;
> War yet shall be, but warriors
>   Are now operatives; War's made
>   Less grand than Peace,
>   And a singe runs through lace and feather.

The poem itself states, as well as illustrates, the assumptions behind Melville's style: a world in which a singe runs through lace and feather demands an appropriate style.

Melville saw, however, another kind of singe running through the lace and feather of life. Every man must confront it, sooner or later, the painful end of illusion, the dire destiny of the passage round the Horn, just as America was confronting it in the Civil War. But not only in the moment of great crisis is there the "singe": in the ordinary course of life, there is a doubleness in things. If Nature seems beneficent and beautiful, that is only one aspect, for, as it is put in "Misgivings," there is "Nature's darker side," and as, in "The Stone Fleet," the sailor says, "Nature is nobody's ally."

Such doubleness lies in history, too. Man is doomed to exert will to control events, but even when he seems to act effectively, the process in which his will operates may be only a mask for a secret process of which he has suspected nothing. So we find it said in "Misgivings," in which, as of 1860, the poet broods on the impending conflict:

> And storms are formed behind the storm we feel:
> The hemlock shakes in the rafter, the oak in the driving
> keel.

And in "The Conflict of Convictions," the wind of History "spins *against* the way it drives." For example, by the victory of "Right" in the Civil War, certain undreamed-of forces may be released so that

> Power unanointed may come—
> Dominion (unsought by the free)
> And the Iron Dome,
> Stronger for stress and strain,
> Fling her huge shadow athwart the main;
> But the Founders' dream shall flee.

But there are other polarities and ambiguities in life. A decision presumably made on idealistic grounds may simply be the reflex of a historical situation. "On the Slain Collegians" shows young men of both North and South "swept by the wind of their place and time." Even if an ethical distinction is to be made at the level of the cause for which war is being waged, at another level such a distinction is irrelevant:

> Warred one for Right, and one for Wrong?
> So be it; but they both were young—
> Each grape to his cluster clung,
> All their elegies are sung.

Each was doomed to cling to his cluster, and in this fact is implicit the polarity of "ideology" ("Law," "Right," or even "Destiny") against human values, human suffering, human aspiration, qualities of personality and spirit.

The human bond may be as important as the bond of ideology. As "On the Photograph of a Corps Commander" puts it:

> Nothing can lift the heart of man
> Like manhood in a fellow-man.

And the fellow-man may be a fellow, not by ideology but only in his manhood. Stonewall Jackson and Lee are noble enemies, are nobly wrong. In "Donelson," we find that the "Rebel," though he is in the wrong, defends "a perverted Bunker Hill." A recognition of the human community is an essential virtue, and the human community is, in one perspective, a community of guilt, as we find in "The Swamp Angel," the poem on the bombardment of Charleston, South Carolina:

> Who weeps for the woeful City
> Let him weep for our guilty kind;
> Who joys at her wild despairing—
> Christ, the Forgiver, convert his mind.

A recognition of the human as distinguished from the ideological makes magnanimity possible, and Melville ends the volume with a poem called "A Meditation," and the lines:

> When Vicksburg fell, and the moody files marched out,
> Silent the victors stood, scorning to raise a shout.

"Man honors man" beyond "cause," as Melville says in "Magnanimity Baffled," knowing, if he is wise, that even the best cause does violence to some values, and that, as William James remarks in "Pragmatism and Religion," after victory "something apparently drastic and bitter always remains in the bottom of the cup."

The most painful polarity of all is that between all values and the blank fact of annihilation. As in "Sheridan at Cedar Creek,"

> There is glory for the brave
> Who lead, and nobly save,
> But no knowledge in the grave
> Where the nameless followers sleep.

But the same fact of annihilation—the subject on which Melville had brooded so much—which appears in this poem as mere blankness may elsewhere be regarded as a peace, with the problem of values in the flux of history resolved, however perilously and equivocally, in the context of natural process. For instance, in "Malvern Hill," the elms remember the horror and heroism of the battle,

> *But sap the twig will fill:*
> *Wag the world how it will,*
> *Leaves must be green in Spring.*

But if death is blankness—or even blankness regarded as elegiac peace—how can values be found in action desperately foredoomed to blankness? The answer is by a stoicism at once self-assertive and self-denying. It is self-assertive in the courage to endure, and by endurance to define its own value, outside of time, as in the poem on the prisoners who died at Andersonville, in Georgia, "On a Natural Monument":

> Their fame is this: they did endure—
> Endure, when fortitude was vain
> To kindle any approving strain
> Which they might hear. To these who rest
> This healing sleep alone was sure.

But stoicism may be self-denying in the will to sink the personal pain in a compassionate and ennobling awareness of the general human lot, as in another poem on a forgotten monument, "An Uninscribed Monument":

> Thou who beholdest, if thy thought,
> Not narrowed down to personal cheer,
> Take in the import of the quiet here—
> The after-quiet—the calm full fraught;
> Thou too wilt silent stand—
> Silent as I, and lonesome as the land.

There is, however, another way of regarding action, another polarity involving it. The act is in time. It is at the knife-edge moment of the present, between the past and the future, and at this moment it both projects and fulfills life. But as the life projected into the future is fulfilled, the act with all its urgencies disappears into the past. Action becomes legend.

This theme is continually implicit in *Battle-Pieces,* but its fullest poetic embodiment is in "Battle of Stone River, Tennessee," which is described in the subtitle as "A View from Oxford Cloisters." Here, half a world away from the battle, a learned don might ironically convert his distance in space into a distance in time, and muse that the present conflict, with all its issues and urgencies, will soon be no more for America than the War of the Roses is for England: "In legend all shall end."

In the very moment of action, action enters into legend:

But Rosecrans in the cedarn glade,
And, deep in denser cypress gloom,
Dark Breckinridge, shall fade away
Or thinly loom.
The pale throngs who in forest cowed
Before the spell of battle's pause,
Forefelt the stillness that shall dwell
On them and on their wars.
North and South shall join the train
Of Yorkist and Lancastrian.

This theme is intimately related to that of the polarity of ideology and human values, as well as to that of ideology and historical necessity:

Our rival Roses warred for Sway—
For Sway, but named the name of Right;
And Passion, scorning pain and death,
Lent sacred fervor to the fight.

In legend, ideology, as well as historical necessity, is bleached out, and we are left to meditate on merely the gestures and stances—the "Passion"—of the old participants: the passion with which they play their roles.

We cannot be too schematic about such polarities as we have been discussing. One pair shades into another. One pole does not cancel out its opposite. All belong to the complex texture of life as lived, to the density and equivocalness of experience. But to live in any full sense demands the effort to comprehend this complexity of texture, this density and equivocalness of experience, and yet not forfeit the ability to act. The man who "sees through it," but who, at the same time, can act, who has a sense of the tragedy of the human plight—that is the hero for Melville. For instance, "The College Colonel":

But all through the Seven Days' Fight,
And deep in the Wilderness grim,

And in the field-hospital tent,
    And Petersburg crater, and dim
Lean brooding in Libby, there came—
    Ah heaven!—what *truth* to him.

Beyond his personal experience and personal heroism and the official celebration, what the young colonel sees through to is the tragic complexity of man's fate, the painful limit of man's rational vision; for one aspect of man's fate is the inevitability of evil, the cost of action, the blind doom which underlies all the superstructures which he erects and must trust in—the secret force which shakes the "oak in the driving keel," or as it is put in "The Apparition," the "unreserve of Ill," the fact that "Solidity's a crust," with a "core of fire below."

In many poems this idea of the ever-presence of evil —evil, shall we say, as the cost of good?—appears; for instance in "Commemorative of a Naval Victory," a poem which one is tempted to call great:

But seldom the laurel wreath is seen
    Unmixed with pensive pansies dark;
There's a light and a shadow on every man
    Who at last attains his lifted mark—
Nursing through night the ethereal spark.
Elate he never can be;
He feels that spirits which glad had hailed his worth,
Sleep in oblivion.—The shark
Glides white through the phosphorous sea.

Many themes are absorbed here into the ghastly whiteness and imperial ease of the gliding shark. More specifically, "The Coming Storm," without the splendid allusiveness of the last poem, states the tragic paradox:

No utter surprise can come to him
    Who reaches Shakspeare's core:
That which we seek and shun is there—
    Man's final lore.

With this stanza we may look at the question of the place of *Battle-Pieces* in the course of Melville's over-all development, and to begin we may turn to a justly celebrated essay, by Henry Alexander Murray, which appears as an introduction to *Pierre; or, the Ambiguities,* which Dr. Murray sees stemming, like *Moby Dick,* from a profound moral conflict in the author's being. He says:

> Moral conflict, if radical and stubborn, results in a division, an inflexible dualism, in all branches of feeling and thought, which so influences the sufferer's apperceptions, that every significant object becomes ambivalent to him, that is, it both attracts and repels him, being composed, as he sees it, of two contrary elements, one good and one evil, which cannot be reconciled or blended. . . .
>
> One whose heart is divided against itself is also determined to interpret every significant situation in which he becomes involved as ambivalent; but here a separation of the two elements may sometimes be effected: the occasion may be apperceived as a choice-point between two paths, one of which must be single-mindedly accepted as true and right, the other wholly rejected as false and wrong. But, after making the seemingly virtuous choice, the man will, sooner or later, begin to see some serious flaw or sin in his elected course, and to recall with self-abasing feelings of regret the merits of the repudiated way. . . .

The end result may be, then, a state of moral paralysis, which accounts for the feeling Pierre discovers, and an inability to discriminate values, which Melville describes as follows:

> For the more that he wrote, and the deeper and the deeper that he dived, Pierre saw the everlasting elusiveness of Truth; the universal lurking insincerity of even the greatest and purest written thoughts.[8]

All has become a dream: "we dream that we dreamed a dream." The frantic and blood-drenched melodrama in which the novel ends is merely an index to the appalling emptiness the hero discovers in his quest for a fundamental meaning in life—and in his own being. And it is usually agreed that between the hero of the novel and the author himself there is a more than ordinary degree of identification, that quite deliberately Melville was writing the most intimate of the several biographies of what Murray calls his "idealized self."

Between *Pierre* and the outbreak of the Civil War lie some ten years of blankness and failure for Melville, and a desperation perhaps approaching madness. We have already remarked that the War was, in a general sense, curative for Melville, but what it most specifically did for him was to lead him to see that the fate of man is to affirm his manhood by action, even in the face of the difficulty of defining truth. Man to be man must try to comprehend the density and equivocalness of experience but at the same time he must not forfeit the ability to act. This is the tragic split in his fate, but at the same time and by the same token it is the challenge to his nobility. In *Pierre,* Melville had depicted a man who, fearing paralysis of the will, drives himself to a frenzy of disastrous action. In "Bartelby," he depicted a man in the grip of that mortal paralysis. *Battle-Pieces,* in which is celebrated the hero who can see the doubleness of life and yet act, may be regarded as the token of Melville's own redemption from the depth into which he had long been staring.

*

Whitman and Melville are the poets of the Civil War, but the difference between them is instructive. Before discussing that difference, I wish, however, to say three things. First, my comparison is of them as poets of the war—though, of course, the poetry of the war cannot be entirely isolated from the body of work of either man. Second, to my mind it is clear that Whitman is the bigger poet. Third, the distinction I am making is, necessarily, one of emphases rather than of absolute differences.

Whitman's poetry of the war I shall call primarily "synthetic." That is, he gives strong representational images—cavalry crossing a ford or a bivouac at night or a dressing station—which draw into focus and unify whatever attitudes and emotions are already available in the reader. If there are tensions and contradictions lurking among these attitudes, such tensions and contradictions are absorbed, purged in the vivid, overmastering immediacy of the image. As for his generalizations and comments, we shall shortly be sampling them. Melville's poetry, on the other hand, is analytic. It does give strong representational images, too; and we have noted Melville's realistic sense, which he shares with Whitman. But Melville often strives to analyze the implications of his images and the attitudes evoked by them; and this interplay of imagery and statement actually exploits the resistance a reader might have to the poem. By way of comparison, we may turn to some of Whitman's poetry not of the war, say in "Song of Myself," and point out that the magnificent and often dramatically moving catalogues of persons and events involve enormous variety and testify to a will to find values in all life and to possess all life, and absorb it. Whitman has the true poetic eye, and poetic sympathy, to present his items without divesting them of their intrinsic and characteristic values, but he never sharpens issues among them that might make possession and absorption difficult. What he does is to celebrate, ultimately, not the items but the will to possess, to absorb. On the other hand, for Melville, the poetry lies in a conflict of values, an inner conflict, and that is what he feels driven, ultimately, to deal with.

To take a simple instance: when Whitman writes a poem about the death letter from the front, the powerful "Come up from the Fields, Father," the family is safely Northern, on a farm in Ohio, and the Northern reader Whitman was writing for could find his patriotism, his selfish interests, and all his human and humane feelings mobilized together and focused in the image—"ritualized." This is not to say that Whitman merely manipulates what are called stock responses in the reader, but it is to say that he was characteristically more concerned with intensity and purity of feeling than with any complexity or painful richness of feeling.

To return to the poem, if Melville had written it, the farm might very well have been in Georgia, and the dead son one of those "Slain Collegians" about whom he did write a poem; then the Northern reader, whose own son had been habitually shot at by the now dead Georgia lad, might have had some divisions of attitude to deal with. Like all decent poetry, that of Melville aims at the moment of poise, of synthesis, but for him the poise and the synthesis are hard-won, and often incomplete and provisional, and the awareness of that fact is the point, the "truth," of the poetry. To summarize, Whitman, in his poems of the War, is ritualistic, Melville is dramatic, ultimately tragic.

The differences we have been talking about in relation to the poetry have some parallel in the difference between their respective brands of Unionism. For Whitman, the Union was a mystique. One aspect of this mystique was, of course, Whitman's democratic faith. Another was his passion for power, not power for himself, but his passion for participation in the power of a unity. In one sense, Whitman welcomed such power merely because it was power, even if he could think of it, too, as susceptible of being "spiritualized" in one way or another, one day or another.

In "Long, Too Long, America," Whitman exhorts America to show the world "what your children en-masse really are." In "Over the Carnage Rose Prophetic a Voice," he says that "affection shall solve the problems of freedom yet," but the reward offered for this achievement is to be power:

> Those who love each other shall become invincible,
> They shall yet make Columbia victorious.

If, in "From Paumanok Starting I Fly Like a Bird," Whitman promises to sing the songs of the individual states, he finds it necessary

> To sing first (to the tap of the war-drum if need be),
> The idea of all, of the Western world one and inseparable.

The "idea of all" becomes, easily, "an idea only," and in "Song of the Banner at Daybreak," Whitman hails the flag waving high in the air as "an idea only"—the pure idea into which all is absorbed, the abstraction in which all distinctions are wiped out:

> Valueless, object of eyes, over all and demanding all—
> (absolute owner of all)—O banner and pennant!
> I too leave the rest—great as it is, it is nothing—houses,
> machines are nothing, I see them not,
> I see but you, O warlike pennant! O banner so broad, with
> stripes, I sing you only,
> Flapping up there in the wind.

On this general point of unity and Union, we may look at Santayana's wickedly astute formulation in "The Poetry of Barbarism." Santayana does not give us the whole truth of Whitman; but what he says is important because by the very obliquity of the angle from which he views the subject, he makes us see so sharply one partial truth which must be reckoned with in any attempt to assess the whole truth. He says that Whitman dreamed of a democracy without distinctions of any kind, where even "Women are to have as nearly as possible the same character as men," and where whatever has kept men apart and "made it impossible for them to be messmates together was to be discarded." On such a basis, of course, unity can exist only by force—or mysticism. To come to Whitman and the Civil War, "when he heard the drum taps so clearly, he could only gaze at the picturesque and terrible aspects of the struggle, and linger among the wounded day after day with a canine devotion; he could not be aroused either to clear thought or to a positive action."

The making of distinctions—that is the very center of Melville's poetry, and of Melville's Unionism. He was a Unionist, but he did not see the Union in mystical terms, or as an absolute, however much a part of his nature may have yearned for that easy solution. There were human values beyond mere unity by the achievement of which the Union must justify itself. Hence, in one perspective at least, the Union could be regarded by Melville as a political arrangement serving certain ends—which it might serve well or ill. As a political arrangement, it might very well, in the ironical course of destiny, change its nature, and the very "power," which Whitman hymned as the blessing to be derived from Union, might well be the bane; and in victory, in power, as we have seen, the "Founders' dream" might flee—a chilling thought that does not disturb Whitman in his poetry of the War, though he does discover some sobering second thoughts in *Democratic Vistas.*

More radically, in "The House-top," the poem on the Draft Riots of 1863 in New York City and their bloody suppression, Melville calls into question the very premise of the democratic faith which was a corollary of Whitman's Unionism. Into the general anarchy, which involved, ironically enough, the widespread lynching of Negroes, "Wise Draco" comes, and with grape-shot from cannon set hub to hub in the streets, corroborated "Calvin's creed" as well as the "cynic tyrannies of honest kings":

. . . the Town, redeemed,
Gives thanks devout; nor, being thankful, heeds
The grimy slur on the Republic's faith implied,
Which holds that Man is naturally good,
And—more—is Nature's Roman, never to be scourged.

William James, in the oration at the dedication of the monument, on the Boston Common, to Robert Gould Shaw and his Negro regiment, the 54th Massachusetts Infantry, says that "the victory to be philosophically prayed for is that of the more inclusive side—the side which even in the hour of triumph will to some degree do justice to the ideals in which the vanquished interests lay." Both Whitman and Melville, both good Unionists, would doubtless have accepted this formulation. But Whitman would have understood it to operate by aggregation, or absorption, and to aim at the wiping out of distinction in the process. Melville would have understood it to operate by an analysis to locate first principles, and by dialectic. We have seen something like this operative in poem after poem, in "The Conflict of Convictions," "The Armies of the Wilderness," "On the Slain Collegians," "The Swamp Angel," "The College Colonel," and "A Meditation." But it appears in many other poems, too. For "clear thought," which Santayana names as one of the two things not granted Whitman to achieve, is at the center of Melville's poetry, the effort to achieve awareness of the distinctions and paradoxes of life and to resolve them.

To that "positive action" which Santayana says Whitman could not be aroused to, Melville, by his positive, masculine, anguished temperament, was committed—committed, we may say, as the very premise of his personal survival. I do not mean to say that, literally, Melville took a more active part in the war, or even to insist on what is obviously true, that Melville had led a more adventurous life. What I mean is that in his fiction he had been concerned with the nature of action and the expense —and affirmation—of spirit in action, and that in the poems of the Civil War he was obsessed with the need to understand the complicated context of what seemed to be a necessary action, and to confront, without refuge in verbal or sentimental solutions, the costs of action.[9] His own yearning for absolutes—including, shall we assume, an absolute of Unionism—was modified by an agonizing awareness of the relativisms of experience. The streak of mysticism in Melville was at war with his ferocious appetite to know. He was a mystic who hated mysticism.

If Melville was, in fact, capable of writing a poem about the America that, after the war, would rise to dominate the world, we must look at what kind of poem it is. In "America" Melville gives us a picture of the standard allegorical female waking from the "foul dream" in which she had seen "earth's foundation bare" (and "slimy" too, if we remember "The Conflict of Convictions"), to stand with "Law on her brow and empire in her eyes."

How drearily *pro forma* all this is! Melville's imagination, with ours, is untouched. The poem might have been written by Longfellow or Lowell to be recited at a victory celebration. Or by Sidney Lanier, Confederate veteran, instead of what he did write, "The Meditation of Columbia," the cantata performed at the opening of the great Centennial in Philadelphia by a chorus of eight hundred voices and an orchestra of a hundred and fifty instruments.[10] "America" does, in fact, have a public and official tone that would have done very well for such an occasion as the Centennial; as its position in the volume *Battle-Pieces* indicates, it is a poem written to resolve—no, gloss over—the very issues raised in the body of the book. Here Melville has substituted ritual—and ritual of a sleazy sort —for insight.

*

The underlying tragic insight of *Battle-Pieces* is, as we have said, the necessity for action in the face of the difficulty of knowing truth. In this situation man becomes fully man only if he submits himself to the complications of the inwardness of life in order to be returned, chastened and enlightened, to the objective world of action. In this case—the case of the Civil War—Melville, speaking for and to the victors, holds that the chastening would lie in the discovery of the victorious *self* as blood kin, in the human plight of virtue-in-guilt and guilt-in-virtue, to the defeated *other*, and that this enlightenment would, in the end, be Melville's way of trying to follow the prescription of William James for doing "justice to the ideals in which the vanquished interests lay."

This theme, in poetic terms, is central to *Battle-Pieces*, but in the "Supplement" Melville addresses himself in plain prose to the same issue. He who had "sung of the soldiers and sailors," now demands, "who shall hymn the politicians?" Melville, identifying his views with those of Lincoln, asks, now that Lincoln is dead, what will they—politicians—do, who are creatures of calculation, ideology, or random passion, who do not "see through it." Melville prays for the Union to be restored in spirit as well as at bayonet point, but this, he says, can be achieved only if the inwardness of the war is understood: "Let us pray that the terrible historic tragedy of our time may not have been enacted without instructing our whole beloved country through terror and pity. . . ." The inwardness of History is, then, the inwardness of tragedy, and it offers the classic catharsis as a basis for facing action in the practical world.

*

In 1866 the inward issues of the Civil War and the classic catharsis were the last things that the ordinary Northern book-buyer, suffering grief, panting for revenge, flushed with victory, or calculating his own profits in the great new boom, wanted to hear about. In the South, where the notion prevailed that certain ambiguities might exist, there were, in 1866, no book-buyers.

Battle-Pieces did, however, receive a few favorable reviews. For instance, *Harper's Monthly* (perhaps not uninfluenced by the fact that Harper's had published the book) declared that Melville had written the "most stirring lyrics of the war." But the general sentiment among reviewers was adverse. The reviewer in the New York *Evening Post,* perhaps William Cullen Bryant, found the thought "vague"; F. B. Sanborn, an abolitionist, quite naturally found that Melville had no "real grasp on the causes or purposes of that struggle"; another reviewer simply pronounced the book "epileptic." As a matter of fact, there were not many reviews of any kind, good or bad, and the troubling presence of *Battle-Pieces* soon faded into the shadows. Only "Sheridan at Cedar Creek," one of the more conventional pieces, lingered on, in uncounted schoolrooms, in the broad daylight of Friday afternoon recitations.

*

When *Battle-Pieces* appeared, Melville had been desperately in need of money as well as appreciation; and with a book on such a topic, and in a period when a volume of poetry not infrequently sold like a popular novel today, Melville's hope, a hope that today would mark a poet as a certifiable lunatic, had some grounding in reality.[11] With this hope blasted, Melville faced the brute fact that he could make neither a living nor a name, by his pen. He had failed, too, in his hope to convert his guttering fame into a competence by means of a consular appointment. He was now ready to descend into his Tartarus, the Customs House of the Port of New York, where he became an inspector—an occupation which, years before, in *Red-*

burn, he had described as more inglorious than "driving geese to water." So now, at the age of forty-seven, at the wage of four dollars a day, Melville made his terms with the world, and with fate.

No, the terms by which Melville was to survive were not quite clear by December 5, 1866, when, already knowing the worst about *Battle-Pieces,* he took his oath as Inspector Number 75. Within a year the terms were clearer; his elder son, Malcolm, with whom Melville had had a good deal of friction, died, the body behind a locked door, in night clothes, pistol in hand, wound in temple. The coroner's jury did revise its original verdict of suicide by saying that, though Malcolm's death was caused by his own hand, it was not clear that "the act was by premeditation or consciously done." But the jury could not revise the facts, and Melville had to live with them.

*

William Ellery Sedwick says that in *Battle-Pieces* Melville had "recanted his mind's Promethean role" affirmed in *Moby Dick:* to say the least, he had decisively modified it, and the death of the son must have modified it even further. But Melville remained a seeker of ultimates, and with his grief he could not rest in the near-Pyrrhonism of his thought in *Battle-Pieces.* He certainly could not rest with the last lines of "The Conflict of Convictions":

> YEA AND NAY—
> EACH HATH HIS SAY;
> BUT GOD HE KEEPS THE MIDDLE WAY.
> NONE WAS BY
> WHEN HE SPREAD THE SKY;
> WISDOM IS VAIN, AND PROPHESY.

Nor could he rest with the humanistic philosophy recurrent in *Battle-Pieces:* though there are no values supernaturally delivered, man may create his own values and in them find self-definition and moral peace. To however noble and grandly tragic a plane this conception of life might be elevated, and however courageously it might be used as a justification for action, the conception was not quite enough to satisfy his eschatological appetite. So we have *Clarel.*

*

Clarel is a monstrously long poem, nearly twenty thousand lines, and as we have seen, it was years in the writing. The writing was for Melville an obsession—and also a refuge, the "other life," the real life into which he might enter at night after the ignominy of the Customs House, with its shadows of political job-ism, small-time financial corruption, and intellectual blankness, a microcosm perfectly reflecting in its scale the temper of the great world outside, the new booming America. Melville was somewhat like Machiavelli, who, after his ruin in the great world, returned to a niggardly property at San Casciano, where he spent his days gossiping or playing bowls with peasants, but at night took off his muddy shoes, bathed and dressed himself in his "curial robes" to commune with the "ancients"—and to write the book in which he tried to make sense of his own experience in the great world. But Melville was not trapped in the ironical role of the failure who writes a handbook for success, like Machiavelli's *Prince;* he was, if anything, trapped in a more profound and painful irony—the role of the failure in the world who, like the fox in the fable of the sour grapes, repudiates the world.

*

In late January 1857, Melville, waiting in Jaffa for return passage to America, had put into his journal his impressions of the Holy Land. Of Jerusalem he wrote: "The color of the whole city is grey and looks at you like a cold grey eye in a cold old man." Of the Church of the Holy Sepulcher, with the hawkers, Turkish police, ignorant pilgrims and ignorant tourists before the Tomb: ". . . you stare for a moment on the ineloquence of the bedizened slab, and glad to come out, wipe your brow glad to escape as from the heat and jam of a show-box . . . . A sickening cheat." Of the Dead Sea, with a hint of the bitterness of his then recent failure: ". . . foam on beach and pebbles like slaver of mad dog . . . carried the bitter of the water in my mouth all day—bitterness of life . . . . Bitter it is to be poor and bitter to be reviled, and oh bitter are these waters of Death, thought I." Of the landscape above the Sea: "Whitish mildew pervading whole tracts of landscape—bleached—leprosy—encrustations of curses."

It was a land of death, but unlike the vision of desolation which Melville had conjured up in the "slag-heap" of his "Encantadas," this land had once been the Promised Land, the land of milk and honey, and the source of the living waters of the spiritual life of the Western World. Here, in the ruined land, with characteristic paradoxicality, Melville was seeking renewal. As the character Rolfe has it in *Clarel:*

> Man sprung from deserts: at the touch
> Of grief or trial overmuch,
> On deserts he falls back at need.

Years later, in his poem, against the background of this land of desert, Melville sets a group of characters who carry on, in their beings and by word, the debate of the modern world. The poem is an important document of our modernity, as it is a document of Melville's own mind. It is, in fact, a precursor of *The Waste Land,* with the same basic image, the same flickering contrasts of the past and the present, the same charade of belief and unbelief.

The main character is Clarel, a disillusioned divinity

student, a sort of "pilgrim-infidel" in the Holy Land, where now all faiths and no-faith mingle in a corrosive fantasy. There is Ruth,[12] the Jewish girl (of American origin) with whom he falls in love and in whom he hopes to find a surrogate for religious values—that recurrent theme in Victorian poetry; Nehemiah, a religious fanatic whose fanaticism has been absorbed into sweetness, who has fled America to be here for the Second Coming; Celio, an Italian ex-Catholic, a hunchback whose deformity is a symbol of his spiritual pain; Vine, an American of "gifts unique" but not clearly defined, a shadowy projection of Hawthorne; Rolfe, another American, who is a mariner, adventurer, and intellectual, who has lived in the Pacific Islands, who, like Melville, has blue eyes, and who, in certain other respects, may be taken as a projection of Melville; a Greek banker and Glaucon, his gay young nephew; Derwent, an Anglican clergyman, who feels that all doubts and difficulties will automatically disappear in time, with "progress"; Margoth, an apostate Jew, a geologist who takes a strictly positivistic view of all matters; Mortmain, a Swede who has been a revolutionist in France but has lost faith in human regeneration; Ungar, of a Maryland Catholic family but with some Indian blood, who now holds no "one elected creed" but retains a strong feeling for the Church, who had been a Confederate officer and is now a soldier of fortune in the Near East, embodying, like Mortmain, a bitter critique of democratic, melioristic modernism. These, and other less important characters, give a shifting chiaroscuro of beliefs and doctrines.

This chiaroscuro actually represents the options in the quest for certainty (and self-definition) which has brought Clarel to the Holy Land, and what drama is here lies in Clarel's spiritual pilgrimage as reflected in the images of the natural, historical, and immediately human world about him. In one sense, Clarel's story is another re-telling of Melville's single great story, which appears in many guises. The shock that Melville, just before entering his teens, received from the bankruptcy, madness, and then the death of his father, determined that story of the youth —the Ishmael—who seeks a way into the world, and an understanding of the world, by seeking a father. Clarel has lost his "God," and he, like the other Ishmaels, is seeking a father.[13]

Clarel's story is also a kind of parable of growing up, and has many dimensions; it is "thick" not "thin," in its implications. Clarel, who has never really been in the world, must now confront the world: first, its blankness, the eyeless and sealed city of Jerusalem, then the horror of the death-in-life of Celio, who rejects the present and the future for the past, and then the horror of the literal death of the man who has not known life. This is the first of a series of deaths, ending in the death of Ruth, and we might trace the stages of Clarel's education by analyzing the meaning of each death in the series, and say that by understanding each death in turn Clarel prepares himself to understand life. In this connection we may remember that the whole poem is pegged to the Christian calendar, with the climax at Easter. The deaths in the poem point to a "resurrection," Clarel, shall we say, dying the deaths and at last being reborn into fulfilled selfhood. This theme is related, of course, to the perspective in which the poem may be regarded as a parable of growing up, for the morbidities of adolescence and the fascination with death are related to the youthful will to shed the husk of the conventional, inherited self and be reborn as the "real self," a mature person.

The theme of death and resurrection implies, then, the theme of sexual maturation. In one sense, the story of Ruth embodies, as we have said, the notion of romantic love as a substitute for religious values, but it also involves the stages in the progress of Clarel toward sexual maturity. In the beginning, when Clarel (who has never known a mother or sister) first meets Ruth, he is drawn, significantly, by the human warmth of Ruth's mother. Then, as a corollary to this fact, when he falls in love with Ruth, he falls in love with an idea, a symbol, and not with a young female of flesh and blood. At this stage there are only hints of the "darker" reality of sex. In this general perspective, the pilgrimage Clarel now makes in the period of Ruth's mourning for her father, when he may not see her, is a preparation for their marriage; he must come to an understanding of the terms on which human love may be significant in itself, not merely as a symbol.

In fact, we may take the whole story of Clarel's development as a narrative presenting the stages of the Oedipal conflict and its resolution. For instance, of fundamental significance are the attitude of Clarel toward the mother of Ruth and his subsequent "idealization" of Ruth, the idealization serving as a denial of the incestuous element here—for if Clarel finds Ruth's mother in the role of his own mother, then his love of Ruth is incestuous.[14] Furthermore, regarded in this perspective and not in isolation, the aura of homosexuality in the episode with Vine (pages 228–31) takes on a new meaning, that of a stage in the development of Clarel (as in one sense, does Melville mean to imply, of all men?) which is to be overpassed. This line of reasoning is supported by the fact that Clarel, just before the episode, has been perplexed by Rolfe, and by Rolfe's views of history and religion, and has said, even in the moment of stumbling upon Vine, that he cannot understand Rolfe. What is meaningful here is that Clarel is not yet ready, as it were, to understand the balanced, mature wisdom of Rolfe, who (like the Druse) embodies the human depth and control which Clarel will come, only in the end, to appreciate. Not being ready now for what Rolfe has to offer, Clarel turns to Vine. Vine, it must be granted, is a man who has his own virtues and powers, and in this episode he can reject Clarel's advances and point him toward the track he must follow to his "resurrection," saying, "Go, live it out"; but Vine, nevertheless, can be exhibited elsewhere in the poem, in a moment of spiritual confusion and distress—a situation in which we never find the totally fulfilled Rolfe. Therefore Vine may be taken as a stage toward Rolfe. Furthermore, it is significant that Rolfe, from whom the immature Clarel turns, is an idealized version of Melville himself; and that only after the full experience of the pilgrimage can Clarel understand Rolfe and be ready to go back to Ruth.

But Clarel never rejoins Ruth alive. Returning at night to Jerusalem, Clarel and his party see lights, then men with mattocks, in the burial ground of the Jews. The corpses that they are about to bury turn out to be those of Ruth and her mother Agar, dead of a fever and grief. For a time, Rolfe, Vine, and Derwent remain with Clarel (in his "martyrdom," his rounding of the Horn), to give what comfort they can. "Friendly they tarried," but are soon drawn back into the necessity of the world, which is characteristically "rent with partings." Clarel is left alone, as man always is in the end, to make what terms he can with the polarities and antinomies of life, and to try to make terms with himself by achieving, if possible, the selfhood of the sort exemplified by the Druse and by Rolfe.

Clarel's terms are made in Passion Week—which thematically gives an image for Clarel's, and the general human, experience. On the Via Crucis, a throng passes, Arabs, Jews, Turks, Christians:

> In varied forms of fate they wend—
> Or man or animal, 'tis one:
> Cross-bearers all, alike they tend
> And follow, slowly follow on.

Facing this image of the natural process of life (natural, as indicated by the fact that both men and animals are among the "varied forms of fate"), Clarel can at last accept, or at least take the first step toward accepting, the role of the mature and self-sufficient man who, without ultimate sanctions, can, like the heroes of *Battle-Pieces,* act—that is, he can go into the "city" of men and accept the human liability.

This fact returns us to the very beginning of the poem, to which the conclusion structurally corresponds. In the first few lines of the poem Clarel is introduced, alone, in a "low chamber" that is "like a tomb new-cut in stone"—the tomb from which, shall we say, he will be resurrected in the end. But let us note that he is not only in a "tomb," but is facing, as we shall soon learn in the poem, the blank eyeless walls of the city.[15] The entombment he suffers is, then, equated with his alienation from the "city" of men and action, with his entrapment in the anguish of self. The resurrection, the release to go into the "city" of men, comes only when he accepts the necessity of nature and at the same time sees in the human communion—even the biologic communion—a redemptive sacrament. He is now prepared to find his fate as a man among men, and this is the climax in which the theme of the philosophical quest and that of human growth are merged. It is a climax in which Clarel-as-Melville and Rolfe-as-Melville merge, too.[16]

But there is one more element to be considered here, and an important one. If we understand Clarel as the son seeking the lost father, we see him learning, in the end, that the fate of the mature and self-sufficient man is to live without a father. And this stage in the story of Melville brings us closer to the last stage, to be found in *Billy Budd,* where the focus is shifted from the questing son to the tragedy of the father whose son has found him.

The entrance into the "city" of men, however, is not quite the end of the poem *Clarel.* There is the Epilogue, in which something of Melville's characteristic doubleness, though now offered by way of comfort, appears. Melville directly addresses the youth who has come to terms with life: "Then keep thy heart, though yet but ill-resigned." By such an animal faith, and such a life-will and self-commanding stoicism,

> Emerge thou mayst from the last whelming sea,
> And prove that death but routs life into victory.

*

Clarel has not fared too well at the hands of the critics, and indeed the poem is, in many respects, far from satisfying. Its mere length makes an outrageous demand on the reader, and does much to prevent him from sensing the truly impressive architectonics of the work. Mere length does create a difficulty here, but worse, the length often results from a technical failure; for instance, the problems of meter and rhyme sometimes force Melville to thin and pad a passage and to confuse an argument or blur a scene. In other words, there is often a lag between Melville's intense intellectual involvement and the emotional involvement required to realize meaning at the poetic level. As *Battle-Pieces*, at its best, had well proved, Melville was capable of work with density of intellectual implication and immediate poetic impact; but here a fatal fatigue seems often to set in, as though a concern with the scale of the whole overawed all energies but those required for the discursive effort. If only he had been able to execute the poem in another temper and at another pace, or having finished a draft, had been able to lay it aside and then come back to it!

The octosyllabic line, prevailingly iambic, with irregular rhyming, has often been suggested as a bad choice for the poem in that it is supposed to make for monotony and cramp. At one time I inclined to that view, but now I strongly feel that the difficulty is, simply, in Melville's handling. Often, the rhyming seems forced or facile, and often the commitment to rhyme or meter is allowed to distort the sense or the structure of the sentence. Often, too, a more tactful and various placement of rhyme, and a more serious scrutiny of the relation of rhyme to syntactic and rhetorical emphases, would have done much to redeem the verse. And there are enough passages that are stylistically effective to sharpen our regret.

At a deeper level, we may assess the damage wrought by Melville's own emphasis on his intellectual involvement, as split off from the poetic involvement, or dramatic involvement: the poem is static. If *Clarel* is rich and dense, it is so only in theme;[17] at the level of action and the realization of human experience, it is thin. The action is conditioned almost totally by thematic considerations. The poem—in contrast with most things in the body of Melville's work, which characteristically grew from a specific germ drawn from life or reading—is deductive. Even the love story of Ruth, which provides the nearest thing in the poem to an action, has little relation to human motives and decisions, certainly none to passion, and its course is, at the literal level, determined by accidents—the death of her father at the hands of Arab raiders and her own death by disease. Ruth is, in fact, only a term in a dialectic: the refuge in romantic love from the despair of unbelief. Ruth's death, appropriately from "natural causes," simply says, thematically, that the attempt to substitute romantic love for metaphysical certainty is vain; for romantic love is embedded in the indifferent texture of nature. Man must, that is, find the answer in a different relation, both to himself and to others.

We may say, even, that the conception of *Clarel* violated Melville's genius, which, as we have suggested earlier, was to take a strong germ of drama, come upon in life or in his reading, and develop it imaginatively for what meanings he might find in its depth. In *Clarel* he reverses this process.[18] The actual journey to the Holy Land had not given him an action; it gave him merely an idea, and all the personal passion and compulsion which drove him to the idea—and to the subsidiary ideas—could do little to infuse life into the poem as long as there was no germ of action to flower in his imagination.

Melville was, in fact, lacking in inventiveness (except insofar as invention might extrapolate detail from a "given" central action), and here, having conceived the poem abstractly, he could not invent a basic action to absorb and vivify the ideas. We do not have a "lived" meaning for the poem—we have a charade of meanings. There are, of course, bits and patches along the way, strokes of imagery and phrase, for Melville's genius could not be denied; but such fragments do not constitute a continuum for the poem, or control the general effect. At the very end, after the death of Ruth, Clarel himself does come to life, but he comes to life after the action, such as it is, is over. The passion here is that of a man looking back on action, not that of a man involved in action. At the end, too, the poem *Clarel* comes to life in what we may call Melville's lyric poem *about* his epic poem, the philosophical lyric which is the Epilogue.

In spite of all criticism, however, *Clarel* remains both fascinating and important—if it is read as what it turned out to be, and not what it set out to be. It is a complex document in literary history and in the history of ideas; and it is, too, the document of a conscience and a consciousness. It reaches back to Byron, to *Childe Harold,* and is more immediately related, though not by imitation, to poems like *In Memoriam,* "Dover Beach," and "The Scholar Gipsy." It casts forward to Thomas Hardy (even to *The Dynasts*), to Ezra Pound and *The Cantos,* and significantly to Eliot and *The Waste Land, Ash Wednesday,* and *Four Quartets.* In itself it is an original and powerfully deployed body of ideas. We can read it in the same spirit we read Carlyle, the Whitman of *Democratic Vistas,* William James, Brooks Adams, Henry Adams, Thorstein Veblen, or more recently, the Edmund Wilson of *Patriotic Gore*. But *Clarel* is not only a document; it is a poem, with its own strange intermittent power, and its chief critic is the ghost of the poem it so violently strives to be, and of the poem it might have been, which haunts us. Even so, that ghost sometimes enters flickeringly into, and vivifies, the poem that is.

The poem is, in fact, more than a body of ideas, for here an idea is always presented as held by a particular person. Melville is attempting a very subtle thing, to see the deep relation of personality and ideas, and the mutual modification implicit in such relation: for instance, in the complexities of the psychology of the character of Clarel or of Mortmain. More and more clearly throughout the book he is trying to show the precise kind of shock that occurs when one character impinges upon another. In this respect *Clarel* reminds us of a novel by Henry James —the kind of novel that seems worlds removed from *Moby Dick* but is a projection of what Melville had attempted in *Pierre*. Further, as a corollary to this, we see that ideas are not merely to be judged abstractly as true or false; in one sense, the personal tone, the quality of the commitment a person has to an idea and the depth and richness of his experience of an idea, are related to the "truth" of an idea. In fact, Walter E. Bezanson, whose edition of *Clarel* is indispensable for anyone who wishes to understand the density and seriousness of the poem, concludes that Melville "goes increasingly from asking whose beliefs are right to asking who is the right kind of man." [19] For instance, the personal aura of Vine or Rolfe is more important than the ideas, as such, which they hold. And *Clarel* itself is an index to the depth of Melville's own experience of his ideas, a mark of the resonance of his commitment to ideas.

To sum up, Melville is trying to show ideas not as abstractions but as a function of the life process; and here, as in so much, he is something of a pioneer. He is one of the makers of modernity, of our consciousness and conscience. But no, we cannot say that of Melville. He did not make anything—except the poetry. And his poetry was, for all practical purposes, lost. The author of *Clarel* was, we might say, a seismograph that nobody looked at.

*

Melville can have had little expectation that *Clarel* would be a success; the very subject matter of the poem was, in a deep sense, the hope that failure might "rout" him into a victory quite different from worldly fame. But with what tormented irony and ambivalence, what sense of concession to weaknesses thought overcome, and what painful evocation of old hopes and despairs, *Clarel* was prepared for the press, we can only guess. It was, after all, the end of many years of intensive work and spiritual struggle, and the moment was heavily charged. In February 1876, when Melville and his wife were sunk in the proofs, Elizabeth Melville surreptitiously wrote a cousin explaining why she could not receive her as a guest in the Melville house:

> Herman, poor fellow, is in such a frightfully nervous state, & particularly now with such an added strain on his mind, that I am actually *afraid* to have anyone here for fear that he will be upset entirely, & not be able to go on with the printing. . . . If ever this dreadful *incubus* of a *book* (I call it so because it has undermined all our happiness) gets off Herman's shoulders I do hope he may be in better mental health . . . pity and pray for your ever affectionate cousin—Lizzie.

Mixed with Melville's other emotions was the bitterness—or perhaps the superstitious impulse—that made him want to print the book anonymously, as he had originally intended with *Pierre*. According to his wife, the publishers overrode this notion, but even so, the book, by a sort of stoic pridefulness, carried no reference to previous work by the author. Furthermore, in a dedication to the late Peter Gansevoort,[20] Melville went beyond the call of gratitude and affection to state flatly that the publication had been paid for by him—a clear warning to the reader that no publisher in his right mind would have independently undertaken such a venture. To compound all this, in a brief and crabbed prefatory note, Melville announced that he was prepared to "dismiss" the book—and by the same token the reader's opinion of it—"content beforehand with whatever future awaits it."

For all practical purposes, no future awaited it. This was the year of the Great Centennial. Did Melville choose the symbolic year to issue the poem so eminently unfitted to grace the particular kind of celebration which was in train? Such a piece of irony would have been in keeping with his cast of mind and the color of his expectations.

The reception accorded to *Clarel* fulfilled what we may take to have been those expectations. Only seven American notices of the book appeared, and the kindest remark offered was that though there was a "vein of earnestness" it was "singularly at variance with the carelessness of execution." Some years after the publication, Melville wrote to an English admirer[21] (there remained a few in England), that the poem was "eminently adapted for unpopularity." He was right for that time. And for this. But we may remember that the edition of *Leaves of Grass* which Whitman issued for the Centennial was only a shade less unpopular than *Clarel*. It was the Gilded Age.

*

If all Melville's work up to the moment in *Clarel* when the hero, now that Ruth is dead, looks back on his experience to assess it, may be regarded as the struggle to find a way by which to live, his late work may be regarded as the struggle to find a way by which to look at life as already lived. In *Battle-Pieces* there had been the pervasive paradox of act and legend, the poise of the instant when the present becomes the past, the act becomes the legend, as in "Battle of Stone River, Tennessee." But after *Clarel,* Melville's poems are of that "legend," and their theme is the question of how to live in the stillness of legend and yet have life.

But the question was not one to be explored only in poetry; it was one central to Melville's personal living. *Clarel* had, with whatever stoical preparation for rejection, been offered to the world, and the world had not wanted it. From this point on, Melville is writing, even more rigorously, for himself. That is, poetry is now a way of life in a personal "stillness," released from dependence on the world. Now he could cultivate his obscurity, like a garden.

By 1885 Melville's wife had inherited enough money to allow him to retire from his post at the Customs House and spend twenty-five dollars a month on books and pictures, that being the sum she set aside for the purpose. The new prosperity, augmented by some other bequests to Melville himself, allowed him also the indulgence of issuing a volume of his own poems—a thing no regular publisher would have dreamed of. The volume is *John Marr and Other Sailors,* which contains some of his finest pieces. It was privately printed in an edition of only twenty-five copies—nothing more, one might say, than a letter to posterity that was scarcely expected to reach the address. And *Timoleon,* which in addition to some poems of the last period includes the group "Fruit of Travel Long Ago," and the famous "Monody" on the death of Hawthorne, of 1864, was issued in the same way, privately and limited to twenty-five copies, in the year of Melville's death, 1891. One notice of *John Marr* had appeared. There was none of *Timoleon.*

Before his death Melville gathered the bulk of his unpublished verse under the title *Weeds and Wildings Chiefly: with a Rose or Two.* Many of these pieces are slight, conventional nature pieces of uncertain date, with only occasional flashes of poetry. But here too the poet may proudly accept his position outside of an age for which he had little but contempt—an age in which "Apollo's bust" is burned to make "lime for Mammon's tower." In "Immolated," presumably written some years earlier, he addresses, in tones reminiscent of Ben Jonson's "Ode: To Himself" and John Marston's "To Oblivion," certain poems he has burned:

> Rest therefore, free from all despite,
> Snugged in the arms of comfortable night.[22]

But with whatever anger and irony such lines had been written, the last poem of this projected collection, "Pontoosuce,"[23] closes with a passage, one of the noblest in Melville's work, that demands to be set against the end of *Clarel.* The lady of the vision he has by the lake in the rich autumn countryside of the Berkshires teaches him the final joy in resignation to the cyclic pulse of the universe:

> She ceased, and nearer slid, and hung
> In dewy guise, then softlier sung:
> "Since light and shade are equal set
> And all revolves, nor more ye know;
> Ah, why should tears the pale cheek fret
> For aught that waneth here below.
> Let go, let go!"
>
> With that, her warm lips thrilled me through,
> She kissed me, while her chaplet cold

Its rootlets brushed against my brow,
With all their humid clinging mould.
She vanished, leaving fragrant breath
And warmth and chill of wedded life and death.

In the new phase, after the failure of *Clarel,* Melville seems to have been nearly immune to shock; and in that immunity, he could look back on old struggles, and write poetry in a new vein, a mixture of gaiety and pathos. In the clearest example of the new mode, we have "Bridegroom Dick," in which the old mariner, sitting with his wife, smokes his pipe and looks back on his adventurous youth, "the May-time o' pennoned young fellows," before the "old order foundered" in the Civil War and "tradition was lost and we learned strange ways." Dick is, of course, a rendering of Melville himself, and the poem is full of references to the literal past he had known, characters and events that we recognize from his earlier work or from the biography. The shocks and struggles of the past are now resolved in memory and the affectionate companionship of the aging wife:

Don't fidget so, wife; an old man's passion
Amounts to no more than this smoke that I puff;
There, there, now, buss me in good old fashion;
A died-down candle will flicker in the snuff.

In this attempt to develop, not the old theme of how to live, but the new theme of how to regard life-as-lived, Melville discovered, paradoxically enough, a new technical freedom, a release into the kind of action that poetry is, a new flash of image and language, a new creative élan. He often managed to purge his language of many of the stale poeticisms and the fillers used to patch out meter. Now, at best, he had learned to sustain a rhythmical and syntactical movement through a series of lines with more freedom than had before been possible for him except in his happiest moments. And in "Bridegroom Dick" there is a remarkable achievement in precise observation, rhythmical variety based on natural speech, and the fusion of a dramatic lingo and a poetic tone, a style reminiscent, in the new form, of effects in *Moby Dick:*

> And ah, for old Lieutenant Chock-a-Block—
> Fast, wife, chock-fast to death's black dock!

Or:

> But fame is a wake that after-wakes cross. . . .

Or:

> With a bead in your eye and beads in your glass,
> And a grip o' the flipper, it was part and pass. . . .

Or:

> "Brown, tie him up."—The cord he brooked:
> How else?—his arms spread apart—never threaping;
> No, never he flinched, never sideways he looked,
> Peeled to the waistband, the marble flesh creeping. . . .

We find many of the same elements in "Tom Deadlight" as well as in "Billy in the Darbies," which we shall discuss later, and in which these elements are absorbed into a more complex and deeply moving poetry.

"Tom Deadlight" is another poem looking back on the action of the past; and in "John Marr" we again find the hero musing, like Dick, on old shipmates. If in "John Marr" the content of the musing is not as strictly personal as in "Bridegroom Dick," the prose headnote, which gives an elaborate setting for the poem, is a thinly disguised picture of Melville. This introduction describes how Marr, too old for the sea, goes West to settle on the prairies, marries, loses wife and child, and now isolated among a "staid people," who are "ascetics by necessity not less than by moral bias" and to whom the sea is but "a rumor traditional and vague," finds no one with whom he can commune. When, at a corn-husking, Marr begins a tale of his past, a blacksmith who at Sunday gatherings is "an earnest exhorter," says chillingly: "Friend, we know nothing of that here."

The world, now that there was no titillation to be had from a young sailor who had consorted with dusky beauties under palm trees, could not concern itself with the vision of a life-possibility Melville had brought back from

> Marquesas and glenned isles that be
> Authentic Edens in a Pagan sea.

Nor could that world, devoutly worshiping the bitch-goddess Success, know what grim joy there might be in looking at "The Tuft of Kelp" to ask:

> All dripping in tangles green,
> Cast up by a lonely sea
> If purer for that, O Weed,
> Bitterer, too, are ye?

Nor could it understand the wisdom learned from the passage around the Horn, the wisdom exemplified in the image of "The Man-of-War Hawk":

> No arrow can reach him; nor thought can attain
> To the placid supreme in the sweep of his reign.

Nor could it see anything except lunacy in the notion of an "asylum" in the "saw-pit mouth" of "The Maldive Shark."

*

Three other poems of the last phase demand special comment, "The Berg," "The Haglets," and "Billy in the Darbies." "The Berg," from *John Marr and Other Sailors,* though very uneven and sometimes awkward in the first half, offers some extremely interesting examples of Melville's style. There is the vivid observation in the "jackstraw needle ice" at the base of the berg, and in the image of the seals "dozing sleek on sliddery ledges." In the last ten lines, which give a strong climax with a haunting shadowy import, we find a powerfully uncoiling movement and some brilliant and original phrasing:

> Hard Berg (methought), so cold, so vast,
> With mortal damps self-overcast;
> Exhaling still thy dankish breath—
> Adrift dissolving, bound for death;
> Though lumpish thou, a lumbering one—
> A lumbering lubbard loitering slow,
> Impingers rue thee and go down,
> Sounding thy precipice below,
> Nor stir the slimy slug that sprawls
> Along thy dead indifference of walls.

The sea slug here and this "indifference" remind us of Thomas Hardy's sea worm, also "slimed" and "indifferent," in "The Convergence of the Twain," his poem on the sinking of the *Titanic:*

> Over the mirrors meant
> To glass the opulent
> The sea-worm crawls—grotesque, slimed, dumb, indifferent.

The ship in Melville's dream is "infatuate," like the *Titanic,* and embodies the "pride of life" that planned and launched the *Titanic,* and both, by doom or brutal contingency, ram, with seeming willfulness, the berg. The poem returns, as do "The Haglets," "Old Counsel," "The Tuft of Kelp," and "Pebbles" in this volume, to Melville's obsessive theme of sudden disaster in the midst of pride and success. But it also re-embodies the theme found in "The Old Stone Fleet," in the words of the old sailor: "Nature is nobody's ally." The sea-floor of "The Berg," like the sea-floor of "The Convergence of the Twain," is the image that man must make terms with if he is to find peace.[24]

*

The image of the sea-floor appears elsewhere, and powerfully, in Melville's poetry of this period, for instance, in "The Haglets," and in "Billy in the Darbies." In these two poems, however, the sea-floor is not the place of mere blankness found in "The Berg," the place of brute ending. The Admiral in "The Haglets," unaware of the fatal birds that follow him, does indeed go down in the moment of his victory and pride, to destruction. But how is that "natural" fact dealt with? Here is the end of the poem:

Ah, for the Plate-Fleet trophy now,
The victor's voucher, flags and arms;
Never they'll hang in Abbey old
And take Time's dust with holier palms;
Nor less content, in liquid night,
Their captor sleeps—the Admiral of the White.

Imbedded deep with shells
And drifted treasure deep,
Forever he sinks deeper in
Unfathomable sleep—
His cannon round him thrown,
His sailors at his feet,
The wizard sea enchanting them
Where never haglets beat.

On nights when meteors play
And light the breakers' dance,
The Oreads from the caves
With silvery elves advance;
And up from ocean stream,
And down from heaven far,
The rays that blend in dream
The abysm and the star.

This is much more complex than "The Berg," with the cluster of thematic implications in the images of the sea-floor, with the paradox of defeat-in-victory and victory-in-defeat, and, in the images of the "abysm" and the "star," not only the paradox of man's fate but—and we should emphasize this—the paradox of his nature. And this idea Melville had already stated in the Epilogue to *Clarel:*

The running battle of the star and clod.

*

"The Haglets," for all its fine flashes and its thematic interest, is not one of Melville's best pieces; nor is its sea-floor as richly freighted as that of "Billy in the Darbies," the poem which "The Haglets" forecasts. "Billy in the Darbies," though it does not have the immediately available power of, say, "The March into Virginia," "The College Colonel," or "Commemoration of a Naval Victory," is certainly Melville's most nearly perfect poem—the poem in which he achieves complete mastery of style and, shall we say, of his life.

"Billy in the Darbies" is described, at the end of *Billy Budd,* as a broadside ballad: some "tarry hand had made some lines which, after circulating among the shipboard crews for a while, finally got rudely printed at Portsmouth." But the poem, which thus appears as a sort of coda to the novel, had been the germ of the whole. If the poem is to be associated with the novel, it is also to be associated, by its "backward-looking" as well as by general subject matter and style, with the constellation of "John Marr," "Tom Deadlight," "Jack Roy," and "Bridegroom Dick." But there is another relation between "Billy in the Darbies" and this group. "John Marr" and "Tom Deadlight" are introduced by prose headnotes which identify the main character and the situation from which the poems spring; and the original version of "Billy in the Darbies" [25] has a headnote of the same order, and may, as has been surmised, have been intended for the collection *John Marr and Other Sailors.*

But if Melville had originally intended to include the ballad in that volume, by the time of its publication, in early 1888, the idea was impractical, for now the headnote had begun to dominate Melville's inspiration, and had, in fact, exfoliated into a manuscript of some 70 pages. By November of that year, the manuscript was to be one of some 150 pages, and the process of development and revision was to continue until terminated by Melville's death in 1891, when the version which we now know, not necessarily to be taken as final, was left among his papers.

The tentative early lines of the poem had, of course, developed too, and as a kind of aside we may say that, in the process of development, the interpenetration of the prose fiction and the poem may give some hint of the relation that, for Melville, existed between the two forms. For instance, *Moby Dick*, a prose work of exposition, character, and action, is conceived "poetically," and in execution the prose often strains toward verse.[26] On the other hand, Melville's best poems, and many others, are, as we have said earlier, anecdotal or dramatic; they have, in other words, a "prose" base. The lyric mood, of unmoored emotion, of abstraction, was not for him; his feelings responded to, and his imagination took fire from, the collisions and tensions of experience as life offered specific, realistic images of them. So, as the prose story of Billy Budd grew in range and depth, the poem, in interpenetration with it, would have grown, not merely preying on it like a clump of mistletoe, but rather, shall we hazard, contributing, in its yeast of feeling, to the whole ferment and expansion.

This returns us to the question of what ordinary factual changes occurred between the early scribbles and the form left at Melville's death. For one thing, though this early Billy is nicknamed "Beauty," as the headnote tells us, and seems to have "a lineage contrasting his lot," he is not the boy of the foretop, a post proper to youth and agility, but is the "Captain of a gun's crew in a seventy-four," that is, an older man in a position of authority requiring experience and judgment and, it may be emphasized, one who has accepted a place, however humble, in the hierarchical system of authority to which Billy is the innocent outsider, a "barbarian." And it might even be suggested that the difference in symbolic aura between the skyey post of the foretopman and that of the gunner is of some significance.[27]

For another difference, this Billy of the first version is, according to Melville's headnote, "condemned at sea to be hung as the ring-leader of an incipient mutiny." In other words, the original Billy is neither young nor innocent, and though there is pathos in the "last eve" of the older and tougher man, the pathos is of a different order, of a simple order resembling that of John Marr or Tom Deadlight, one that the Melville who had written *White-Jacket* might deeply feel, but one that implies none of the issues raised by the outraged innocence of the later Billy caught in the trap of the world.

It may seem strange that Melville, with his feeling for the dramatic, the dense, and the paradoxical, ever conceived the story in such simple terms, even in the first fragment. But on second thought, as we set the earliest version in the context of the feeling that dominates the constellation of poems with which it is associated, the reason is clear. The headnote is not a story, it is merely the context for a poem, a poem not to deal with the dramatic content of life but with the elegiac mood of "backward-looking" on life, a mood in which dramatic issues would dissolve. Not the mutineer's own story and its issues, but his recollections, the pathos of the past in its past-ness, would, presumably, be in focus.

The movement, however, from the early version forward to the form which we now have, is a movement toward the development of the dramatic content. But this new emphasis on dramatic content is, at the same time, kept in the context of the "backward-looking": the story has happened long ago. We are invited to look at the "inside narrative," at the truth hidden in Time. In other words, the elegiac mood, something of the pathos of pastness, remains; but as the realistic headnote was to give a context for the elegiac, now, by the reversal of emphasis, the elegiac tone gives a context for the dramatic story which the headnote becomes, and thus we are brought, in another way, to the problem of "action" and "legend" which we have encountered in *Battle-Pieces.* Within the "legend" of life yet lie the grim issues that were life, and with which one must make terms if "reconciliation" to experience is to be more than a sentimental escape into the mere "legend." So with the story of Billy Budd, both novel and poem, we go beyond the feeling and attitude of the constellation of poems from which it sprang.

If under the elegiac mood Melville first conceived his old mutineer, he early began to modify this Billy and to complicate the story. By early 1888, Billy is young and innocent, Claggart has appeared as the adversary (though as yet unanalyzed) and is struck dead in the presence of Vere. In this version Vere has no real role in the story but is merely the instrument of execution; and the end of the story does not come with the ballad, but with the news report in a "naval chronicle" which gives the "outside narrative," the world's institutional view of the event, in contrast to the "inside narrative." [28]

At this point it may be useful to remember that Melville had mutiny in the family history, in the case of Philip Spencer, son of John C. Spencer, then Secretary of War, who, at the age of eighteen, as a midshipman on the training brig *Somers* of the United States Navy, was hanged at sea, on December 1, 1842, with two members of the crew accused of conspiring with him to seize the brig and hoist the Jolly Roger. Guert Gansevoort, Melville's cousin on his mother's side and a lieutenant and second in command on the *Somers,* had been the senior member of the "council" of officers which Captain Mackenzie, knowing he had no legal right to convoke a court-martial, had requested to advise him, and Guert was certainly a key figure in the tragic sequel. The case was mysterious and shocking, and resulted in acrimonious public debate and in the sensational court-martial of Mackenzie, where Guert played a prominent and, it may seem, a not entirely creditable part as witness for the defense. Guert, appearing as the character Tom Tight in "Bridegroom Dick," is unwilling, even years after the event, to discuss it.

But the *Somers* case cannot be taken as *the* source of *Billy Budd.* Both the story and the poem are too deeply grounded in Melville's earlier work and experience. Claggart goes back to the Master-at-Arms of *White-Jacket* and, as Hayford and Sealts argue, to one Sterrit, who had been Master-at-Arms on the *Constitution* and who was thought by the sailors to be in league with the devil. So Claggart goes back, too, to the "shark's white fin"—he is the shark that "glides through the phosphorous sea," he is what shakes "the oak in the driving keel," he is, in spite of and beyond all hints of psychological explanation or literary sources, evil metaphysically conceived. As for Vere, he faces in a new form, transferred from history to a personal story, some of the polarities and issues of *Battle-Pieces;* and the resolution here is merely a projection, in another and deeper tonality, of the resolution at the end of *Clarel,* the hope that death but routs life into victory.

Billy Budd may, however, be more intimately related to Melville's personal history and development. Billy, as we learn in Chapter 2, has qualities that suggest a mother "eminently favored by Love and Graces," and a "lineage in direct contradiction to his lot." In Chapter 22, Melville says that Vere, in his private interview with Billy, would "have concealed nothing from the condemned one," and one of the things presumably not concealed was the fact of Vere's fatherhood: "He was old enough to have been Billy's father," and Vere "may in the end have caught Billy to his heart, even as Abraham may have caught young Isaac on the brink of offering him up in obedience to the exacting behest."

It is true that the blood relationship is not positively stated in the story. Thematically, however, it is not important that the relationship be biological. Spiritually and morally, it is there beyond the shadow of a doubt. If Melville did not mean the relationship, however conceived, to have significance, why mention it at all?

This father-son theme has some bearing, in fact, on the much-debated question of the theme of reconciliation in *Billy Budd*. Here we may remember that the tough old Billy of the first scribbled version is scarcely a son figure. We cannot know precisely the date when Melville first meditated the change in the character of Billy, but we can be fairly confident that the change took place in the period between 1886 and late 1887, and we do know that an event of great personal importance for Melville took place early in 1886. Melville's second son, Stanwix, died in San Francisco, at the age of thirty-five. He, like Malcolm, was doomed to frustration and a tragic end—an unstable, undependable wanderer and ne'er-do-well. It would seem natural that the news of this death, which prostrated Melville's wife, would have revived for him all the old painful debates about his own connection with Malcolm's fate, now compounded by similar debates concerning the fate of Stanwix.[29] Would it even have made him think of the parallel between himself and Stanwix: how his own father had been a failure, how he, Melville, had been a wanderer and ne'er-do-well, and in the end a "failure," too? How much would this repetition have made the story of Stanwix (or the story of Billy Budd, and of Vere, too) seem a matter of doom rather than of an easily defined culpable responsibility? To paraphrase a line from "Bridegroom Dick," there in reference to the divided loyalties of the Civil War, both Billy and Vere, like Malcolm and Melville, were "trapped" in "fate," and "jammed" in the "strait"—were caught in the kind of dilemma that had always stirred Melville's imagination.

Such speculations, which are characteristic of Melville's work, would easily lead to, or support, a change in the conception of the nature and role of the condemned sailor. In such a context, too, it would not be illogical to suppose that the death of Stanwix (and the revived memories of the death of Malcolm) would set Melville's mind toward that younger "mutineer" who, in the family history and already in the poem "Bridegroom Dick," was waiting to be assimilated into the novel. Philip Spencer, like both Malcolm and Stanwix, had been a difficult and wayward son and like them, was a figure in a tragic father-son story; for the elder Spencer, after trouble with Philip, had as a matter of discipline sent him into the Navy, and to his death, and must have had to live with some sense of his own failure in comprehension, sympathy, and judgment.[30]

But here another consideration arises. Philip Spencer, Malcolm, and Stanwix all had been wayward, and Billy is not. Billy does, however, have a defect: he stutters. This seemingly trivial thing is fatal for him. It is true, as some critics have pointed out, that the stutter may well have been intended, symbolically, to be something more than trivial, to be, like the little hand-shaped spot on the fair cheek of the heroine in Hawthorne's story "The Birthmark," a sign of mortality and the human taint, even of Original Sin; and it has been argued with plausibility that, psychoanalytically regarded, the stutter conspires with the psychic censor of the stutterer to prevent the expression of a buried hostility—in this case toward the figures of authority. But at the practical daytime level of the story we take the stutter as something morally neutral, like the color of one's hair—or like the defect of being cross-eyed, from which Philip Spencer suffered (made worse by a bad operation), and which, in a sense, was his doom. His doom, not merely as might be supposed, because it might well have aggravated his drinking and angers and general instabilities, but because his look—"the most infernal expression I ever beheld on a human face"—was used by Guert Gansevoort (as by Captain Mackenzie) to condemn him to be hanged: "It satisfied me of his guilt."

Thus Billy is damned not only by his "barbarian" innocence that makes him a natural victim of the rules of the civilized world, and by metaphysical evil in the person of Claggart, but by his physical defect, his stutter, as Philip Spencer is damned by his squint. He is triply damned—and ultimately guiltless. Does Melville mean to imply, by the reordering of things, that even the waywardness of Malcolm and Stanwix—or even of Philip Spencer, for that matter—is a similar doom, and that in the recognition of doom reconciliation is possible?[31] Even reconciliation with the self—for Vere, the "father" in the story, is doomed, too. For he is not only a father, but the captain of a man-of-war at a certain historical moment, and all his awareness and sensibility merely heighten his anguish at being caught in the jaws of a dilemma.[32] Father and son are both "cross-bearers," and in the recognition of that fact is the ultimate reconciliation, here as in *Clarel*.

So *Billy Budd* is a father-son story, an Abraham-Isaac story. It is, in other words, another and more complicated embodiment of Melville's germ story, the Ishmael story, the story of the search by the son for the lost father. But it differs from the previous examples of that germ story in two crucial respects. Here the son finds the father, and the father recognizes the son. That is the scene that Melville did not—or could not—write. It is the encounter behind the locked door of the Captain's cabin. Is this the dream of the reconciling end of the search for the father that Melville, the son, never found in life? Is it also the dream of reconciliation that Melville, the father, looking back on the locked door beyond which Malcolm lay, a boy as rebellious and wayward as poor young Philip Spencer hanged at the yard-arm of the *Somers*, had to dream at last, before he himself could die? And if we should say to him that the dream has no more validity than that endowed by his need to dream it, might he not reply that the only wisdom we have is forced on us, that we are "routed" into it?

In any case, when Billy's body swings in the dawn light, we have come a long way from the moment when the arm of Tashtego, reaching up through the surface of the sea, nails the wing of the screaming "sky-hawk" to the mast. And Melville has come a long way from the moment when he broke in the door of Malcolm's room.[33]

We have been speaking of the story of Billy Budd, not specifically of the poem, but the two are, in the end, aspects of a single intuition and single work. Without the story the poem could not fully deliver itself. But this is not to say that the poem is a mere appendage.

Though from the first the prose story and the poem may be thought of as interpenetrating in the process of creation, in another sense, it may be said that the story provides the "materials" and "issues" in the way that life provides such things to art, and art demands such things of life: the story here is the "postulated life" which the poem refracts in "art," in much the same way as the battles of the Civil War are refracted in art. "Billy in the Darbies" absorbs the materials and issues of the story into a new medium, with a new density and intonation, which become, in fact, a new perspective of meaning. It is by the poem that we might claim to know, in spite of whatever built-in ironies and ambiguities may be in the story, what the final meaning amounts to: reconciliation or the possibility of reconciliation.

The poem is on page 349.

With continuing inspection, the reader becomes more and more aware of the levels of meaning aqueously shifting in the depth of the poem—the subtle characterization of Billy, the personal pathos, the flow of image and rhythm, the delicate interplay of the hinted-at individual story and the generalized implication of the images of suffering and redemption, the contrast between the human bond in Billy's affectionate relation with his messmates and the existential loneliness somehow resolved in the twin images of Billy "aloft from alow" and of Billy "fast asleep."

The shifting and teasing allusiveness of the poem, and the sense of depth, derive, in part at least, from the connection with the events of the novel. But such qualities also bear some relation to the fact that the poem is both popular and sophisticated; it is, dramatically, the musings of the ignorant boy Billy, and never gives the impression of violating the required decorum, but it is also a poem that embodies an extremely complex attitude toward experience, and under the simple surface, very complex stylistic elements; it is at once a broadside ballad and a high poetic elegy, like "Lycidas," from which, in fact, it draws certain effects. In one sense, it is similar to the poems of Chatterton, to "The Ancient Mariner," and to "La Belle Dame Sans Merci," poems which, in combining the resonance of both popular and art poetry, evoke a mixture of different and sometimes contradictory expectations in the reader, and a complicated interplay, of fusion and contrast, in the fulfillment.[34]

In the beginning we learn that the Chaplain has prayed, and that Billy is humbly grateful. Then comes the phrase, "But, look—" and the word *but* sets the moonlight now stealing in to "silver" the nook in contrast to the prayer. Is it in contrast in the sense that the moonbeam indicates that God responds directly, without the Chaplain's institutional mediation, to the natural innocence of Billy? Such a reading would, of course, be related to the theme as developed in the fictional treatment—and to Captain Vere's dilemma of justice and mercy in contrast to institutional considerations. Or is the meaning of the moonbeam to be thought of as suggesting also a more radical contrast—the contrast between the reconciliation which the Chaplain offers in theological terms and one which may come in natural terms? Without rejecting the theological reading, we may say that the second seems more central to the poem, which can be thought of as existing between the two polar images of the body swung transcendently "aloft from alow," and the body in the oozy weeds.[35] But we shall return to this.

The image of the "jewel-block" offers the next point of focus in the poem. Literally, a jewel-block is the pulley at the end of the main and fore-topsail yards, but Billy, in a blend of self-pity and self-commanding humor, stumbles, as it were, upon the pun, and for us he becomes the jewel, white, glimmering, pure—and to pun again, "pendant," hanging both as pearl and as executed man, precious in his role as the "hanged man."

But the pearl is also the eardrop given to Bristol Molly, and in contrast to the implications of transcendence in the image, the thought turns to the warm actuality of life in the person of Molly—and of Billy, too, who, after all, is just a youthful sailor, not a Christ-figure after all, but a sailor who has found such natural satisfactions as he might with a Molly who probably was no better than she should have been. And this flash of realism returns Billy—and us—to the grim reality of the present moment, in the pun on *suspend,* which continues, with a more sardonic intonation, the basic idea of the two previous puns.

Just as the mind of Billy has turned from the literal jewel-block and its grim connotations to the thought of Bristol Molly, so now, turning from the grim humor of the pun on *suspend,* he reaches out again toward life and human warmth, this time toward his messmates. This relationship carries over some charge of feeling from the story, but even without that, much is conveyed by the tone of affection and the awareness of a common human lot in the ritual of their parting. Hennig Cohen, in his edition of the poems, has proposed that the "bit o' biscuit" and the "last parting cup" bear a "suggestion of the last sacrament with its implications of immortality."[36] But Billy's role may be more than that of a mere sufferer. In the novel, which is the context of the poem, we find such a passage as: "At the same moment it chanced that the vapory fleece hanging low in the East, was shot through with some soft glory as of the fleece of the Lamb of God seen in mystical vision and simultaneously therewith, watched by the wedged mass of upturned faces, Billy ascended; and ascending, took the full rose of the dawn." And in reference to the spar from which Billy had been suspended: "To them [the sailors of the fleet] a chip of it was a piece of the Cross." This would seem to suggest that Billy has something of a Christlike role, that of a sufferer who, though merely human and secular, somehow suffers, in his guiltlessness, for others.

If the poem may be thought of as existing in the tension between the two images, that of the body swung transcendently aloft and that of the body in the weeds on the sea-floor, then we must ask what, if anything, does the poem make of this polarity? Mr. Cohen suggests that the "consolation" offered by the hint of "resurrection" in the "aloft" is "qualified by the harsh fact that Billy is raised on high by the hangman's rope and the possibility that the 'oozy weeds' which twist about him as he sinks to sleep are fetters additional to the darbies which bind his wrists." In other words, Mr. Cohen would seem to emphasize the impossibility—or perhaps only the difficulty—of reconciling the elements in the polarity. Certainly the difficulty should not be underemphasized; it would not have been in Melville's nature to do so, and to read the poem we must try to explore the terms by which a reconciliation may be possible.

Perhaps the best way to explore the question is to look at the weeds. They are, indeed, fetters—a meaning which the word *twist,* coming just after Billy's request that the sentry ease the darbies, amply supports. But is that the only meaning here? Let us look at the whole passage (line 27 to the end). In the first two lines, Billy, like a baby, is being put into his hammock and dropped "deep"—deep fathoms down; but the dropping, with the repetition of "fathoms down," is down to sleep. Billy feels the sleep already on him, and when he asks the sentry to ease him, the phrase "just ease" is significant in that it implies that there is really not much that needs doing, an implication that reduces the inimical weight of the darbies, and later, it should be pointed out, the inimical weight of the weeds as surrogate darbies; and in this sense, there is again the suggestion of Billy in the role of the "baby," and the sentry in the role of the "nurse"—the nurse making the baby comfortable for sleep. (In this connection it may be worth remembering that Billy is also "Baby Budd" in the story, a fact here echoed in the treatment and tone.) Furthermore, in the last line, the statement that Billy is sleepy is not put into opposition to the weeds; the statement and the weeds are connected by an *and,* not set apart by a *but,* the weeds being, as it were, *with* the sleep and not *against* it.

Here, then, is not a sharply discriminated opposition but an effect of sequence and flow. This effect is made more significant by another factor, the prevailing vowel-run of the whole passage, from line 27 to the end. In line

27 the *e* of *me* is repeated in the second *me*, and again in *deep*. This is picked up in line 28 with *dream* and *asleep;* in line 29 with *feel* and *stealing;* in line 30 with *ease* and *these;* in line 31 with *me;* and in line 32 with *sleepy, weeds,* and again *me*. This is not to suggest that a certain sound automatically carries a specific content, as in a code (*weeds* is a word neither sleepy nor wakeful), but it is to say that here the sound has been specifically charged with a series of related meanings, beginning with *me*, which is Billy: *me-deep-dream-asleep-feel-stealing-ease-these-sleepy*. By the time we come to *weeds,* the literal meaning of the word is impregnated with what we may call the audio-symbolic meaning; and thus the inimical meaning of the weeds as fetters binding the dead man is interpenetrated and substantially canceled by the beneficent meaning, a meaning last echoed in *me* just before the word *twist*.

By way of support to such reading, we may notice, too, that the somnolence of the first two lines is reinforced by the repetition of the droning *m*'s and *d*'s, which reappear at the end. For further incidental support, we may observe how the word *oozy* in the phrase "oozy weeds," though inimical in itself, picks up and echoes the beneficent word *sleepy* just before. True, the word *twist* ends the line, and the poem, with a last painful touch—but with a painfulness only like the memory of pain, a reminder of the cost of peace, for Billy is now asleep.

*

Let us return to the relation between the images of Billy "aloft" and of Billy deep in the oozy weeds. In the first, as in the "bit o' biscuit" and the "last parting cup," there is, as Mr. Cohen points out, the hint of "resurrection." But here we must read "resurrection" (and all the implications of the Christ image) as metaphorical. I should, in fact, prefer to the word *resurrection* the word *transcendence,* as avoiding the theological connotation, for that would seem merely a distraction from what I take to be the main line of meaning. In the opening scene, in which the Chaplain's prayer and the moonbeams "astray" appear, the contrast may be taken to give a grounding for the naturalistic "transcendence" as opposed to a theological notion. But a firmer grounding is found in the body of Melville's work. In *Battle-Pieces,* it is man's vision of his role—in history, in relation to other men, and in self-definition—that offers the possibility of transcendence. In *Clarel,* what in the end remains of theology is nothing more than a "natural" theology, not different from metaphor. In "Venice," which presumably dates from the time when Melville, among the dunes of Southport, told Hawthorne that he had made up his mind "to be annihilated," the continuity between the work of the coral worm and the "reefs of palaces" implies the monistic view that the highest aspirations and values of man, which are apt to be thought of as setting man off from nature, are, in themselves, merely a natural development.[37] And the vision of "Pontoosuce" is one of man in nature.

There is, of course, a contrast between what transcendence is possible for man, and the harsh facts of his natural condition. The transcendence is hard to come by, and Mr. Cohen is again right in pointing out the "harsh fact that Billy is raised on high by the hangman's rope." But in a final sense, the transcendence is not "qualified by harsh fact"; the transcendence is made possible by it—that is, by the redemptive recognition, in the harsh fact, of the human bond. Only by pressure and in pain is man "routed" into a knowledge of his fate, and into whatever triumph, however limited and qualified, is possible in it. We remember the shared experience of the soldiers in *Battle-Pieces;* and the motley crowd of Jew, Christian, Arab, and Turk on the Via Crucis, in their "varied forms of fate," whom Clarel recognizes as "cross-bearers all," and we may remember that in this recognition he takes the first step toward whatever peace is to be possible for him. In the same spirit, we remember Billy with the "bit o' biscuit" and the "parting cup." So if we do not have the image of the body on the sea-floor, in the darbies and caught in the weeds, with the history that brought the body there, the image of the body "aloft" is meaningless.

But what sort of meaning may be found here?

In trying to answer the question we must remember that we are not to expect some sort of schematic reading of Melville's poem, or of his fiction. We are, rather, to hope at best for terms in which the complexity of experience may be discussed; and in that spirit we may, as we have suggested earlier, regard Billy "aloft" and Billy "alow" as the two poles of meaning, with the recognition that life involves complications and is an ever-shifting process. In other words, we must not think of one image as canceling out the other, as in mathematics, nor think of one as provisional and the other final in any chronological sense. No, they are both ever-present and ever-significant, demanding constant re-inspection.

To look for a moment at the two poles of the process, we may think of Billy "alow" as the image implying all the natural suffering that may make possible the image of Billy "aloft" in dawn light in unsuffering transcendence. At the same time, each image has its own characteristic peace, but a peace that always carries with it the mark of its cost. Each image is of a dead man.

Man, as we have seen from the Civil War poems, has these two sorts of peace possible to him, what we may call the peace of nature and the peace of vision. There is, as we find it in the scene on the sea-floor in "The Haglets," the "abysm" and the "star," and if, in one sense, the abysm is death, blankness, ending, it is also a peace and inculcates its own kind of wisdom, the wisdom of "Let go, let go!" in "Pontoosuce," the wisdom of the pilot fish in the jaws of the Maldive shark, the Lucretian wisdom, the wisdom of man's acceptance of his place in nature as his peace.

But what of the "star"? It has its wisdom, too, the wisdom of accepting, not only man's place in nature, but a need in his nature, the need for the formulation of an idea, the need for a set of values by which he may regard himself, the need for a significant role in the universe. In the complexity of man's nature and experience, the need for one wisdom and the need for the other are, in spite of the apparent contradiction, inextricably mingled to give what, in the Epilogue of *Clarel,* is called the "running battle of the star and clod."

But man yearns for more than a mingling; he yearns for a unifying. In the depth of the "wizard sea" of "The Haglets," the sea in which the magic of reconciliation of our conflicting needs may be found, we meet

> The rays that blend in dream
> The abysm and the star.

And that is what we meet in "Billy in the Darbies." The poem itself is such a dream.

*

Melville died on September 28, 1891. It developed that he was not entirely forgotten. The New York *Daily Tribune,* in its obituary notice, remarked that he had "won considerable fame as an author by the publication of a book in 1847 entitled 'Typee.' " Then added: "This was his best work, although he has since written a number of other stories, which were published more for private than public circulation." *The New York Times,* too, ran an obituary notice. It was entitled: "A Tribute to the late Henry Melville." At the last minute, however, the mistake in the name was corrected by blurring out all the letters of "Henry" except the *H.*

Notes to the Introduction

1 Jean Simon, in *Herman Melville, marin, métaphysicien, et poète* (1939), goes so far as to argue that the first half of *Clarel* was done between the return from the Holy Land in 1857 and *Battle-Pieces,* which appeared in 1866. Howard C. Horsford, in his Introduction to the edition of *Melville's Journal of a Visit to Europe and the Levant,* claims that *Clarel* was begun in the early 1860's and finished in the early 1870's. Walter Bezanson, in his indispensable study of *Clarel* which introduces his edition of the poem, dates the beginning of work after Melville had taken his job as an inspector of customs, that is, on December 5, 1866. Melville may, of course, have been long considering a poem on his journey to the Holy Land, but to me there is a strong presumption that Bezanson is right, based on the difference between *Battle-Pieces* and *Clarel.* In *Battle-Pieces* we still find strongly marked some of the romantic faith in democracy and in the future of America (and the Western World) which had belonged to the country in the days before the Civil War. In *Clarel* this faith is subjected to recurrent and mordant criticism of the sort that was becoming characteristic of many of the more sensitive and perceptive observers of the Gilded Age. Furthermore, the effect of *Battle-Pieces* is of a work in which ideas spring, dramatically and inductively, from the result of a mind grappling immediately with experience. *Clarel* is very different; it is basically schematic and intellectual. It would seem to be, in one perspective at least, a kind of philosophical commentary developing from *Battle-Pieces.*

2 An echo of Marvell appears, oddly enough, in *Billy Budd,* in the name of "Starry Vere," drawn from Marvell's poem, "Upon Appleton House." In "The Genesis of *Billy Budd,*" by Charles R. Anderson (*American Literature,* November 1940), the prototype of Melville's Captain Edward Fairfax Vere is identified as Sir William George Fairfax, commander of the *Indefatigable,* whose career and that of the fictional Vere are closely parallel.

3 The full title gives a fair description of the work: *Rebellion Record: A Diary of American Events, with Documents, Narratives, Illustrative Incidents, Poetry, Etc.*, ed. by Frank Moore. The work was issued in 12 volumes, the first in 1861, the last in 1868. It is not unreasonable to suppose that Melville, poring over this work, found in it—and in its ghastly poetry—the idea for *Battle-Pieces*, for Melville's book does give, like the *Rebellion Record*, a log of the war. And furthermore, the *Record* may well have directed Melville's imagination to certain episodes and emphases, for instance the Battle of Ball's Bluff, which, though of no great military importance, had a great psychological impact, and of which there is a good account in the *Record*, or the sinking of the *Cumberland*, an event treated by several poems in the *Record*. The sinking of the *Cumberland* would, in any case, have been a subject natural to Melville, but "The Swamp Angel," one of Melville's better poems, almost certainly was suggested by the *Record*, as was, in part at least, "A Meditation." In the notes on particular poems I have indicated the kinds of suggestions offered by the *Record*.

4 One biographer, Leon Howard, suggests that in the autumn of 1865, having written a number of the poems and now being out of debt to Harper's, Melville proposed a volume, and that the firm suggested that some of the poems be offered in *Harper's New Monthly Magazine* to test the public reaction. In any case, in 1866 the following poems appeared: "The March to the Sea," February; "The Cumberland," March; "Philip" (later "Sheridan at Cedar Creek"), April; "Chattanooga," June; "Gettysburg," July. It is probably a compliment to the editorial astuteness of the publishers (or of Melville?) that these poems, with the slim exception of a few lines at the end of "Philip," have not the slightest hint of the qualities that make *Battle-Pieces* memorable; these pieces are, without exception, "official" celebrations of Federal victories, with no undertone or overtone of irony of any sort, and without any embarrassing suggestion of poetic talent.

5 The last line is, strictly speaking, tetrameter, but the pauses and weightings are such that it "feels" like pentameter.

6 But the glory, as Charles Feidelson has suggested to me, is diminished, or ironically qualified, by being "belaurelled"—thus honored, shall we say, at the very moment that it is reduced to the irrelevance of nonaction.

7 In a rather poor poem, not here printed, called "The Fortitude of the North, under the Disaster of the Second Manassas," there is an echo to "The March into Virginia" in the line: "The Cape-of-Storms is proof to every throe."

8 How close this is, even in phrase, to much of Conrad, particularly in *Lord Jim*.

9 Charles Feidelson observes that before *Battle-Pieces* Melville had "already given up his own positive mode of action—defeated, I'd say, primarily by the difficulty of acting in the face of his own problematic inwardness. I don't think he ever regarded his poems as major acts in the same way as he regarded his fiction, and I believe this is reflected in the tone of the poems." I should certainly not deny that Melville's attitude toward "action" changed after *Moby Dick*, but I feel that it changed again at a point which I am inclined to locate toward the end of *Clarel* (see pp. 270–72). But what I mean to claim here is that *Battle-Pieces* is concerned with the theme of action in the way I have stated above. The quotations here are from notes provided by Charles Feidelson.

10 Lowell had been invited to compose a hymn for the occasion but refused. Whittier accepted. Both Lowell and Longfellow were invited to compose an ode for the Fourth of July of the Centennial and both refused.

11 For example, Whittier's *Snow-Bound* made the author modestly well off, even in the first year of circulation. *Snow-Bound* appeared, appropriately enough, the same year as *Battle-Pieces,* at the very moment when the new urban world of big industry and rampant finance capitalism was coming into its own, and many citizens, even as they enjoyed the benefits of the new order which the Civil War had ushered in, could look back nostalgically on the innocent world of their own, and the nation's, childhood. *Snow-Bound* was their voice. As for *Battle-Pieces,* it forbade any such romantic escape into the past. It insisted, instead, on a closer look at the inner meaning of the present. It was, in fact, a voice inimical to easy innocence, and to the happy gospel of having one's cake and eating it too.

12 Ruth is the daughter of Nathan; he, born in the Middle West, of Puritan ancestry and upbringing, is a quester who has run through various beliefs, including pantheism, and winds up a convert to Judaism, and a Zionist, with a Jewish wife, Agar, who quite unwillingly has accompanied him to the Holy Land. The story of Nathan, with its echo of the religious fer-

ment in America, is one of the more interesting ones, historically, in *Clarel;* it is, in one sense, to be paired with that of Ungar.

13 In *Pierre* we find that the hero loses his God in discovering the sin of his father: he now may become a "railing atheist" and find evil, metaphysical evil, triumphantly afoot in the world, and everything in life "saturate and soaking with lies." Clarel himself does not reach this state, but when we first see him he lives in a blank world, the world of the eyeless walls. The cause of his plight is not revealed to us, but in Mortmain the loss of faith is clearly related to the evil in his parents. With Clarel himself we have a teasing omission—a blank place in the picture which we are invited to fill in.

14 There is an interesting parallel between Melville and Hawthorne in the constant repetition of the theme of the lost father, and of the Oedipal theme, with the corollary in the theme of incest. For Hawthorne, the fullest analyses of this appear in "Hawthorne's Unfinished Work," by John H. Lamont, M.D. (*Harvard Medical Alumni Bulletin,* xxxvi, 1962), and *The Sins of the Fathers,* by Frederick C. Crews.

15 The blank eyeless walls that Clarel confronts remind us of the walls that poor Bartelby gazes at during life and of the fact that, in death, he lies with "his head touching the cold stone" of the prison wall. Bartelby is never resurrected from his tomb, and *Clarel* may be taken as the sequel in which the alienated man is resurrected. See "Melville's Parable of the Walls," by Leo Marx, in *Sewanee Review,* Vol. LXI (1953).

16 In *Pierre* the relation of the hero and his "lovely immaculate mother" is developed in considerable detail: he is completely dominated by the charming and strong-willed widow, in a love "not to be limited in duration by that climax which is so fatal to ordinary love." The fiancée Lucy, who, being chosen by the mother, is really an extension of her, is scarcely presented as a sexual object, for to Pierre the "husbandly embrace" may be regarded as an "impious thing." It is the arrival of Isabel that breaks the mother's domination, but even here the union is not "impious"; Pierre may feel the sexual impulse toward his wife, but rejects it on the grounds that she is his half-sister (and here we may remember the triangle of Clarel-Agar-Ruth). As Murray suggests, the fear of incest may be merely an alibi, another "ambiguity." Murray also remarks that after the arrival of Isabel the development of Pierre is

short-circuited; he is freed from his mother, but the damage has been done, and hence the violent and hysterical action of the second half of the novel.

Clarel has another interesting relation to *Pierre,* and to *Battle-Pieces* as well. To begin with *Battle-Pieces,* that work has no "hero," no person presented in the process of learning (or failing to learn) the wisdom embodied in the work. We have only the shadowy presence of the author struggling for meaning. But in *Clarel,* this defect, by intention at least, is remedied: we have a hero whose education we can follow. In *Pierre,* as we have said, the identification of the author and the hero is almost complete, and the work is something very close to the avowed exploration of the unconscious of the author.

In *Pierre* there is a further sharpening of focus: As Melville says of the work on the book which Pierre is writing, what "absorbs the time and life of Pierre, is not the book but the primitive elementalizing of the strange stuff, which in the act of attempting that book, has upheaved and upgushed in his soul." Melville's intention was, according to Murray, "to set forth in symbols, allegories, and expository passages his discoveries in the world of mind," for the book that Pierre, in the novel, is attempting to write is the novel that Melville, in real life, is attempting to write.

This fact about *Pierre* leads to another contrast with *Clarel.* In the latter, we are increasingly aware of the distance between the author and the hero; the author accepts the responsibility of his superior wisdom, analyzes Clarel, and at the end, in the Epilogue, summarizes to him, in direct address, the meaning of his experience. To compound and emphasize this detachment, as it were, we find intruded into the work a double of the author, an idealized self—Rolfe. Pierre ends in grievous error and in a moral paralysis relieved only by the desperate melodrama of murder and suicide; but Clarel, with the model of Rolfe (among others) before him, moves toward the wisdom that will enable him to survive. He has overpassed what Melville elsewhere ("In a Bye-Canal") has called the "peril in man."

Related to this difference between the heroes of *Pierre* and *Clarel* is another, more general difference between the two works. Murray, in the essay already mentioned, says that the worst features of *Pierre* (the lack of art, of dramatic control) as well as the best (the force of a profound and pioneering work in depth psychology) are due to Melville's "unconditional surrender to the forces of the unconscious." If this is true—and I accept it—then in *Clarel* (as well as, necessarily, *Battle-Pieces*) we find the deliberate choice of a method that would avoid such a surrender: the author is detached from the hero, both literally and in the dramatic embodiment of Rolfe. The unconscious is used in the poem, but is used objectively, "analyzed."

In regard to my general reading of *Clarel*, the question may reasonably be asked: How do we know that Melville was conscious of all this? Or to state the matter another way: How do we know that Melville intended all this?

One way, and the fundamental way, to answer such questions is to say that what counts is not the degree of consciousness (or of clarity of intention) that the writer actually had during the process of creation, but the degree (or clarity) of expressive integration in the work as it is delivered. What I have tried to do is to indicate what, insofar as the theme is concerned, I take to be the expressive integration of the poem.

Aside, however, from that reply to the question, we do have, in the case of *Clarel*, some reason to assume a certain degree of consciousness on Melville's part, probably a high degree, for *Pierre*, as Murray has ably argued, is not only the product, but the embodiment, of a high degree of consciousness—of even a morbid self-consciousness. It would seem almost inconceivable that Melville, now dealing with related issues, should not have something, to say the least, of the same awareness provoked by the earlier experience in creation. Futhermore, the fact that, under the circumstances of failure, poverty, pressure of time, and emotional strain, *Clarel* got written at all might argue that Melville brought to it the sort of obsessive and probing intensity that carried him through *Moby Dick* and *Pierre*. Obsessive intensity in itself does not, of course, necessarily imply consciousness—but in this case it would, on the record, seem to do so.

17 I have tried to suggest the degree of dialectical thrust in the poem, but it is true that because of diffuseness and technical ineptitude, this thrust is often blurred or lost, unless we are willing to use the scalpel to exposé it. And even then, what we sometimes uncover is a defect in the articulation of the structure.

18 It is true, we must remember, that in some of the later

fiction, notably *The Confidence Man,* and in sketches like "The Lightning Rod Man" and "The Bell Tower," Melville had already taken a deductive approach, perhaps under the influence of Hawthorne's work. If this is true, Melville had done it under a misapprehension of the inner springs of Hawthorne's finer achievements.

19 In *Battle-Pieces,* in the distinction between the "human" and the "ideological," Melville had, of course, been moving toward this.

20 A personal letter of thanks to his uncle for his act of generosity—not the first—runs:

> 26 August, 1875
>
> My dear Uncle Peter:
>
> Last evening I received through a note from Mr. Lansing a check for $1200, which he says you requested him to send me.—I shall at once deposit the money in a Savings Bank, there to remain till needed for the purpose designed.
>
> And now, My Dear Uncle, in receiving this generous gift from you, so much enhanced by the circumstances, I feel the same sentiments which I expressed to you in person at Albany when you so kindly made known your intention. I will not repeat them here; but only pray God to bless you, and have you in His keeping.
>
> With respect and true affection,
> Your nephew,
> Herman Melville.

The donor was dead before the publication of *Clarel* the next year.

21 Charles James Billson, a classicist recently graduated from Oxford, and a lawyer. Letter of October 10, 1884. As late as 1890 Havelock Ellis wrote Melville an admiring letter, asking for information about his ancestry. Ellis was then interested in exploring a possible relation between race and literary talent. The letter is in the Houghton Library, at Harvard.

22 It is assumed that the burning of the poems took place when Melville left Arrowhead, in October 1863. But if so, this was not the first time Melville had disposed of his work in such a summary fashion; there is a letter to Thomas, on May 25, 1862, in which Melville says that he had sold his "doggeral" [*sic*] at ten cents a pound to a trunk maker for lining.

23 There is no unanimity among critics for the date of this poem. Some date it very early.

24 In general, Melville and Hardy have much in common—their thirst for ultimates and their metaphysical cast of mind, their stoicism and irony, their combination of compassion and grudging "meliorism," their collocations of realistic and conventionally poetic elements, their wrenching of rhythms, their idiosyncratic vocabularies (for instance, see "lumbering lubbard" and "impingers rue thee," among other examples in "The Berg"), their isolation from prevailing styles and attitudes of their time, the fact that both were self-educated, and even the fact that both made the real commitment to poetry, not in the flush of youth, but in middle life.

25 Harrison Hayford and Merton M. Sealts, Jr., in their *Billy Budd, Sailor: An Inside Narrative,* give a fascinating account of the origin and growth of the novel.

26 Some of Melville's fiction is, of course, more prosaic ("Bartleby the Scrivener" or *The Confidence Man,* for instance), and that was the last direction of his work in fiction, until *Billy Budd,* in which there is some return to the earlier way of thinking.

27 And of course, Jack Chase, the godly creature to whom *Billy Budd* is dedicated, was "Captain of the Maintop in the year 1843 in the U. S. Frigate United States."

28 This element remains in the novel, but is put in a less significant position, in Chapter 29.

29 A close and astute student of Melville has objected here that Melville would not, in all probability, have been much affected by the fate of his sons, or daughters for that matter; that he was an "unnatural" father, made life at home very difficult for his children, and was the chief cause of the failure of Stanwix and the suicide of Malcolm, who was in terror of him. These facts are, indeed, on the record. But, with the full and humbling recognition of them, as of the fact that matters of human and literary motive always lie in a shadowland, I should argue my position as follows:

Melville did deliberately draw the father-son theme into a story where it was not even hinted at in the original form with which he began to work. It is not unusual, of course, for such an obsessive theme (and there should be little debate that this theme was obsessive for Melville) to attach itself to material that, off-hand, does not seem to invite it. But two facts here do seem worthy of comment: that the death of Stanwix did occur during the period when Melville was moving toward the alteration of the original tough old Billy into the new innocent, young Billy, and that Melville did reverse the focus of interest, in his obsessive theme, from that of son seeking father to that of the father's attitude toward the son who finds him. What I suggest is that even if the death of Stanwix came *after* the process of the change of Billy had begun, the death *may* still have provoked the shift of the focus of interest, and that even if the death came *after* that shift of focus had begun, it would still, almost inevitably, have effects that would coalesce with, and intensify, that process. Given the uncertainty about dates, this is what we can, with a high degree of probability, now claim.

What I have been rehearsing is, however, not an answer, but the preparation for an answer, to the original objection based on Melville's defective paternal sense. It seems to me that Melville's record as an unnatural father, instead of being an objection to my line of speculation, may very well support it, that it may be closely related to the fact that Melville did change the focus of interest in the father-son theme and turn Vere into what is, when stripped of all explanation and extenuation, a son-killer. It may be countered here that Melville may have done this merely to heighten his drama, but I should reply that, though technical considerations do sometimes have decisive effects on themes and meanings, they work in terms of what is psychologically available, at greater or lesser remove; and that, if the change of focus came here as a direct result of a technical consideration (the wish to heighten dramatic tension), the particular change clearly did involve what was psychologically available, and available at a minimal remove. Furthermore, and more crucially, if Melville, caught in the self-absorption of his anguish, was an unnatural father, this does not mean that he would not know the anguish of that self-absorption. The need to break out of the self, to identify the self with a fate beyond the personal fate ("Not narrowed down to personal cheer," as it is put in "An Uninscribed Monument") is a theme that lies, as I have tried to indicate, at the very center of *Battle-Pieces* and of *Clarel* (and it might be added, of *Moby*

Dick and *Pierre* as well). Art is often confessional and penitential, and self-criticism, even self-denigration, can be as central a dynamic in literature as self-justification. In fact, the sense of guilt may sometimes lead to the yearning projection of the self-that-might-have-been, the idealized self acting out a redemptive drama. That is, art can be as readily summoned to repair the defects of our own moral nature as to repair, according to the standard formula, the defects of nature. How rarely, indeed, do we find an easy equation between the virtues celebrated in a literary work and the private life of the author! Rather, cads and monsters often make the best idealists on the printed page. Strip the "ethereal" Shelley of his poems, and what do we have? Or strip the "compassionate" Dreiser. And the most touching lullaby in English poetry was composed by Robert Greene, who married a gentlewoman, wasted her dowry, and removed himself from her bed and the family circle to the taverns, where he famously died of the "surfeit of Rhenish wine and pickled herring." And if Melville was an unnatural father, there still lie among his papers the letters to his children written aboard the *Meteor,* in 1860. The two letters to Malcolm give the events of the voyage that would appeal to an eleven-year-old, the sight of Tierra del Fuego, the weather off the terrible Horn, and the death and sea-burial of the sailor Ray, who fell from the rigging while furling the topsails in rough weather and crashed to the deck at the feet of "Uncle Tom." In the second letter Melville does lecture Malcolm:

> I hope you have called to mind what I said to you about your behaviour previous to my going away. I hope that you have been obedient to your mother and helped her all you could and saved her trouble. Now is the time to show what you are—whether you are a good, honorable boy, or a good-for-nothing one. Any boy of your age, who disobeys his mother, or worries her, or is disrespectful to her—such a boy is a poor shabby fellow, and if you know any such boys, you ought to cut their acquaintance.

But the letter concludes:

> I think of you and Stanwix and Bessie and Fanny very often, and often long to be with you. But it cannot be

at present. The picture which I have of you and the rest, I look at sometimes, till the faces almost seem real.— Now, my Dear Boy, good bye, and God bless you—

Your affectionate father
H. Melville.

The letter to Bessie is carefully printed out so that she could read it herself. He tells of the birds that follow the ship, says that every time he uses the little bag she had made for him he thinks of her, and ends by saying that he hopes she takes good care of little Fanny and that when they go up the hill, where the strawberries are, they "go this way"—and there is a sketch of two little girls going hand in hand up a hill.

Among the papers there is, too, a little present Melville had sent for Fanny's delight—the fin of a baby flying fish, dry, translucent, light as air.

Nothing is simple.

30 In connection with the process by which Melville altered the conception and meaning of Billy, we should perhaps note that during this period, two magazine articles revived interest in the *Somers* case, "Mutiny on the Somers," by Lt. H. D. Smith, in the *American Magazine*, June 1888, and "The Murder of Philip Spencer," by Gail Hamilton (Mary Abigail Dodge, a friend of the aging Whittier, who may have fancied herself as more than his friend), in the *Cosmopolitan Magazine*, in three installments beginning June 1889. Smith's article comes early enough to have a possible though not a necessary relation to the development of Vere's character, in sympathetically emphasizing the responsibility of command. Hamilton's article, though its date makes conjecture of relationship difficult, and though it is a telling attack on Mackenzie and Gansevoort, is consistent on certain important points with Melville's treatment of the story, for instance, in its emphasis on the possibility of mental imbalance in Mackenzie, a question raised about Vere.

Neither article is, of course, necessary to establish some relation between *Billy Budd* and the *Somers* case. Melville has referred to the case as early as *White-Jacket*, where, in discussing the barbarity of the Articles of War, he writes: "The well-known case of a United States brig furnishes a memorable example, which at any moment may be repeated. Three men, in a time of peace, were then hung at the yard-arm, merely because, in the Captain's judgment, it became necessary to hang them. To this day the question of their complete guilt is socially discussed." (Ch. lxxii.) The contrast between Melville's view of the case here and that in "Bridegroom Dick" is marked. In spite of the savage handling of Mackenzie (and Guert) by various writers, including James Fenimore Cooper (see *The Cruise of the Somers: Illustrative of the Despotism of the Quarter Deck; and of the Unmanly Conduct of Captain Mackenzie*), the family had clung to the belief that Guert's action was approved by God, and Melville's shift in attitude between *White Jacket* and "Bridegroom Dick" may have been conditioned by this fact. Furthermore, the attitude in *White-Jacket* is polemical and not dramatic. By the time we get to *Billy Budd,* where Melville again refers to the *Somers* case (Ch. 21), the belittling remark that the men were hanged "merely because, in the Captain's judgment, it became necessary," has changed to a discussion of the "obscuring smoke" of ignorance in which a commander must sometimes make crucial decisions. Without the "obscuring smoke," not only of ignorance but of moral complexity, there would be no role for Vere, and no story as we now have it. As for a specific judgment in *Billy Budd* on the *Somers* case, Melville merely dismisses the topic with the strange and ambiguous words: "History, and here cited without a comment." Revived speculations about Mackenzie's role, and that of Guert, may well have contributed to the development of the character and story of Vere; and even such a thing as the parallel in the fact that both Mackenzie (who was an author) and Vere are anomalously bookish becomes curiously teasing.

31 As a matter of fact, Stanwix did have certain physical disabilities that bear on his confused life. He gave up working in Allan Melville's law office because of deafness, and gave up a later attempt to become a dentist because he was near-sighted.

As a parallel to the general question of doom and reconciliation for Stanwix, Malcolm, Spencer, and Billy, we may look back on what is said about the mutineers of the Nore. In *Billy Budd,* Chapter 3, we find that the same men who, at the Nore, "converted into irony" the "patriotic devotion" celebrated in certain popular songs were, in another ironic shift, to help "win a coronet for Nelson at the Nile, and the naval crown of crowns for him at Trafalgar." The irony behind this superficial irony is that the same human quality—"pugnacious instinct"—which leads, at one moment, to mutiny at the Nore may, at another moment, lead to the patriotic heroism at Trafalgar. Or, again, in the same chapter, it is said that the Nore mutiny was analogous to a "contagious fever"; in other words, in both "instinct" and "fever" are implied elements of "doom" beyond moral responsibility.

In the treatment of Claggart, in Chapter 12, the question is put more explicitly. Claggart, too, is "doomed": "With no power to annul the elemental evil in him, though readily enough he could hide it; apprehending the good, but powerless to be it; a nature like Claggart's, surcharged with energy as such natures almost invariably are, what recourse is left to it but to recoil upon itself and, like the scorpion for which the Creator alone is responsible, act out to the end the part allotted to it." But the theme of responsibility runs on into Chapter 13, in the discussion of the spilled soup. It is a "mere accident," we are told, but Claggart must have taken it as the "sly escape of spontaneous feeling . . . more or less answering to the antipathy in his own." Are the "mere accident" and the "sly escape" of feeling to be taken as mutually exclusive interpretations? Or can they co-exist in the same act? But the theme permeates the story. We remember that when, in Chapter 1, Billy had given the "buffer" on the *Rights of Man* the terrible drubbing, his arm had simply come flying out; and the Captain says of the event: "I dare say he never meant to do quite as much as he did . . ." This is simply a muted parallel to the killing of Claggart. Again, in Chapters 20 and 21, when the surgeon questions Vere's sanity, the same question, in another form, is raised.

32 There is a fascinating parallel between the roles of Billy and Captain Vere, and those of Natty Bumppo and Judge Templeton in *The Pioneers*, of Cooper. Natty, though chronologically old, is a child in the ways of the world, with the "natural" virtues of the forest; he is the "innocent," the "barbarian," confronted by the complex, ambiguous, and often paradoxical demands of the civilized order. Judge Templeton, like Captain Vere, is fully aware of, and appreciative of, the virtues of the "innocent." Furthermore, if Judge Templeton is not the father of Natty, his role, as the carrier of traditional wisdom, is paternal; he must see over and beyond Natty. More specifically, the Judge does have a "paternal" obligation to Natty, in that Natty has saved the life of his child Elizabeth and is, therefore, assimilated, symbolically speaking, to her.

The Judge, like Captain Vere, must go beyond his appreciation of innocence, and beyond his personal obligation, to affirm social continuity and defend the community. If, in *The Pioneers,* the end of the matter is pathos rather than tragedy, this does not deny the fact that Judge Templeton is caught in the same cleft stick as Captain Vere, and that the moral and philosophical content of both episodes is the same.

We may say, indeed, that the two episodes, one early and one late in the 19th century, are the two great seminal trial scenes in American literature. They are both concerned with a basic issue and obsessive theme of the American story. In both episodes, it is America that is, in one sense, on trial. Not that America is the accused. America is both the accused *and* the judge before whom the accused stands, and both collaborate in enacting the drama of America. Let us not forget that in any trial, the judge is on trial as well as the accused.

Huckleberry Finn, though not a novel involving a trial, does involve, we may point out, the same basic theme as *The Pioneers* and *Billy Budd.*

33 The theme of reconciliation in *Billy Budd* (as in "Billy in the Darbies") is not universally accepted. A number of critics have undertaken to persuade us that the story is, in a greater or lesser degree, an exercise in irony. It is not that they maintain, merely, that the story is full of ironical contrasts, dilemmas, and paradoxes (as it clearly is). What they maintain is that it does not mean what it obviously says, what it obviously says being that Vere, a decent and thoughtful man, sacrifices Billy, whom, in one perspective, he knows to be guiltless, and whom he loves as a "father," to a necessary definition of justice, and that Billy accepts his fate and blesses the instrument of it. The most radical proponent of this ironical view is Lawrance Thompson, the author of *Melville's Quarrel with God,* who, by working from a set of rather peculiar assumptions, arrives at the conclusion that *Billy Budd* summarizes what he regards as Melville's life-long obsession:

> Motivated by his mingled disillusionment, hate, skepticism, agnosticism, wistfulness, Melville projected his complex narratives not merely because he was caught on the horns of what some like to view as a profoundly ambiguous paradox but also because he took comfort and delight in employing ambiguities and equivocations as stylistic devices for hoodwinking and deceiving those

> readers whom he hated because they would be inclined to resent the dark implications of his single thematic concern. His obsession, which remained quite constant, achieved an increasingly Schopenhauerish intensity of hate toward the end of his life. On the last page of the manuscript of *Billy Budd* he wrote, 'END OF BOOK April 19th, 1891.'

Some of the questions raised by the "ironists" are, however, fruitful if taken in the context of the whole story, or of Melville's work in general. The story does not, indeed, offer any easy "solution"; ironic contrasts do lie in the very tissue of the conception of the story (and of the poem, too), and in one sense what the story says is that the only "solution" lies in the stance one may take toward the "insoluble."

The poem is not to be taken as fully defining that stance, for the stance is implicit in the direction and conclusion of the whole action. But the poem is important in that it gives an air of acceptance on the part of the person who would have the greatest difficulty in accepting the values embodied in the action. It is true, of course, that the ballad is not spoken *by* Billy but is composed *about* him. But even if we accept the notion that this "fictitious" Billy does not speak the language of the literal Billy, nor have the same cast of mind, this Billy, in his "satirical turns," does dramatize, first, the difficulty of the struggle of the literal Billy to come to terms with his fate, and second, the pathos in his acceptance of the values implicit in that fate.

In this connection, the placement of the poem has some importance in our reading of it. Since it is at the end, we read it *after* the cry "God bless Captain Vere!" and *after* we know the peculiar physiological features of Billy's death, and we read the poem as permeated with that knowledge. But though the poem comes, in placement, *after* the cry of blessing and the death, it is a narrative cut-back, which gives us a version of Billy's experience on the night before his death, the experience that leads to the cry of blessing and the peaceful death. In other words, the poem traces, in terms of Billy's own sensibility, the growth of the feeling of acceptance which has already been fictionally rendered. The poem is, then, the "innermost" part of the "inside story" of Billy, and as such was finally chosen as the thing on which the whole should come to focus.

I say "finally chosen," for during the several stages of the process of composition, according to the analysis by Hayford and Sealts, the work did not end with the poem but with the news account, which now constitutes the penultimate chapter. The news account is, of course, the "outermost" part of the "outside story" of Billy, being official, remote, and dehumanized, and it does afford a savagely ironical contrast to the "inside story," which is the content avowed in Melville's final subtitle, "An Inside Narrative." If the work did come to rest on the news story, there might be more, though not decisive, reasons for accepting the readings offered by the ironists. But Melville did elect the poem as the final focus for the whole, and what we carry away is the image of Billy given therein. As for what further revisions Melville might have made had he lived, we certainly cannot argue with any certainty beyond the text as it now stands. Furthermore, the direction of Melville's reworkings seems clear and coherent.

When I say "clear and coherent," I do not mean to deny the contrasts the ironists dwell on, or those offered by Paul Brodtkorb, Jr., in "The Definitive *Billy Budd:* 'But aren't it all sham?'" (PMLA, Dec. 1967, vol. lxxxii) to indicate that the text as we have it may be regarded as composed of various strata of development often inconsistent with each other. But it does seem to me that to schematize the contrasts as sets of options (conservative versus radical, etc.) violates the nature of the story, a story which, as Hayford and Sealts put it, is about a "problematic world." They write: "But the rhetorical question 'Who in the rainbow can draw the line . . . ?' should be a warning to critics who find the lines of demarcation in the story easy to determine and who suppose Melville's own attitude was altogether clear cut."

I should go further and say that the story is a clear and coherent development of the theme which haunts *Battle-Pieces* and *Clarel.* Both of those works are concerned with the problematical nature of the world; they are about the fact that we do not find values "clear cut." Life is a tissue of polarities, ironies, contradictions, and its tragic nature derives from the fact that in this realm of ambiguity we must, in the end, act. Melville's hero is, as I have said, the man who, fully aware of the context and the cost of action, can yet act. It may be objected that Clarel bears little relation to the warriors of *Battle-Pieces* who, in spite of all ambiguities, can act—that Clarel, in fact, doesn't "do" anything. But he does enter the "city" of men, and that act, small as it may literally seem, means, in the context of the poem, the acceptance of the necessity for action: he has been "resurrected." He can now follow Vine's counsel and "live it out."

I should add that I do not see the psychoanalytical view of *Billy Budd*, any more than that of the ironists, as necessarily invalidating the theme of reconciliation. If the story of Billy is, like that of Clarel, a story of the groping movement toward maturity, then the "hostility" presumably indicated by the stutter is what is resolved behind the door of the Captain's cabin. The Oedipal conflict is overpassed: Billy is initiated into the world of manhood, the "father" offers both "love" and "law," and now Billy, in accepting the "doom" of the world, can bless the father. If Billy, being put to sleep at the end of the poem, is an echo of "Baby Budd" of the early stage of the story, that fact is now profoundly modified.

34 Critics have pointed out the possible relation of another poem on the death of a sailor, "Tom Bowling," by Charles Dibdin, to "Billy in the Darbies," emphasizing the "aloft" and "alow":

> His form was of the manliest beauty,
> His heart was kind and soft;
> Faithful below, he did his duty;
> But now he's gone aloft.

35 To consider further the reading of the passage, we should note that the "moonshine," whatever the nature of the comfort it may be taken to imply, will "die in the dawning of Billy's last day." That is, against any comfort of reconciliation, there is to be considered the brutal "daylight" fact of death. The discussion in Chapter 24 of *Billy Budd* on the point of Billy's innocence is fairly general. The Chaplain is said to feel that he has "no consolation to proffer which could result in a peace transcending that which he beheld"; and to feel that "innocence was an even better thing than religion with which to go to Judgment." Billy is like a "superior savage" or a "barbarian"—a "natural" man.

36 Presumably by "last sacrament" is here intended the viaticum, with its use of bread and wine.

37 It is possible that the last stanza of "The Haglets" implies such an idea—the idea that the "rays" that blend the "abysm" and the "star" are, in themselves, "natural."

FROM

Battle-Pieces and Aspects of the War

1866

The Portent

(1859)

Hanging from the beam,
Slowly swaying (such the law),
Gaunt the shadow on your green,
Shenandoah!
The cut is on the crown
(Lo, John Brown),
And the stabs shall heal no more.

Hidden in the cap
Is the anguish none can draw;
So your future veils its face,
Shenandoah!
But the streaming beard is shown
(Weird John Brown),
The meteor of the war.

Misgivings

(1860)

When ocean-clouds over inland hills
Sweep storming in late autumn brown,
And horror the sodden valley fills,
And the spire falls crashing in the town,
I muse upon my country's ills—
The tempest bursting from the waste of Time
On the world's fairest hope linked with man's foulest crime.

Nature's dark side is heeded now—
(Ah! optimist-cheer disheartened flown)—
A child may read the moody brow
Of yon black mountain lone.
With shouts the torrents down the gorges go,
And storms are formed behind the storm we feel:
The hemlock shakes in the rafter, the oak in the driving keel.

The Conflict of Convictions

(1860–1)

On starry heights
  A bugle wails the long recall;
Derision stirs the deep abyss,
  Heaven's ominous silence over all.
Return, return, O eager Hope,
  And face man's latter fall.
Events, they make the dreamers quail;
Satan's old age is strong and hale,
A disciplined captain, gray in skill,
And Raphael a white enthusiast still;
Dashed aims, at which Christ's martyrs pale,
Shall Mammon's slaves fulfill?

  (*Dismantle the fort,*
  Cut down the fleet—
  Battle no more shall be!
  While the fields for fight in æons to come
  Congeal beneath the sea.)

The terrors of truth and dart of death
  To faith alike are vain;
Though comets, gone a thousand years,
    Return again,
Patient she stands—she can no more—
And waits, nor heeds she waxes hoar.

  (*At a stony gate,*
  A statue of stone,
  Weed overgrown—
  Long 'twill wait!)

But God his former mind retains,
  Confirms his old decree;
The generations are inured to pains,
  And strong Necessity
Surges, and heaps Time's strand with wrecks.
  The People spread like a weedy grass,
  The thing they will they bring to pass,
And prosper to the apoplex.
The rout it herds around the heart,
  The ghost is yielded in the gloom;
Kings wag their heads—Now save thyself
  Who wouldst rebuild the world in bloom.

  (*Tide-mark*
  And top of the ages' strife,
  Verge where they called the world to come,
  The last advance of life—
  Ha ha, the rust on the Iron Dome!)

Nay, but revere the hid event;
  In the cloud a sword is girded on,
I mark a twinkling in the tent
  Of Michael the warrior one.
Senior wisdom suits not now,
The light is on the youthful brow.

  (*Ay, in caves the miner see:*
  His forehead bears a blinking light;
  Darkness so he feebly braves—
  A meagre wight!)

But He who rules is old—is old;
Ah! faith is warm, but heaven with age is cold.

  (*Ho ho, ho ho,*
  The cloistered doubt

Of olden times
Is blurted out!)

The Ancient of Days forever is young,
Forever the scheme of Nature thrives;
I know a wind in purpose strong—
It spins *against* the way it drives.
What if the gulfs their slimed foundations bare?
So deep must the stones be hurled
Whereon the throes of ages rear
The final empire and the happier world.

(*The poor old Past,*
The Future's slave,
She drudged through pain and crime
To bring about the blissful Prime,
Then—perished. There's *a grave!*)

Power unanointed may come—
Dominion (unsought by the free)
And the Iron Dome,
Stronger for stress and strain,
Fling her huge shadow athwart the main;
But the Founders' dream shall flee.
Age after age shall be
As age after age has been,
(From man's changeless heart their way they win);
And death be busy with all who strive—
Death, with silent negative.

YEA AND NAY—
EACH HATH HIS SAY;
BUT GOD HE KEEPS THE MIDDLE WAY.
NONE WAS BY
WHEN HE SPREAD THE SKY;
WISDOM IS VAIN, AND PROPHESY.

The March into Virginia

Ending in the First Manassas

(JULY, 1861)

Did all the lets and bars appear
To every just or larger end,
Whence should come the trust and cheer?
Youth must its ignorant impulse lend—
Age finds place in the rear.
All wars are boyish, and are fought by boys,
The champions and enthusiasts of the state:
Turbid ardors and vain joys
Not barrenly abate—
Stimulants to the power mature,
Preparatives of fate.

Who here forecasteth the event?
What heart but spurns at precedent
And warnings of the wise,
Contemned foreclosures of surprise?
The banners play, the bugles call,
The air is blue and prodigal.
No berrying party, pleasure-wooed,
No picnic party in the May,
Ever went less loth than they
Into that leafy neighborhood.
In Bacchic glee they file toward Fate,
Moloch's uninitiate;
Expectancy, and glad surmise
Of battle's unknown mysteries.
All they feel is this: 'tis glory,
A rapture sharp, though transitory,
Yet lasting in belaureled story.

So they gayly go to fight,
Chatting left and laughing right.

But some who this blithe mood present,
    As on in lightsome files they fare,
Shall die experienced ere three days are spent—
    Perish, enlightened by the vollied glare;
Or shame survive, and, like to adamant,
    The throe of Second Manassas share.

Ball's Bluff

A Reverie

(OCTOBER, 1861)

One noonday, at my window in the town,
I saw a sight—saddest that eyes can see—
Young soldiers marching lustily
Unto the wars,
With fifes, and flags in mottoed pageantry;
While all the porches, walks, and doors
Were rich with ladies cheering royally.

They moved like Juny morning on the wave,
Their hearts were fresh as clover in its prime
(It was the breezy summer time),
Life throbbed so strong,
How should they dream that Death in a rosy clime
Would come to thin their shining throng?
Youth feels immortal, like the gods sublime.

Weeks passed; and at my window, leaving bed,
By night I mused, of easeful sleep bereft,
On those brave boys (Ah War! thy theft);
Some marching feet
Found pause at last by cliffs Potomac cleft;
Wakeful I mused, while in the street
Far footfalls died away till none were left.

Dupont's Round Fight

(NOVEMBER, 1861)

In time and measure perfect moves
    All Art whose aim is sure;
Evolving rhyme and stars divine
    Have rules, and they endure.

Nor less the Fleet that warred for Right,
    And, warring so, prevailed
In geometric beauty curved,
    And in an orbit sailed.

The rebel at Port Royal felt
    The Unity overawe,
And rued the spell. A type was here,
    And victory of LAW.

The Stone Fleet

An Old Sailor's Lament

(DECEMBER, 1861)

I have a feeling for those ships,
    Each worn and ancient one,
With great bluff bows, and broad in the beam:
    Ay, it was unkindly done.
                But so they serve the Obsolete—
                Even so, Stone Fleet!

You'll say I'm doting; do but think
    I scudded round the Horn in one—
The Tenedos, a glorious
    Good old craft as ever run—
                Sunk (how all unmeet!)
                With the Old Stone Fleet.

An India ship of fame was she,
    Spices and shawls and fans she bore;
A whaler when her wrinkles came—
    Turned off! till, spent and poor,
                Her bones were sold (escheat)!
                Ah! Stone Fleet.

Four were erst patrician keels
    (Names attest what families be),
The Kensington, and Richmond too,
    Leonidas, and Lee:
                But now they have their seat
                With the Old Stone Fleet.

To scuttle them—a pirate deed—
    Sack them, and dismast;

They sunk so slow, they died so hard,
  But gurgling dropped at last.
    Their ghosts in gales repeat
    Woe's us, Stone Fleet!

And all for naught. The waters pass—
  Currents will have their way;
Nature is nobody's ally; 'tis well;
  The harbor is bettered—will stay.
    A failure, and complete,
    Was your Old Stone Fleet.

Donelson

(FEBRUARY, 1862)

The bitter cup
    Of that hard countermand
Which gave the Envoys up,
Still was wormwood in the mouth,
    And clouds involved the land,
When, pelted by sleet in the icy street,
    About the bulletin-board a band
Of eager, anxious people met,
And every wakeful heart was set
On latest news from West or South.
"No seeing here," cries one—"don't crowd"—
"You tall man, pray you, read aloud."

IMPORTANT.

We learn that General Grant,
Marching from Henry overland,
And joined by a force up the Cumberland sent
(Some thirty thousand the command),
On Wednesday a good position won—
Began the siege of Donelson.

This stronghold crowns a river-bluff,
A good broad mile of leveled top;
Inland the ground rolls off
Deep-gorged, and rocky, and broken up—
A wilderness of trees and brush.
The spaded summit shows the roods
Of fixed intrenchments in their hush;
Breast-works and rifle-pits in woods
Perplex the base.—

The welcome weather
Is clear and mild; 'tis much like May.
The ancient boughs that lace together
Along the stream, and hang far forth,
Strange with green mistletoe, betray
A dreamy contrast to the North.

Our troops are full of spirits—say
The siege won't prove a creeping one.
They purpose not the lingering stay
Of old beleaguerers; not that way;
But, full of vim *from Western prairies won,*
They'll make, ere long, a dash at Donelson.

Washed by the storm till the paper grew
Every shade of a streaky blue,
That bulletin stood. The next day brought
A second.

LATER FROM THE FORT.
Grant's investment is complete—
A semicircular one.
Both wings the Cumberland's margin meet,
Then, backward curving, clasp the rebel seat.
On Wednesday this good work was done;
But of the doers some lie prone.
Each wood, each hill, each glen was fought for;
The bold inclosing line we wrought for
Flamed with sharpshooters. Each cliff cost
A limb or life. But back we forced
Reserves and all; made good our hold;
And so we rest.

Events unfold.
On Thursday added ground was won,
A long bold steep: we near the Den.
Later the foe came shouting down
In sortie, which was quelled; and then
We stormed them on their left.
A chilly change in the afternoon;
The sky, late clear, is now bereft
Of sun. Last night the ground froze hard—
Rings to the enemy as they run
Within their works. A ramrod bites
The lip it meets. The cold incites
To swinging of arms with brisk rebound.
Smart blows 'gainst lusty chests resound.

Along the outer line we ward
A crackle of skirmishing goes on.
Our lads creep round on hand and knee,
They fight from behind each trunk and
stone;
And sometimes, flying for refuge, one
Finds 'tis an enemy shares the tree.
Some scores are maimed by boughs shot off
In the glades by the Fort's big gun.
We mourn the loss of Colonel Morrison,
Killed while cheering his regiment on.
Their far sharpshooters try our stuff;
And ours return them puff for puff:
'Tis diamond-cutting-diamond work.
Woe on the rebel cannoneer
Who shows his head. Our fellows lurk
Like Indians that waylay the deer
By the wild salt-spring.—The sky is dun,
Foredooming the fall of Donelson.
Stern weather is all unwonted here.
The people of the country own

We brought it. Yea, the earnest North
Has elementally issued forth
To storm this Donelson.

FURTHER.

A yelling rout
Of ragamuffins broke profuse
To-day from out the Fort.
Sole uniform they wore, a sort
Of patch, or white badge (as you choose)
Upon the arm. But leading these,
Or mingling, were men of face
And bearing of patrician race,
Splendid in courage and gold lace—
The officers. Before the breeze
Made by their charge, down went our line;
But, rallying, charged back in force,
And broke the sally; yet with loss.
This on the left; upon the right
Meanwhile there was an answering fight;
Assailants and assailed reversed.
The charge too upward, and not down—
Up a steep ridge-side, toward its crown,
A strong redoubt. But they who first
Gained the fort's base, and marked the trees
Felled, heaped in horned perplexities,
And shagged with brush; and swarming there
Fierce wasps whose sting was present death—
They faltered, drawing bated breath,
And felt it was in vain to dare;
Yet still, perforce, returned the ball,
Firing into the tangled wall
Till ordered to come down. They came;
But left some comrades in their fame,
Red on the ridge in icy wreath

And hanging gardens of cold Death.
But not quite unavenged these fell;
Our ranks once out of range, a blast
Of shrapnel and quick shell
Burst on the rebel horde, still massed,
Scattering them pell-mell.
(This fighting—judging what we read—
Both charge and countercharge,
Would seem but Thursday's told at large,
Before in brief reported.—Ed.)
Night closed in about the Den
Murky and lowering. Ere long, chill rains.
A night not soon to be forgot,
Reviving old rheumatic pains
And longings for a cot.
No blankets, overcoats, or tents.
Coats thrown aside on the warm march here—
We looked not then for changeful cheer;
Tents, coats, and blankets too much care.
No fires; a fire a mark presents;
Near by, the trees show bullet-dents.
Rations were eaten cold and raw.
The men well soaked, came snow; and more—
A midnight sally. Small sleeping done—
But such is war;
No matter, we'll have Fort Donelson.

"Ugh! ugh!
'Twill drag along—drag along,"
Growled a cross patriot in the throng,
His battered umbrella like an ambulance-cover
Riddled with bullet-holes, spattered all over.

"Hurrah for Grant!" cried a stripling shrill;
Three urchins joined him with a will,
And some of taller stature cheered.
Meantime a Copperhead passed; he sneered.
    "Win or lose," he pausing said,
"Caps fly the same; all boys, mere boys;
Any thing to make a noise.
    Like to see the list of the dead;
These '*craven Southerners*' hold out;
Ay, ay, they'll give you many a bout."
    "We'll beat in the end, sir,"
Firmly said one in staid rebuke,
A solid merchant, square and stout.
    "And do you think it? that way tend, sir?"
Asked the lean Copperhead, with a look
Of splenetic pity. "Yes, I do."
His yellow death's head the croaker shook:
"The country's ruined, that I know."
A shower of broken ice and snow,
    In lieu of words, confuted him;
They saw him hustled round the corner go,
    And each by-stander said—Well suited him.

Next day another crowd was seen
In the dark weather's sleety spleen.
Bald-headed to the storm came out
A man, who, 'mid a joyous shout;
Silently posted this brief sheet:

GLORIOUS VICTORY OF THE FLEET!

FRIDAY'S GREAT EVENT!

THE ENEMY'S WATER-BATTERIES BEAT!

WE SILENCED EVERY GUN!

THE OLD COMMODORE'S COMPLIMENTS SENT
PLUMP INTO DONELSON!

"Well, well, go on!" exclaimed the crowd
To him who thus much read aloud.
"That's all," he said. "What! nothing more?"
"Enough for a cheer, though—hip, hurrah!
"But here's old Baldy come again—
"More news!"—And now a different strain.

(*Our own reporter a dispatch compiles,*
As best he may, from varied sources.)

Large re-enforcements have arrived—
Munitions, men, and horses—
For Grant, and all debarked, with stores.

The enemy's field-works extend six miles—
The gate still hid; so well contrived.

Yesterday stung us; frozen shores
Snow-clad, and through the drear defiles
And over the desolate ridges blew
A Lapland wind.
The main affair
Was a good two hours' steady fight
Between our gun-boats and the Fort.
The Louisville's wheel was smashed
outright.
A hundred-and-twenty-eight-pound ball
Came planet-like through a starboard port,
Killing three men, and wounding all
The rest of that gun's crew,
(*The captain of the gun was cut in two*);
Then splintering and ripping went—
Nothing could be its continent.

In the narrow stream the Louisville,
Unhelmed, grew lawless; swung around,
And would have thumped and drifted, till
All the fleet was driven aground,
But for the timely order to retire.

Some damage from our fire, 'tis thought,
Was done the water-batteries of the Fort.

Little else took place that day,
Except the field artillery in line
Would now and then—for love, they say—
Exchange a valentine.

The old sharpshooting going on.
Some plan afoot as yet unknown;
So Friday closed round Donelson.

LATER.
Great suffering through the night—
A stinging one. Our heedless boys
Were nipped like blossoms. Some dozen
Hapless wounded men were frozen.
During day being struck down out of sight,
And help-cries drowned in roaring noise,
They were left just where the skirmish
shifted—
Left in dense underbrush snow-drifted.
Some, seeking to crawl in crippled plight,
So stiffened—perished.
Yet in spite
Of pangs for these, no heart is lost.
Hungry, and clothing stiff with frost,
Our men declare a nearing sun
Shall see the fall of Donelson.

And this they say, yet not disown
The dark redoubts round Donelson,
And ice-glazed corpses, each a stone—
A sacrifice to Donelson;
They swear it, and swerve not, gazing on
A flag, deemed black, flying from Donelson.
Some of the wounded in the wood
Were cared for by the foe last night,
Though he could do them little needed good,
Himself being all in shivering plight.
The rebel is wrong, but human yet;
He's got a heart, and thrusts a bayonet.
He gives us battle with wondrous will—
This bluff's a perverted Bunker Hill.

The stillness stealing through the throng
The silent thought and dismal fear revealed;
They turned and went,
Musing on right and wrong
And mysteries dimly sealed—
Breasting the storm in daring discontent;
The storm, whose black flag showed in heaven,
As if to say no quarter there was given
To wounded men in wood,
Or true hearts yearning for the good—
All fatherless seemed the human soul.
But next day brought a bitterer bowl—
On the bulletin-board this stood:

Saturday morning at 3 A.M.
A stir within the Fort betrayed
That the rebels were getting under arms;
Some plot these early birds had laid.
But a lancing sleet cut him who stared
Into the storm. After some vague alarms,
Which left our lads unscared,

Out sallied the enemy at dim of dawn,
With cavalry and artillery, and went
In fury at our environment.
Under cover of shot and shell
Three columns of infantry rolled on,
Vomited out of Donelson—
Rolled down the slopes like rivers of hell,
Surged at our line, and swelled and poured
Like breaking surf. But unsubmerged
Our men stood up, except where roared
The enemy through one gap. We urged
Our all of manhood to the stress,
But still showed shattered in our desperateness.
Back set the tide,
But soon afresh rolled in;
And so it swayed from side to side—
Far batteries joining in the din,
Though sharing in another fray—
Till all became an Indian fight,
Intricate, dusky, stretching far away,
Yet not without spontaneous plan
However tangled showed the plight:
Duels all over 'tween man and man,
Duels on cliff-side, and down in ravine,
Duels at long range, and bone to bone;
Duels every where flitting and half unseen.
Only by courage good as their own,
And strength outlasting theirs,
Did our boys at last drive the rebels off.
Yet they went not back to their distant lairs
In strong-hold, but loud in scoff
Maintained themselves on conquered ground—
Uplands; built works, or stalked around.

Our right wing bore this onset. Noon
Brought calm to Donelson.

The reader ceased; the storm beat hard;
'Twas day, but the office-gas was lit;
Nature retained her sulking-fit,
In her hand the shard.
Flitting faces took the hue
Of that washed bulletin-board in view,
And seemed to bear the public grief
As private, and uncertain of relief;
Yea, many an earnest heart was won,
As broodingly he plodded on,
To find in himself some bitter thing,
Some hardness in his lot as harrowing
As Donelson.
That night the board stood barren there,
Oft eyed by wistful people passing,
Who nothing saw but the rain-beads chasing
Each other down the wafered square,
As down some storm-beat grave-yard stone.
But next day showed—

MORE NEWS LAST NIGHT.

STORY OF SATURDAY AFTERNOON.

VICISSITUDES OF THE WAR.

The damaged gun-boats can't wage fight
For days; so says the Commodore.
Thus no diversion can be had.
Under a sunless sky of lead
Our grim-faced boys in blackened plight

Gaze toward the ground they held before,
And then on Grant. He marks their mood,
And hails it, and will turn the same to good.
Spite all that they have undergone,
Their desperate hearts are set upon
This winter fort, this stubborn fort,
This castle of the last resort,
This Donelson.

1 *P.M.*

An order given
Requires withdrawal from the front
Of regiments that bore the brunt
Of morning's fray. Their ranks all riven
Are being replaced by fresh, strong men.
Great vigilance in the foeman's Den;
He snuffs the stormers. Need it is
That for that fell assault of his,
That rout inflicted, and self-scorn—
Immoderate in noble natures, torn
By sense of being through slackness overborne—
The rebel be given a quick return:
The kindest face looks now half stern.
Balked of their prey in airs that freeze,
Some fierce ones glare like savages.
And yet, and yet, strange moments are—
Well—blood, and tears, and anguished War!
The morning's battle-ground is seen
In lifted glades, like meadows rare;
The blood-drops on the snow-crust there
Like clover in the white-weed show—
Flushed fields of death, that call again—
Call to our men, and not in vain,
For that way must the stormers go.

3 *P.M.*
The work begins.
Light drifts of men thrown forward, fade
In skirmish-line along the slope,
Where some dislodgments must be made
Ere the stormer with the strong-hold cope.

Lew Wallace, moving to retake
The heights late lost—
(*Herewith a break.*
Storms at the West derange the wires.
Doubtless, ere morning, we shall hear
The end; we look for news to cheer—
Let Hope fan all her fires.)

Next day in large bold hand was seen
The closing bulletin:

VICTORY!
Our troops have retrieved the day
By one grand surge along the line;
The spirit that urged them was divine.
The first works flooded, naught could stay
The stormers: on! still on!
Bayonets for Donelson!

Over the ground that morning lost
Rolled the blue billows, tempest-tossed,
Following a hat on the point of a sword.
Spite shell and round-shot, grape and
canister,
Up they climbed without rail or banister—
Up the steep hill-sides long and broad,
Driving the rebel deep within his works.
'Tis nightfall; not an enemy lurks

In sight. The chafing men
Fret for more fight:
"To-night, to-night let us take the Den!"
But night is treacherous, Grant is wary;
Of brave blood be a little chary.
Patience! the Fort is good as won;
To-morrow, and into Donelson.

LATER AND LAST.

THE FORT IS OURS.

A flag came out at early morn
Bringing surrender. From their towers
Floats out the banner late their scorn.
In Dover, hut and house are full
Of rebels dead or dying.
The National flag is flying
From the crammed court-house pinnacle.
Great boat-loads of our wounded go
To-day to Nashville. The sleet-winds blow;
But all is right: the fight is won,
The winter-fight for Donelson.
Hurrah!
The spell of old defeat is broke,
The habit of victory begun;
Grant strikes the war's first sounding stroke
At Donelson.

For lists of killed and wounded, see
The morrow's dispatch: to-day 'tis victory.

The man who read this to the crowd
Shouted as the end he gained;
And though the unflagging tempest rained,
They answered him aloud.

And hand grasped hand, and glances met
In happy triumph; eyes grew wet.
O, to the punches brewed that night
Went little water. Windows bright
Beamed rosy on the sleet without,
And from the deep street came the frequent
        shout;
While some in prayer, as these in glee,
Blessed heaven for the winter-victory.
But others were who wakeful laid
    In midnight beds, and early rose,
    And, feverish in the foggy snows,
Snatched the damp paper—wife and maid.
    The death-list like a river flows
        Down the pale sheet,
And there the whelming waters meet.

    Ah God! may Time with happy haste
    Bring wail and triumph to a waste,
        And war be done;
    The battle flag-staff fall athwart
    The curs'd ravine, and wither; naught
        Be left of trench or gun;
    The bastion, let it ebb away,
    Washed with the river bed; and Day
        In vain seek Donelson.

The Temeraire

(Supposed to have been suggested to an Englishman of the old order by the fight of the Monitor and Merrimac)

The gloomy hulls, in armor grim,
  Like clouds o'er moors have met,
And prove that oak, and iron, and man
  Are tough in fibre yet.

But Splendors wane. The sea-fight yields
  No front of old display;
The garniture, emblazonment,
  And heraldry all decay.

Towering afar in parting light,
  The fleets like Albion's forelands shine—
The full-sailed fleets, the shrouded show
  Of Ships-of-the-Line.

The fighting Temeraire,
  Built of a thousand trees,
Lunging out her lightnings,
  And beetling o'er the seas—
O Ship, how brave and fair,
  That fought so oft and well,
On open decks you manned the gun
    Armorial.
What cheerings did you share,
  Impulsive in the van,
When down upon leagued France and Spain
  We English ran—
The freshet at your bowsprit
  Like the foam upon the can.

Bickering, your colors
    Licked up the Spanish air,
You flapped with flames of battle-flags—
    Your challenge, Temeraire!
The rear ones of our fleet
    They yearned to share your place,
Still vying with the Victory
    Throughout that earnest race—
The Victory, whose Admiral,
    With orders nobly won,
Shone in the globe of the battle glow—
    The angel in that sun.
Parallel in story,
    Lo, the stately pair,
As late in grapple ranging,
    The foe between them there—
When four great hulls lay tiered,
And the fiery tempest cleared,
And your prizes twain appeared,
        Temeraire!

But Trafalgar' is over now,
    The quarter-deck undone;
The carved and castled navies fire
    Their evening-gun.
O, Titan Temeraire,
    Your stern-lights fade away;
Your bulwarks to the years must yield,
    And heart-of-oak decay.
A pigmy steam-tug tows you,
    Gigantic, to the shore—
Dismantled of your guns and spars,
    And sweeping wings of war.
The rivets clinch the iron-clads,
    Men learn a deadlier lore;

But Fame has nailed your battle-flags—
    Your ghost it sails before:
O, the navies old and oaken,
    O, the Temeraire no more!

A Utilitarian View of the Monitor's Fight

Plain be the phrase, yet apt the verse,
    More ponderous than nimble;
For since grimed War here laid aside
His Orient pomp, 'twould ill befit
        Overmuch to ply
    The rhyme's barbaric cymbal.

Hail to victory without the gaud
    Of glory; zeal that needs no fans
Of banners; plain mechanic power
Plied cogently in War now placed—
        Where War belongs—
    Among the trades and artisans.

Yet this was battle, and intense—
    Beyond the strife of fleets heroic;
Deadlier, closer, calm 'mid storm;
No passion; all went on by crank,
        Pivot, and screw,
    And calculations of caloric.

Needless to dwell; the story's known.
    The ringing of those plates on plates
Still ringeth round the world—
The clangor of that blacksmiths' fray.
        The anvil-din
    Resounds this message from the Fates:

War shall yet be, and to the end;
    But war-paint shows the streaks of weather;

War yet shall be, but warriors
Are now but operatives; War's made
        Less grand than Peace,
    And a singe runs through lace and feather.

Shiloh

A Requiem

(APRIL, 1862)

Skimming lightly, wheeling still,
The swallows fly low
Over the field in clouded days,
The forest-field of Shiloh—
Over the field where April rain
Solaced the parched ones stretched in pain
Through the pause of night
That followed the Sunday fight
Around the church of Shiloh—
The church so lone, the log-built one,
That echoed to many a parting groan
And natural prayer
Of dying foemen mingled there—
Foemen at morn, but friends at eve—
Fame or country least their care:
(What like a bullet can undeceive!)
But now they lie low,
While over them the swallows skim,
And all is hushed at Shiloh.

Malvern Hill

(JULY, 1862)

Ye elms that wave on Malvern Hill
In prime of morn and May,
Recall ye how McClellan's men
Here stood at bay?
While deep within yon forest dim
Our rigid comrades lay—
Some with the cartridge in their mouth,
Others with fixed arms lifted South—
Invoking so
The cypress glades? Ah wilds of woe!

The spires of Richmond, late beheld
Through rifts in musket-haze,
Were closed from view in clouds of dust
On leaf-walled ways,
Where streamed our wagons in caravan;
And the Seven Nights and Days
Of march and fast, retreat and fight,
Pinched our grimed faces to ghastly plight—
Does the elm wood
Recall the haggard beards of blood?

The battle-smoked flag, with stars eclipsed,
We followed (it never fell!)—
In silence husbanded our strength—
Received their yell;
Till on this slope we patient turned
With cannon ordered well;
Reverse we proved was not defeat;

But ah, the sod what thousands meet!—
        Does Malvern Wood
Bethink itself, and muse and brood?

We elms of Malvern Hill
    Remember every thing;
But sap the twig will fill:
Wag the world how it will,
    Leaves must be green in Spring.

Battle of Stone River, Tennessee

A View from Oxford Cloisters

(JANUARY, 1863)

With Tewksbury and Barnet heath
  In days to come the field shall blend,
The story dim and date obscure;
  In legend all shall end.
Even now, involved in forest shade
  A Druid-dream the strife appears,
The fray of yesterday assumes
  The haziness of years.
    In North and South still beats the vein
    Of Yorkist and Lancastrian.

Our rival Roses warred for Sway—
  For Sway, but named the name of Right;
And Passion, scorning pain and death,
  Lent sacred fervor to the fight.
Each lifted up a broidered cross,
  While crossing blades profaned the sign;
Monks blessed the fratricidal lance,
  And sisters scarfs could twine.
    Do North and South the sin retain
    Of Yorkist and Lancastrian?

But Rosecrans in the cedarn glade,
  And, deep in denser cypress gloom,
Dark Breckinridge, shall fade away
    Or thinly loom.
The pale throngs who in forest cowed
  Before the spell of battle's pause,
Forefelt the stillness that shall dwell
  On them and on their wars.

North and South shall join the train
Of Yorkist and Lancastrian.

But where the sword has plunged so deep,
And then been turned within the wound
By deadly Hate; where Climes contend
On vasty ground—
No warning Alps or seas between,
And small the curb of creed or law,
And blood is quick, and quick the brain;
Shall North and South their rage deplore,
And reunited thrive amain
Like Yorkist and Lancastrian?

The House-top

A Night Piece

(JULY, 1863)

No sleep. The sultriness pervades the air
And binds the brain—a dense oppression, such
As tawny tigers feel in matted shades,
Vexing their blood and making apt for ravage.
Beneath the stars the roofy desert spreads
Vacant as Libya. All is hushed near by.
Yet fitfully from far breaks a mixed surf
Of muffled sound, the Atheist roar of riot.
Yonder, where parching Sirius set in drought,
Balefully glares red Arson—there—and there.
The Town is taken by its rats—ship-rats
And rats of the wharves. All civil charms
And priestly spells which late held hearts in awe—
Fear-bound, subjected to a better sway
Than sway of self; these like a dream dissolve,
And man rebounds whole æons back in nature.
Hail to the low dull rumble, dull and dead,
And ponderous drag that shakes the wall.
Wise Draco comes, deep in the midnight roll
Of black artillery; he comes, though late;
In code corroborating Calvin's creed
And cynic tyrannies of honest kings;
He comes, nor parlies; and the Town, redeemed,
Gives thanks devout; nor, being thankful, heeds
The grimy slur on the Republic's faith implied,
Which holds that Man is naturally good,
And—more—is Nature's Roman, never to be scourged.

The Armies of the Wilderness

(1863–4)

I

Like snows the camps on Southern hills
    Lay all the winter long,
Our levies there in patience stood—
    They stood in patience strong.
On fronting slopes gleamed other camps
    Where faith as firmly clung:
Ah, froward kin! so brave amiss—
    The zealots of the Wrong.

In this strife of brothers
    (God, hear their country call),
However it be, whatever betide,
    Let not the just one fall.

Through the pointed glass our soldiers saw
    The base-ball bounding sent;
They could have joined them in their sport
    But for the vale's deep rent.
And others turned the reddish soil,
    Like diggers of graves they bent:
The reddish soil and trenching toil
        Begat presentiment.

Did the Fathers feel mistrust?
    Can no final good be wrought?
Over and over, again and again
    Must the fight for the Right be fought?

They lead a Gray-back to the crag:
"Your earth-works yonder—tell us, man!"
"A prisoner—no deserter, I,
Nor one of the tell-tale clan."
His rags they mark: "True-blue like you
Should wear the color—your Country's, man!"
He grinds his teeth: "However that be,
Yon earth-works have their plan."

Such brave ones, foully snared
By Belial's wily plea,
Were faithful unto the evil end—
Feudal fidelity.

"Well, then, your camps—come, tell the names!"
Freely he leveled his finger then:
"Yonder—see—are our Georgians; on the crest,
The Carolinians; lower, past the glen,
Virginians—Alabamians—Mississippians—
Kentuckians
(Follow my finger)—Tennesseeans; and the
ten
Camps *there*—ask your grave-pits; they'll tell.
Halloa! I see the picket-hut, the den
Where I last night lay." "Where's Lee?"
"In the hearts and bayonets of all yon men!"

The tribes swarm up to war
As in ages long ago,
Ere the palm of promise leaved
And the lily of Christ did blow.

Their mounted pickets for miles are spied
Dotting the lowland plain,
The nearer ones in their veteran-rags—
Loutish they loll in lazy disdain.

But ours in perilous places bide
With rifles ready and eyes that strain
Deep through the dim suspected wood
Where the Rapidan rolls amain.

The Indian has passed away,
But creeping comes another—
Deadlier far. Picket,
Take heed—take heed of thy brother!

From a wood-hung height, an outpost lone,
Crowned with a woodman's fort,
The sentinel looks on a land of dole,
Like Paran, all amort.
Black chimneys, gigantic in moor-like wastes,
The scowl of the clouded sky retort;
The hearth is a houseless stone again—
Ah! where shall the people be sought?

Since the venom such blastment deals,
The South should have paused, and thrice,
Ere with heat of her hate she hatched
The egg with the cockatrice.

A path down the mountain winds to the glade
Where the dead of the Moonlight Fight lie low;
A hand reaches out of the thin-laid mould
As begging help which none can bestow.
But the field-mouse small and busy ant
Heap their hillocks, to hide if they may the
woe:
By the bubbling spring lies the rusted canteen,
And the drum which the drummer-boy dying
let go.

Dust to dust, and blood for blood—
Passion and pangs! Has Time
Gone back? or is this the Age
Of the world's great Prime?

The wagon mired and cannon dragged
Have trenched their scar; the plain
Tramped like the cindery beach of the damned—
A site for the city of Cain.
And stumps of forests for dreary leagues
Like a massacre show. The armies have lain
By fires where gums and balms did burn,
And the seeds of Summer's reign.

Where are the birds and boys?
Who shall go chestnutting when
October returns? The nuts—
O, long ere they grow again.

They snug their huts with the chapel-pews,
In court-houses stable their steeds—
Kindle their fires with indentures and bonds,
And old Lord Fairfax's parchment deeds;
And Virginian gentlemen's libraries old—
Books which only the scholar heeds—
Are flung to his kennel. It is ravage and range,
And gardens are left to weeds.

Turned adrift into war
Man runs wild on the plain,
Like the jennets let loose
On the Pampas—zebras again.

Like the Pleiads dim, see the tents through the
storm—

Aloft by the hill-side hamlet's graves,
On a head-stone used for a hearth-stone there
The water is bubbling for punch for our
braves.
What if the night be drear, and the blast
Ghostly shrieks? their rollicking staves
Make frolic the heart; beating time with their
swords,
What care they if Winter raves?

Is life but a dream? and so,
In the dream do men laugh aloud?
So strange seems mirth in a camp,
So like a white tent to a shroud.

II

The May-weed springs; and comes a Man
And mounts our Signal Hill;
A quiet Man, and plain in garb—
Briefly he looks his fill,
Then drops his gray eye on the ground,
Like a loaded mortar he is still:
Meekness and grimness meet in him—
The silent General.

Were men but strong and wise,
Honest as Grant, and calm,
War would be left to the red and black ants,
And the happy world disarm.

That eve a stir was in the camps,
Forerunning quiet soon to come
Among the streets of beechen huts
No more to know the drum.
The weed shall choke the lowly door,
And foxes peer within the gloom,

Till scared perchance by Mosby's prowling men,
　Who ride in the rear of doom.

　Far West, and farther South,
　　Wherever the sword has been,
　Deserted camps are met,
　　And desert graves are seen.

The livelong night they ford the flood;
　With guns held high they silent press,
Till shimmers the grass in their bayonets' sheen—
　On Morning's banks their ranks they dress;
Then by the forests lightly wind,
　Whose waving boughs the pennons seem to
　　bless,
Borne by the cavalry scouting on—
　Sounding the Wilderness.

　Like shoals of fish in spring
　　That visit Crusoe's isle,
　The host in the lonesome place—
　　The hundred thousand file.

The foe that held his guarded hills
　Must speed to woods afar;
For the scheme that was nursed by the Culpepper
　　hearth
　With the slowly-smoked cigar—
The scheme that smouldered through winter long
　Now bursts into act—into war—
The resolute scheme of a heart as calm
　As the Cyclone's core.

　The fight for the city is fought
　　In Nature's old domain;

Man goes out to the wilds,
And Orpheus' charm is vain.

In glades they meet skull after skull
Where pine-cones lay—the rusted gun,
Green shoes full of bones, the mouldering coat
And cuddled-up skeleton;
And scores of such. Some start as in dreams,
And comrades lost bemoan:
By the edge of those wilds Stonewall had charged—
But the Year and the Man were gone.

At the height of their madness
The night winds pause,
Recollecting themselves;
But no lull in these wars.

A gleam!—a volley! And who shall go
Storming the swarmers in jungles dread?
No cannon-ball answers, no proxies are sent—
They rush in the shrapnel's stead.
Plume and sash are vanities now—
Let them deck the pall of the dead;
They go where the shade is, perhaps into Hades,
Where the brave of all times have led.

There's a dust of hurrying feet,
Bitten lips and bated breath,
And drums that challenge to the grave,
And faces fixed, forefeeling death.

What husky huzzahs in the hazy groves—
What flying encounters fell;
Pursuer and pursued like ghosts disappear
In gloomed shade—their end who shall tell?

The crippled, a ragged-barked stick for a crutch,
    Limp to some elfin dell—
Hobble from the sight of dead faces—white
    As pebbles in a well.

    Few burial rites shall be;
        No priest with book and band
    Shall come to the secret place
        Of the corpse in the foeman's land.

Watch and fast, march and fight—clutch your
        gun!
    Day-fights and night-fights; sore is the stress;
Look, through the pines what line comes on?
    Longstreet slants through the hauntedness!
'Tis charge for charge, and shout for yell:
    Such battles on battles oppress—
But Heaven lent strength, the Right strove well,
    And emerged from the Wilderness.

    Emerged, for the way was won;
        But the Pillar of Smoke that led
    Was brand-like with ghosts that went up
            Ashy and red.

None can narrate that strife in the pines,
    A seal is on it—Sabæan lore!
Obscure as the wood, the entangled rhyme
    But hints at the maze of war—
Vivid glimpses or livid through peopled gloom,
    And fires which creep and char—
A riddle of death, of which the slain
        Sole solvers are.

On the Photograph of a Corps Commander

Ay, man is manly. Here you see
   The warrior-carriage of the head,
And brave dilation of the frame;
   And lighting all, the soul that led
In Spottsylvania's charge to victory,
   Which justifies his fame.

A cheering picture. It is good
   To look upon a Chief like this,
In whom the spirit moulds the form.
   Here favoring Nature, oft remiss,
With eagle mien expressive has endued
   A man to kindle strains that warm.

Trace back his lineage, and his sires,
   Yeoman or noble, you shall find
Enrolled with men of Agincourt,
   Heroes who shared great Harry's mind.
Down to us come the knightly Norman fires,
   And front the Templars bore.

Nothing can lift the heart of man
   Like manhood in a fellow-man.
The thought of heaven's great King afar
   But humbles us—too weak to scan;
But manly greatness men can span,
   And feel the bonds that draw.

The Swamp Angel

There is a coal-black Angel
    With a thick Afric lip,
And he dwells (like the hunted and harried)
    In a swamp where the green frogs dip.
But his face is against a City
    Which is over a bay of the sea,
And he breathes with a breath that is blastment,
    And dooms by a far decree.

By night there is fear in the City,
    Through the darkness a star soareth on;
There's a scream that screams up to the zenith,
    Then the poise of a meteor lone—
Lighting far the pale fright of the faces,
    And downward the coming is seen;
Then the rush, and the burst, and the havoc,
    And wails and shrieks between.

It comes like the thief in the gloaming;
    It comes, and none may foretell
The place of the coming—the glaring;
    They live in a sleepless spell
That wizens, and withers, and whitens;
    It ages the young, and the bloom
Of the maiden is ashes of roses—
    The Swamp Angel broods in his gloom.

Swift is his messengers' going,
    But slowly he saps their halls,

As if by delay deluding.
    They move from their crumbling walls
Farther and farther away;
    But the Angel sends after and after,
By night with the flame of his ray—
    By night with the voice of his screaming—
Sends after them, stone by stone,
    And farther walls fall, farther portals,
And weed follows weed through the Town.

Is this the proud City? the scorner
    Which never would yield the ground?
Which mocked at the coal-black Angel?
    The cup of despair goes round.
Vainly she calls upon Michael
    (The white man's seraph was he),
For Michael has fled from his tower
    To the Angel over the sea.

Who weeps for the woeful City
    Let him weep for our guilty kind;
Who joys at her wild despairing—
    Christ, the Forgiver, convert his mind.

The College Colonel

He rides at their head;
A crutch by his saddle just slants in view,
One slung arm is in splints, you see,
Yet he guides his strong steed—how coldly too.

He brings his regiment home—
Not as they filed two years before,
But a remnant half-tattered, and battered, and worn,
Like castaway sailors, who—stunned
By the surf's loud roar,
Their mates dragged back and seen no more—
Again and again breast the surge,
And at last crawl, spent, to shore.

A still rigidity and pale—
An Indian aloofness lones his brow;
He has lived a thousand years
Compressed in battle's pains and prayers,
Marches and watches slow.

There are welcoming shouts, and flags;
Old men off hat to the Boy,
Wreaths from gay balconies fall at his feet,
But to *him*—there comes alloy.

It is not that a leg is lost,
It is not that an arm is maimed,

It is not that the fever has racked—
    Self he has long disclaimed.

But all through the Seven Days' Fight,
    And deep in the Wilderness grim,
And in the field-hospital tent,
    And Petersburg crater, and dim
Lean brooding in Libby, there came—
    Ah heaven!—what *truth* to him.

"The Coming Storm:"

A Picture by S. R. Gifford, and owned by E.B.
Included in the N.A. Exhibition, April, 1865

All feeling hearts must feel for him
    Who felt this picture. Presage dim—
Dim inklings from the shadowy sphere
    Fixed him and fascinated here.

A demon-cloud like the mountain one
    Burst on a spirit as mild
As this urned lake, the home of shades.
    But Shakspeare's pensive child

Never the lines had lightly scanned,
    Steeped in fable, steeped in fate;
The Hamlet in his heart was 'ware,
    Such hearts can antedate.

No utter surprise can come to him
    Who reaches Shakspeare's core;
That which we seek and shun is there—
        Man's final lore.

"Formerly a Slave"

An idealized Portrait, by E. Vedder, in the Spring Exhibition of the National Academy, 1865

The sufferance of her race is shown,
  And retrospect of life,
Which now too late deliverance dawns upon;
  Yet is she not at strife.

Her children's children they shall know
  The good withheld from her;
And so her reverie takes prophetic cheer—
  In spirit she sees the stir

Far down the depth of thousand years,
  And marks the revel shine;
Her dusky face is lit with sober light,
  Sibylline, yet benign.

On the Slain Collegians

Youth is the time when hearts are large,
        And stirring wars
Appeal to the spirit which appeals in turn
        To the blade it draws.
If woman incite, and duty show
    (Though made the mask of Cain),
Or whether it be Truth's sacred cause,
        Who can aloof remain
That shares youth's ardor, uncooled by the snow
        Of wisdom or sordid gain?

The liberal arts and nurture sweet
Which give his gentleness to man—
    Train him to honor, lend him grace
Through bright examples meet—
That culture which makes never wan
With underminings deep, but holds
    The surface still, its fitting place,
    And so gives sunniness to the face
And bravery to the heart; what troops
    Of generous boys in happiness thus bred—
    Saturnians through life's Tempe led,
Went from the North and came from the South,
With golden mottoes in the mouth,
    To lie down midway on a bloody bed.

Woe for the homes of the North,
And woe for the seats of the South:
All who felt life's spring in prime,

And were swept by the wind of their place and
time—
All lavish hearts, on whichever side,
Of birth urbane or courage high,
Armed them for the stirring wars—
Armed them—some to die.
Apollo-like in pride,
Each would slay his Python—caught
The maxims in his temple taught—
Aflame with sympathies whose blaze
Perforce enwrapped him—social laws,
Friendship and kin, and by-gone days—
Vows, kisses—every heart unmoors,
And launches into the seas of wars.
What could they else—North or South?
Each went forth with blessings given
By priests and mothers in the name of Heaven;
And honor in both was chief.
Warred one for Right, and one for Wrong?
So be it; but they both were young—
Each grape to his cluster clung,
All their elegies are sung.

The anguish of maternal hearts
Must search for balm divine;
But well the striplings bore their fated parts
(The heavens all parts assign)—
Never felt life's care or cloy.
Each bloomed and died an unabated Boy;
Nor dreamed what death was—thought it mere
Sliding into some vernal sphere.
They knew the joy, but leaped the grief,
Like plants that flower ere comes the leaf—
Which storms lay low in kindly doom,
And kill them in their flush of bloom.

America

I

Where the wings of a sunny Dome expand
I saw a Banner in gladsome air—
Starry, like Berenice's Hair—
Afloat in broadened bravery there;
With undulating long-drawn flow,
As rolled Brazilian billows go
Voluminously o'er the Line.
The Land reposed in peace below;
    The children in their glee
Were folded to the exulting heart
    Of young Maternity.

II

Later, and it streamed in fight
    When tempest mingled with the fray,
And over the spear-point of the shaft
    I saw the ambiguous lightning play.
Valor with Valor strove, and died:
Fierce was Despair, and cruel was Pride;
And the lorn Mother speechless stood,
Pale at the fury of her brood.

III

Yet later, and the silk did wind
        Her fair cold form;
Little availed the shining shroud,
    Though ruddy in hue, to cheer or warm.
A watcher looked upon her low, and said—

She sleeps, but sleeps, she is not dead.
But in that sleep contortion showed
The terror of the vision there—
  A silent vision unavowed,
Revealing earth's foundation bare,
  And Gorgon in her hidden place.
It was a thing of fear to see
  So foul a dream upon so fair a face,
And the dreamer lying in that starry shroud.

IV

But from the trance she sudden broke—
The trance, or death into promoted life;
At her feet a shivered yoke,
And in her aspect turned to heaven
  No trace of passion or of strife—
A clear calm look. It spake of pain,
But such as purifies from stain—
Sharp pangs that never come again—
  And triumph repressed by knowledge meet,
Power dedicate, and hope grown wise,
  And youth matured for age's seat—
Law on her brow and empire in her eyes.
  So she, with graver air and lifted flag;
While the shadow, chased by light,
Fled along the far-drawn height,
  And left her on the crag.

The Fortitude of the North

under the Disaster of the Second Manassas

They take no shame for dark defeat
    While prizing yet each victory won,
Who fight for the Right through all retreat,
    Nor pause until their work is done.
The Cape-of-Storms is proof to every throe;
    Vainly against that foreland beat
Wild winds aloft and wilder waves below:
    The black cliffs gleam through rents in sleet
When the livid Antarctic storm-clouds glow.

Inscription

for Marye's Heights, Fredericksburg

To them who crossed the flood
And climbed the hill, with eyes
    Upon the heavenly flag intent,
    And through the deathful tumult went
Even unto death: to them this Stone—
Erect, where they were overthrown—
    Of more than victory the monument.

An Uninscribed Monument

on One of the Battle-fields of the Wilderness

Silence and Solitude may hint
(Whose home is in yon piny wood)
What I, though tableted, could never tell—
The din which here befell,
And striving of the multitude.
The iron cones and spheres of death
Set round me in their rust,
These, too, if just,
Shall speak with more than animated breath.
Thou who beholdest, if thy thought,
Not narrowed down to personal cheer,
Take in the import of the quiet here—
The after-quiet—the calm full fraught;
Thou too wilt silent stand—
Silent as I, and lonesome as the land.

A Requiem

for Soldiers Lost in Ocean Transports

When, after storms that woodlands rue,
To valleys comes atoning dawn,
The robins blithe their orchard-sports renew;
And meadow-larks, no more withdrawn,
Caroling fly in the languid blue;
The while, from many a hid recess,
Alert to partake the blessedness,
The pouring mites their airy dance pursue.
So, after ocean's ghastly gales,
When laughing light of hoyden morning breaks,
Every finny hider wakes—
From vaults profound swims up with glittering
scales;
Through the delightsome sea he sails,
With shoals of shining tiny things
Frolic on every wave that flings
Against the prow its showery spray;
All creatures joying in the morn,
Save them forever from joyance torn,
Whose bark was lost where now the dolphins
play;
Save them that by the fabled shore,
Down the pale stream are washed away,
Far to the reef of bones are borne;
And never revisits them the light,
Nor sight of long-sought land and pilot more;
Nor heed they now the lone bird's flight
Round the lone spar where mid-sea surges pour.

On a Natural Monument

in a Field of Georgia

No trophy this—a Stone unhewn,
    And stands where here the field immures
The nameless brave whose palms are won.
Outcast they sleep; yet fame is nigh—
    Pure fame of deeds, not doers;
Nor deeds of men who bleeding die
    In cheer of hymns that round them float:
In happy dreams such close the eye.
But withering famine slowly wore,
    And slowly fell disease did gloat.
Even Nature's self did aid deny;
They choked in horror the pensive sigh.
    Yea, off from home sad Memory bore
(Though anguished Yearning heaved that way),
Lest wreck of reason might befall.
    As men in gales shun the lee shore,
Though there the homestead be, and call,
And thitherward winds and waters sway—
As such lorn mariners, so fared they.
But naught shall now their peace molest.
    Their fame is this: they did endure—
Endure, when fortitude was vain
To kindle any approving strain
Which they might hear. To these who rest,
    This healing sleep alone was sure.

Commemorative of a Naval Victory

Sailors there are of gentlest breed,
    Yet strong, like every goodly thing;
The discipline of arms refines,
    And the wave gives tempering.
    The damasked blade its beam can fling;
It lends the last grave grace:
The hawk, the hound, and sworded nobleman
    In Titian's picture for a king,
Are of hunter or warrior race.

In social halls a favored guest
    In years that follow victory won,
How sweet to feel your festal fame
    In woman's glance instinctive thrown:
    Repose is yours—your deed is known,
It musks the amber wine;
It lives, and sheds a light from storied days
    Rich as October sunsets brown,
Which make the barren place to shine.

But seldom the laurel wreath is seen
    Unmixed with pensive pansies dark;
There's a light and a shadow on every man
    Who at last attains his lifted mark—
    Nursing through night the ethereal spark.
Elate he never can be;
He feels that spirits which glad had hailed his
        worth,
    Sleep in oblivion.—The shark
Glides white through the phosphorus sea.

The Scout toward Aldie

The cavalry-camp lies on the slope
    Of what was late a vernal hill,
But now like a pavement bare—
An outpost in the perilous wilds
    Which ever are lone and still;
        But Mosby's men are there—
        Of Mosby best beware.

Great trees the troopers felled, and leaned
    In antlered walls about their tents;
Strict watch they kept; 'twas *Hark!* and *Mark!*
Unarmed none cared to stir abroad
    For berries beyond their forest-fence:
        As glides in seas the shark,
        Rides Mosby through green dark.

All spake of him, but few had seen
    Except the maimed ones or the low;
Yet rumor made him every thing—
A farmer—woodman—refugee—
    The man who crossed the field but now;
        A spell about his life did cling—
        Who to the ground shall Mosby bring?

The morning-bugles lonely play,
    Lonely the evening-bugle calls—
Unanswered voices in the wild;
The settled hush of birds in nest
    Becharms, and all the wood enthralls:

Memory's self is so beguiled
That Mosby seems a satyr's child.

They lived as in the Eerie Land—
The fire-flies showed with fairy gleam;
And yet from pine-tops one might ken
The Capitol Dome—hazy—sublime—
A vision breaking on a dream:
So strange it was that Mosby's men
Should dare to prowl where the Dome was
seen.

A scout toward Aldie broke the spell.—
The Leader lies before his tent
Gazing at heaven's all-cheering lamp
Through blandness of a morning rare;
His thoughts on bitter-sweets are bent:
His sunny bride is in the camp—
But Mosby—graves are beds of damp!

The trumpet calls; he goes within;
But none the prayer and sob may know:
Her hero he, but bridegroom too.
Ah, love in a tent is a queenly thing,
And fame, be sure, refines the vow;
But fame fond wives have lived to rue,
And Mosby's men fell deeds can do.

Tan-tara! tan-tara! tan-tara!
Mounted and armed he sits a king;
For pride she smiles if now she peep—
Elate he rides at the head of his men;
He is young, and command is a boyish thing:
They file out into the forest deep—
Do Mosby and his rangers sleep?

The sun is gold, and the world is green,
Opal the vapors of morning roll;
The champing horses lightly prance—
Full of caprice, and the riders too
Curving in many a caricole.
But marshaled soon, by fours advance—
Mosby had checked that airy dance.

By the hospital-tent the cripples stand—
Bandage, and crutch, and cane, and sling,
And palely eye the brave array;
The froth of the cup is gone for them
(Caw! caw! the crows through the blueness
wing):
Yet these were late as bold, as gay;
But Mosby—a clip, and grass is hay.

How strong they feel on their horses free,
Tingles the tendoned thigh with life;
Their cavalry-jackets make boys of all—
With golden breasts like the oriole;
The chat, the jest, and laugh are rife.
But word is passed from the front—a call
For order; the wood is Mosby's hall.

To which behest one rider sly
(Spurred, but unarmed) gave little heed—
Of dexterous fun not slow or spare,
He teased his neighbors of touchy mood,
Into plungings he pricked his steed:
A black-eyed man on a coal-black mare,
Alive as Mosby in mountain air.

His limbs were long, and large, and round;
He whispered, winked—did all but shout:
A healthy man for the sick to view;

The taste in his mouth was sweet at morn;
Little of care he cared about.
And yet of pains and pangs he knew—
In others, maimed by Mosby's crew.

The Hospital Steward—even he
(Sacred in person as a priest),
And on his coat-sleeve broidered nice
Wore the caduceus, black and green.
No wonder he sat so light on his beast;
This cheery man in suit of price
Not even Mosby dared to slice.

They pass the picket by the pine
And hollow log—a lonesome place;
His horse adroop, and pistol clean;
'Tis cocked—kept leveled toward the wood;
Strained vigilance ages his childish face.
Since midnight has that stripling been
Peering for Mosby through the green.

Splashing they cross the freshet-flood,
And up the muddy bank they strain;
A horse at a spectral white-ash shies—
One of the span of the ambulance,
Black as a hearse. They give the rein:
Silent speed on a scout were wise,
Could cunning baffle Mosby's spies.

Rumor had come that a band was lodged
In green retreats of hills that peer
By Aldie (famed for the swordless charge).
Much store they'd heaped of captured arms
And, peradventure, pilfered cheer;
For Mosby's lads oft hearts enlarge
In revelry by some gorge's marge.

"Don't let your sabres rattle and ring;
To his oat-bag let each man give heed—
There now, that fellow's bag's untied,
Sowing the road with the precious grain.
Your carbines swing at hand—you need!
Look to yourselves, and your nags beside,
Men who after Mosby ride."

Picked lads and keen went sharp before—
A guard, though scarce against surprise;
And rearmost rode an answering troop,
But flankers none to right or left.
No bugle peals, no pennon flies:
Silent they sweep, and fain would swoop
On Mosby with an Indian whoop.

On, right on through the forest land,
Nor man, nor maid, nor child was seen—
Not even a dog. The air was still;
The blackened hut they turned to see,
And spied charred benches on the green;
A squirrel sprang from the rotting mill
Whence Mosby sallied late, brave blood to spill.

By worn-out fields they cantered on—
Drear fields amid the woodlands wide;
By cross-roads of some olden time,
In which grew groves; by gate-stones down—
Grassed ruins of secluded pride:
A strange lone land, long past the prime,
Fit land for Mosby or for crime.

The brook in the dell they pass. One peers
Between the leaves: "Ay, there's the place—
There, on the oozy ledge—'twas there

We found the body (Blake's, you know);
Such whirlings, gurglings round the face—
Shot drinking! Well, in war all's fair—
So Mosby says. The bough—take care!"

Hard by, a chapel. Flower-pot mould
Danked and decayed the shaded roof;
The porch was punk; the clapboards spanned
With ruffled lichens gray or green;
Red coral-moss was not aloof;
And mid dry leaves green dead-man's-hand
Groped toward that chapel in Mosby-land.

They leave the road and take the wood,
And mark the trace of ridges there—
A wood where once had slept the farm—
A wood where once tobacco grew
Drowsily in the hazy air,
And wrought in all kind things a calm—
Such influence, Mosby! bids disarm.

To ease even yet the place did woo—
To ease which pines unstirring share,
For ease the weary horses sighed:
Halting, and slackening girths, they feed,
Their pipes they light, they loiter there;
Then up, and urging still the Guide,
On, and after Mosby ride.

This Guide in frowzy coat of brown,
And beard of ancient growth and mould,
Bestrode a bony steed and strong,
As suited well with bulk he bore—
A wheezy man with depth of hold
Who jouncing went. A staff he swung—
A wight whom Mosby's wasp had stung.

Burnt out and homeless—hunted long!
That wheeze he caught in autumn-wood
Crouching (a fat man) for his life,
And spied his lean son 'mong the crew
That probed the covert. Ah! black blood
Was his 'gainst even child and wife—
Fast friends to Mosby. Such the strife.

A lad, unhorsed by sliding girths,
Strains hard to readjust his seat
Ere the main body show the gap
'Twixt them and the rear-guard; scrub-oaks near
He sidelong eyes, while hands move fleet;
Then mounts and spurs. One drops his
cap—
"Let Mosby find!" nor heeds mishap.

A gable time-stained peeps through trees:
"You mind the fight in the haunted house?
That's it; we clenched them in the room—
An ambuscade of ghosts, we thought,
But proved sly rebels on a bouse!
Luke lies in the yard." The chimneys loom:
Some muse on Mosby—some on doom.

Less nimbly now through brakes they wind,
And ford wild creeks where men have
drowned;
They skirt the pool, avoid the fen,
And so till night, when down they lie,
Their steeds still saddled, in wooded ground:
Rein in hand they slumber then,
Dreaming of Mosby's cedarn den.

But Colonel and Major friendly sat
Where boughs deformed low made a seat.

The Young Man talked (all sworded and spurred)
Of the partisan's blade he longed to win,
And frays in which he meant to beat.
The grizzled Major smoked, and heard:
"But what's that—Mosby?" "No, a bird."

A contrast here like sire and son,
Hope and Experience sage did meet;
The Youth was brave, the Senior too;
But through the Seven Days one had served,
And gasped with the rear-guard in retreat:
So he smoked and smoked, and the wreath
he blew—
"Any *sure* news of Mosby's crew?"

He smoked and smoked, eying the while
A huge tree hydra-like in growth—
Moon-tinged—with crook'd boughs rent or
lopped—
Itself a haggard forest. "Come!"
The Colonel cried, "to talk you're loath;
D'ye hear? I say he must be stopped,
This Mosby—caged, and hair close
cropped."

"Of course; but what's that dangling there?"
"Where?" "From the tree—that gallows-bough;
"A bit of frayed bark, is it not?"
"Ay—or a rope; did *we* hang last?—
Don't like my neckerchief any how;"
He loosened it: "O ay, we'll stop
This Mosby—but that vile jerk and drop!"

By peep of light they feed and ride,
Gaining a grove's green edge at morn,
And mark the Aldie hills uprear

And five gigantic horsemen carved
Clear-cut against the sky withdrawn;
Are more behind? an open snare?
Or Mosby's men but watchmen there?

The ravaged land was miles behind,
And Loudon spread her landscape rare;
Orchards in pleasant lowlands stood,
Cows were feeding, a cock loud crew,
But not a friend at need was there;
The valley-folk were only good
To Mosby and his wandering brood.

What best to do? what mean yon men?
Colonel and Guide their minds compare;
Be sure some looked their Leader through;
Dismounted, on his sword he leaned
As one who feigns an easy air;
And yet perplexed he was they knew—
Perplexed by Mosby's mountain-crew.

The Major hemmed as he would speak,
But checked himself, and left the ring
Of cavalrymen about their Chief—
Young courtiers mute who paid their court
By looking with confidence on their king;
They knew him brave, foresaw no grief—
But Mosby—the time to think is brief.

The Surgeon (sashed in sacred green)
Was glad 'twas not for *him* to say
What next should be; if a trooper bleeds,
Why he will do his best, as wont,
And his partner in black will aid and pray;
But judgment bides with him who leads,
And Mosby many a problem breeds.

This Surgeon was the kindliest man
    That ever a callous trade professed;
He felt for him, that Leader young,
And offered medicine from his flask:
    The Colonel took it with marvelous zest.
        For such fine medicine good and strong,
        Oft Mosby and his foresters long.

A charm of proof. "Ho, Major, come—
    Pounce on yon men! Take half your troop,
Through the thickets wind—pray speedy be—
And gain their rear. And, Captain Morn,
    Picket these roads—all travelers stop;
        The rest to the edge of this crest with me,
        That Mosby and his scouts may see."

Commanded and done. Ere the sun stood steep,
    Back came the Blues, with a troop of Grays,
Ten riding double—luckless ten!—
Five horses gone, and looped hats lost,
    And love-locks dancing in a maze—
        Certes, but sophomores from the glen
        Of Mosby—not his veteran men.

"Colonel," said the Major, touching his cap,
    "We've had our ride, and here they are."
"Well done! how many found you there?"
"As many as I bring you here."
    "And no one hurt?" "There'll be no scar—
        One fool was battered." "Find their lair?"
        "Why, Mosby's brood camp every where."

He sighed, and slid down from his horse,
    And limping went to a spring-head nigh.
"Why, bless me, Major, not hurt, I hope?"
"Battered my knee against a bar

When the rush was made; all right by-and-
by.—
Halloa! they gave you too much rope—
Go back to Mosby, eh? elope?"

Just by the low-hanging skirt of wood
The guard, remiss, had given a chance
For a sudden sally into the cover—
But foiled the intent, nor fired a shot,
Though the issue was a deadly trance;
For, hurled 'gainst an oak that humped
low over,
Mosby's man fell, pale as a lover.

They pulled some grass his head to ease
(Lined with blue shreds a ground-nest
stirred).
The Surgeon came—"Here's a to-do!"
"Ah!" cried the Major, darting a glance,
"This fellow's the one that fired and spurred
Down hill, but met reserves below—
My boys, not Mosby's—so we go!"

The Surgeon—bluff, red, goodly man—
Kneeled by the hurt one; like a bee
He toiled. The pale young Chaplain too—
(Who went to the wars for cure of souls,
And his own student-ailments)—he
Bent over likewise; spite the two,
Mosby's poor man more pallid grew.

Meanwhile the mounted captives near
Jested; and yet they anxious showed;
Virginians; some of family-pride,
And young, and full of fire, and fine
In open feature and cheek that glowed;

And here thralled vagabonds now they ride—
But list! one speaks for Mosby's side.

"Why, three to one—your horses strong—
Revolvers, rifles, and a surprise—
Surrender we account no shame!
We live, are gay, and life is hope;
We'll fight again when fight is wise.
There are plenty more from where we came;
But go find Mosby—start the game!"

Yet one there was who looked but glum;
In middle-age, a father he,
And this his first experience too:
"They shot at my heart when my hands were up—
This fighting's crazy work, I see!"
But noon is high; what next to do?
The woods are mute, and Mosby is the foe.

"Save what we've got," the Major said;
"Bad plan to make a scout too long;
The tide may turn, and drag them back,
And more beside. These rides I've been,
And every time a mine was sprung.
To rescue, mind, they won't be slack—
Look out for Mosby's rifle-crack."

"We'll welcome it! give crack for crack!
Peril, old lad, is what I seek."
"O then, there's plenty to be had—
By all means on, and have our fill!"
With that, grotesque, he writhed his neck,

Showing a scar by buck-shot made—
Kind Mosby's Christmas gift, he said.

"But, Colonel, my prisoners—let a guard
Make sure of them, and lead to camp.
That done, we're free for a dark-room fight
If so you say." The other laughed;
"Trust me, Major, nor throw a damp.
But first to try a little sleight—
Sure news of Mosby would suit me quite."

Herewith he turned—"Reb, have a dram?"
Holding the Surgeon's flask with a smile
To a young scapegrace from the glen.
"O yes!" he eagerly replied,
"And thank you, Colonel, but—any guile?
For if you think we'll blab—why, then
You don't know Mosby or his men."

The Leader's genial air relaxed.
"Best give it up," a whisperer said.
"By heaven, I'll range their rebel den!"
"They'll treat you well," the captive cried;
"They're all like us—handsome—well bred:
In wood or town, with sword or pen,
Polite is Mosby, bland his men."

"Where were you, lads, last night?—come, tell!"
"We?—at a wedding in the Vale—
The bridegroom our comrade; by his side
Belisent, my cousin—O, so proud
Of her young love with old wounds pale—
A Virginian girl! God bless her pride—
Of a crippled Mosby-man the bride!"

"Four walls shall mend that saucy mood,
And moping prisons tame him down,"
Said Captain Cloud. "God help that day,"
Cried Captain Morn, "and he so young.
But hark, he sings—a madcap one!"
"O we multiply merrily in the May,
The birds and Mosby's men, they say!"

While echoes ran, a wagon old,
Under stout guard of Corporal Chew
Came up; a lame horse, dingy white,
With clouted harness; ropes in hand,
Cringed the humped driver, black in hue;
By him (for Mosby's band a sight)
A sister-rebel sat, her veil held tight.

"I picked them up," the Corporal said,
"Crunching their way over stick and root,
Through yonder wood. The man here—Cuff—
Says they are going to Leesburg town."
The Colonel's eye took in the group;
The veiled one's hand he spied—enough!
Not Mosby's. Spite the gown's poor stuff,

Off went his hat: "Lady, fear not;
We soldiers do what we deplore—
I must detain you till we march."
The stranger nodded. Nettled now,
He grew politer than before:—
"'Tis Mosby's fault, this halt and search:"
The lady stiffened in her starch.

"My duty, madam, bids me now
Ask what may seem a little rude.
Pardon—that veil—withdraw it, please
(Corporal! make every man fall back);

Pray, now, I do but what I should;
Bethink you, 'tis in masks like these
That Mosby haunts the villages."

Slowly the stranger drew her veil,
And looked the Soldier in the eye—
A glance of mingled foul and fair;
Sad patience in a proud disdain,
And more than quietude. A sigh
She heaved, as if all unaware,
And far seemed Mosby from her care.

She came from Yewton Place, her home,
So ravaged by the war's wild play—
Campings, and foragings, and fires—
That now she sought an aunt's abode.
Her kinsmen? In Lee's army, they.
The black? A servant, late her sire's.
And Mosby? Vainly he inquires.

He gazed, and sad she met his eye;
"In the wood yonder were you lost?"
No; at the forks they left the road
Because of hoof-prints (thick they were—
Thick as the words in notes thrice crossed),
And fearful, made that episode.
In fear of Mosby? None she showed.

Her poor attire again he scanned:
"Lady, once more; I grieve to jar
On all sweet usage, but must plead
To have what peeps there from your dress;
That letter—'tis justly prize of war."
She started—gave it—she must need.
" 'Tis not from Mosby? May I read?"

And straight such matter he perused
That with the Guide he went apart.
The Hospital Steward's turn began:
"Must squeeze this darkey; every tap
Of knowledge we are bound to start."
"Garry," she said, "tell all you can
Of Colonel Mosby—that brave man."

"Dun know much, sare; and missis here
Know less dan me. But dis I know—"
"Well, what?" "I dun know what I know."
"A knowing answer!" The hump-back coughed,
Rubbing his yellowish wool like tow.
"Come—Mosby—tell!" "O dun look so!
My gal nursed missis—let we go."

"Go where?" demanded Captain Cloud;
"Back into bondage? Man, you're free!"
"Well, *let* we free!" The Captain's brow
Lowered; the Colonel came—had heard:
"Pooh! pooh! his simple heart I see—
A faithful servant.—Lady" (a bow),
"Mosby's abroad—with us you'll go.

"Guard! look to your prisoners; back to camp!
The man in the grass—can he mount and away?
Why, how he groans!" "Bad inward bruise—
Might lug him along in the ambulance."
"Coals to Newcastle! let him stay.
Boots and saddles!—our pains we lose,
Nor care I if Mosby hear the news!"

But word was sent to a house at hand,
And a flask was left by the hurt one's side.
They seized in that same house a man,

Neutral by day, by night a foe—
So charged his neighbor late, the Guide.
A grudge? Hate will do what it can;
Along he went for a Mosby-man.

No secrets now; the bugle calls;
The open road they take, nor shun
The hill; retrace the weary way.
But one there was who whispered low,
"This is a feint—we'll back anon;
Young Hair-Brains don't retreat, they say;
A brush with Mosby is the play!"

They rode till eve. Then on a farm
That lay along a hill-side green,
Bivouacked. Fires were made, and then
Coffee was boiled; a cow was coaxed
And killed, and savory roasts were seen;
And under the lee of a cattle-pen
The guard supped freely with Mosby's
men.

The ball was bandied to and fro;
Hits were given and hits were met:
"Chickamauga, Feds—take off your hat!"
"But the Fight in the Clouds repaid you, Rebs!"
"Forgotten about Manassas yet?"
Chatting and chaffing, and tit for tat,
Mosby's clan with the troopers sat.

"Here comes the moon!" a captive cried;
"A song! what say? Archy, my lad!"
Hailing the still one of the clan
(A boyish face with girlish hair),
"Give us that thing poor Pansy made

Last year." He brightened, and began;
And this was the song of Mosby's man:

Spring is come; she shows her pass—
Wild violets cool!
South of woods a small close grass—
A vernal wool!
Leaves are a'bud on the sassafras—
They'll soon be full:
Blessings on the friendly screen—
I'm for the South! says the leafage green.

Robins! fly, and take your fill
Of out-of-doors—
Garden, orchard, meadow, hill,
Barns and bowers;
Take your fill, and have your will—
Virginia's yours!
But, bluebirds! keep away, and fear
The ambuscade in bushes here.

"A green song that," a sergeant said;
"But where's poor Pansy? gone, I fear."
"Ay, mustered out at Ashby's Gap."
"I see; now for a live man's song;
Ditty for ditty—prepare to cheer.
My bluebirds, you can fling a cap!
You barehead Mosby-boys—why—clap!"

Nine Blue-coats went a-nutting
Slyly in Tennessee—
Not for chestnuts—better than that—
Hush, you bumble-bee!
Nutting, nutting—
All through the year there's nutting!

A tree they spied so yellow,
Rustling in motion queer;
In they fired, and down they dropped—
Butternuts, my dear!
Nutting, nutting—
Who'll 'list to go a-nutting?

Ah! why should good fellows foemen be?
And who would dream that foes they were—
Larking and singing so friendly then—
A family likeness in every face.
But Captain Cloud made sour demur:
"Guard! keep your prisoners *in* the pen,
And let none talk with Mosby's men."

That captain was a valorous one
(No irony, but honest truth),
Yet down from his brain cold drops distilled,
Making stalactites in his heart—
A conscientious soul, forsooth;
And with a formal hate was filled
Of Mosby's band; and some he'd killed.

Meantime the lady rueful sat,
Watching the flicker of a fire
Where the Colonel played the outdoor host
In brave old hall of ancient Night.
But ever the dame grew shyer and shyer,
Seeming with private grief engrossed—
Grief far from Mosby, housed or lost.

The ruddy embers showed her pale.
The Soldier did his best devoir:
"Some coffee?—no?—a cracker?—one?"
Cared for her servant—sought to cheer:
"I know, I know—a cruel war!

        But wait—even Mosby'll eat his bun;
        The Old Hearth—back to it anon!"

But cordial words no balm could bring;
    She sighed, and kept her inward chafe,
And seemed to hate the voice of glee—
Joyless and tearless. Soon he called
    An escort: "See this lady safe
        In yonder house.—Madam, you're free.
        And now for Mosby.—Guide! with me."

("A night-ride, eh?") "Tighten your girths!
    But, buglers! not a note from you.
Fling more rails on the fires—a blaze!"
("Sergeant, a feint—I told you so—
    Toward Aldie again. Bivouac, adieu!")
        After the cheery flames they gaze,
        Then back for Mosby through the maze.

The moon looked through the trees, and tipped
    The scabbards with her elfin beam;
The Leader backward cast his glance,
Proud of the cavalcade that came—
    A hundred horses, bay and cream:
        "Major! look how the lads advance—
        Mosby we'll have in the ambulance!"

"No doubt, no doubt:—was that a hare?—
    First catch, then cook; and cook him brown."
"Trust me to catch," the other cried—
"The lady's letter!—a dance, man, dance
    This night is given in Leesburg town!"
        "He'll be there too!" wheezed out the
            Guide;
        "That Mosby loves a dance and ride!"

"The lady, ah!—the lady's letter—
A *lady*, then, is in the case,"
Muttered the Major. "Ay, her aunt
Writes her to come by Friday eve
(To-night), for people of the place,
At Mosby's last fight jubilant,
A party give, though table-cheer be scant."

The Major hemmed. "Then this night-ride
We owe to her?—One lighted house
In a town else dark.—The moths, begar!
Are not quite yet all dead!" "How? how?"
"A mute, meek, mournful little mouse!—
Mosby has wiles which subtle are—
But woman's wiles in wiles of war!"

"Tut, Major! by what craft or guile—"
"Can't tell! but he'll be found in wait.
Softly we enter, say, the town—
Good! pickets post, and all so sure—
When—crack! the rifles from every gate,
The Gray-backs fire—dash up and down—
Each alley unto Mosby known!"

"Now, Major, now—you take dark views
Of a moonlight night." "Well, well, we'll see,"
And smoked as if each whiff were gain.
The other mused; then sudden asked,
"What would you do in grand decree?"
"I'd beat, if I could, Lee's armies—then
Send constables after Mosby's men."

"Ay! ay!—you're odd." The moon sailed up;
On through the shadowy land they went.
"Names must be made and printed be!"

Hummed the blithe Colonel. "Doc, your flask!
    Major, I drink to your good content.
        My pipe is out—enough for me!
        One's buttons shine—does Mosby see?

"But what comes here?" A man from the front
    Reported a tree athwart the road.
"Go round it, then; no time to bide;
All right—go on! Were one to stay
    For each distrust of a nervous mood,
        Long miles we'd make in this our ride
        Through Mosby-land.—On! with the
            Guide!"

Then sportful to the Surgeon turned:
    "Green sashes hardly serve by night!"
"Nor bullets nor bottles," the Major sighed,
"Against these moccasin-snakes—such foes
    As seldom come to solid fight:
        They kill and vanish; through grass they
            glide;
        Devil take Mosby!"—his horse here shied.

"Hold! look—the tree, like a dragged balloon;
    A globe of leaves—some trickery here;
My nag is right—best now be shy."
A movement was made, a hubbub and snarl;
    Little was plain—they blindly steer.
        The Pleiads, as from ambush sly,
        Peep out—Mosby's men in the sky!

As restive they turn, how sore they feel,
    And cross, and sleepy, and full of spleen,
And curse the war. "Fools, North and South!"
Said one right out. "O for a bed!
    O now to drop in this woodland green!"

He drops as the syllables leave his
mouth—
Mosby speaks from the undergrowth—

Speaks in a volley! out jets the flame!
Men fall from their saddles like plums from
trees;
Horses take fright, reins tangle and bind;
"Steady—dismount—form—and into the wood!"
They go, but find what scarce can please:
Their steeds have been tied in the field
behind,
And Mosby's men are off like the wind.

Sound the recall! vain to pursue—
The enemy scatters in wilds he knows,
To reunite in his own good time;
And, to follow, they need divide—
To come lone and lost on crouching foes:
Maple and hemlock, beech and lime,
Are Mosby's confederates, share the crime.

"Major," burst in a bugler small,
"The fellow we left in Loudon grass—
Sir Slyboots with the inward bruise,
His voice I heard—the very same—
Some watchword in the ambush pass;
Ay, sir, we had him in his shoes—
We caught him—Mosby—but to lose!"

"Go, go!—these saddle-dreamers! Well,
And here's another.—Cool, sir, cool!"
"Major, I saw them mount and sweep,
And one was humped, or I mistake,
And in the skurry dropped his wool."

"A wig! go fetch it:—the lads need sleep;
They'll next see Mosby in a sheep!

"Come, come, fall back! reform your ranks—
All's jackstraws here! Where's Captain Morn?—
We've parted like boats in a raging tide!
But stay—the Colonel—did he charge?
And comes he there? 'Tis streak of dawn;
Mosby is off, the woods are wide—
Hist! there's a groan—this crazy ride!"

As they searched for the fallen, the dawn grew chill;
They lay in the dew: "Ah! hurt much, Mink?
And—yes—the Colonel!" Dead! but so calm
That death seemed nothing—even death,
The thing we deem every thing heart can think;
Amid wilding roses that shed their balm,
Careless of Mosby he lay—in a charm!

The Major took him by the hand—
Into the friendly clasp it bled
(A ball through heart and hand he rued):
"Good-by!" and gazed with humid glance;
Then in a hollow revery said,
"The weakest thing is lustihood;
But Mosby"—and he checked his mood.

"Where's the advance?—cut off, by heaven!
Come, Surgeon, how with your wounded there?"
"The ambulance will carry all."
"Well, get them in; we go to camp.
Seven prisoners gone? for the rest have care."

Then to himself, "This grief is gall;
That Mosby!—I'll cast a silver ball!"

"Ho!" turning—"Captain Cloud, you mind
The place where the escort went—so shady?
Go, search every closet low and high,
And barn, and bin, and hidden bower—
Every covert—find that lady!
And yet I may misjudge her—ay,
Women (like Mosby) mystify.

"We'll see. Ay, Captain, go—with speed!
Surround and search; each living thing
Secure; that done, await us where
We last turned off. Stay! fire the cage
If the birds be flown." By the cross-road
spring
The bands rejoined; no words; the glare
Told all. Had Mosby plotted there?

The weary troop that wended now—
Hardly it seemed the same that pricked
Forth to the forest from the camp:
Foot-sore horses, jaded men;
Every backbone felt as nicked,
Each eye dim as a sick-room lamp,
All faces stamped with Mosby's stamp.

In order due the Major rode—
Chaplain and Surgeon on either hand;
A riderless horse a negro led;
In a wagon the blanketed sleeper went;
Then the ambulance with the bleeding band;
And, an emptied oat-bag on each head,
Went Mosby's men, and marked the dead.

What gloomed them? what so cast them down,
And changed the cheer that late they took,
As double-guarded now they rode
Between the files of moody men?
Some sudden consciousness they brook,
Or dread the sequel. That night's blood
Disturbed even Mosby's brotherhood.

The flagging horses stumbled at roots,
Floundered in mires, or clinked the stones;
No rider spake except aside;
But the wounded cramped in the ambulance,
It was horror to hear their groans—
Jerked along in the woodland ride,
While Mosby's clan their revery hide.

The Hospital Steward—even he—
Who on the sleeper kept his glance,
Was changed; late bright-black beard and eye
Looked now hearse-black; his heavy heart,
Like his fagged mare, no more could dance;
His grape was now a raisin dry:
'Tis Mosby's homily—*Man must die.*

The amber sunset flushed the camp
As on the hill their eyes they fed;
The pickets dumb looks at the wagon dart;
A handkerchief waves from the bannered tent—
As white, alas! the face of the dead:
Who shall the withering news impart?
The bullet of Mosby goes through heart
to heart!

They buried him where the lone ones lie
(Lone sentries shot on midnight post)—
A green-wood grave-yard hid from ken,

Where sweet-fern flings an odor nigh—
    Yet held in fear for the gleaming ghost!
        Though the bride should see threescore
            and ten,
        She will dream of Mosby and his men.

Now halt the verse, and turn aside—
    The cypress falls athwart the way;
No joy remains for bard to sing;
And heaviest dole of all is this,
    That other hearts shall be as gay
        As hers that now no more shall spring:
        To Mosby-land the dirges cling.

Lee in the Capitol

(APRIL, 1866)

Hard pressed by numbers in his strait,
Rebellion's soldier-chief no more contends—
Feels that the hour is come of Fate,
Lays down one sword, and widened warfare ends.
The captain who fierce armies led
Becomes a quiet seminary's head—
Poor as his privates, earns his bread.
In studious cares and aims engrossed,
Strives to forget Stuart and Stonewall dead—
Comrades and cause, station and riches lost,
And all the ills that flock when fortune's fled.
No word he breathes of vain lament,
Mute to reproach, nor hears applause—
His doom accepts, perforce content,
And acquiesces in asserted laws;
Secluded now would pass his life,
And leave to time the sequel of the strife.

But missives from the Senators ran;
Not that they now would gaze upon a swordless foe,
And power made powerless and brought low:
Reasons of state, 'tis claimed, require the man.
Demurring not, promptly he comes
By ways which show the blackened homes,
And—last—the seat no more his own,
But Honor's; patriot grave-yards fill

The forfeit slopes of that patrician hill,
　　And fling a shroud on Arlington.
The oaks ancestral all are low;
No more from the porch his glance shall go
Ranging the varied landscape o'er,
Far as the looming Dome—no more.
One look he gives, then turns aside,
Solace he summons from his pride:
"So be it! They await me now
Who wrought this stinging overthrow;
They wait me; not as on the day
Of Pope's impelled retreat in disarray—
By me impelled—when toward yon Dome
The clouds of war came rolling home."
The burst, the bitterness was spent,
The heart-burst bitterly turbulent,
And on he fared.
　　　　　　　　In nearness now
　　He marks the Capitol—a show
Lifted in amplitude, and set
With standards flushed with the glow of
　　　　Richmond yet;
　　Trees and green terraces sleep below.
Through the clear air, in sunny light,
The marble dazes—a temple white.

Intrepid soldier! had his blade been drawn
For yon starred flag, never as now
Bid to the Senate-house had he gone,
But freely, and in pageant borne,
As when brave numbers without number,
　　　　massed,
Plumed the broad way, and pouring passed—
Bannered, beflowered—between the shores
Of faces, and the dinn'd huzzas,

And balconies kindling at the sabre-flash,
'Mid roar of drums and guns, and cymbal-crash,
While Grant and Sherman shone in blue—
Close of the war and victory's long review.

Yet pride at hand still aidful swelled,
And up the hard ascent he held.
The meeting follows. In his mien
The victor and the vanquished both are seen—
All that he is, and what he late had been.
Awhile, with curious eyes they scan
The Chief who led invasion's van—
Allied by family to one,
Founder of the Arch the Invader warred upon:
Who looks at Lee must think of Washington;
In pain must think, and hide the thought,
So deep with grievous meaning it is fraught.

Secession in her soldier shows
Silent and patient; and they feel
    (Developed even in just success)
Dim inklings of a hazy future steal;
    Their thoughts their questions well express:
"Does the sad South still cherish hate?
Freely will Southern men with Northern mate?
The blacks—should we our arm withdraw,
Would that betray them? some distrust your law.
And how if foreign fleets should come—
Would the South then drive her wedges home?"
And more hereof. The Virginian sees—
Replies to such anxieties.
Discreet his answers run—appear
Briefly straightforward, coldly clear.

"If now," the Senators, closing, say,
"Aught else remain, speak out, we pray."

Hereat he paused; his better heart
Strove strongly then; prompted a worthier part
Than coldly to endure his doom.
Speak out? Ay, speak, and for the brave,
Who else no voice or proxy have;
Frankly their spokesman here become,
And the flushed North from her own victory
save.
That inspiration overrode—
Hardly it quelled the galling load
Of personal ill. The inner feud
He, self-contained, a while withstood;
They waiting. In his troubled eye
Shadows from clouds unseen they spy;
They could not mark within his breast
The pang which pleading thought oppressed:
He spoke, nor felt the bitterness die.

"My word is given—it ties my sword;
Even were banners still abroad,
Never could I strive in arms again
While you, as fit, that pledge retain.
Our cause I followed, stood in field and gate—
All's over now, and now I follow Fate.
But this is naught. A People call—
A desolated land, and all
The brood of ills that press so sore,
The natural offspring of this civil war,
Which ending not in fame, such as might rear
Fitly its sculptured trophy here,
Yields harvest large of doubt and dread
To all who have the heart and head
To feel and know. How shall I speak?
Thoughts knot with thoughts, and utterance
check.
Before my eyes there swims a haze,

Through mists departed comrades gaze—
First to encourage, last that shall upbraid!
How shall I speak? The South would fain
Feel peace, have quiet law again—
Replant the trees for homestead-shade.
  You ask if she recants: she yields.
Nay, and would more; would blend anew,
As the bones of the slain in her forests do,
Bewailed alike by us and you.
  A voice comes out from these charnel-fields,
A plaintive yet unheeded one:
'Died all in vain? both sides undone?'
Push not your triumph; do not urge
Submissiveness beyond the verge.
Intestine rancor would you bide,
Nursing eleven sliding daggers in your side?
Far from my thought to school or threat;
I speak the things which hard beset.
Where various hazards meet the eyes,
To elect in magnanimity is wise.
Reap victory's fruit while sound the core;
What sounder fruit than re-established law?
I know your partial thoughts do press
Solely on us for war's unhappy stress;
But weigh—consider—look at all,
And broad anathema you'll recall.
The censor's charge I'll not repeat,
That meddlers kindled the war's white heat—
Vain intermeddlers and malign,
Both of the palm and of the pine;
I waive the thought—which never can be rife—
Common's the crime in every civil strife:
But this I feel, that North and South were
    driven
By Fate to arms. For *our* unshriven,

What thousands, truest souls, were tried—
    As never may any be again—
All those who stemmed Secession's pride,
But at last were swept by the urgent tide
    Into the chasm. I know their pain.
A story here may be applied:
'In Moorish lands there lived a maid
    Brought to confess by vow the creed
    Of Christians. Fain would priests persuade
That now she must approve by deed
    The faith she kept. "What deed?" she asked.
"Your old sire leave, nor deem it sin,
    And come with us." Still more they tasked
The sad one: "If heaven you'd win—
    Far from the burning pit withdraw,
Then must you learn to hate your kin,
    Yea, side against them—such the law,
For Moor and Christian are at war."
"Then will I never quit my sire,
But here with him through every trial go,
Nor leave him though in flames below—
God help me in his fire!" '
So in the South; vain every plea
'Gainst Nature's strong fidelity;
    True to the home and to the heart,
Throngs cast their lot with kith and kin,
    Foreboding, cleaved to the natural part—
Was this the unforgivable sin?
These noble spirits are yet yours to win.
Shall the great North go Sylla's way?
Proscribe? prolong the evil day?
Confirm the curse? infix the hate?
In Union's name forever alienate?
From reason who can urge the plea—
Freemen conquerors of the free?

When blood returns to the shrunken vein,
Shall the wound of the Nation bleed again?
Well may the wars wan thought supply,
And kill the kindling of the hopeful eye,
Unless you do what even kings have done
In leniency—unless you shun
To copy Europe in her worst estate—
Avoid the tyranny you reprobate."

He ceased. His earnestness unforeseen
Moved, but not swayed their former mien;
    And they dismissed him. Forth he went
Through vaulted walks in lengthened line
Like porches erst upon the Palatine:
    Historic reveries their lesson lent,
    The Past her shadow through the Future
        sent.

But no. Brave though the Soldier, grave his
        plea—
    Catching the light in the future's skies,
Instinct disowns each darkening prophecy:
    Faith in America never dies;
Heaven shall the end ordained fulfill,
We march with Providence cheery still.

A MEDITATION:

ATTRIBUTED TO A NORTHERNER AFTER ATTENDING THE LAST OF TWO FUNERALS FROM THE SAME HOMESTEAD—THOSE OF A NATIONAL AND A CONFEDERATE OFFICER (BROTHERS), HIS KINSMEN, WHO HAD DIED FROM THE EFFECTS OF WOUNDS RECEIVED IN THE CLOSING BATTLES

A Meditation

How often in the years that close,
  When truce had stilled the sieging gun,
The soldiers, mounting on their works,
  With mutual curious glance have run
From face to face along the fronting show,
And kinsman spied, or friend—even in a foe.

What thoughts conflicting then were shared,
  While sacred tenderness perforce
Welled from the heart and wet the eye;
  And something of a strange remorse
Rebelled against the sanctioned sin of blood,
And Christian wars of natural brotherhood.

Then stirred the god within the breast—
  The witness that is man's at birth;
A deep misgiving undermined
  Each plea and subterfuge of earth;
They felt in that rapt pause, with warning rife,
Horror and anguish for the civil strife.

Of North or South they recked not then,
  Warm passion cursed the cause of war:
Can Africa pay back this blood
  Spilt on Potomac's shore?

Yet doubts, as pangs, were vain the strife to
stay,
And hands that fain had clasped again could
slay.

How frequent in the camp was seen
The herald from the hostile one,
A guest and frank companion there
When the proud formal talk was done;
The pipe of peace was smoked even 'mid the
war,
And fields in Mexico again fought o'er.

In Western battle long they lay
So near opposed in trench or pit,
That foeman unto foeman called
As men who screened in tavern sit:
"You bravely fight" each to the other said—
"Toss us a biscuit!" o'er the wall it sped.

And pale on those same slopes, a boy—
A stormer, bled in noon-day glare;
No aid the Blue-coats then could bring,
He cried to them who nearest were,
And out there came 'mid howling shot and shell
A daring foe who him befriended well.

Mark the great Captains on both sides,
The soldiers with the broad renown—
They all were messmates on the Hudson's
marge,
Beneath one roof they laid them down;
And, free from hate in many an after pass,
Strove as in school-boy rivalry of the class.

A darker side there is; but doubt
    In Nature's charity hovers there:
If men for new agreement yearn,
    Then old upbraiding best forbear:
"The South's the sinner!" Well, so let it be;
But shall the North sin worse, and stand the
        Pharisee?

O now that brave men yield the sword,
    Mine be the manful soldier-view;
By how much more they boldly warred,
    By so much more is mercy due:
When Vicksburg fell, and the moody files
        marched out,
Silent the victors stood, scorning to raise a shout.

Supplement to *Battle-Pieces*

Were I fastidiously anxious for the symmetry of this book, it would close with the notes.* But the times are such that patriotism—not free from solicitude—urges a claim overriding all literary scruples.

It is more than a year since the memorable surrender, but events have not yet rounded themselves into completion. Not justly can we complain of this. There has been an upheaval affecting the basis of things; to altered circumstances complicated adaptations are to be made; there are difficulties great and novel. But is Reason still waiting for Passion to spend itself? We have sung of the soldiers and sailors, but who shall hymn the politicians?

In view of the infinite desirableness of Re-establishment, and considering that, so far as feeling is concerned, it depends not mainly on the temper in which the South regards the North, but rather conversely; one who never was a blind adherent feels constrained to submit some thoughts, counting on the indulgence of his countrymen.

And, first, it may be said that, if among the feelings and opinions growing immediately out of a great civil convulsion, there are any which time shall modify or do away, they are presumably those of a less temperate and charitable cast.

There seems no reason why patriotism and narrowness should go together, or why intellectual impartiality should be confounded with political trimming, or why serviceable truth should keep cloistered because not partisan. Yet the work of Reconstruction, if admitted to be feasible at all,

* In the original edition of *Battle-Pieces,* Melville's notes preceded the Supplement.

demands little but common sense and Christian charity. Little but these? These are much.

Some of us are concerned because as yet the South shows no penitence. But what exactly do we mean by this? Since down to the close of the war she never confessed any for braving it, the only penitence now left her is that which springs solely from the sense of discomfiture; and since this evidently would be a contrition hypocritical, it would be unworthy in us to demand it. Certain it is that penitence, in the sense of voluntary humiliation, will never be displayed. Nor does this afford just ground for unreserved condemnation. It is enough, for all practical purposes, if the South have been taught by the terrors of civil war to feel that Secession, like Slavery, is against Destiny; that both now lie buried in one grave; that her fate is linked with ours; and that together we comprise the Nation.

The clouds of heroes who battled for the Union it is needless to eulogize here. But how of the soldiers on the other side? And when of a free community we name the soldiers, we thereby name the people. It was in subserviency to the slave-interest that Secession was plotted; but it was under the plea, plausibly urged, that certain inestimable rights guaranteed by the Constitution were directly menaced, that the people of the South were cajoled into revolution. Through the arts of the conspirators and the perversity of fortune, the most sensitive love of liberty was entrapped into the support of a war whose implied end was the erecting in our advanced century of an Anglo-American empire based upon the systematic degradation of man.

Spite this clinging reproach, however, signal military virtues and achievements have conferred upon the Confederate arms historic fame, and upon certain of the commanders a renown extending beyond the sea—a renown which we of the North could not suppress, even if we would. In personal character, also, not a few of the military leaders of the South enforce forbearance; the memory of others the North refrains from disparaging; and some, with more or less of reluctance, she can respect. Posterity, sympathizing with our convictions, but removed from our passions, may perhaps go farther here. If George IV. could, out of the graceful instinct of a gentleman, raise an honorable monument in the great fane of Christendom over the remains of the enemy of his dynasty, Charles Edward, the invader of England and victor in the rout at Preston Pans—upon whose head the king's ancestor but one reign removed had set a price—is it probable that the grandchildren of General Grant will pursue with rancor, or slur by sour neglect, the memory of Stonewall Jackson?

But the South herself is not wanting in recent histories and biographies which record the deeds of her chieftains —writings freely published at the North by loyal houses, widely read here, and with a deep though saddened interest. By students of the war such works are hailed as welcome accessories, and tending to the completeness of the record.

Supposing a happy issue out of present perplexities, then, in the generation next to come, Southerners there will be yielding allegiance to the Union, feeling all their interests bound up in it, and yet cherishing unrebuked that kind of feeling for the memory of the soldiers of the fallen Confederacy that Burns, Scott, and the Ettrick Shepherd felt for the memory of the gallant clansmen ruined through their fidelity to the Stuarts—a feeling whose passion was tempered by the poetry imbuing it, and which in no wise affected their loyalty to the Georges, and which, it may be added, indirectly contributed excellent things to literature. But, setting this view aside, dishonorable would it be in the South were she willing to abandon to shame the memory of brave men who with signal personal disinterestedness warred in her behalf, though from motives, as we believe, so deplorably astray.

Patriotism is not baseness, neither is it inhumanity. The mourners who this summer bear flowers to the mounds of the Virginian and Georgian dead are, in their domestic bereavement and proud affection, as sacred in the eye of Heaven as are those who go with similar offerings of tender grief and love into the cemeteries of our Northern martyrs. And yet, in one aspect, how needless to point the contrast.

Cherishing such sentiments, it will hardly occasion surprise that, in looking over the battle-pieces in the foregoing collection, I have been tempted to withdraw or modify some of them, fearful lest in presenting, though but dramatically and by way of a poetic record, the passions and epithets of civil war, I might be contributing to a bitterness which every sensible American must wish at an end. So, too, with the emotion of victory as reproduced on some pages, and particularly toward the close. It should not be construed into an exultation misapplied —an exultation as ungenerous as unwise, and made to minister, however indirectly, to that kind of censoriousness too apt to be produced in certain natures by success after trying reverses. Zeal is not of necessity religion, neither is it always of the same essence with poetry or patriotism.

There were excesses which marked the conflict, most of which are perhaps inseparable from a civil strife so intense and prolonged, and involving warfare in some border countries new and imperfectly civilized. Barbarities also there were, for which the Southern people collectively can hardly be held responsible, though perpetrated by ruffians in their name. But surely other qualities—exalted ones—courage and fortitude matchless, were likewise displayed, and largely; and justly may these be held the characteristic traits, and not the former.

In this view, what Northern writer, however patriotic, but must revolt from acting on paper a part any way akin to that of the live dog to the dead lion; and yet it is right to rejoice for our triumph, so far as it may justly imply an advance for our whole country and for humanity.

Let it be held no reproach to any one that he pleads for reasonable consideration for our late enemies, now stricken down and unavoidably debarred, for the time, from speaking through authorized agencies for themselves. Nothing has been urged here in the foolish hope of conciliating those men—few in number, we trust—who have resolved never to be reconciled to the Union. On such hearts every thing is thrown away except it be religious commiseration, and the sincerest. Yet let them call to mind that unhappy Secessionist, not a military man, who with impious alacrity fired the first shot of the Civil War at Sumter, and a little more than four years afterward fired the last one into his own heart at Richmond.

Noble was the gesture into which patriotic passion surprised the people in a utilitarian time and country; yet the glory of the war falls short of its pathos—a pathos which now at last ought to disarm all animosity.

How many and earnest thoughts still rise, and how hard to repress them. We feel what past years have been, and years, unretarded years, shall come. May we all have moderation; may we all show candor. Though, perhaps, nothing could ultimately have averted the strife, and though to treat of human actions is to deal wholly with second causes, nevertheless, let us not cover up or try to extenuate what, humanly speaking, is the truth—namely, that those unfraternal denunciations, continued through years, and which at last inflamed to deeds that ended in bloodshed, were reciprocal; and that, had the preponderating strength and the prospect of its unlimited increase lain on the other side, on ours might have lain those actions which now in our late opponents we stigmatize under the name of Rebellion. As frankly let us own—what it would be unbecoming to parade were foreigners concerned—that our triumph was won not more by skill and bravery than by superior resources and crushing numbers; that it was a triumph, too, over a people for years politically misled by designing men, and also by some honestly-erring men, who from their position could not have been otherwise than broadly influential; a people who, though, indeed, they sought to perpetuate the curse of slavery, and even extend it, were not the authors of it, but (less fortunate, not less righteous than we) were the fated inheritors; a people who, having a like origin with ourselves, share essentially in whatever worthy qualities we may possess. No one can add to the lasting reproach which hopeless defeat has now cast upon Secession by withholding the recognition of these verities.

Surely we ought to take it to heart that that kind of pacification, based upon principles operating equally all over the land, which lovers of their country yearn for, and which our arms, though signally triumphant, did not bring about, and which law-making, however anxious, or energetic, or repressive, never by itself can achieve, may yet be largely aided by generosity of sentiment public and private. Some revisionary legislation and adaptive is indispensable; but with this should harmoniously work another kind of prudence, not unallied with entire magnanimity. Benevolence and policy—Christianity and Machiavelli—dissuade from penal severities toward the subdued. Abstinence here is as obligatory as considerate care for our unfortunate fellow-men late in bonds, and, if observed, would equally prove to be wise forecast. The great qualities of the South, those attested in the War, we can perilously alienate, or we may make them nationally available at need.

The blacks, in their infant pupilage to freedom, appeal to the sympathies of every humane mind. The paternal guardianship which for the interval government exercises over them was prompted equally by duty and benevolence.

Yet such kindliness should not be allowed to exclude kindliness to communities who stand nearer to us in nature. For the future of the freed slaves we may well be concerned; but the future of the whole country, involving the future of the blacks, urges a paramount claim upon our anxiety. Effective benignity, like the Nile, is not narrow in its bounty, and true policy is always broad. To be sure, it is vain to seek to glide, with moulded words, over the difficulties of the situation. And for them who are neither partisans, nor enthusiasts, nor theorists, nor cynics, there are some doubts not readily to be solved. And there are fears. Why is not the cessation of war now at length attended with the settled calm of peace? Wherefore in a clear sky do we still turn our eyes toward the South, as the Neapolitan, months after the eruption, turns his toward Vesuvius? Do we dread lest the repose may be deceptive? In the recent convulsion has the crater but shifted? Let us revere that sacred uncertainty which forever impends over men and nations. Those of us who always abhorred slavery as an atheistical iniquity, gladly we join in the exulting chorus of humanity over its downfall. But we should remember that emancipation was accomplished not by deliberate legislation; only through agonized violence could so mighty a result be effected. In our natural solicitude to confirm the benefit of liberty to the blacks, let us forbear from measures of dubious constitutional rightfulness toward our white countrymen—measures of a nature to provoke, among other of the last evils, exterminating hatred of race toward race. In imagination let us place ourselves in the unprecedented position of the Southerners—their position as regards the millions of ignorant manumitted slaves in their midst, for whom some of us now claim the suffrage. Let us be Christians toward our fellow-whites, as well as philanthropists toward the blacks, our fellow-men. In all things, and toward all, we are enjoined to do as we would be done by. Nor should we forget that benevolent desires, after passing a certain point, can not undertake their own fulfillment without incurring the risk of evils beyond those sought to be remedied. Something may well be left to the graduated care of future legislation, and to heaven. In one point of view the coexistence of the two races in the South—whether the negro be bond or free—seems (even as it did to Abraham Lincoln) a grave evil. Emancipation has ridded the country of the reproach, but not wholly of the calamity. Especially in the present transition period for both races in the South, more or less of trouble may not unreasonably be anticipated; but let us not hereafter be too swift to charge the blame exclusively in any one quarter. With certain evils men must be more or less patient. Our institutions have a potent digestion, and may in time convert and assimilate to good all elements thrown in, however originally alien.

But, so far as immediate measures looking toward permanent Re-establishment are concerned, no consideration should tempt us to pervert the national victory into oppression for the vanquished. Should plausible promise of eventual good, or a deceptive or spurious sense of duty, lead us to essay this, count we must on serious consequences, not the least of which would be divisions among the Northern adherents of the Union. Assuredly, if any honest Catos there be who thus far have gone with us, no longer will they do so, but oppose us, and as resolutely as hitherto they have supported. But this path of thought leads toward those waters of bitterness from which one can only turn aside and be silent.

But supposing Re-establishment so far advanced that the Southern seats in Congress are occupied, and by men qualified in accordance with those cardinal principles of representative government which hitherto have prevailed in the land—what then? Why, the Congressmen elected by the people of the South will—represent the people of the South. This may seem a flat conclusion; but, in view of the last five years, may there not be latent significance in it? What will be the temper of those Southern members? and, confronted by them, what will be the mood of our own representatives? In private life true reconciliation seldom follows a violent quarrel; but, if subsequent intercourse be unavoidable, nice observances and mutual are indispensable to the prevention of a new rupture. Amity itself can only be maintained by reciprocal respect, and true friends are punctilious equals. On the floor of Congress North and South are to come together after a passionate duel, in which the South, though proving her valor, has been made to bite the dust. Upon differences in debate shall acrimonious recriminations be exchanged? shall censorious superiority assumed by one section provoke defiant self-assertion on the other? shall Manassas and Chickamauga be retorted for Chattanooga and Richmond? Under the supposition that the full Congress will be composed of gentlemen, all this is impossible. Yet, if otherwise, it needs no prophet of Israel to foretell the end. The maintenance of Congressional decency in the future will rest mainly with the North. Rightly will more forbearance be required from the North than the South, for the North is victor.

But some there are who may deem these latter thoughts inapplicable, and for this reason: Since the test-oath operatively excludes from Congress all who in any way participated in Secession, therefore none but Southerners wholly in harmony with the North are eligible to seats. This is true for the time being. But the oath is alterable; and in the wonted fluctuations of parties not improbably it will undergo alteration, assuming such a form, perhaps, as not to bar the admission into the National Legislature of men who represent the populations lately in revolt. Such a result would involve no violation of the principles of democratic government. Not readily can one perceive how the political existence of the millions of late Secessionists can permanently be ignored by this Republic. The years of the war tried our devotion to the Union; the time of peace may test the sincerity of our faith in democracy.

In no spirit of opposition, not by way of challenge, is any thing here thrown out. These thoughts are sincere ones; they seem natural—inevitable. Here and there they must have suggested themselves to many thoughtful patriots. And, if they be just thoughts, ere long they must have that weight with the public which already they have had with individuals.

For that heroic band—those children of the furnace who, in regions like Texas and Tennessee, maintained their fidelity through terrible trials—we of the North felt for them, and profoundly we honor them. Yet passionate sympathy, with resentments so close as to be almost domestic in their bitterness, would hardly in the present juncture tend to discreet legislation. Were the Unionists and Secessionists but as Guelphs and Ghibellines? If not, then far be it from a great nation now to act in the spirit that animated a triumphant town-faction in the Middle Ages. But crowding thoughts must at last be checked; and, in times like the present, one who desires to be impartially just in the expression of his views, moves as among sword-points presented on every side.

Let us pray that the terrible historic tragedy of our time may not have been enacted without instructing our whole beloved country through terror and pity; and may fulfillment verify in the end those expectations which kindle the bards of Progress and Humanity.

THE END

FROM *Clarel*

1876

If during the period in which this work has remained unpublished, though not undivulged, any of its properties have by a natural process exhaled; it yet retains, I trust, enough of original life to redeem it at least from vapidity. Be that as it may, I here dismiss the book—content beforehand with whatever future awaits it.

FROM PART I

Jerusalem

I : THE HOSTEL

In chamber low and scored by time,
Masonry old, late washed with lime—
Much like a tomb new-cut in stone;
Elbow on knee, and brow sustained
All motionless on sidelong hand,
A student sits, and broods alone.
  The small deep casement sheds a ray
Which tells that in the Holy Town
It is the passing of the day—
The Vigil of Epiphany.
Beside him in the narrow cell
His luggage lies unpacked; thereon
The dust lies, and on him as well—
The dust of travel. But anon
His face he lifts—in feature fine,
Yet pale, and all but feminine
But for the eye and serious brow—
Then rises, paces to and fro,
And pauses, saying, "Other cheer
Than that anticipated here,
By me the learner, now I find.
Theology, art thou so blind?
What means this naturalistic knell
In lieu of Siloh's oracle
Which here should murmur? Snatched from
  grace,
And waylaid in the holy place!
Not thus it was but yesterday
Off Jaffa on the clear blue sea;
Nor thus, my heart, it was with thee

Landing amid the shouts and spray;
Nor thus when mounted, full equipped,
Out through the vaulted gate we slipped
Beyond the walls where gardens bright
With bloom and blossom cheered the sight.
"The plain we crossed. In afternoon,
How like our early autumn bland—
So softly tempered for a boon—
The breath of Sharon's prairie land!
And was it, yes, her titled Rose,
That scarlet poppy oft at hand?
Then Ramleh gleamed, the sail-white town
At even. There I watched day close
From the fair tower, the suburb one:
Seaward and dazing set the sun:
Inland I turned me toward the wall
Of Ephraim, stretched in purple pall.
Romance of mountains! But in end
What change the near approach could lend.
"The start this morning—gun and lance
Against the quarter-moon's low tide;
The thieves' huts where we hushed the ride;
Chill day-break in the lorn advance;
In stony strait the scorch of noon,
Thrown off by crags, reminding one
Of those hot paynims whose fierce hands
Flung showers of Afric's fiery sands
In face of that crusader-king,
Louis, to wither so his wing;
And, at the last, aloft for goal,
Like the ice-bastions round the Pole,
Thy blank, blank towers, Jerusalem!"

Again he droops, with brow on hand.
But, starting up, "Why, well I knew
Salem to be no Samarcand;

'Twas scarce surprise; and yet first view
Brings this eclipse. Needs be my soul,
Purged by the desert's subtle air
From bookish vapors, now is heir
To nature's influx of control;
Comes likewise now to consciousness
Of the true import of that press
Of inklings which in travel late
Through Latin lands, did vex my state,
And somehow seemed clandestine. Ah!
These under-formings in the mind.
Banked corals which ascend from far,
But little heed men that they wind
Unseen, unheard—till lo, the reef—
The reef and breaker, wreck and grief.
But here unlearning, how to me
Opes the expanse of time's vast sea!
Yes, I am young, but Asia old.
The books, the books not all have told.
  "And, for the rest, the facile chat
Of overweenings—what was that
The grave one said in Jaffa lane
Whom there I met, my countryman,
But new-returned from travel here;
Some word of mine provoked the strain;
His meaning now begins to clear:
Let me go over it again:—
  "Our New World's worldly wit so shrewd
Lacks the Semitic reverent mood,
Unworldly—hardly may confer
Fitness for just interpreter
Of Palestine. Forego the state
Of local minds inveterate,
Tied to one poor and casual form.
To avoid the deep saves not from storm.
  "Those things he said, and added more;

No clear authenticated lore
I deemed. But now, need now confess
My cultivated narrowness,
Though scarce indeed of sort he meant?
'Tis the uprooting of content!"
So he, the student. 'Twas a mind,
Earnest by nature, long confined
Apart like Vesta in a grove
Collegiate, but let to rove
At last abroad among mankind,
And here in end confronted so
By the true genius, friend or foe,
And actual visage of a place
Before but dreamed of in the glow
Of fancy's spiritual grace.
Further his meditations aim,
Reverting to his different frame
Bygone. And then: "Can faith remove
Her light, because of late no plea
I've lifted to her source above?"
Dropping thereat upon the knee,
His lips he parted; but the word
Against the utterance demurred
And failed him. With infirm intent
He sought the house-top. Set of sun:
His feet upon the yet warm stone,
He, Clarel, by the coping leant,
In silent gaze. The mountain town,
A walled and battlemented one,
With houseless suburbs front and rear,
And flanks built up from steeps severe,
Saddles and turrets the ascent—
Tower which rides the elephant.
Hence large the view. There where he stood,
Was Acra's upper neighborhood.
The circling hills he saw, with one

Excelling, ample in its crown,
Making the uplifted city low
By contrast—Olivet. The flow
Of eventide was at full brim;
Overlooked, the houses sloped from him—
Terraced or domed, unchimnied, gray,
All stone—a moor of roofs. No play
Of life; no smoke went up, no sound
Except low hum, and that half drowned.

The inn abutted on the pool
Named Hezekiah's, a sunken court
Where silence and seclusion rule,
Hemmed round by walls of nature's sort,
Base to stone structures seeming one
E'en with the steeps they stand upon.

As a three-decker's stern-lights peer
Down on the oily wake below,
Upon the sleek dark waters here
The inn's small lattices bestow
A rearward glance. And here and there
In flaws the languid evening air
Stirs the dull weeds adust, which trail
In festoons from the crag, and veil
The ancient fissures, overtopped
By the tall convent of the Copt,
Built like a light-house o'er the main.

Blind arches showed in walls of wane,
Sealed windows, portals masoned fast,
And terraces where nothing passed
By parapets all dumb. No tarn
Among the Kaatskills, high above
Farm-house and stack, last lichened barn
And log-bridge rotting in remove—
More lonesome looks than this dead pool
In town where living creatures rule.

Not here the spell might he undo;

The strangeness haunted him and grew.
    But twilight closes. He descends
And toward the inner court he wends.

IV : OF THE CRUSADERS

When sighting first the towers afar
Which girt the object of the war
And votive march—the Saviour's Tomb,
What made the red-cross knights so shy?
And wherefore did they doff the plume
And baldrick, kneel in dust, and sigh?
    Hardly it serves to quote Voltaire
And say they were freebooters—hence,
Incapable of awe or sense
Pathetic; no, for man is heir
To complex moods; and in that age
Belief devout and bandit rage
Frequent were joined; and e'en to-day
At shrines on the Calabrian steep—
Not insincere while feelings sway—
The brigand halts to adore, to weep.
Grant then the worst—is all romance
Which claims that the crusader's glance
Was blurred by tears?
                                        But if that round
Of disillusions which accrue
In this our day, imply a ground
For more concern than Tancred knew,
Thinking, yet not as in despair,
Of Christ who suffered for him there
Upon the crag; then, own it true,
Cause graver much than his is ours
At least to check the hilarious heart
Before these memorable towers.
    But wherefore this? such theme why start?

Because if here in many a place
The rhyme—much like the knight indeed—
Abjure brave ornament, 'twill plead
Just reason, and appeal for grace.

XVII : NATHAN

Nathan had sprung from worthy stock—
Austere, ascetical, but free,
Which hewed their way from sea-beat rock
Wherever woods and winter be.
    The pilgrim-keel in storm and stress
Had erred, and on a wilderness.
But shall the children all be schooled
By hap which their forefathers ruled?
Those primal settlers put in train
New emigrants which inland bore;
From these too, emigrants again
Westward pressed further; more bred more;
At each remove a goodlier wain,
A heart more large, an ampler shore,
With legacies of farms behind;
Until in years the wagons wind
Through parks and pastures of the sun,
Warm plains as of Esdraleon:
'Tis nature in her best benign.
Wild, wild in symmetry of mould,
With freckles on her tawny gold,
The lily alone looks pantherine—
The libbard-lily. Never broods
The gloom here of grim hemlock woods
Breeding the witchcraft-spell malign;
But groves like isles in Grecian seas,
Those dotting isles, the Sporades.
But who the gracious charm may tell—
Long rollings of the vast serene—

The prairie in her swimming swell
Of undulation.
Such glad scene
Was won by venturers from far
Born under that severer star
The landing patriarchs knew. In fine,
To Illinois—a turf divine
Of promise, how auspicious spread,
Ere yet the cities rose thereon—
From Saco's mountain wilds were led
The sire of Nathan, wife and son;
Life's lot to temper so, and shun
Mountains whose camp withdrawn was set
Above one vale he would forget.
After some years their tale had told,
He rested; lay forever stilled
With sachems and mound-builders old.
The son was grown; the farm he tilled;
A stripling, but of manful ways,
Hardy and frugal, oft he filled
The widow's eyes with tears of praise.
An only child, with her he kept
For *her* sake part, the Christian way,
Though frequent in his bosom crept
Precocious doubt unbid. The sway
He felt of his grave life, and power
Of vast space, from the log-house door
Daily beheld. Three Indian mounds
Against the horizon's level bounds
Dim showed across the prairie green
Like dwarfed and blunted mimic shapes
Of Pyramids at distance seen
From the broad Delta's planted capes
Of vernal grain. In nearer view
With trees he saw them crowned, which drew
From the red sagamores of eld

Entombed within, the vital gum
Which green kept each mausoleum.
    Hard by, as chanced, he once beheld
Bones like sea corals; one bleached skull
A vase vined round and beautiful
With flowers; felt, with bated breath
The floral revelry over death.
    And other sights his heart had thrilled;
Lambs had he known by thunder killed,
Innocents—and the type of Christ
Betrayed. Had not such things sufficed
To touch the young pure heart with awe,
Memory's mint could move him more.
In prairie twilight, summer's own,
The last cow milked, and he alone
In barn-yard dreamy by the fence,
Contrasted, came a scene immense:
The great White Hills, mount flanked by mount,
The Saco and Ammonoosuc's fount;
Where, in September's equinox
Nature hath put such terror on
That from his mother man would run—
Our mother, Earth: the founded rocks
Unstable prove: the Slide! the Slide!
Again he saw the mountain side
Sliced open; yet again he stood
Under its shadow, on the spot—
Now waste, but once a cultured plot,
Though far from village neighborhood—
Where, nor by sexton hearsed at even,
Somewhere his uncle slept; no mound,
Since not a trace of him was found,
So whelmed the havoc from the heaven.
    This reminiscence of dismay,
These thoughts unhinged him. On a day
Waiting for monthly grist at mill

In settlement some miles away,
It chanced, upon the window-sill
A dusty book he spied, whose coat,
Like the Scotch miller's powdered twill,
The mealy owner might denote.
Called off from reading, unaware
The miller e'en had left it there.
A book all but forsaken now
For more advanced ones not so frank,
Nor less in vogue and taking rank;
And yet it never shall outgrow
That infamy it first incurred,
Though—viewed in light which moderns know—
Capricious infamy absurd.
  The blunt straightforward Saxon tone,
Work-a-day language, even his own,
The sturdy thought, not deep but clear,
The hearty unbelief sincere,
Arrested him much like a hand
Clapped on the shoulder. Here he found
Body to doubt, rough standing-ground.
After some pages brief were scanned,
"Wilt loan me this?" he anxious said.
The shrewd Scot turned his square, strong head—
The book he saw, in troubled trim,
Fearing for Nathan, even him
So young, and for the mill, may be,
Should his unspoken heresy
Get bruited so. The lad but part
Might penetrate that senior heart.
Vainly the miller would dissuade;
Pledge gave he, and the loan was made.
  Reclined that night by candle dim
He read, then slept, and woke afraid:
The White Hill's slide! the Indian skull!

But this wore off; and unto him
Came acquiescence, which tho' dull
Was hardly peace. An altered earth
Sullen he tilled, in Adam's frame
When thrust from Eden out to dearth
And blest no more, and wise in shame.
The fall! nor aught availed at need
To Nathan, not each filial deed
Done for his mother, to allay
This ill. But tho' the Deist's sway,
Broad as the prairie fire, consumed
Some pansies which before had bloomed
Within his heart; it did but feed
To clear the soil for upstart weed.
    Yes, ere long came replacing mood.
The god, expelled from given form,
Went out into the calm and storm.
Now, ploughing near the isles of wood
In dream he felt the loneness come,
In dream regarded there the loam
Turned first by him. Such mental food
Need quicken, and in natural way,
Each germ of Pantheistic sway,
Whose influence, nor always drear,
Tenants our maiden hemisphere;
As if, dislodged long since from cells
Of Thracian woodlands, hither stole—
Hither, to renew their old control—
Pan and the pagan oracles.
    How frequent when Favonius low
Breathed from the copse which mild did wave
Over his father's sylvan grave,
And stirred the corn, he stayed the hoe,
And leaning, listening, felt a thrill
Which heathenized against the will.

Years sped. But years attain not truth,
Nor length of life avails at all;
But time instead contributes ruth:
His mother—her the garners call:
When sicklemen with sickles go,
The churl of nature reaps her low.
Let now the breasts of Ceres swell—
In shooks, with golden tassels gay,
The Indian corn its trophies ray
About the log-house; is it well
With death's ripe harvest?—To believe,
Belief to win nor more to grieve!
But how? a sect about him stood
In thin and scattered neighborhood;
Uncanny, and in rupture new;
Nor were all lives of members true
And good. For them who hate and heave
Contempt on rite and creed sublime,
Yet to their own rank fable cleave—
Abject, the latest shame of time;
These quite repelled, for still his mind
Erring, was of no vulgar kind.
Alone, and at Doubt's freezing pole
He wrestled with the pristine forms
Like the first man. By inner storms
Held in solution, so his soul
Ripened for hour of such control
As shapes, concretes. The influence came,
And from a source that well might claim
Surprise.
'Twas in a lake-port new,
A mart for grain, by chance he met
A Jewess who about him threw
Else than Nerea's amorous net
And dubious wile. 'Twas Miriam's race:
A sibyl breathed in Agar's grace—

A sibyl, but a woman too;
He felt her grateful as the rains
To Rephaim and the Rama plains
In drought. Ere won, herself did woo:
"Wilt join my people?" Love is power;
Came the strange plea in yielding hour.
Nay, and turn Hebrew? But why not?
If backward still the inquirer goes
To get behind man's present lot
Of crumbling faith; for rear-wall shows
Far behind Rome and Luther—what?
The crag of Sinai. Here then plant
Thyself secure: 'tis adamant.
    Still as she dwelt on Zion's story
He felt the glamour, caught the gleam;
All things but these seemed transitory—
Love, and his love's Jerusalem.
And interest in a mitred race,
With awe which to the fame belongs,
These in receptive heart found place
When Agar chanted David's songs.
    'Twas passion. But the Puritan—
Mixed latent in his blood—a strain
How evident, of Hebrew source;
'Twas that, diverted here in force,
Which biased—hardly might do less.
Hereto append, how earnestness,
Which disbelief for first-fruits bore,
Now, in recoil, by natural stress
Constrained to faith—to faith in more
Than prior disbelief had spurned;
As if, when he toward credence turned,
Distance therefrom but gave career
For impetus that shot him sheer
Beyond. Agar rejoiced; nor knew
How such a nature, charged with zeal,

Might yet overpass that limit due
Observed by her. For woe or weal
They wedded, one in heart and creed.
Transferring fields with title-deed,
From rustic life he quite withdrew—
Traded, and throve. Two children came:
Sedate his heart, nor sad the dame.
But years subvert; or he outgrew
(While yet confirmed in all the myth)
The mind infertile of the Jew.
His northern nature, full of pith,
Vigor and enterprise and will,
Having taken thus the Hebrew bent,
Might not abide inactive so
And but the empty forms fulfill:
Needs utilize the mystic glow—
For nervous energies find vent.
　　The Hebrew seers announce in time
The return of Judah to her prime;
Some Christians deemed it then at hand.
Here was an object: Up and do!
With seed and tillage help renew—
Help reinstate the Holy Land.
　　Some zealous Jews on alien soil
Who still from Gentile ways recoil,
And loyally maintain the dream,
Salute upon the Paschal day
With *Next year in Jerusalem!*
Now Nathan turning unto her,
Greeting his wife at morning ray,
Those words breathed on the Passover;
But she, who mutely startled lay,
In the old phrase found import new,
In the blithe tone a bitter cheer
That did the very speech subdue.
She kenned her husband's mind austere,

Had watched his reveries grave; he meant
No flourish mere of sentiment.
Then what to do? or how to stay?
Decry it? that would faith unsay.
Withstand him? but she gently loved.
And so with Agar here it proved,
As oft it may, the hardy will
Overpowered the deep monition still.

Enough; fair fields and household charms
They quit, sell all, and cross the main
With Ruth and a young child in arms.
A tract secured on Sharon's plain,
Some sheds he built, and ground walled in
Defensive; toil severe but vain.
The wandering Arabs, wonted long
(Nor crime they deemed it, crime nor sin)
To scale the desert convents strong—
In sly foray leaped Nathan's fence
And robbed him; and no recompense
Attainable where law was none
Or perjured. Resolute hereon,
Agar, with Ruth and the young child,
He lodged within the stronghold town
Of Zion, and his heart exiled
To abide the worst on Sharon's lea.
Himself and honest servants three
Armed husbandmen became, as erst
His sires in Pequod wilds immersed.
Hittites—foes pestilent to God
His fathers old those Indians deemed:
Nathan the Arabs here esteemed
The same—slaves meriting the rod;
And out he spake it; which bred hate
The more imperiling his state.
With muskets now his servants slept;

Alternate watch and ward they kept
In grounds beleaguered. Not the less
Visits at stated times he made
To them in Zion's walled recess.
Agar with sobs of suppliance prayed
That he would fix there: "Ah, for good
Tarry! abide with us, thine own;
Put not these blanks between us; should
Such space be for a shadow thrown?
Quit Sharon, husband; leave to brood;
Serve God by cleaving to thy wife,
Thy children. If come fatal strife—
Which I forebode—nay!" and she flung
Her arms about him there, and clung.
  She plead. But tho' his heart could feel,
'Twas mastered by inveterate zeal.
Even the nursling's death ere long
Balked not his purpose tho' it wrung.

  But Time the cruel, whose smooth way
Is feline, patient for the prey
That to this twig of being clings;
And Fate, which from her ambush springs
And drags the loiterer soon or late
Unto a sequel unforeseen;
These doomed him and cut short his date;
But first was modified the lien
The husband had on Agar's heart;
And next a prudence slid athwart—
After distrust. But be unsaid
That steep toward which the current led.
Events shall speak.
                And now the guide,
Who did in sketch this tale begin,
Parted with Clarel at the inn;
And ere long came the eventide.

FROM PART II

The Wilderness

IV : OF MORTMAIN

"Our friend there—he's a little queer,"
To Rolfe said Derwent riding on;
"Beshrew me, there is in his tone
Naught of your new world's chanticleer.
Who's the eccentric? can you say?"
    "Partly; but 'tis at second hand.
At the Black Jew's I met with one
Who, in response to my demand,
Did in a strange disclosure run
Respecting him."—"Repeat it, pray."—
And Rolfe complied. But here receive
Less the details of narrative
Than what the drift and import may convey.

    A Swede he was—illicit son
Of noble lady, after-wed,
Who, for a cause over which be thrown
Charity of oblivion dead,—
Bore little love, but rather hate,
Even practiced to ensnare his state.
His father, while not owning, yet
In part discharged the natural debt
Of duty; gave him liberal lore
And timely income; but no more.
    Thus isolated, what to bind
But the vague bond of human kind?
The north he left, to Paris came—
Paris, the nurse of many a flame
Evil and good. This son of earth,
This Psalmanazer, made a hearth

In warm desires and schemes for man:
Even *he* was an Arcadian.
Peace and good will was his acclaim—
If not in words, yet in the aim:
Peace, peace on earth: that note he thrilled,
But scarce in way the cherubs trilled
To Bethlehem and the shepherd band.
Yet much his theory could tell;
And he expounded it so well,
Disciples came. He took his stand.
　Europe was in a decade dim:
Upon the future's trembling rim
The comet hovered. His a league
Of frank debate and close intrigue:
Plot, proselyte, appeal, denounce—
Conspirator, pamphleteer, at once,
And prophet. Wear and tear and jar
He met with coffee and cigar:
These kept awake the man and mood
And dream. That uncreated Good
He sought, whose absence is the cause
Of creeds and Atheists, mobs and laws.
Precocities of heart outran
The immaturities of brain.
　Along with each superior mind
The vain, foolhardy, worthless, blind,
With Judases, are nothing loath
To clasp pledged hands and take the oath
Of aim, the which, if just, demands
Strong hearts, brows deep, and priestly hands.
Experience with her sharper touch
Stung Mortmain: Why, if men prove such,
Dote I? love theory overmuch?
Yea, also, whither will advance
This Revolution sprung in France
So many years ago? where end?

That current takes me. Whither tend?
Come, thou who makest such hot haste
To forge the future—weigh the past.
    Such frame he knew. And timed event
Cogent a further question lent:
Wouldst meddle with the state? Well, mount
Thy guns; how many men dost count?
Besides, there's more that here belongs:
Be many questionable wrongs:
By yet more questionable war,
Prophet of peace, these wouldst thou bar?
The world's not new, nor new thy plea.
Tho' even shouldst thou triumph, see,
Prose overtakes the victor's songs:
Victorious right may need redress:
No failure like a harsh success.
Yea, ponder well the historic page:
Of all who, fired with noble rage,
Have warred for right without reprieve,
How many spanned the wings immense
Of Satan's muster, or could cheat
His cunning tactics of retreat
And ambuscade? Oh, now dispense!
The world is portioned out, believe:
The good have but a patch at best,
The wise their corner; for the rest—
Malice divides with ignorance.
And what is stable? find one boon
That is not lackey to the moon
Of fate. The flood ebbs out—the ebb
Floods back; the incessant shuttle shifts
And flies, and wears and tears the web.
Turn, turn thee to the proof that sifts:
What if the kings in Forty-eight
Fled like the gods? even as the gods
Shall do, return they made; and sate

And fortified their strong abodes;
And, to confirm them there in state,
Contrived new slogans, apt to please—
Pan and the tribal unities.
Behind all this still works some power
Unknowable, thou'lt yet adore.
That steers the world, not man. States drive;
The crazy rafts with billows strive.—
Go, go—absolve thee. Join that band
That wash them with the desert sand
For lack of water. In the dust
Of wisdom sit thee down, and rust.

So mused he—solitary pined.
Tho' his apostolate had thrown
New prospects ope to Adam's kind,
And fame had trumped him far and free—
Now drop he did—a clod unknown;
Nay, rather, he would not disown
Oblivion's volunteer to be;
Like those new-world discoverers bold
Ending in stony convent cold,
Or dying hermits; as if they,
Chastised to Micah's mind austere,
Remorseful felt that ampler sway
Their lead had given for old career
Of human nature.
But this man
No cloister sought. He, under ban
Of strange repentance and last dearth,
Roved the gray places of the earth.
And what seemed most his heart to wring
Was some unrenderable thing:
'Twas not his bastardy, nor bale
Medean in his mother pale,
Nor thwarted aims of high design;

But deeper—deep as nature's mine.
Tho' frequent among kind he sate
Tranquil enough to hold debate,
His moods he had, mad fitful ones,
Prolonged or brief, outbursts or moans;
And at such times would hiss or cry:
"Fair Circe—goddess of the sty!"
More frequent this: "Mock worse than wrong:
The Syren's kiss—the Fury's thong!"

Such he. Tho' scarce as such portrayed
In full by Rolfe, yet Derwent said
At close: "There's none so far astray,
Detached, abandoned, as might seem,
As to exclude the hope, the dream
Of fair redemption. One fine day
I saw at sea, by bit of deck—
Weedy—adrift from far away—
The dolphin in his gambol light
Through showery spray, arch into sight:
He flung a rainbow o'er that wreck."

XXII : CONCERNING HEBREWS

As by the wood drifts thistle-down
And settles on soft mosses fair,
Stillness was wafted, dropped and sown;
Which stillness Vine, with timorous air
Of virgin tact, thus brake upon,
Nor with chance hint: "One can't forbear
Thinking that Margoth is—a *Jew.*"
Hereat, as for response, they view
The priest.
"And, well, why me?" he cried;
"With one consent why turn to *me?*
Am I professional? Nay, free!

I grant that here by Judah's side
Queerly it jars with frame implied
To list this geologic Jew
His way Jehovah's world construe:
In Gentile 'twould not seem so odd.
But here may preconceptions thrall?
Be many Hebrews we recall
Whose contrast with the breastplate bright
Of Aaron flushed in altar-light,
And Horeb's Moses, rock and rod,
Or closeted alone with God,
Quite equals Margoth's in its way:
At home we meet them every day.
The Houndsditch clothesman scarce would seem
Akin to seers. For one, I deem
Jew banker, merchant, statesman—these,
With artist, actress known to fame,
All strenuous in each Gentile aim,
Are Nature's off-hand witnesses
There's nothing mystic in her reign:
Your Jew's like wheat from Pharaoh's tomb:
Sow it in England, what will come?
The weird old seed yields market grain."
    Pleased by his wit while some recline,
A smile uncertain lighted Vine,
But died away.
                    "Jews share the change,"
Derwent proceeded: "Range, they range—
In liberal sciences they roam;
They're leavened, and it works, believe;
Signs are, and such as scarce deceive;
From Holland, that historic home
Of erudite Israel, many a tome
Talmudic, shipped is over sea
For antiquarian rubbish."
                              "Rest!"

Cried Rolfe; "e'en that indeed may be,
Nor less the Jew keep fealty
To ancient rites. Aaron's gemmed vest
Will long outlive Genevan cloth—
Nothing in Time's old camphor-chest
So little subject to the moth.
But Rabbis have their troublers too.
Nay, if thro' dusty stalls we look,
Haply we disinter to view
More than one bold freethinking Jew
That in his day with vigor shook
Faith's leaning tower."
"Which stood the throe,"
Here Derwent in appendix: "look,
Faith's leaning tower was founded so:
Faith leaned from the beginning; yes,
If slant, she holds her steadfastness."
"May be;" and paused: "but wherefore clog?—
Uriel Acosta, he was one
Who troubled much the synagogue—
Recanted then, and dropped undone:
A suicide. There's Heine, too,
(In lineage crossed by blood of Jew,)
Pale jester, to whom life was yet
A tragic farce; whose wild death-rattle,
In which all voids and hollows met,
Desperately maintained the battle
Betwixt the dirge and castanet.
But him leave to his Paris stone
And rail, and friendly wreath thereon.
Recall those Hebrews, which of old
Sharing some doubts we moderns rue,
Would fain Eclectic comfort fold
By grafting slips from Plato's palm
On Moses' melancholy yew:

But did they sprout? So *we* seek balm
By kindred graftings. Is that true?"
"Why ask? But see: there lived a Jew—
No Alexandrine Greekish one—
You know him—Moses Mendelssohn."
"Is't him you cite? True spirit staid,
He, though his honest heart was scourged
By doubt Judaic, never laid
His burden at Christ's door; he urged—
'Admit the mounting flames enfold
My basement; wisely shall my feet
The attic win, for safe retreat?' "
"And *he* said that? Poor man, he's cold.
But was not this that Mendelssohn
Whose Hebrew kinswoman's Hebrew son,
Baptized to Christian, worthily won
The good name of Neander so?"
"If that link were, well might one urge
From such example, thy strange flow,
Conviction! Breaking habit's tether,
Sincerest minds will yet diverge
Like chance-clouds scattered by mere weather;
Nor less at one point still they meet:
The self-hood keep they pure and sweet."

"But Margoth," in reminder here
Breathed Vine, as if while yet the ray
Lit Rolfe, to try his further cheer:
"But Margoth!"
"He, poor sheep astray,
The Levitic cipher quite erased,
On what vile pig-weed hath he grazed.
Not his Spinosa's starry brow
(A non-conformer, ye'll allow),
A lion in brain, in life a lamb,
Sinless recluse of Amsterdam;

Who, in the obscure and humble lane,
Such strangers seemed to entertain
As sat by tent beneath the tree
On Mamre's plain—mysterious three,
The informing guests of Abraham.
But no, it had but ill beseemed
If God's own angels so could list
To visit one, Pan's Atheist.
That high intelligence but dreamed—
Above delusion's vulgar plain
Deluded still. The erring twain,
Spinosa and poor Margoth here,
Both Jews, which in dissent do vary:
In these what parted poles appear—
The blind man and the visionary."
"And whose the eye that sees aright.
If any?" Clarel eager asked.
Aside Rolfe turned as overtasked;
And none responded. 'Twas like night
Descending from the seats of light,
Or seeming thence to fall. But here
Sedate a kindly tempered look
Private and confidential spoke
From Derwent's eyes, Clarel to cheer:
Take heart; something to fit thy youth
Instill I may, some saving truth—
Not best just now to volunteer.
Thought Clarel: Pray, and what wouldst prove?
Thy faith an over-easy glove.

Meanwhile Vine had relapsed. They saw
In silence the heart's shadow draw—
Rich shadow, such as gardens keep
In bower aside, where glow-worms peep
In evening over the virgin bed

Where dark-green periwinkles sleep—
Their bud the Violet of the Dead.

XXVII : VINE AND CLAREL

While now, to serve the pilgrim train,
The Arabs willow branches hew,
(For palms they serve in dearth of true),
Or, kneeling by the margin, stoop
To brim memorial bottles up;
And the Greek's wine entices two:
Apart see Clarel here incline,
Perplexed by that Dominican,
Nor less by Rolfe—capricious man:
"I cannot penetrate him.—Vine?"
    As were Venetian slats between,
He espied him through a leafy screen,
Luxurious there in umbrage thrown,
Light sprays above his temples blown—
The river through the green retreat
Hurrying, reveling by his feet.
    Vine looked an overture, but said
Nothing, till Clarel leaned—half laid—
Beside him: then "We dream, or be
In sylvan John's baptistery:
May Pisa's equal beauty keep?—
But how bad habits persevere!
I have been moralizing here
Like any imbecile: as thus:
Look how these willows over-weep
The waves, and plain: 'Fleet so from us?
And wherefore? whitherward away?
Your best is here where wildings sway
And the light shadow's blown about;
Ah, tarry, for at hand's a sea
Whence ye shall never issue out

Once in.' They sing back: 'So let be!
We mad-caps hymn it as we flow—
Short life and merry! be it so!' "
    Surprised at such a fluent turn,
The student did but listen—learn.

    Putting aside the twigs which screened,
Again Vine spake, and lightly leaned
"Look; in yon vault so leafy dark,
At deep end lit by gemmy spark
Of mellowed sunbeam in a snare;
Over the stream—ay, just through there—
The sheik on that celestial mare
Shot, fading.—Clan of outcast Hagar,
Well do ye come by spear and dagger!
Yet in your bearing ye outvie
Our western Red Men, chiefs that stalk
In mud paint—whirl the tomahawk.—
But in these Nimrods noted you
The natural language of the eye,
Burning or liquid, flame or dew,
As still the changeable quick mood
Made transit in the wayward blood?
Methought therein one might espy,
For all the wildness, thoughts refined
By the old Asia's dreamful mind;
But hark—a bird?"
                                        Pure as the rain
Which diamondeth with lucid grain,
The white swan in the April hours
Floating between two sunny showers
Upon the lake, while buds unroll;
So pure, so virginal in shrine
Of true unworldliness looked Vine.
Ah, clear sweet ether of the soul
(Mused Clarel), holding him in view.

Prior advances unreturned
Not here he recked of, while he yearned—
O, now but for communion true
And close; let go each alien theme;
Give me thyself!
                                        But Vine, at will
Dwelling upon his wayward dream,
Nor as suspecting Clarel's thrill
Of personal longing, rambled still;
"Methinks they show a lingering trace
Of some quite unrecorded race
Such as the Book of Job implies.
What ages of refinings wise
Must have forerun what there is writ—
More ages than have followed it.
At Lydda late, as chance would have,
Some tribesmen from the south I saw,
Their tents pitched in the Gothic nave,
The ruined one. Disowning law,
Not lawless lived they; no, indeed;
Their chief—why, one of Sydney's clan,
A slayer, but chivalric man;
And chivalry, with all that breed
Was Arabic or Saracen
In source, they tell. But, as men stray
Further from Ararat away
Pity it were did they recede
In carriage, manners, and the rest;
But no, for ours the palm indeed
In bland amenities far West!
Come now, for pastime let's complain;
Grudged thanks, Columbus, for thy main!
Put back, as 'twere—assigned by fate
To fight crude Nature o'er again,
By slow degrees we re-create.
But then, alas, in Arab camps

No lack, they say, no lack of scamps."
    Divided mind knew Clarel here;
The heart's desire did interfere.
Thought he, How pleasant in another
Such sallies, or in thee, if said
After confidings that should wed
Our souls in one:—Ah, call me *brother!*—
So feminine his passionate mood
Which, long as hungering unfed,
All else rejected or withstood.
    Some inklings he let fall. But no:
Here over Vine there slid a change—
A shadow, such as thin may show
Gliding along the mountain-range
And deepening in the gorge below.
    Does Vine's rebukeful dusking say—
Why, on this vernal bank to-day,
Why bring oblations of thy pain
To one who hath his share? here fain
Would lap him in a chance reprieve?
Lives none can help ye; that believe.
Art thou the first soul tried by doubt?
Shalt prove the last? Go, live it out.
But for thy fonder dream of love
In man toward man—the soul's caress—
The negatives of flesh should prove
Analogies of non-cordialness
In spirit.—E'en such conceits could cling
To Clarel's dream of vain surmise
And imputation full of sting.
But, glancing up, unwarned he saw
What serious softness in those eyes
Bent on him. Shyly they withdraw.
Enslaver, wouldst thou but fool me
With bitter-sweet, sly sorcery,
Pride's pastime? or wouldst thou indeed,

Since things unspoken may impede,
Let flow thy nature but for bar?
Nay, dizzard, sick these feelings are;
How findest place within thy heart
For such solicitudes apart
From Ruth?—Self-taxings. . . .

XXXI : THE INSCRIPTION

While yet Rolfe's foot in stirrup stood,
Ere the light vault that wins the seat,
Derwent was heard: "What's this we meet?
A Cross? and—if one could but spell—
Inscription Sinaitic? Well,
Mortmain is nigh—*his* crazy freak;
Whose else? A closer view I'll seek;
I'll climb."
                    In moving there aside
The rock's turned brow he had espied;
In rear this rock hung o'er the waste
And Nehemiah in sleep embraced
Below. The forepart gloomed Lot's wave
So nigh, the tide the base did lave.
Above, the sea-face smooth was worn
Through long attrition of that grit
Which on the waste of winds is borne.
And on the tablet high of it—
Traced in dull chalk, such as is found
Accessible in upper ground—
Big there between two scrawls, below
And over—a cross; three stars in row
Upright, two more for thwarting limb
Which drooped oblique.
                                        At Derwent's cry
The rest drew near; and every eye

Marked the device.—Thy passion's whim,
Wild Swede, mused Vine in silent heart.
"Looks like the *Southern Cross* to me,"
Said Clarel; "so 'tis down in chart."
"And so," said Rolfe, " 'tis set in sky—
Though error slight of place prevail
In midmost star here chalked. At sea,
Bound for Peru, when south ye sail,
Startling that novel cluster strange
Peers up from low; then as ye range
Cape-ward still further, brightly higher
And higher the stranger doth aspire,
'Till off the Horn, when at full hight
Ye slack your gaze as chilly grows the night.
But Derwent—see!"
The priest having gained
Convenient lodge the text below,
They called: "What's that in curve contained
Above the stars? Read: we would know."
"Runs thus: *By one who wails the loss,*
This altar to the Slanting Cross."
"Ha! under that?" "Some crow's-foot scrawl."
"Decipher, quick! we're waiting all."
"Patience: for ere one try rehearse,
'Twere well to make it out. 'Tis verse."
"Verse, say you? Read." " 'Tis mystical:

" 'Emblazoned bleak in austral skies—
A heaven remote, whose starry swarm
Like Science lights but cannot warm—
Translated Cross, hast thou withdrawn,
Dim paling too at every dawn,
With symbols vain once counted wise,
And gods declined to heraldries?
Estranged, estranged: can friend prove so?

Aloft, aloof, a frigid sign:
How far removed, thou Tree divine,
Whose tender fruit did reach so low—
Love apples of New-Paradise!
About the wide Australian sea
The planted nations yet to be—
When, ages hence, they lift their eyes,
Tell, what shall they retain of thee?
But class thee with Orion's sword?
In constellations unadored,
Christ and the Giant equal prize?
The atheist cycles—*must* they be?
Fomentors as forefathers we?' "

"Mad, mad enough," the priest here cried,
Down slipping by the shelving brinks;
"But 'tis not Mortmain," and he sighed.
"Not Mortmain?" Rolfe exclaimed. "Methinks,"
The priest, " 'tis hardly in his vein."
"How? fraught with feeling is the strain?
His heart's not ballasted with stone—
He's crank." "Well, well, e'en let us own
That Mortmain, Mortmain is the man.
We've then a pledge here at a glance
Our comrade's met with no mischance.
Soon he'll rejoin us." "There, amen!"
"But now to wake Nehemiah in den
Behind here.—But kind Clarel goes.
Strange how he naps nor trouble knows
Under the crag's impending block,
Nor fears its fall, nor recks of shock."

Anon they mount; and much advance
Upon that chalked significance.
The student harks, and weighs each word,
Intent, he being newly stirred.

But tarries Margoth? Yes, behind
He lingers. He placards his mind:
Scaling the crag he rudely scores
With the same chalk (how here abused!)
Left by the other, after used,
A sledge or hammer huge as Thor's;
A legend lending—this, to wit:
"I, Science, I whose gain's thy loss,
I slanted thee, thou Slanting Cross."
But sun and rain, and wind, with grit
Driving, these haste to cancel it.

XXXIV : MORTMAIN REAPPEARS

While now at poise the wings of shade
Outstretched overhang each ridge and glade,
Mortmain descends from Judah's hight
Through sally-port of minor glens:
Against the background of black dens
Blacker the figure glooms enhanced.
Relieved from anxious fears, the group
In friendliness would have advanced
To greet, but shrank or fell adroop.
Like Hecla ice inveined with marl
And frozen cinders showed his face
Rigid and darkened. Shunning parle
He seated him aloof in place,
Hands clasped about the knees drawn up
As round the cask the binding hoop—
Condensed in self, or like a seer
Unconscious of each object near,
While yet, informed, the nerve may reach
Like wire under wave to furthest beach.
By what brook Cherith had he been,
Watching it shrivel from the scene—
Or voice aerial had heard,

That now he murmured the wild word;
"But, hectored by the impious years,
What god invoke, for leave to unveil
That gulf whither tend these modern fears,
And deeps over which men crowd the sail?
    Up, as possessed, he rose anon,
And crying to the beach went down:
"Repent! repent in every land
Or hell's hot kingdom is at hand!
Yea, yea,
In pause of the artillery's boom,
While now the armed world holds its own,
The comet peers, the star dips down;
Flicker the lamps in Syria's tomb,
While Anti-Christ and Atheist set
On Anarch the red coronet!"

    "Mad John," sighed Rolfe, "dost there betray
The dire *Vox Clamans* of our day?"
    "Why heed him?" Derwent breathed: "alas!
Let him alone, and it will pass.—
What would he now?" Before the bay
Low bowed he there, with hand addressed
To scoop. "Unhappy, hadst thou best?"
Djalea it was; then calling low
Unto a Bethlehemite whose brow
Was wrinkled like the bat's shrunk hide—
"Your salt-song, Beltha: warn and chide."

    "Would ye know what bitter drink
        They gave to Christ upon the Tree?
    Sip the wave that laps the brink
        Of Siddim: taste, and God keep ye!
    It drains the hills where alum's hid—
    Drains the rock-salt's ancient bed;
        Hither unto basin fall

The torrents from the steeps of gall—
Here is Hades' water-shed.
Sinner, would ye that your soul
Bitter were and like the pool?
Sip the Sodom waters dead;
But never from thy heart shall haste
The Marah—yea, the after-taste."

He closed.—Arrested as he stooped,
Did Mortmain his pale hand recall?
No; undeterred the wave he scooped,
And tried it—madly tried the gall.

XXXVI : SODOM

Full night. The moon has yet to rise;
The air oppresses, and the skies
Reveal beyond the lake afar
One solitary tawny star—
Complexioned so by vapors dim,
Whereof some hang above the brim
And nearer waters of the lake,
Whose bubbling air-beads mount and break
As charged with breath of things alive.

In talk about the Cities Five
Engulfed, on beach they linger late.
And he, the quaffer of the brine,
Puckered with that heart-wizening wine
Of bitterness, among them sate
Upon a camel's skull, late dragged
From forth the wave, the eye-pits slagged
With crusted salt.—"What star is yon?"
And pointed to that single one
Befogged above the sea afar.
"It might be Mars, so red it shines,"

One answered; "duskily it pines
In this strange mist."—"It is the star
Called Wormwood. Some hearts die in thrall
Of waters which yon star makes gall;"
And, lapsing, turned, and made review
Of what that wickedness might be
Which down on these ill precincts drew
The flood, the fire; put forth new plea,
Which not with Writ might disagree;
Urged that those malefactors stood
Guilty of sins scarce scored as crimes
In any statute known, or code—
Nor now, nor in the former times:
Things hard to prove: decorum's wile,
Malice discreet, judicious guile;
Good done with ill intent—reversed:
Best deeds designed to serve the worst;
And hate which under life's fair hue
Prowls like the shark in sunned Pacific blue.
    He paused, and under stress did bow,
Lank hands enlocked across the brow.
    "Nay, nay, thou sea,
'Twas not all carnal harlotry,
But sins refined, crimes of the spirit,
Helped earn that doom ye here inherit:
Doom well imposed, though sharp and dread,
In some god's reign, some god long fled.—
Thou gaseous puff of mineral breath
Mephitical; thou swooning flaw
That fann'st me from this pond of death;
Wert thou that venomous small thing
Which tickled with the poisoned straw?
Thou, stronger, but who yet couldst start
Shrinking with sympathetic sting,
While willing the uncompunctious dart!
Ah, ghosts of Sodom, how ye thrill

About me in this peccant air,
Conjuring yet to spare, but spare!
Fie, fie, that didst in formal will
Plot piously the posthumous snare.
And thou, the mud-flow—evil mass
Of surest-footed sluggishness
Swamping the nobler breed—art there?
Moan, Burker of kind heart: all's known
To Him; with thy connivers, moan.—
Sinners—expelled, transmuted souls
Blown in these airs, or whirled in shoals
Of gurgles which your gasps send up,
Or on this crater marge and cup
Slavered in slime, or puffed in stench—
Not ever on the tavern bench
Ye lolled. Few dicers here, few sots,
Few sluggards, and no idiots.
'Tis *thou* who servedst Mammon's hate
Or greed through forms which holy are—
Black slaver steering by a star,
'Tis *thou*—and all like thee in state.
Who knew the world, yet varnished it;
Who traded on the coast of crime
Though landing not; who did outwit
Justice, his brother, and the time—
These, chiefly these, to doom submit.
But who the manifold may tell?
And sins there be inscrutable,
Unutterable."
                    Ending there
He shrank, and like an osprey gray
Peered on the wave. His hollow stare
Marked then some smaller bubbles play
In cluster silvery like spray:
"Be these the beads on the wives'-wine,
Tofana-brew?—O fair Medea—

O soft man-eater, furry-fine:
Oh, be thou Jael, be thou Leah—
Unfathomably shallow!—No!
Nearer the core than man can go
Or Science get—nearer the slime
Of nature's rudiments and lime
In chyle before the bone. Thee, thee,
In thee the filmy cell is spun—
The mould thou art of what men be:
Events are all in thee begun—
By thee, through thee!—Undo, undo,
Prithee, undo, and still renew
The fall forever!"
On his throne
He lapsed; and muffled came the moan
How multitudinous in sound,
From Sodom's wave. He glanced around:
They all had left him, one by one.
Was it because he open threw
The inmost to the outward view?
Or did but pain at frenzied thought,
Prompt to avoid him, since but naught
In such case might remonstrance do?
But none there ventured idle plea,
Weak sneer, or fraudful levity.

Two spirits, hovering in remove,
Sad with inefficacious love,
Here sighed debate: "Ah, Zoima, say;
Be it far from me to impute a sin,
But may a sinless nature win
Those deeps he knows?"—"Sin shuns that way;
Sin acts the sin, but flees the thought
That sweeps the abyss that sin has wrought.
Innocent be the heart and true—
Howe'er it feed on bitter bread—

That, venturous through the Evil led,
Moves as along the ocean's bed
Amid the dragon's staring crew."

XXXIX : OBSEQUIES

The camel's skull upon the beach
No more the sluggish waters reach—
No more the languid waters lave;
Not now they wander in and out
Of those void chambers walled about—
So dull the calm, so dead the wave.
Above thick mist how pallid looms,
While the slurred day doth wanly break,
Ammon's long ridge beyond the lake.

Down to the shrouded margin comes
Lone Vine—and starts: not at the skull,
The camel's, for that bides the same
As when overnight 'twas Mortmain's stool.
But, nigh it—how *that* object name?
Slant on the shore, ground-curls of mist
Enfold it, as in amethyst
Subdued, small flames in dead of night
Lick the dumb back-log ashy white.
What is it?—paler than the pale
Pervading vapors, which so veil,
That some peak-tops are islanded
Baseless above the dull, dull bed
Of waters, which not e'en transmit
One ripple 'gainst the cheek of It.

The start which the discoverer gave
Was physical—scarce shocked the soul,
Since many a prior revery grave
Forearmed against alarm's control.

To him, indeed, each lapse and end
Meet—in harmonious method blend.
Lowly he murmured, "Here is balm:
Repose is snowed upon repose—
Sleep upon sleep; it is the calm
And incantation of the close."
    The others, summoned to the spot,
Were staggered: Nehemiah? no!
The innocent and sinless—what!—
Pale lying like the Assyrian low?

    The Swede stood by; nor after-taste
Extinct was of the liquid waste
Nor influence of that Wormwood Star
Whereof he spake. All overcast—
His genial spirits meeting jar—
Derwent on no unfeeling plea
Held back. Mortmain, relentless: "See:
To view death on the bed—at ease—
A dream, and draped; to minister
To inheriting kin; to comfort *these*
In chamber comfortable:—*here*
The elements all that unsay!
The first man dies. Thus Abel lay."
    The sad priest, rightly to be read
Scarce hoping,—pained, dispirited—
Was dumb. And Mortmain went aside
In thrill by only Vine espied:
Alas (thought Vine) thou bitter Swede,
Into thine armor dost thou bleed?

    Intent but poised, the Druse looked on:
"The sheath: the sword?"
                                        "Ah, whither gone?"
Clarel, and bowed him there and kneeled:
"Whither art gone? thou friendliest mind

Unfriended—what friend now shalt find?
Robin or raven, hath God a bird
To come and strew thee, lone interred,
With leaves, when here left far behind?"
 "He's gone," the Jew; "czars, stars must go
Or change! All's chymestry. Aye so."—
"*Resurget*"—faintly Derwent there.
"*In pace*"—Vine, nor more would dare.

 Rolfe in his reaching heart did win
Prelude remote, yet gathering in:
"Moist, moist with sobs and balsam shed—
Warm tears, cold odors from the urn—
They hearsed in heathen Rome their dead
All hopeless of the soul's return.
Embracing them, in marble set,
The mimic gates of Orcus met—
The Pluto-bolt, the fatal one
Wreathed over by the hung festoon.
How fare we *now*? But were it clear
In nature or in lore devout
That parted souls live on in cheer,
Gladness would be—shut pathos out.
His poor thin life: the end? no more?
The end here by the Dead Sea shore?"
 He turned him, as awaiting nod
Or answer from earth, air, or skies;
But be it ether or the clod,
The elements yield no replies.
 Cross-legged on a cindery hight,
Belex, the fatalist, smoked on.
Slow whiffs; and then, "It needs be done:
Come, beach the loins there, Bethlehemite."—

 Inside a hollow free from stone
With camel-ribs they scooped a trench;

And Derwent, rallying from blench
Of Mortmain's brow, and nothing loth
Tacit to vindicate the cloth,
Craved they would bring to him the Book,
Now ownerless. The same he took,
And thence had culled brief service meet,
But closed, reminded of the psalm
Heard when the salt fog shrunk the palm—
They wending toward these waters' seat—
Raised by the saint, as e'en it lent
A voice to low presentiment:
Naught better might one here repeat:
"Though through the valley of the shade
I pass, no evil do I fear;
His candle shineth on my head:
Lo, he is with me, even here."

That o'er, they kneeled—with foreheads bare
Bowed as he made the burial prayer.
Even Margoth bent him; but 'twas so
As some hard salt at sea will do
Holding the narrow plank that bears
The shotted hammock, while brief prayers
Are by the master read mid war
Relentless of wild elements—
The sleet congealing on the spar:
It was a sulking reverence.
The body now the Arabs placed
Within the grave, and then with haste
Had covered, but for Rolfe's restraint:
"The Book!"—The Bible of the saint—
With that the relics there he graced,
Yea, put it in the hand: "Since now
The last long journey thou dost go,
Why part thee from thy friend and guide!
And better guide who knoweth? Bide."

They closed. And came a rush, a roar—
Aloof, but growing more and more,
Nearer and nearer. They invoke
The long Judaic range, the hight
Of nearer mountains hid from sight
By the blind mist. Nor spark nor smoke
Of that plunged wake their eyes might see;
But, hoarse in hubbub, horribly,
With all its retinue around—
Flints, dust, and showers of splintered stone,
An avalanche of rock down tore,
In somerset from each rebound—
Thud upon thump—down, down and down—
And landed. Lull. Then shore to shore
Rolled the deep echo, fold on fold,
Which, so reverberated, bowled
And bowled far down the long El Ghor.

They turn; and, in that silence sealed,
What works there from behind the veil?
A counter object is revealed—
A thing of heaven, and yet how frail:
Up in thin mist above the sea
Humid is formed, and noiselessly,
The fog-bow: segment of an oval
Set in a colorless removal
Against a vertical shaft, or slight
Slim pencil of an aqueous light.
Suspended there, the segment hung
Like to the May-wreath that is swung
Against the pole. It showed half spent—
Hovered and trembled, paled away, and—went.

FROM PART III

Mar Saba

V : THE HIGH DESERT

Where silence and the legend dwell,
A cleft in Horeb is, they tell,
Through which upon one happy day
(The sun on his heraldic track
Due sign having gained in Zodiac)
A sunbeam darts, which slants away
Through ancient carven oriel
Or window in the Convent there,
Illuming so with annual flush
The somber vaulted chamber spare
Of Catherine's Chapel of the Bush—
The Burning Bush. Brief visitant,
It makes no lasting covenant;
It brings, but cannot leave, the ray.
To hearts which here the desert smote
So came, so went the Cypriote.
Derwent deep felt it; and, as fain
His prior spirits to regain;
Impatient too of scenes which led
To converse such as late was bred,
Moved to go on. But some declined.
So, for relief to heart which pined,
Belex he sought, by him sat down
In cordial ease upon a stone
Apart, and heard his stories free
Of Ibrahim's wild infantry.

The rest abide. To these there comes,
As down on Siddim's scene they peer,
The contrast of their vernal homes—

Field, orchard, and the harvest cheer.
At variance in their revery move
The spleen of nature and her love:
At variance, yet entangled too—
Like wrestlers. Here in apt review
They call to mind Abel and Cain—
Ormuzd involved with Ahriman
In deadly lock. Were those gods gone?
Or under other names lived on?
The theme they started. 'Twas averred
That, in old Gnostic pages blurred,
Jehovah was construed to be
Author of evil, yea, its god;
And Christ divine his contrary:
A god was held against a god,
But Christ revered alone. Herefrom,
If inference availeth aught
(For still the topic pressed they home)
The two-fold Testaments become
Transmitters of Chaldaic thought
By implication. If no more
Those Gnostic heretics prevail
Which shook the East from shore to shore,
Their strife forgotten now and pale;
Yet, with the sects, that old revolt
Now reappears, if in assault
Less frank: none say Jehovah's evil,
None gainsay that he bears the rod;
Scarce that; but there's dismission civil,
And Jesus is the indulgent God.
This change, this dusking change that slips
(Like the penumbra o'er the sun),
Over the faith transmitted down;
Foreshadows it complete eclipse?
    Science and Faith, can these unite?
Or is that priestly instinct right

(Right as regards conserving still
The Church's reign) whose strenuous will
Made Galileo pale recite
The Penitential Psalms in vest
Of sackcloth; which to-day would blight
Those potent solvents late expressed
In laboratories of the West?
    But in her Protestant repose
Snores faith toward her mortal close?
Nay, like a sachem petrified,
Encaved found in the mountain-side,
Perfect in feature, true in limb,
Life's full similitude in him,
Yet all mere stone—is faith dead *now*,
A petrifaction? Grant it so,
Then what's in store? what shapeless birth?
Reveal the doom reserved for earth?
How far may seas retiring go?
    But, to redeem us, shall we say
That faith, undying, does but range,
Casting the skin—the creed. In change
Dead always does some creed delay—
Dead, not interred, though hard upon
Interment's brink? At Saint Denis
Where slept the Capets, sire and son,
Eight centuries of lineal clay,
On steps that led down into vault
The prince inurned last made a halt,
The coffin left they there, 'tis said,
Till the inheritor was dead;
Then, not till then 'twas laid away.
But if no more the creeds be linked,
If the long line's at last extinct,
If time both creed and faith betray,
Vesture and vested—yet again
What interregnum or what reign

Ensues? Or does a period come?
The Sibyl's books lodged in the tomb?
Shall endless time no more unfold
Of truth at core? Some things discerned
By the far Noahs of India old—
Earth's first spectators, the clear-eyed
Unvitiated, unfalsified
Seers at first hand—shall these be learned
Though late, even by the New World, say,
Which now contemns?
But what shall stay
The fever of advance? London immense
Still wax for aye? A check: but whence?
How of the teeming Prairie-Land?
There shall the plenitude expand
Unthinned, unawed? Or does it need
Only that men should breed and breed
To enrich those forces into play
Which in past times could oversway
Pride at his proudest? Do they come,
The locusts, only to the bloom?
Prosperity sire them?
Thus they swept,
Nor sequence held, consistent tone—
Imagination wildering on
Through vacant halls which faith once kept
With ushers good.
Themselves thus lost,
At settled hearts they wonder most.
For those (they asked) who still adhere
In homely habit's dull delay,
To dreams dreamed out or passed away;
Do these, our pagans, all appear
Much like each poor and busy one
Who when the Tartar took Pekin,
(If credence hearsay old may win)

Knew not the fact—so vast the town
The multitude, the maze, the din?
    Still laggeth in deferred adieu
The A. D. (Anno Domini)
Overlapping into era new
Even as the Roman A. U. C.
Yet ran for time, regardless all
That Christ was born, and after fall
Of Rome itself?
                                    But now our age,
So infidel in equipage,
While carrying still the Christian name—
For all its self-asserted claim,
How fares it, tell? Can the age stem
Its own conclusions? is't a king
Awed by his conquests which enring
With menaces his diadem?
Bright visions of the times to be—
Must these recoil, ere long be cowed
Before the march in league avowed
Of Mammon and Democracy?
    In one result whereto we tend
Shall Science disappoint the hope,
Yea, to confound us in the end,
New doors to superstition ope?
    As years, as years and annals grow,
And action and reaction vie,
And never men attain, but know
How waves on waves forever die;
Does all more enigmatic show? . . .

FROM PART IV

Bethlehem

XX : DERWENT AND UNGAR

"Not thou com'st in the still small voice,"
Said Derwent, "thou queer Mexican!"
And followed him with eyes: "This man,"
And turned here, "he likes not grave talk,
The settled undiluted tone;
It does his humorous nature balk.
'Twas ever to his sly rebuff,
While yet obstreperous in praise,
Taking that dusty pinch of snuff.
An oddity, he has his ways;
Yet trust not, friends, the half he says;
Not he would do a weasel harm;
A secret agent of Reform;
At least, that is my theory."
    "The quicksilver is quick to skim,"
Ungar remarked, with eye on him.
    "Yes, nature has her levity,"
Dropped Derwent.
                        Nothing might disarm
The other; he: "Your word *reform:*
What meaning's to that word assigned?
From Luther's great initial down,
Through all the series following on,
The impetus augments—the blind
Precipitation: blind, for tell
Whitherward does the surge impel?
The end, the aim? 'Tis mystery."
    "Oh, no. Through all methinks I see
The object clear: belief revised,
Men liberated—equalized

In happiness. No mystery,
Just none at all; plain sailing."
"Well,
Assume this: is it feasible?
Your methods? These are of the world:
Now the world cannot save the world;
And Christ renounces it. His faith,
Breaking with every mundane path,
Aims straight at heaven. To founded thrones
He says: Trust not to earthly stanchions;
And unto poor and houseless ones—
My Father's house has many mansions.
Warning and solace be but this;
No thought to mend a world amiss."
"Ah now, ah now!" plead Derwent.
"Nay,
Test further; take another way:
Go ask Aurelius Antonine—
A Cæsar wise, grave, just, benign,
Lord of the world—why, in the calm
Which through his reign the empire graced—
Why he, that most considerate heart
Superior, and at vantage placed,
Contrived no secular reform,
Though other he knew not, nor balm."
"Alas," cried Derwent (and, in part,
As vainly longing for retreat)
"Though good Aurelius was a man
Matchless in mind as sole in seat,
Yet pined he under numbing ban
Of virtue without Christian heat:
As much you intimated too,
Just saying that no balm he knew.
Howbeit, true reform goes on
By Nature; doing, never done.
Mark the advance: creeds drop the hate;

Events still liberalize the state."
"But tell: do men now more cohere
In bonds of duty which sustain?
Cliffs crumble, and the parts regain
A liberal freedom, it is clear.
And for conventicles—I fear,
Much as a hard heart aged grown
Abates in rigor, losing tone;
So sects decrepit, at death's door,
Dote into peace through loss of power."
"You put it so," said Derwent light:
"No more developments to cite?"
"Ay, quench the true, the mock sun fails
Therewith. Much so, Hypocrisy,
The false thing, wanes just in degree
That Faith, the true thing, wanes: each pales.
There's *one* development; 'tis seen
In masters whom not low ye rate:
What lack, in some outgivings late,
Of the old Christian style toward men—
I do not mean the wicked ones,
But Pauperism's unhappy sons
In cloud so blackly ominous,
Grimy in Mammon's English pen—
Collaterals of his overplus:
How worse than them Immanuel fed
On hill-top—helped and comforted.
Thou, Poverty, erst free from shame,
Even sacred through the Saviour's claim,
Professed by saints, by sages prized—
A pariah now, and bastardized!
Reactions from the Christian plan
Bear others further. Quite they shun
A god to name, or cite a man
Save Greek, heroical, a Don:
'Tis Plato's aristocratic tone

All recognition they forego
Of Evil; supercilious skim
With spurious wing of seraphim
The last abyss. Freemen avow
Belief in right divine of Might,
Yet spurn at kings. This is the light—
Divine the darkness. Mark the way
The Revolution, whose first mode,
Ere yet the maniacs overrode,
Despite the passion of the dream
Evinced no disrespect for God;
Mark how, in our denuding day,
E'en with the masses, as would seem,
It tears the fig-leaf quite away.
Contrast these incidents: The mob,
The Paris mob of Eighty-nine,
Haggard and bleeding, with a throb
Burst the long Tuileries. In shrine
Of chapel there, they saw the Cross
And Him thereon. Ah, bleeding Man,
The people's friend, thou bled'st for us
Who here bleed, too! Ragged they ran—
They took the crucifix; in van
They put it, marched with drum and psalm
And throned it in their Notre Dame.
But yesterday—how did they then,
In new uprising of the Red,
The offspring of those Tuileries men?
They made a clothes-stand of the Cross
Before the church; and, on that head
Which bowed for them, could wanton toss
The sword-belt, while the gibing sped.
Transcended rebel angels! Woe
To us; without a God, 'tis woe!"

XXI : UNGAR AND ROLFE

"Such earnestness! such wear and tear,
And man but a thin gossamer!"
So here the priest aside; then turned,
And, starting: "List! the vesper-bell?
Nay, nay—the hour is passed. But, oh,
He must have supped, Don Hannibal,
Ere now. Come, friends, and shall we go?
This hot discussion, let it stand
And cool; to-morrow we'll remand."
"Not yet, I pray," said Rolfe; "a word;"
And turned toward Ungar; "be adjured,
And tell us if for earth may be
In ripening arts, no guarantee
Of happy sequel."
"Arts are tools;
But tools, they say are to the strong:
Is Satan weak? weak is the Wrong?
No blessed augury overrules:
Your arts advance in faith's decay:
You are but drilling the new Hun
Whose growl even now can some dismay;
Vindictive in his heart of hearts,
He schools him in your mines and marts—
A skilled destroyer."
"But, need own
That portent does in no degree
Westward impend, across the sea."
"Over there? And do ye not forebode?
Against pretenses void or weak
The impieties of 'Progress' speak.
What say *these*, in effect, to God?
'How profits it? And who art Thou
That we should serve Thee? Of Thy ways

No knowledge we desire; *new* ways
We have found out, and better. Go—
Depart from us; we do erase
Thy sinecure: behold, the sun
Stands still no more in Ajalon:
Depart from us!'—And if He do?
(And that He may, the Scripture says)
Is aught betwixt ye and the hells?
For He, nor in irreverent view,
'Tis He distills that savor true
Which keeps good essences from taint;
Where He is not, corruption dwells,
And man and chaos are without restraint."
"Oh, oh, you do but generalize
In void abstractions."
"Hypothesize:
If be a people which began
Without impediment, or let
From any ruling which fore-ran;
Even striving all things to forget
But this—the excellence of man
Left to himself, his natural bent,
His own devices and intent;
And if, in satire of the heaven,
A world, a new world have been given
For stage whereon to deploy the event;
If such a people be—well, well,
One hears the kettle-drums of hell!
Exemplary act awaits its place
In drama of the human race."
"Is such act certain?" Rolfe here ran;
"Not much is certain."
"God is—man.
The human nature, the divine—
Have both been proved by many a sign.
'Tis no astrologer and star.

The world has now so old become,
Historic memory goes so far
Backward through long defiles of doom;
Whoso consults it honestly
That mind grows prescient in degree;
For man, like God, abides the same
Always, through all variety
Of woven garments to the frame."
"Yes, God is God, and men are men,
Forever and for aye. What then?
There's Circumstance—there's Time; and these
Are charged with store of latencies
Still working in to modify.
For mystic text that you recall,
Dilate upon, and e'en apply—
(Although I seek not to decry)
Theology's scarce practical.
But leave this: the New World's the theme,
Here, to oppose your dark extreme.
(Since an old friend is good at need)
To an old thought I'll fly. Pray, heed:
Those waste-weirs which the New World yields
To inland freshets—the free vents
Supplied to turbid elements;
The vast reserves—the untried fields;
These long shall keep off and delay
The class-war, rich-and-poor-man fray
Of history. From that alone
Can serious trouble spring. Even that
Itself, this good result may own—
The first firm founding of the state."
Here ending, with a watchful air
Inquisitive, Rolfe waited him.
And Ungar:
"True heart do ye bear
In this discussion? or but trim

To draw my monomania out,
For monomania, past doubt,
Some of ye deem it. Yet I'll on.
Yours seems a reasonable tone;
But in the New World things make haste:
Not only men, the *state* lives fast—
Fast breeds the pregnant eggs and shells,
The slumberous combustibles
Sure to explode. 'Twill come, 'twill come!
One demagogue can trouble much:
How of a hundred thousand such?
And universal suffrage lent
To back them with brute element
Overwhelming? What shall bind these seas
Of rival sharp communities
Unchristianized? Yea, but 'twill come!"
"What come?"
"Your Thirty Years (of) War."
"Should fortune's favorable star
Avert it?"
"Fortune? nay, 'tis doom."
"Then what comes after? spasms but tend
Ever, at last, to quiet."
"Know,
Whatever happen in the end,
Be sure 'twill yield to one and all
New confirmation of the fall
Of Adam. Sequel may ensue,
Indeed, whose germs one now may view:
Myriads playing pygmy parts—
Debased into equality:
In glut of all material arts
A civic barbarism may be:
Man disennobled—brutalized
By popular science—Atheized

Into a smatterer—"
"Oh, oh!"
"Yet knowing all self need to know
In self's base little fallacy;
Dead level of rank commonplace:
An Anglo-Saxon China, see,
May on your vast plains shame the race
In the Dark Ages of Democracy."

America!
In stilled estate,
On him, half-brother and co-mate—
In silence, and with vision dim
Rolfe, Vine, and Clarel gazed on him;
They gazed, nor one of them found heart
To upbraid the crotchet of his smart,
Bethinking them whence sole it came,
Though birthright he renounced in hope,
Their sanguine country's wonted claim.
Nor dull they were in honest tone
To some misgivings of their own:
They felt how far beyond the scope
Of elder Europe's saddest thought
Might be the New World's sudden brought
In youth to share old age's pains—
To feel the arrest of hope's advance,
And squandered last inheritance;
And cry—"To Terminus build fanes!
Columbus ended earth's romance:
No New World to mankind remains!"

XXX : THE VALLEY OF DECISION

Delay!—Shall flute from forth the Gate
Issue, to warble welcome here—

Upon this safe returning wait
In gratulation? And, for cheer,
When inn they gain, there shall they see
The door-post wreathed?
Howe'er it be,
Through Clarel a revulsion ran,
Such as may seize debarking man
First hearing on Coquimbo's ground
That subterranean sullen sound
Which dull foreruns the shock. His heart,
In augury fair arrested here,
Upbraided him: Fool! and didst part
From Ruth? Strangely a novel fear
Obtruded—petty, and yet worse
And more from reason too averse,
Than that recurrent haunting bier
Molesting him erewhile. And yet
It was but irritation, fret—
Misgiving that the lines he writ
Upon the eve before the start
For Siddim, failed, or were unfit—
Came short of the occasion's tone:
To leave her, leave her in grief's smart:
To leave her—her, the stricken one:
Now first to feel full force of it!
Away! to be but there, but there!
Vain goadings: yet of love true part.
But then the pledge with letter sent,
Though but a trifle, still might bear
A token in dumb argument
Expressive more than words.
With knee
Straining against the saddle-brace,
He urges on; till, near the place
Of Hebrew graves, a light they see

Moving, and figures dimly trace:
Some furtive strange society.
Yet nearer as they ride, the light
Shuts down. "Abide!" enjoined the Druse;
"Waylayers these are none, but Jews,
Or I mistake, who here by night
Have stolen to do grave-digger's work.
During late outbreak in the town
The bigot in the baser Turk
Was so inflamed, some Hebrews dread
Assault, even here among their dead.
Abide a space; let me ride on."
    Up pushed he, spake, allayed the fright
Of them who had shut down the light
At sound of comers.
                                        Close they draw—
Advancing, lit by fan-shaped rays
Shot from a small dark-lantern's jaw
Presented pistol-like. They saw
Mattocks and men, in outline dim
On either ominous side of him
From whom went forth that point of blaze.
Resting from labor, each one stays
His implement on grave-stones old.
New-dug, between these, they behold
Two narrow pits: and (nor remote)
Twin figures on the ground they note
Folded in cloaks.
                                    "And who rest there?"
Rolfe sidelong asked.
                                            "Our friends; have care!"
Replied the one that held in view
The lantern, slanting it a'shift,
Plainer disclosing them, and, too,
A broidered scarf, love's first chance gift,

The student's (which how well he knew!)
Binding one mantle's slender span.
With piercing cry, as one distraught,
Down from his horse leaped Clarel—ran,
And hold of that cloak instant caught,
And bared the face. Then (like a man
Shot through the heart, but who retains
His posture) rigid he remains—
The mantle's border in his hand,
His glazed eyes unremoved. The band
Of Jews—the pilgrims—all look on
Shocked or amazed.
But speech he won:
"No—yes: enchanted here!—her name?"
"Ruth, Nathan's daughter," said a Jew
Who kenned him now—the youth that came
Oft to the close; "but, thou—forbear;
The dawn's at hand and haste is due:
See, by her side, 'tis Agar there."
"Ruth? Agar?—*art* thou God?—But ye—
All swims, and I but blackness see.—
How happed it? speak!"
"The fever—grief:
'Twere hard to tell; was no relief."
"And ye—your tribe—'twas *ye* denied
Me access to this virgin's side
In bitter trial: take my curse!—
O blind, blind, barren universe!
Now am I like a bough torn down,
And I must wither, cloud or sun!—
Had I been near, this had not been.
Do spirits look down upon this scene?—
The message? some last word was left?"
"For thee? no, none; the life was reft
Sudden from Ruth; and Agar died

Babbling of gulls and ocean wide—
Out of her mind."
"And here's the furl
Of Nathan's faith: then perish faith—
'Tis perjured!—Take me, take me, Death!
Where Ruth is gone, me thither whirl,
Where'er it be!"
"Ye do outgo
Mad Korah. Boy, this is the Dale
Of Doom, God's last assizes; so,
Curb thee; even if sharp grief assail,
Respect these precincts lest thou know
An ill."
"Give way, quit thou our dead!"
Menaced another, striding out;
"Art thou of us? turn thee about!"
"Spurn—I'll endure; all spirit's fled
When one fears nothing.—Bear with me,
Yet bear!—Conviction is not gone
Though faith's gone: that which shall not be
Still *ought* to be!"
But here came on,
With heavy footing, hollow heard,
Hebrews, which bare rude slabs, to place
Athwart the bodies when interred,
That earth should weigh not on the face;
For coffin was there none; and all
Was make-shift in this funeral.
Uncouthly here a Jew began
To re-adjust Ruth's cloak. Amain
Did Clarel push him; and, in hiss:
"Not thou—for me!—Alone, alone
In such bride-chamber to lie down!
Nay, leave one hand out—like to this—
That so the bridegroom may not miss

To kiss it first, when soon he comes.—
But 'tis not she!" and hid his face.

They laid them in the under-glooms—
Each pale one in her portioned place.
The gravel, from the bank raked down,
Dull sounded on those slabs of stone,
Grave answering grave—dull and more dull,
Each mass growing more, till either pit was full.

As up from Kedron dumb they drew,
Then first the shivering Clarel knew
Night's damp. The Martyr's port is won—
Stephen's; harsh grates the bolt withdrawn;
And, over Olivet, comes on
Ash Wednesday in the gray of dawn.

XXXI : DIRGE

Stay, Death. Not mine the Christus-wand
Wherewith to charge thee and command:
I plead. Most gently hold the hand
Of her thou leadest far away;
Fear thou to let her naked feet
Tread ashes—but let mosses sweet
Her footing tempt, where'er ye stray.
Shun Orcus; win the moonlit land
Belulled—the silent meadows lone,
Where never any leaf is blown
From lily-stem in Azrael's hand.
There, till her love rejoin her lowly
(Pensive, a shade, but all her own)
On honey feed her, wild and holy;
Or trance her with thy choicest charm.
And if, ere yet the lover's free,
Some added dusk thy rule decree—

That shadow only let it be
Thrown in the moon-glade by the palm.

XXXII : PASSION WEEK

Day passed; and passed a second one,
A third—fourth—fifth; and bound he sate
In film of sorrow without moan—
Abandoned, in the stony strait
Of mutineer thrust on wild shore,
Hearing, beyond the roller's froth,
The last dip of the parting oar.
Alone, for all had left him so;
Though Rolfe, Vine, Derwent—each was loth,
How loth to leave him, or to go
Be first. From Vine he caught new sense
Developed through fate's pertinence.
Friendly they tarried—blameless went:
Life, avaricious, still demands
Her own, and more; the world is rent
With partings.
But, since all are gone,
Why lingers he, the stricken one?
Why linger where no hope can be?
Ask grief, love ask—fidelity
In dog that by the corse abides
Of shepherd fallen—abides, abides
Though autumn into winter glides,
Till on the mountain all is chill
And snow-bound, and the twain lie still.

How oft through Lent the feet were led
Of this chastised and fasting one
To neutral silence of the dead
In Kedron's gulf. One morn he sate
Down poring toward it from the gate

Sealed and named Golden. There a tomb,
Erected in time's recent day,
In block along the threshold lay
Impassable. From Omar's bloom
Came birds which lit, nor dreamed of harm,
On neighboring stones. His visage calm
Seemed not the one which late showed play
Of passion's throe; but here divine
No peace; ignition in the mine
Announced is by the rush, the roar:
These end; yet may the coal burn on—
Still slumberous burn beneath the floor
Of pastures where the sheep lie down.
    Ere long a cheerful choral strain
He hears; 'tis an Armenian train
Embowered in palms they bear, which (green,
And shifting oft) reveal the mien
Of flamens tall and singers young
In festal robes: a rainbow throng.
Like dolphins off Madeira seen
Which quick the ship and shout dismay.
With the blest anthem, censers sway,
Whose opal vapor, spiral borne,
Blends with the heavens' own azure Morn
Of Palms; for 'twas Palm Sunday bright,
Though thereof he, oblivious quite,
Knew nothing, nor that here they came
In memory of the green acclaim
Triumphal, and hosanna-roll
Which hailed Him on the ass's foal.
    But unto Clarel that bright view
Into a dusk reminder grew:
He saw the tapers—saw again
The censers, singers, and the wreath
And litter of the bride of death
Pass through the Broken Fountain's lane;

In treble shrill and bass how deep
The men and boys he heard again
The undetermined contest keep
About the bier—the bier Armenian.
Yet dull, in torpor dim, he knew
The futile omen in review.

Yet three more days, and leadenly
From over Mary's port and arch,
On Holy Thursday, he the march
Of friars beheld, with litany
Filing beneath his feet, and bent
With crosses craped to sacrament
Down in the glenned Gethsemane.
Yes, Passion Week; the altars cower—
Each shrine a dead dismantled bower.

But when Good Friday dirged her gloom
Ere brake the morning, and each light
Round Calvary faded and the TOMB,
What exhalations met his sight:—
Illusion of grief's wakeful doom:
The dead walked. There, amid the train,
White Nehemiah he saw again—
With charnel beard; and Celio passed
As in a dampened mirror glassed;
Gleamed Mortmain, pallid as wolf-bone
Which bleaches where no man hath gone;
And Nathan in his murdered guise—
Sullen, and Hades in his eyes;
Poor Agar, with such wandering mien
As in her last blank hour was seen.
And each and all kept lonely state,
Yea, man and wife passed separate.
But Ruth—ah, how estranged in face!
He knew her by no earthly grace:

Nor might he reach to her in place.
And languid vapors from them go
Like thaw-fogs curled from dankish snow.

Where, where now He who helpeth us,
The Comforter?—Tell, Erebus!

XXXIII : EASTER

BUT ON THE THIRD DAY CHRIST AROSE;
And, in the town He knew, the rite
Commemorative eager goes
Before the hour. Upon the night
Between the week's last day and first,
No more the Stabat is dispersed
Or Tenebræ. And when the day,
The Easter, falls in calendar
The same to Latin and the array
Of all schismatics from afar—
Armenians, Greeks from many a shore—
Syrians, Copts—profusely pour
The hymns: 'tis like the choric gush
Of torrents Alpine when they rush
To swell the anthem of the spring.
That year was now. Throughout the fane,
Floor, and arcades in double ring
About the gala of THE TOMB,
Blazing with lights, behung with bloom—
What child-like thousands roll the strain,
The hallelujah after pain,
Which in all tongues of Christendom
Still through the ages has rehearsed
That Best, the outcome of the Worst.
Nor blame them who by lavish rite
Thus greet the pale victorious Son,
Since Nature times the same delight,

And rises with the Emerging One;
Her passion-week, her winter mood
She slips, with crape from off the Rood.
    In soft rich shadow under dome,
With gems and robes repletely fine,
The priests like birds Brazilian shine:
And moving tapers charm the sight,
Enkindling the curled incense-fume:
A dancing ray, Auroral light.

Burn on the hours, and meet the day.
The morn invites; the suburbs call
The concourse to come forth—this way!
Out from the gate by Stephen's wall,
They issue, dot the hills, and stray
In bands, like sheep among the rocks;
And the Good Shepherd in the heaven,
To whom the charge of these is given,
The Christ, ah! counts He there His flocks?
    But they, at each suburban shrine,
Grateful adore that Friend benign;
Though chapel now and cross divine
Too frequent show neglected; nay,
For charities of early rains
Rim them about with vernal stains,
Forerunners of maturer May,
When those red flowers, which so can please,
(*Christ's-Blood-Drops* named—anemones),
Spot Ephraim and the mountain-way.
    But heart bereft is unrepaid
Though Thammuz' spring in Thammuz' glade
Invite; then how in Joel's glen?
What if dyed shawl and bodice gay
Make bright the black dell? what if they
In distance clear diminished be
To seeming cherries dropped on pall

Borne graveward under laden tree?
The cheer, so human, might not call
The maiden up; *Christ is arisen:*
But Ruth, may Ruth so burst the prison?

The rite supreme being ended now,
Their confluence here the nations part:
Homeward the tides of pilgrims flow,
By contrast making the walled town
Like a depopulated mart;
More like some kirk on week-day lone,
On whose void benches broodeth still
The brown light from November hill.

But though the freshet quite be gone—
Sluggish, life's wonted stream flows on.

XXXIV : VIA CRUCIS

Some leading thoroughfares of man
In wood-path, track, or trail began;
Though threading heart of proudest town,
They follow in controlling grade
A hint or dictate, nature's own,
By man, as by the brute, obeyed.

Within Jerusalem a lane,
Narrow, nor less an artery main
(Though little knoweth it of din),
In parts suggests such origin.
The restoration or repair,
Successive through long ages there,
Of city upon city tumbled,
Might scarce divert that thoroughfare,
Whose hill abideth yet unhumbled
Above the valley-side it meets.

Pronounce its name, this natural street's:
The *Via Crucis*—even the way
Tradition claims to be the one
Trod on that Friday far away
By Him our pure exemplar shown.

'Tis Whitsun-tide. From paths without,
Through Stephen's gate—by many a vein
Convergent brought within this lane,
Ere sun-down shut the loiterer out—
As 'twere a frieze, behold the train!
Bowed water-carriers; Jews with staves,
Infirm gray monks; over-loaded slaves;
Turk soldiers—young, with home-sick eyes;
A Bey, bereaved through luxuries;
Strangers and exiles; Moslem dames
Long-veiled in monumental white,
Dumb from the mounds which memory claims;
A half-starved vagrant Edomite;
Sore-footed Arab girls, which toil
Depressed under heap of garden-spoil;
The patient ass with panniered urn;
Sour camels humped by heaven and man,
Whose languid necks through habit turn
For ease—for ease they hardly gain.
In varied forms of fate they wend—
Or man or animal, 'tis one:
Cross-bearers all, alike they tend
And follow, slowly follow on.

But, lagging after, who is he
Called early every hope to test,
And now, at close of rarer quest,
Finds so much more the heavier tree?
From slopes whence even Echo's gone,
Wending, he murmurs in low tone:

"They wire the world—far under sea
They talk; but never comes to me
A message from beneath the stone."

Dusked Olivet he leaves behind,
And, taking now a slender wynd,
Vanishes in the obscurer town.

XXXV : EPILOGUE

If Luther's day expand to Darwin's year,
Shall that exclude the hope—foreclose the fear?

Unmoved by all the claims our times avow,
The ancient Sphinx still keeps the porch of
shade;
And comes Despair, whom not her calm may
cow,
And coldly on that adamantine brow
Scrawls undeterred his bitter pasquinade.
But Faith (who from the scrawl indignant turns)
With blood warm oozing from her wounded trust,
Inscribes even on her shards of broken urns
The sign o' the cross—*the spirit above the dust!*

Yea, ape and angel, strife and old debate—
The harps of heaven and dreary gongs of hell;
Science the feud can only aggravate—
No umpire she betwixt the chimes and knell:
The running battle of the star and clod
Shall run forever—if there be no God.

Degrees we know, unknown in days before;
The light is greater, hence the shadow more;
And tantalized and apprehensive Man
Appealing—Wherefore ripen us to pain?

Seems there the spokesman of dumb Nature's
train.
But through such strange illusions have they
passed
Who in life's pilgrimage have baffled striven—
Even death may prove unreal at the last,
And stoics be astounded into heaven.

Then keep thy heart, though yet but ill-
resigned—
Clarel, thy heart, the issues there but mind;
That like the crocus budding through the snow—
That like a swimmer rising from the deep—
That like a burning secret which doth go
Even from the bosom that would hoard and keep;
Emerge thou mayst from the last whelming sea,
And prove that death but routs life into victory.

FROM

John Marr and Other Sailors with Some Sea-Pieces

1888

John Marr

John Marr, toward the close of the last century born in America of a mother unknown, and from boyhood up to maturity a sailor under divers flags, disabled at last from further maritime life by a crippling wound received at close quarters with pirates of the Keys, eventually betakes himself for a livelihood to less active employment ashore. There, too, he transfers his rambling disposition acquired as a sea-farer.

After a variety of removals, at first as a sailmaker from sea-port to sea-port, then adventurously inland as a rough bench-carpenter, he, finally, in the last-named capacity, settles down about the year 1838 upon what was then a frontier-prairie, sparsely sprinkled with small oak-groves and yet fewer log-houses of a little colony but recently from one of our elder inland States. Here, putting a period to his rovings, he marries.

Ere long a fever, the bane of new settlements on teeming loam, and whose sallow livery was certain to show itself, after an interval, in the complexions of too many of these people, carries off his young wife and infant child. In one coffin, put together by his own hands, they are committed with meager rites to the earth—another mound, though a small one, in the wide prairie, nor far from where the mound-builders of a race only conjecturable had left their pottery and bones, one common clay, under a strange terrace serpentine in form.

With an honest stillness in his general mien—swarthy and black-browed, with eyes that could soften or flash, but never harden, yet disclosing at times a melancholy depth —this kinless man had affections which, once placed, not readily could be dislodged or resigned to a substituted object. Being now arrived at middle-life, he resolves never to quit the soil that holds the only beings ever connected with him by love in the family tie. His log-house he lets to a new-comer, one glad enough to get it, and dwells with the household.

While the acuter sense of his bereavement becomes mollified by time, the void at heart abides. Fain, if possible, would he fill that void by cultivating social relations yet nearer than before with a people whose lot he purposes sharing to the end—relations superadded to that mere work-a-day bond arising from participation in the same outward hardships, making reciprocal helpfulness a matter of course. But here, and nobody to blame, he is obstructed.

More familiarly to consort, men of a practical turn must sympathetically converse, and upon topics of real life. But, whether as to persons or events, one cannot always be talking about the present, much less speculating about the future; one must needs recur to the past, which, with the mass of men, where the past is in any personal way a common inheritance, supplies to most practical natures the basis of sympathetic communion.

But the past of John Marr was not the past of these pioneers. Their hands had rested on the plow-tail, his upon the ship's helm. They knew but their own kind and their own usages; to him had been revealed something of the checkered globe. So limited unavoidably was the mental reach, and by consequence the range of sympathy, in this particular band of domestic emigrants, hereditary tillers of the soil, that the ocean, but a hearsay to their fathers, had now through yet deeper inland removal become to themselves little more than a rumor traditional and vague.

They were a staid people; staid through habituation to monotonous hardship; ascetics by necessity not less than through moral bias; nearly all of them sincerely, however narrowly, religious. They were kindly at need, after their fashion; but to a man wonted—as John Marr in his previous homeless sojournings could not but have been —to the free-and-easy tavern-clubs affording cheap recreation of an evening in certain old and comfortable sea-port towns of that time, and yet more familiar with the companionship afloat of the sailors of the same period, something was lacking. That something was geniality, the flower of life springing from some sense of joy in it, more or less. This their lot could not give to these hard-working endurers of the dispiriting malaria,—men to whom a holiday never came,—and they had too much of uprightness and no art at all or desire to affect what they did not really feel. At a corn-husking, their least grave of gatherings, did the lone-hearted mariner seek to divert his own thoughts from sadness, and in some degree interest theirs, by adverting to aught removed from the crosses and trials of their personal surroundings, naturally enough he would slide into some marine story or picture, but would soon recoil upon himself and be silent, finding no encouragement to proceed. Upon one such occasion an elderly man—a blacksmith, and at Sunday gatherings an earnest exhorter—honestly said to him, "Friend, we know nothing of that here."

Such unresponsiveness in one's fellow-creatures set apart from factitious life, and by their vocation—in those days little helped by machinery—standing, as it were, next of kin to Nature; this, to John Marr, seemed of a piece with the apathy of Nature herself as envisaged to him here on a prairie where none but the perished mound-builders had as yet left a durable mark.

The remnant of Indians thereabout—all but exterminated in their recent and final war with regular white troops, a war waged by the Red Men for their native soil and natural rights—had been coerced into the occupancy of wilds not very far beyond the Mississippi—wilds *then*, but now the seats of municipalities and States. Prior to that, the bisons, once streaming countless in processional herds, or browsing as in an endless battle-line over these vast aboriginal pastures, had retreated, dwindled in number, before the hunters, in main a race distinct from the agricultural pioneers, though generally their advance-guard. Such a double exodus of man and beast left the plain a desert, green or blossoming indeed, but almost as forsaken as the Siberian Obi. Save the prairie-hen, sometimes startled from its lurking-place in the rank grass; and, in their migratory season, pigeons, high overhead on the wing, in dense multitudes eclipsing the day like a passing storm-cloud; save these—there being no wide woods with their underwood—birds were strangely few.

Blank stillness would for hours reign unbroken on this prairie. "It is the bed of a dried-up sea," said the companionless sailor—no geologist—to himself, musing at twilight upon the fixed undulations of that immense alluvial expanse bounded only by the horizon, and missing there the stir that, to alert eyes and ears, animates at all times the apparent solitudes of the deep.

But a scene quite at variance with one's antecedents may yet prove suggestive of them. Hooped round by a level rim, the prairie was to John Marr a reminder of ocean.

With some of his former shipmates, *chums* on certain cruises, he had contrived, prior to this last and more remote removal, to keep up a little correspondence at odd intervals. But from tidings of anybody or any sort he, in common with the other settlers, was now cut off; quite cut off, except from such news as might be conveyed over the grassy billows by the last-arrived prairie-schooner—the vernacular term, in those parts and times, for the emigrant-wagon arched high over with sailcloth and voyaging across the vast champaign. There was no reachable post-office as yet; not even the rude little receptive box with lid and leather hinges, set up at convenient intervals on a stout stake along some solitary green way, affording a perch for birds, and which, later in the unintermitting advance of the frontier, would perhaps decay into a mossy monument, attesting yet another successive overleaped limit of civilized life; a life which in America can to-day hardly be said to have any western bound but the ocean that washes Asia. Throughout these plains, now in places overpopulous with towns overopulent; sweeping plains, elsewhere fenced off in every direction into flourishing farms—pale townsmen and hale farmers alike, in part, the descendants of the first sallow settlers; a region that half a century ago produced little for the sustenance of man, but to-day launching its superabundant wheat-harvest on the world;—of this prairie, now everywhere intersected with wire and rail, hardly can it be said that at the period here written of there was so much as a traceable road. To the long-distance traveler the oak-groves, wide apart, and varying in compass and form; these, with recent settlements, yet more widely separate, offered some landmarks; but otherwise he steered by the sun. In early midsummer, even going but from one log-encampment to the next, a journey it might be of hours or good part of a day, travel was much like navigation. In some more enriched depressions between the long, green, graduated swells, smooth as those of ocean becalmed receiving and subduing to its own tranquillity the voluminous surge raised by some far-off hurricane of days previous, here one would catch the first indication of advancing strangers either in the distance, as a far sail at sea, by the glistening white canvas of the wagon, the wagon itself wading through the rank vegetation and hidden by it, or, failing that, when near to, in the ears of the team, peaking, if not above the tall tiger-lilies, yet above the yet taller grass.

Luxuriant, this wilderness; but, to its denizen, a friend left behind anywhere in the world seemed not alone absent to sight, but an absentee from existence.

Though John Marr's shipmates could not all have departed life, yet as subjects of meditation they were like phantoms of the dead. As the growing sense of his environment threw him more and more upon retrospective musings, these phantoms, next to those of his wife and child, became spiritual companions, losing something of their first indistinctness and putting on at last a dim semblance of mute life; and they were lit by that aureola circling over any object of the affections in the past for reunion with which an imaginative heart passionately yearns.

*

He invokes these visionary ones,—striving, as it were, to get into verbal communion with them, or, under yet stronger illusion, reproaching them for their silence:—

Since as in night's deck-watch ye show,
Why, lads, so silent here to me,
Your watchmate of times long ago?

Once, for all the darkling sea,
You your voices raised how clearly,
Striking in when tempest sung;
Hoisting up the storm-sail cheerly,
Life is storm—let storm! you rung.
Taking things as fated merely,
Child-like though the world ye spanned;
Nor holding unto life too dearly,
Ye who held your lives in hand—
Skimmers, who on oceans four
Petrels were, and larks ashore.

O, not from memory lightly flung,
Forgot, like strains no more availing,
The heart to music haughtier strung;

Nay, frequent near me, never staleing,
Whose good feeling kept ye young.
Like tides that enter creek or stream,
Ye come, ye visit me, or seem
Swimming out from seas of faces,
Alien myriads memory traces,
To enfold me in a dream!

I yearn as ye. But rafts that strain,
Parted, shall they lock again?
Twined we were, entwined, then riven,
Ever to new embracements driven,
Shifting gulf-weed of the main!
And how if one here shift no more,
Lodged by the flinging surge ashore?

Nor less, as now, in eve's decline,
Your shadowy fellowship is mine.
Ye float around me, form and feature:—
Tattooings, ear-rings, love-locks curled;
Barbarians of man's simpler nature,
Unworldly servers of the world.
Yea, present all, and dear to me,
Though shades, or scouring China's sea.

Whither, whither, merchant-sailors,
Whitherward now in roaring gales?
Competing still, ye huntsman-whalers,
In leviathan's wake what boat prevails?
And man-of-war's men, whereaway?
If now no dinned drum beat to quarters
On the wilds of midnight waters—
Foemen looming through the spray;
Do yet your gangway lanterns, streaming,
Vainly strive to pierce below,

When, tilted from the slant plank gleaming,
A brother you see to darkness go?

But, gunmates lashed in shotted canvas,
If where long watch-below ye keep,
Never the shrill "*All hands up hammocks!*"
Breaks the spell that charms your sleep,
And summoning trumps might vainly call,
And booming guns implore—
A beat, a heart-beat musters all,
One heart-beat at heart-core.
It musters. But to clasp, retain;
To see you at the halyards main—
To hear your chorus once again!

Bridegroom Dick

(1876)

Sunning ourselves in October on a day
Balmy as spring, though the year was in decay,
I lading my pipe, she stirring her tea,
My old woman she says to me,
"Feel ye, old man, how the season mellows?"
And why should I not, blessed heart alive,
Here mellowing myself, past sixty-five,
To think o' the May-time o' pennoned young
        fellows
This stripped old hulk here for years may survive.

Ere yet, long ago, we were spliced, Bonny Blue,
(Silvery it gleams down the moon-glade o' time,
Ah, sugar in the bowl and berries in the prime!)
Coxswain I o' the Commodore's crew,—
Under me the fellows that manned his fine gig,
Spinning him ashore, a king in full fig.
Chirrupy even when crosses rubbed me,
Bridegroom Dick lieutenants dubbed me.
Pleasant at a yarn, Bob o' Linkum in a song,
Diligent in duty and nattily arrayed,
Favored I was, wife, and *fleeted* right along;
And though but a tot for such a tall grade,
A high quartermaster at last I was made.

All this, old lassie, you have heard before,
But you listen again for the sake e'en o' me;
No babble stales o' the good times o' yore
To Joan, if Darby the babbler be.

Babbler?—O' what? Addled brains, they forget!
O—quartermaster I; yes, the signals set,
Hoisted the ensign, mended it when frayed,
Polished up the binnacle, minded the helm,
And prompt every order blithely obeyed.
To me would the officers say a word cheery—
Break through the starch o' the quarter-deck realm;
His coxswain late, so the Commodore's pet.
Ay, and in night-watches long and weary,
Bored night to death with the naval etiquette,
Yearning, too, for fun, some younker, a cadet,
Dropping for time each vain bumptious trick,
Boy-like would unbend to Bridegroom Dick.
But a limit there was—a check, d' ye see:
Those fine young aristocrats knew their degree.

Well, stationed aft where their lordships keep,—
Seldom going forward excepting to sleep,—
I, boozing now on by-gone years,
My betters recall along with my peers.
Recall them? Wife, but I see them plain:
Alive, alert, every man stirs again.
Ay, and again on the lee-side pacing,
My spy-glass carrying, a truncheon in show,
Turning at the taffrail, my footsteps retracing,
Proud in my duty, again methinks I go.
And Dave, Dainty Dave, I mark where he stands,
Our trim sailing-master, to time the high-noon,
That thingumbob sextant perplexing eyes and hands,
Squinting at the sun, or twigging o' the moon;
Then, touching his cap to Old Chock-a-Block
Commanding the quarter-deck,—"Sir, twelve o'clock."

Where sails he now, that trim sailing-master,
Slender, yes, as the ship's sky-s'l pole?
Dimly I mind me of some sad disaster—
Dainty Dave was dropped from the navy-roll!
And ah, for old Lieutenant Chock-a-Block—
Fast, wife, chock-fast to death's black dock!
Buffeted about the obstreperous ocean,
Fleeted his life, if lagged his promotion.
Little girl, they are all, all gone, I think,
Leaving Bridegroom Dick here with lids that
wink.

Where is Ap Catesby? The fights fought of yore
Famed him, and laced him with epaulets, and
more.
But fame is a wake that after-wakes cross,
And the waters wallow all, and laugh *Where's
the loss?*
But John Bull's bullet in his shoulder bearing
Ballasted Ap in his long sea-faring.
The middies they ducked to the man who had
messed
With Decatur in the gun-room, or forward
pressed
Fighting beside Perry, Hull, Porter, and the rest.

Humped veteran o' the Heart-o'-Oak war,
Moored long in haven where the old heroes are,
Never on *you* did the iron-clads jar!
Your open deck when the boarder assailed,
The frank old heroic hand-to-hand then availed.

But where's Guert Gan? Still heads he the van?
As before Vera-Cruz, when he dashed splashing
through

The blue rollers sunned, in his brave gold-and-blue,
And, ere his cutter in keel took the strand,
Aloft waved his sword on the hostile land!
Went up the cheering, the quick chanticleering;
All hands vying—all colors flying:
"Cock-a-doodle-doo!" and "Row, boys, row!"
"Hey, Starry Banner!" "Hi, Santa Anna!"—
Old Scott's young dash at Mexico.

Fine forces o' the land, fine forces o' the sea,
Fleet, army, and flotilla—tell, heart o' me,
Tell, if you can, whereaway now they be!

But ah, how to speak of the hurricane unchained—
The Union's strands parted in the hawser over-strained;
Our flag blown to shreds, anchors gone altogether—
The dashed fleet o' States in Secession's foul weather.

Lost in the smother o' that wide public stress,
In hearts, private hearts, what ties there were snapped!
Tell, Hal—vouch, Will, o' the ward-room mess,
On you how the riving thunder-bolt clapped.
With a bead in your eye and beads in your glass,
And a grip o' the flipper, it was part and pass:
"Hal, must it be? Well, if come indeed the shock,
To North or to South, let the victory cleave,
Vaunt it he may on his dung-hill the cock,
But *Uncle Sam's* eagle never crow will, believe."

Sentiment: ay, while suspended hung all,
Ere the guns against Sumter opened there the
ball,
And partners were taken, and the red dance
began,
War's red dance o' death!—Well, we, to a man,
We sailors o' the North, wife, how could we
lag?—
Strike with your kin, and you stick to the flag!
But to sailors o' the South that easy way was
barred.
To some, dame, believe (and I speak o' what I
know),
Wormwood the trial and the Uzzite's black shard;
And the faithfuller the heart, the crueller the
throe.
Duty? It pulled with more than one string,
This way and that, and anyhow a sting.
The flag and your kin, how be true unto both?
If one plight ye keep, then ye break the other
troth.
But elect here they must, though the casuists
were out;
Decide—hurry up—and throttle every doubt.

Of all these thrills thrilled at keelson, and throes,
Little felt the shoddyites a-toasting o' their toes;
In mart and bazar Lucre chuckled the huzza,
Coining the dollars in the bloody mint of war.
But in men, gray knights o' the Order o' Scars,
And brave boys bound by vows unto Mars,
Nature grappled honor, intertwisting in the
strife:—
But some cut the knot with a thoroughgoing
knife.

For how when the drums beat? How in the fray
In Hampton Roads on the fine balmy day?

There a lull, wife, befell—drop o' silence in the din.
Let us enter that silence ere the belchings re-begin.—
Through a ragged rift aslant in the cannonade's smoke
An iron-clad reveals her repellent broadside
Bodily intact. But a frigate, all oak,
Shows honeycombed by shot, and her deck crimson-dyed.
And a trumpet from port of the iron-clad hails,
Summoning the other, whose flag never trails:
"Surrender that frigate, Will! Surrender,
Or I will sink her—*ram,* and end her!"
'T was Hal. And Will, from the naked heart-o'-oak,
Will, the old messmate, minus trumpet, spoke,
Informally intrepid,—"Sink her, and be damned!"
Enough. Gathering way, the iron-clad *rammed.*
The frigate, heeling over, on the wave threw a dusk.
Not sharing in the slant, the clapper of her bell
The fixed metal struck—uninvoked struck the knell
Of the *Cumberland* stilettoed by the *Merrimac's* tusk;
While, broken in the wound underneath the gun-deck,
Like a sword-fish's blade in leviathan waylaid,
The tusk was left infixed in the fast-foundering wreck.
There, dungeoned in the cockpit, the wounded go down,

And the chaplain with them. But the surges uplift
The prone dead from deck, and for moment they drift
Washed with the swimmers, and the spent swimmers drown.
Nine fathom did she sink,—erect, though hid from light
Save her colors unsurrendered and spars that kept the height.

Nay, pardon, old aunty!—Wife, never let it fall,
That big started tear that hovers on the brim;
I forgot about your nephew and the *Merrimac's* ball;
No more then of her, since it summons up him.

But talk o' fellows' hearts in the wine's genial cup:—
Trap them in the fate, jam them in the strait,
Guns speak their hearts then, and speak right up.

The troublous colic o' intestine war
It sets the bowels o' affection ajar.
But, lord, old dame, so spins the whizzing world,
A humming-top, ay, for the little boy-gods
Flogging it well with their smart little rods,
Tittering at time and the coil uncurled.

Now, now, sweetheart, you sidle away,
No, never you like *that* kind o' *gay;*
But sour if I get, giving truth her due,
Honey-sweet forever, wife, will Dick be to *you!*

But avast with the War! Why recall racking days
Since set up anew are the ship's started stays?

Nor less, though the gale we have left behind,
Well may the heave o' the sea remind.
It irks me now, as it troubled me then,
To think o' the fate in the madness o' men.
If Dick was with Farragut on the night-river,
When the boom-chain we burst in the fire-raft's glare,
That blood-dyed the visage as red as the liver;
In the *Battle for the Bay* too if Dick had a share,
And saw one aloft a-piloting the war—
Trumpet in the whirlwind, a Providence in place—
Our Admiral old whom the captains huzza,
Dick joys in the man nor brags about the race.

But better, wife, I like to booze on the days
Ere the Old Order foundered in these very frays,
And tradition was lost and we learned strange ways.
Often I think on the brave cruises then;
Re-sailing them in memory, I hail the press o' men
On the gunned promenade where rolling they go,
Ere the dog-watch expire and break up the show.
The Laced Caps I see between forward guns;
Away from the powder-room they puff the cigar;
"Three days more, hey, the donnas and the dons!"
"Your Xeres widow, will you hunt her up, Starr?"
The Laced Caps laugh, and the bright waves too;
Very jolly, very wicked, both sea and crew,
Nor heaven looks sour on either, I guess,
Nor Pecksniff he bosses the gods' high mess.

Wistful ye peer, wife, concerned for my head,
And how best to get me betimes to my bed.

But king o' the club, the gayest golden spark,
Sailor o' sailors, what sailor do I mark?
Tom Tight, Tom Tight, no fine fellow finer,
A cutwater-nose, ay, a spirited soul;
But, boozing away at the well-brewed bowl,
He never bowled back from that voyage to China.

Tom was lieutenant in the brig-o'-war famed
When an officer was hung for an arch-mutineer,
But a mystery cleaved, and the captain was blamed,
And a rumpus too raised, though his honor it was clear.
And Tom he would say, when the mousers would try him,
And with cup after cup o' Burgundy ply him:
"Gentlemen, in vain with your wassail you beset,
For the more I tipple, the tighter do I get."
No blabber, no, not even with the can—
True to himself and loyal to his clan.

Tom blessed us starboard and d——d us larboard,
Right down from rail to the streak o' the garboard.
Nor less, wife, we liked him.—Tom was a man
In contrast queer with Chaplain Le Fan,
Who blessed us at morn, and at night yet again,
D——ning us only in decorous strain;
Preaching 'tween the guns—each cutlass in its place—
From text that averred old Adam a hard case.

I see him—Tom—on *horse-block* standing,
Trumpet at mouth, thrown up all amain,
An elephant's bugle, vociferous demanding

Of topmen aloft in the hurricane of rain,
"Letting that sail there your faces flog?
Manhandle it, men, and you'll get the good
grog!"
O Tom, but he knew a blue-jacket's ways,
And how a lieutenant may genially haze;
Only a sailor sailors heartily praise.

Wife, where be all these chaps, I wonder?
Trumpets in the tempest, terrors in the fray,
Boomed their commands along the deck like
thunder;
But silent is the sod, and thunder dies away.

But Captain Turret, "*Old Hemlock*" tall,
(A leaning tower when his tank brimmed all,)
Manœuvre out alive from the war did he?
Or, too old for that, drift under the lee?
Kentuckian colossal, who, touching at Madeira,
The huge puncheon shipped o' prime *Santa-Clara;*
Then rocked along the deck so solemnly!
No whit the less though judicious was enough
In dealing with the Finn who made the great
huff;
Our three-decker's giant, a grand boatswain's
mate,
Manliest of men in his own natural senses;
But driven stark mad by the devil's drugged stuff,
Storming all aboard from his run-ashore late,
Challenging to battle, vouchsafing no pretenses.
A reeling King Ogg, delirious in power,
The quarter-deck carronades he seemed to make
cower.
"Put him in *brig* there!" said Lieutenant Marrot.
"Put him in *brig!*" back he mocked like a parrot;
"Try it, then!" swaying a fist like Thor's sledge,

And making the pigmy constables hedge—
Ship's-corporals and the master-at-arms.
"In *brig* there, I say!"—They dally no more;
Like hounds let slip on a desperate boar,
Together they pounce on the formidable Finn,
Pinion and cripple and hustle him in.
Anon, under sentry, between twin guns,
He slides off in drowse, and the long night runs.

Morning brings a summons. Whistling it calls,
Shrilled through the pipes of the boatswain's four aids;
Thrilled down the hatchways along the dusk halls:
Muster to the Scourge!—Dawn of doom and its blast!
As from cemeteries raised, sailors swarm before the mast,
Tumbling up the ladders from the ship's nether shades.

Keeping in the background and taking small part,
Lounging at their ease, indifferent in face,
Behold the trim marines uncompromised in heart;
Their Major, buttoned up, near the staff finds room—
The staff o' lieutenants standing grouped in their place.
All the Laced Caps o' the ward-room come,
The Chaplain among them, disciplined and dumb.
The blue-nosed boatswain, complexioned like slag,
Like a blue Monday shows—his implements in bag.
Executioners, his aids, a couple by him stand,

At a nod there the thongs to receive from his
hand.
Never venturing a caveat whatever may betide,
Though functionally here on humanity's side,
The grave Surgeon shows, like the formal
physician
Attending the rack o' the Spanish Inquisition.

The angel o' the "brig" brings his prisoner up;
Then, steadied by his old *Santa-Clara*, a sup,
Heading all erect, the ranged assizes there,
Lo, Captain Turret, and under starred bunting,
(A florid full face and fine silvered hair,)
Gigantic the yet greater giant confronting.

Now the culprit he liked, as a tall captain can
A Titan subordinate and true *sailor-man;*
And frequent he'd shown it—no worded advance,
But flattering the Finn with a well-timed glance.
But what of that now? In the martinet-mien
Read the *Articles of War*, heed the naval routine;
While, cut to the heart a dishonor there to win,
Restored to his senses, stood the Anak Finn;
In racked self-control the squeezed tears peeping,
Scalding the eye with repressed inkeeping.
Discipline must be; the scourge is deemed due.
But ah for the sickening and strange heart-
benumbing,
Compassionate abasement in shipmates that
view;
Such a grand champion shamed there suc-
cumbing!

"Brown, tie him up."—The cord he brooked:
How else?—his arms spread apart—never
threaping;

No, never he flinched, never sideways he looked,
Peeled to the waistband, the marble flesh creeping,
Lashed by the sleet the officious winds urge.
In function his fellows their fellowship merge—
The twain standing nigh—the two boatswain's mates,
Sailors of his grade, ay, and brothers of his mess.
With sharp thongs adroop the junior one awaits
The word to uplift.

"Untie him—so!
Submission is enough.—Man, you may go."
Then, promenading aft, brushing fat Purser Smart,
"Flog? Never meant it—had n't any heart.
Degrade that tall fellow?"—Such, wife, was he,
Old Captain Turret, who the brave wine could stow.
Magnanimous, you think?—But what does Dick see?
Apron to your eye! Why, never fell a blow;
Cheer up, old wifie, 't was a long time ago.

But where's that sore one, crabbed and severe,
Lieutenant Don Lumbago, an arch scrutineer?
Call the roll to-day, would he answer—*Here!*
When the *Blixum's* fellows to quarters mustered
How he'd lurch along the lane of gun-crews clustered,
Testy as touchwood, to pry and to peer.
Jerking his sword underneath larboard arm,
He ground his worn grinders to keep himself calm.
Composed in his nerves, from the fidgets set free,

Tell, Sweet Wrinkles, alive now is he,
In Paradise a parlor where the even tempers be?

Where's Commander All-a-Tanto?
Where's Orlop Bob singing up from below?
Where's Rhyming Ned? has he spun his last
canto?
Where's Jewsharp Jim? Where's Rigadoon Joe?
Ah, for the music over and done,
The band all dismissed save the droned
trombone!
Where 's Glen o' the gun-room, who loved
Hot-Scotch—
Glen, prompt and cool in a perilous watch?
Where 's flaxen-haired Phil? a gray lieutenant?
Or rubicund, flying a dignified pennant?
But where sleeps his brother?—the cruise it was
o'er,
But ah, for death's grip that welcomed him
ashore!
Where 's Sid, the cadet, so frank in his brag,
Whose toast was audacious—"*Here 's Sid, and
Sid 's flag!*"
Like holiday-craft that have sunk unknown,
May a lark of a lad go lonely down?
Who takes the census under the sea?
Can others like old ensigns be,
Bunting I hoisted to flutter at the gaff—
Rags in end that once were flags
Gallant streaming from the staff?
Such scurvy doom could the chances deal
To Top-Gallant Harry and Jack Genteel?

Lo, Genteel Jack in hurricane weather,
Shagged like a bear, like a red lion roaring;
But O, so fine in his chapeau and feather,

In port to the ladies never once *jawing;*
All bland *politesse,* how urbane was he—
"Oui, mademoiselle"—"Ma chère amie!"

'T was Jack got up the ball at Naples,
Gay in the old *Ohio* glorious;
His hair was curled by the berth-deck barber,
Never you'd deemed him a cub of rude Boreas;
In tight little pumps, with the grand dames in
rout,
A-flinging his shapely foot all about;
His watch-chain with love's jeweled tokens
abounding,
Curls ambrosial shaking out odors,
Waltzing along the batteries, astounding
The gunner glum and the grim-visaged loaders.

Wife, where be all these blades, I wonder,
Pennoned fine fellows, so strong, so gay?
Never their colors with a dip dived under;
Have they hauled them down in a lack-lustre
day,
Or beached their boats in the Far, Far Away?

Hither and thither, blown wide asunder,
Where's this fleet, I wonder and wonder.
Slipt their cables, rattled their adieu,
(Whereaway pointing? to what rendezvous?)
Out of sight, out of mind, like the crack
Constitution,
And many a keel time never shall renew—
Bon Homme Dick o' the buff Revolution,
The *Black Cockade* and the staunch *True-Blue.*

Doff hats to Decatur! But where is his blazon?
Must merited fame endure time's wrong—

Glory's ripe grape wizen up to a raisin?
Yes! for Nature teems, and the years are strong,
And who can keep the tally o' the names that
fleet along!

But his frigate, wife, his bride? Would black-
smiths brown
Into smithereens smite the solid old renown?

Rivetting the bolts in the iron-clad's shell,
Hark to the hammers with a *rat-tat-tat;*
"Handier a *derby* than a laced cocked hat!
The *Monitor* was ugly, but she served us right
well,
Better than the *Cumberland,* a beauty and the
belle."

Better than the Cumberland!—Heart alive in me!
That battlemented hull, Tantallon o' the sea,
Kicked in, as at Boston the taxed chests o' tea!
Ay, spurned by the *ram,* once a tall, shapely
craft,
But lopped by the *Rebs* to an iron-beaked raft—
A blacksmith's unicorn armed *cap-a-pie.*

Under the water-line a *ram's* blow is dealt:
And foul fall the knuckles that strike below the
belt.
Nor brave the inventions that serve to replace
The openness of valor while dismantling the
grace.

Aloof from all this and the never-ending game,
Tantamount to teetering, plot and counterplot;
Impenetrable armor—all-perforating shot;
Aloof, bless God, ride the war-ships of old,

A grand fleet moored in the roadstead of fame;
Not submarine sneaks with *them* are enrolled;
Their long shadows dwarf us, their flags are as
flame.

Don't fidget so, wife; an old man's passion
Amounts to no more than this smoke that I puff;
There, there, now, buss me in good old fashion;
A died-down candle will flicker in the snuff.

But one last thing let your old babbler say,
What Decatur's coxswain said who was long ago
hearsed,
"Take in your flying-kites, for there comes a
lubber's day
When gallant things will go, and the three-
deckers first."

My pipe is smoked out, and the grog runs slack;
But booze away, wife, at your blessed Bohea;
This empty can here must needs solace me—
Nay, sweetheart, nay; I take that back;
Dick drinks from your eyes and he finds no lack!

Tom Deadlight

(1810)

During a tempest encountered homeward-bound from the Mediterranean, a grizzled petty-officer, one of the two captains of the forecastle, dying at night in his hammock, swung in the *sick-bay* under the tiered gun-decks of the British *Dreadnaught*, 98, wandering in his mind, though with glimpses of sanity, and starting up at whiles, sings by snatches his good-bye and last injunctions to two messmates, his watchers, one of whom fans the fevered tar with the flap of his old sou'-wester. Some names and phrases, with here and there a line, or part of one; these, in his aberration, wrested into incoherency from their original connection and import, he involuntarily derives, as he does the measure, from a famous old sea-ditty, whose cadences, long rife, and now humming in the collapsing brain, attune the last flutterings of distempered thought.

Farewell and adieu to you noble hearties,—
    Farewell and adieu to you ladies of Spain,
For I've received orders for to sail for the
        Deadman,
    But hope with the grand fleet to see you
        again.

I have hove my ship to, with main-top-sail aback,
        boys;
    I have hove my ship to, for to strike sound-
        ings clear—
The black scud a' flying; but, by God's blessing,
        dam' me,

Right up the Channel for the Deadman I'll
steer.

I have worried through the waters that are called
the Doldrums,
And growled at Sargasso that clogs while ye
grope—
Blast my eyes, but the light-ship is hid by the
mist, lads:—
Flying Dutchman—odds bobbs—off the Cape
of Good Hope!

But what's this I feel that is fanning my cheek,
Matt?
The white goney's wing?—how she rolls!—
't is the Cape!—
Give my kit to the mess, Jock, for kin none is
mine, none;
And tell *Holy Joe* to avast with the crape.

Dead reckoning, says *Joe*, it won't do to go by;
But they doused all the glims, Matt, in sky
t' other night.
Dead reckoning is good for to sail for the Dead-
man;
And Tom Deadlight he thinks it may reckon
near right.

The signal!—it streams for the grand fleet to
anchor.
The captains—the trumpets—the hullabaloo!
Stand by for blue-blazes, and mind your shank-
painters,
For the Lord High Admiral, he's squinting
at you!

But give me my *tot,* Matt, before I roll over;
Jock, let's have your flipper, it's good for to feel;
And don't sew me up without *baccy* in mouth, boys,
And don't blubber like lubbers when I turn up my keel.

Jack Roy

Kept up by relays of generations young
Never dies at halyards the blithe chorus sung;
While in sands, sounds, and seas where the storm-petrels cry,
Dropped mute around the globe, these halyard singers lie.
Short-lived the clippers for racing-cups that run,
And speeds in life's career many a lavish mother's-son.

But thou, manly king o' the old *Splendid's* crew,
The ribbons o' thy hat still a-fluttering, should fly—
A challenge, and forever, nor the bravery should rue.
Only in a tussle for the starry flag high,
When 't is piety to do, and privilege to die,
Then, only then, would heaven think to lop
Such a cedar as the captain o' the *Splendid's* main-top:
A belted sea-gentleman; a gallant, off-hand
Mercutio indifferent in life's gay command.
Magnanimous in humor; when the splintering shot fell,
"Tooth-picks a-plenty, lads; thank 'em with a shell!"

Sang Larry o' the Cannakin, smuggler o' the wine,
At mess between guns, lad in jovial recline:

"In Limbo our Jack he would chirrup up a
cheer,
The martinet there find a chaffing mutineer;
From a thousand fathoms down under hatches o'
your Hades,
He'd ascend in love-ditty, kissing fingers to your
ladies!"

Never relishing the knave, though allowing for
the menial,
Nor overmuch the king, Jack, nor prodigally
genial.
Ashore on liberty, he flashed in escapade,
Vaulting over life in its levelness of grade,
Like the dolphin off Africa in rainbow a-sweep-
ing—
Arch iridescent shot from seas languid sleeping.

Larking with thy life, if a joy but a toy,
Heroic in thy levity wert thou, Jack Roy.

The Haglets

By chapel bare, with walls sea-beat,
The lichened urns in wilds are lost
About a carved memorial stone
That shows, decayed and coral-mossed,
A form recumbent, swords at feet,
Trophies at head, and kelp for a winding-sheet.

I invoke thy ghost, neglected fane,
Washed by the waters' long lament;
I adjure the recumbent effigy
To tell the cenotaph's intent—
Reveal why fagotted swords are at feet,
Why trophies appear and weeds are the winding-
sheet.

By open ports the Admiral sits,
And shares repose with guns that tell
Of power that smote the arm'd Plate Fleet
Whose sinking flag-ship's colors fell;
But over the Admiral floats in light
His squadron's flag, the red-cross Flag of the
White.

The eddying waters whirl astern,
The prow, a seedsman, sows the spray;
With bellying sails and buckling spars
The black hull leaves a Milky Way;
Her timbers thrill, her batteries roll,
She revelling speeds exulting with pennon at
pole.

But ah, for standards captive trailed
For all their scutcheoned castles' pride—
Castilian towers that dominate Spain,
Naples, and either Ind beside;
Those haughty towers, armorial ones,
Rue the salute from the Admiral's dens of guns.

Ensigns and arms in trophy brave,
Braver for many a rent and scar,
The captor's naval hall bedeck,
Spoil that insures an earldom's star—
Toledoes great, grand draperies too,
Spain's steel and silk, and splendors from Peru.
But crippled part in splintering fight,
The vanquished flying the victor's flags,
With prize-crews, under convoy-guns,
Heavy the fleet from Opher drags—
The Admiral crowding sail ahead,
Foremost with news who foremost in conflict
sped.
But out from cloistral gallery dim,
In early night his glance is thrown;
He marks the vague reserve of heaven,
He feels the touch of ocean lone;
Then turns, in frame part undermined,
Nor notes the shadowing wings that fan behind.

There, peaked and gray, three haglets fly,
And follow, follow fast in wake
Where slides the cabin-lustre shy,
And sharks from man a glamour take,
Seething along the line of light
In lane that endless rules the war-ship's flight.
The sea-fowl here, whose hearts none know,
They followed late the flag-ship quelled,
(As now the victor one) and long

Above her gurgling grave, shrill held
With screams their wheeling rites—then sped
Direct in silence where the victor led.
    Now winds less fleet, but fairer, blow,
A ripple laps the coppered side,
While phosphor sparks make ocean gleam,
Like camps lit up in triumph wide;
With lights and tinkling cymbals meet
Acclaiming seas the advancing conqueror greet.

But who a flattering tide may trust,
Or favoring breeze, or aught in end?—
Careening under startling blasts
The sheeted towers of sails impend;
While, gathering bale, behind is bred
A livid storm-bow, like a rainbow dead.
    At trumpet-call the topmen spring;
And, urged by after-call in stress,
Yet other tribes of tars ascend
The rigging's howling wilderness;
But ere yard-ends alert they win,
Hell rules in heaven with hurricane-fire and din.
    The spars, athwart at spiry height,
Like quaking Lima's crosses rock;
Like bees the clustering sailors cling
Against the shrouds, or take the shock
Flat on the swept yard-arms aslant,
Dipped like the wheeling condor's pinions gaunt.

A lull! and tongues of languid flame
Lick every boom, and lambent show
Electric 'gainst each face aloft;
The herds of clouds with bellowings go:
The black ship rears—beset—harassed,
Then plunges far with luminous antlers vast.
    In trim betimes they turn from land,

Some shivered sails and spars they stow;
One watch, dismissed, they troll the can,
While loud the billow thumps the bow—
Vies with the fist that smites the board,
Obstreperous at each reveller's jovial word.
Of royal oak by storms confirmed,
The tested hull her lineage shows:
Vainly the plungings whelm her prow—
She rallies, rears, she sturdier grows;
Each shot-hole plugged, each storm-sail home,
With batteries housed she rams the watery
dome.

Dim seen adrift through driving scud,
The wan moon shows in plight forlorn;
Then, pinched in visage, fades and fades
Like to the faces drowned at morn,
When deeps engulfed the flag-ship's crew,
And, shrilling round, the inscrutable haglets
flew.
And still they fly, nor now they cry,
But constant fan a second wake,
Unflagging pinions ply and ply,
Abreast their course intent they take;
Their silence marks a stable mood,
They patient keep their eager neighborhood.
Plumed with a smoke, a confluent sea,
Heaved in a combing pyramid full,
Spent at its climax, in collapse
Down headlong thundering stuns the hull:
The trophy drops; but, reared again,
Shows Mars' high-altar and contemns the main.

Rebuilt it stands, the brag of arms,
Transferred in site—no thought of where

The sensitive needle keeps its place,
And starts, disturbed, a quiverer there;
The helmsman rubs the clouded glass—
Peers in, but lets the trembling portent pass.
  Let pass as well his shipmates do
(Whose dream of power no tremors jar)
Fears for the fleet convoyed astern:
"Our flag they fly, they share our star;
Spain's galleons great in hull are stout:
Manned by our men—like us they'll ride it out."
  To-night's the night that ends the week—
Ends day and week and month and year:
A fourfold imminent flickering time,
For now the midnight draws anear:
Eight bells! and passing-bells they be—
The Old Year fades, the Old Year dies at sea.

He launched them well. But shall the New
Redeem the pledge the Old Year made,
Or prove a self-asserting heir?
But healthy hearts few qualms invade:
By shot-chests grouped in bays 'tween guns
The gossips chat, the grizzled, sea-beat ones.
  And boyish dreams some graybeards blab:
"To sea, my lads, we go no more
Who share the Acapulco prize;
We'll all night in, and bang the door;
Our ingots red shall yield us bliss:
Lads, golden years begin to-night with this!"
  Released from deck, yet waiting call,
Glazed caps and coats baptized in storm,
A watch of Laced Sleeves round the board
Draw near in heart to keep them warm:
"Sweethearts and wives!" clink, clink, they meet,
And, quaffing, dip in wine their beards of sleet.

"Ay, let the star-light stay withdrawn,
So here her hearth-light memory fling,
So in this wine-light cheer be born,
And honor's fellowship weld our ring—
Honor! our Admiral's aim foretold:
A tomb or a trophy, and lo, 't is a trophy and
gold!"
But he, a unit, sole in rank,
Apart needs keep his lonely state,
The sentry at his guarded door
Mute as by vault the sculptured Fate;
Belted he sits in drowsy light,
And, hatted, nods—the Admiral of the White.
He dozes, aged with watches passed—
Years, years of pacing to and fro;
He dozes, nor attends the stir
In bullioned standards rustling low,
Nor minds the blades whose secret thrill
Perverts overhead the magnet's Polar will;—

Less heeds the shadowing three that ply
And follow, follow fast in wake,
Untiring wing and lidless eye—
Abreast their course intent they take;
Or sigh or sing, they hold for good
The unvarying flight and fixed inveterate mood.
In dream at last his dozings merge,
In dream he reaps his victory's fruit:
The Flags-o'-the-Blue, the Flags-o'-the-Red,
Dipped flags of his country's fleets salute
His Flag-o'-the-White in harbor proud—
But why should it blench? Why turn to a
painted shroud?
The hungry seas they hound the hull,
The sharks they dog the haglets' flight;
With one consent the winds, the waves

In hunt with fins and wings unite,
While drear the harps in cordage sound
Remindful wails for old Armadas drowned.

Ha—yonder! are they Northern Lights?
Or signals flashed to warn or ward?
Yea, signals lanced in breakers high;
But doom on warning follows hard:
While yet they veer in hope to shun,
They strike! and thumps of hull and heart are
one.
But beating hearts a drum-beat calls
And prompt the men to quarters go;
Discipline, curbing nature, rules—
Heroic makes who duty know:
They execute the trump's command,
Or in peremptory places wait and stand.
Yet cast about in blind amaze—
As through their watery shroud they peer:
"We tacked from land: then how betrayed?
Have currents swerved us—snared us here?"
None heed the blades that clash in place
Under lamps dashed down that lit the magnet's
case.

Ah, what may live, who mighty swim,
Or boat-crew reach that shore forbid,
Or cable span? Must victors drown—
Perish, even as the vanquished did?
Man keeps from man the stifled moan;
They shouldering stand, yet each in heart how
lone.
Some heaven invoke; but rings of reefs
Prayer and despair alike deride
In dance of breakers forked or peaked,
Pale maniacs of the maddened tide;

While, strenuous yet some end to earn,
The haglets spin, though now no more astern.
  Like shuttles hurrying in the looms
Aloft through rigging frayed they ply—
Cross and recross—weave and inweave,
Then lock the web with clinching cry
Over the seas on seas that clasp
The weltering wreck where gurgling ends the
    gasp.

Ah, for the Plate-Fleet trophy now,
The victor's voucher, flags and arms;
Never they'll hang in Abbey old
And take Time's dust with holier palms;
Nor less content, in liquid night,
Their captor sleeps—the Admiral of the White.

Imbedded deep with shells
And drifted treasure deep,
Forever he sinks deeper in
Unfathomable sleep—
His cannon round him thrown,
His sailors at his feet,
The wizard sea enchanting them
Where never haglets beat.

On nights when meteors play
And light the breakers' dance,
The Oreads from the caves
With silvery elves advance;
And up from ocean stream,
And down from heaven far,
The rays that blend in dream
The abysm and the star.

The Man-of-War Hawk

Yon black man-of-war hawk that wheels in the
light
O'er the black ship's white sky-s'l, sunned cloud
to the sight,
Have we low-flyers wings to ascend to his height?

No arrow can reach him; nor thought can attain
To the placid supreme in the sweep of his reign.

Old Counsel

OF THE YOUNG MASTER OF A WRECKED CALIFORNIA CLIPPER

Come out of the Golden Gate,
Go round the Horn with streamers,
Carry royals early and late;
But, brother, be not over-elate—
All hands save ship! has startled dreamers.

The Tuft of Kelp

All dripping in tangles green,
    Cast up by a lonely sea,
If purer for that, O Weed,
    Bitterer, too, are ye?

The Maldive Shark

About the Shark, phlegmatical one,
Pale sot of the Maldive sea,
The sleek little pilot-fish, azure and slim,
How alert in attendance be.
From his saw-pit of mouth, from his charnel of
maw
They have nothing of harm to dread,
But liquidly glide on his ghastly flank
Or before his Gorgonian head;
Or lurk in the port of serrated teeth
In white triple tiers of glittering gates,
And there find a haven when peril 's abroad,
An asylum in jaws of the Fates!

They are friends; and friendly they guide him
to prey,
Yet never partake of the treat—
Eyes and brains to the dotard lethargic and dull,
Pale ravener of horrible meat.

To Ned

Where is the world we roved, Ned Bunn?
Hollows thereof lay rich in shade
By voyagers old inviolate thrown
    Ere Paul Pry cruised with Pelf and Trade.
To us old lads some thoughts come home
Who roamed a world young lads no more shall
        roam.

Nor less the satiate year impends
    When, wearying of routine-resorts,
The pleasure-hunter shall break loose,
    Ned, for our Pantheistic ports:—
Marquesas and glenned isles that be
Authentic Edens in a Pagan sea.

The charm of scenes untried shall lure,
    And, Ned, a legend urge the flight—
The Typee-truants under stars
    Unknown to Shakespere's *Midsummer-Night;*
And man, if lost to Saturn's Age,
Yet feeling life no Syrian pilgrimage.

But, tell, shall he, the tourist, find
    Our isles the same in violet-glow
Enamoring us what years and years—
    Ah, Ned, what years and years ago!
Well, Adam advances, smart in pace,
But scarce by violets that advance you trace.

But we, in anchor-watches calm,
    The Indian Psyche's languor won,
And, musing, breathed primeval balm
    From Edens ere yet overrun;
Marvelling mild if mortal twice,
Here and hereafter, touch a Paradise.

Crossing the Tropics

(FROM *"The Saya-y-Manto"*)

While now the Pole Star sinks from sight
The Southern Cross it climbs the sky;
But losing thee, my love, my light,
O bride but for one bridal night,
The loss no rising joys supply.

Love, love, the Trade Winds urge abaft,
And thee, from thee, they steadfast waft.

By day the blue and silver sea
And chime of waters blandly fanned—
Nor these, nor Gama's stars to me
May yield delight, since still for thee
I long as Gama longed for land.

I yearn, I yearn, reverting turn,
My heart it streams in wake astern.

When, cut by slanting sleet, we swoop
Where raves the world's inverted year,
If roses all your porch shall loop,
Not less your heart for me will droop
Doubling thc world's last outpost drear.

O love, O love, these oceans vast:
Love, love, it is as death were past!

The Berg

(A DREAM)

I saw a ship of martial build
(Her standards set, her brave apparel on)
Directed as by madness mere
Against a stolid iceberg steer,
Nor budge it, though the infatuate ship went
down.
The impact made huge ice-cubes fall
Sullen, in tons that crashed the deck;
But that one avalanche was all—
No other movement save the foundering wreck.

Along the spurs of ridges pale,
Not any slenderest shaft and frail,
A prism over glass-green gorges lone,
Toppled; nor lace of traceries fine,
Nor pendant drops in grot or mine
Were jarred, when the stunned ship went down.

Nor sole the gulls in cloud that wheeled
Circling one snow-flanked peak afar,
But nearer fowl the floes that skimmed
And crystal beaches, felt no jar.
No thrill transmitted stirred the lock
Of jack-straw needle-ice at base;
Towers undermined by waves—the block
Atilt impending—kept their place.
Seals, dozing sleek on sliddery ledges
Slipt never, when by loftier edges
Through very inertia overthrown,
The impetuous ship in bafflement went down.

Hard Berg (methought), so cold, so vast,
With mortal damps self-overcast;
Exhaling still thy dankish breath—
Adrift dissolving, bound for death;
Though lumpish thou, a lumbering one—
A lumbering lubbard loitering slow,
Impingers rue thee and go down,
Sounding thy precipice below,
Nor stir the slimy slug that sprawls
Along thy dead indifference of walls.

FROM *Pebbles*

V

Implacable I, the old implacable Sea:
  Implacable most when most I smile serene—
Pleased, not appeased, by myriad wrecks in me.

VII

Healed of my hurt, I laud the inhuman Sea—
Yea, bless the Angels Four that there convene;
For healed I am even by their pitiless breath
Distilled in wholesome dew named rosmarine.

FROM *Timoleon, Etc.*

1891

After the Pleasure Party

LINES TRACED
UNDER AN IMAGE OF
AMOR THREATENING

Fear me, virgin whosoever
Taking pride from love exempt,
Fear me, slighted. Never, never
Brave me, nor my fury tempt:
Downy wings, but wroth they beat
Tempest even in reason's seat.

Behind the house the upland falls
With many an odorous tree—
White marbles gleaming through green halls,
Terrace by terrace, down and down,
And meets the starlit Mediterranean Sea.

'Tis Paradise. In such an hour
Some pangs that rend might take release.
Nor less perturbed who keeps this bower
Of balm, nor finds balsamic peace?
From whom the passionate words in vent
After long revery's discontent?

Tired of the homeless deep,
Look how their flight yon hurrying billows urge,
Hitherward but to reap
Passive repulse from the iron-bound verge!
Insensate, can they never know
'Tis mad to wreck the impulsion so?
An art of memory is, they tell:
But to forget! forget the glade

Wherein Fate sprung Love's ambuscade,
To flout pale years of cloistral life
And flush me in this sensuous strife.
'Tis Vesta struck with Sappho's smart.
No fable her delirious leap:
With more of cause in desperate heart,
Myself could take it—but to sleep!

Now first I feel, what all may ween,
That soon or late, if faded e'en,
One's sex asserts itself. Desire,
The dear desire through love to sway,
Is like the Geysers that aspire—
Through cold obstruction win their fervid way.
But baffled here—to take disdain,
To feel rule's instinct, yet not reign;
To dote, to come to this drear shame—
Hence the winged blaze that sweeps my soul
Like prairie fires that spurn control,
Where withering weeds incense the flame.

And kept I long heaven's watch for this,
Contemning love, for this, even this?
O terrace chill in Northern air,
O reaching ranging tube I placed
Against yon skies, and fable chased
Till, fool, I hailed for sister there
Starred Cassiopea in Golden Chair.
In dream I throned me, nor I saw
In cell the idiot crowned with straw.

And yet, ah yet scarce ill I reigned,
Through self-illusion self-sustained,
When now—enlightened, undeceived—
What gain I barrenly bereaved!

Than this can be yet lower decline—
Envy and spleen, can these be mine?

The peasant girl demure that trod
Beside our wheels that climbed the way,
And bore along a blossoming rod
That looked the sceptre of May-Day—
On her—to fire this petty hell,
His softened glance how moistly fell!
The cheat! on briars her buds were strung;
And wiles peeped forth from mien how meek.
The innocent bare-foot! young, so young!
To girls, strong man's a novice weak.
To tell such beads! And more remain,
Sad rosary of belittling pain.

When after lunch and sallies gay
Like the Decameron folk we lay
In sylvan groups; and I——let be!
O, dreams he, can he dream that one
Because not roseate feels no sun?
The plain lone bramble thrills with Spring
As much as vines that grapes shall bring.

Me now fair studies charm no more.
Shall great thoughts writ, or high themes sung
Damask wan cheeks—unlock his arm
About some radiant ninny flung?
How glad with all my starry lore,
I'd buy the veriest wanton's rose
Would but my bee therein repose.

Could I remake me! or set free
This sexless bound in sex, then plunge
Deeper than Sappho, in a lunge
Piercing Pan's paramount mystery!

For, Nature, in no shallow surge
Against thee either sex may urge,
Why hast thou made us but in halves—
Co-relatives? This makes us slaves.
If these co-relatives never meet
Self-hood itself seems incomplete.
And such the dicing of blind fate
Few matching halves here meet and mate.
What Cosmic jest or Anarch blunder
The human integral clove asunder
And shied the fractions through life's gate?

Ye stars that long your votary knew
Rapt in her vigil, see me here!
Whither is gone the spell ye threw
When rose before me Cassiopea?
Usurped on by love's stronger reign—
But lo, your very selves do wane:
Light breaks—truth breaks! Silvered no more,
But chilled by dawn that brings the gale
Shivers yon bramble above the vale,
And disillusion opens all the shore.

One knows not if Urania yet
The pleasure-party may forget;
Or whether she lived down the strain
Of turbulent heart and rebel brain;
For Amor so resents a slight,
And her's had been such haught disdain,
He long may wreak his boyish spite,
And boy-like, little reck the pain.

One knows not, no. But late in Rome
(For queens discrowned a congruous home)

Entering Albani's porch she stood
Fixed by an antique pagan stone
Colossal carved. No anchorite seer,
Not Thomas a Kempis, monk austere,
Religious more are in their tone;
Yet far, how far from Christian heart
That form august of heathen Art.
Swayed by its influence, long she stood,
Till surged emotion seething down,
She rallied and this mood she won:

    Languid in frame for me,
To-day by Mary's convent shrine,
Touched by her picture's moving plea
In that poor nerveless hour of mine,
I mused—A wanderer still must grieve.
Half I resolved to kneel and believe,
Believe and submit, the veil take on.
But thee, armed Virgin! less benign,
Thee now I invoke, thou mightier one.
Helmeted woman—if such term
Befit thee, far from strife
Of that which makes the sexual feud
And clogs the aspirant life—
O self-reliant, strong and free,
Thou in whom power and peace unite,
Transcender! raise me up to thee,
Raise me and arm me!

                                        Fond appeal.
For never passion peace shall bring,
Nor Art inanimate for long
Inspire. Nothing may help or heal
While Amor incensed remembers wrong.
Vindictive, not himself he'll spare;

For scope to give his vengeance play
Himself he'll blaspheme and betray.

Then for Urania, virgins everywhere,
O pray! Example take too, and have care.

The Ravaged Villa

In shards the sylvan vases lie,
    Their links of dance undone,
And brambles wither by thy brim,
    Choked fountain of the sun!
The spider in the laurel spins,
    The weed exiles the flower:
And, flung to kiln, Apollo's bust
    Makes lime for Mammon's tower.

Monody

To have known him, to have loved him
After loneness long;
And then to be estranged in life,
And neither in the wrong;
And now for death to set his seal—
Ease me, a little ease, my song!

By wintry hills his hermit-mound
The sheeted snow-drifts drape,
And houseless there the snow-bird flits
Beneath the fir-trees' crape:
Glazed now with ice the cloistral vine
That hid the shyest grape.

Art

In placid hours well-pleased we dream
Of many a brave unbodied scheme.
But form to lend, pulsed life create,
What unlike things must meet and mate:
A flame to melt—a wind to freeze;
Sad patience—joyous energies;
Humility—yet pride and scorn;
Instinct and study; love and hate;
Audacity—reverence. These must mate,
And fuse with Jacob's mystic heart,
To wrestle with the angel—Art.

Venice

With Pantheist energy of will
    The little craftsman of the Coral Sea
Strenuous in the blue abyss,
Up-builds his marvelous gallery
    And long arcade,
Erections freaked with many a fringe
    Of marble garlandry,
Evincing what a worm can do.

Laborious in a shallower wave,
    Advanced in kindred art,
A prouder agent proved Pan's might
When Venice rose in reefs of palaces.

In a Bye-Canal

A swoon of noon, a trance of tide,
The hushed siesta brooding wide
    Like calms far off Peru;
No floating wayfarer in sight,
Dumb noon, and haunted like the night
    When Jael the wiled one slew.

A languid impulse from the oar
Plied by my indolent gondolier
Tinkles against a palace hoar,
    And, hark, response I hear!
A lattice clicks; and lo, I see
Between the slats, mute summoning me,
What loveliest eyes of scintillation,
What basilisk glance of conjuration!

    Fronted I have, part taken the span
Of portents in nature and peril in man.
I have swum—I have been
Twixt the whale's black flukes and the white
        shark's fin;
The enemy's desert have wandered in,
And there have turned, have turned and
        scanned,
Following me how noiselessly,
Envy and Slander, lepers hand in hand.
All this. But at the latticed eye—
"Hey! Gondolier, you sleep, my man;
Wake up!" And, shooting by, we ran;
The while I mused, This, surely now,

Confutes the Naturalists, allow!
Sirens, true sirens verily be,
Sirens, waylayers in the sea.

Well, wooed by these same deadly misses,
Is it shame to run?
No! flee them did divine Ulysses,
  Brave, wise, and Venus' son.

In a Church of Padua

In vaulted place where shadows flit,
An upright sombre box you see:
A door, but fast, and lattice none,
But punctured holes minutely small
In lateral silver panel square
Above a kneeling-board without,
Suggest an aim if not declare.

Who bendeth here the tremulous knee
No glimpse may get of him within,
And he immured may hardly see
The soul confessing there the sin;
Nor yields the low-sieved voice a tone
Whereby the murmurer may be known.

Dread diving-bell! In thee inurned
What hollows the priest must sound,
Descending into consciences
Where more is hid than found.

FROM *The Parthenon*

I : SEEN ALOFT FROM AFAR

Estranged in site,
Aerial gleaming, warmly white,
You look a suncloud motionless
In noon of day divine;
Your beauty charmed enhancement takes
In Art's long after-shine.

FROM

Uncollected Poems

Immolated

Children of my happier prime,
When One yet lived with me, and threw
Her rainbow over life and time,
Even Hope, my bride, and mother to you!
O, nurtured in sweet pastoral air,
And fed on flowers and light, and dew
Of morning meadows—spare, Ah, spare
Reproach; spare, and upbraid me not
That, yielding scarce to reckless mood
But jealous of your future lot,
I sealed you in a fate subdued.
Have I not saved you from the drear
Theft and ignoring which need be
The triumph of the insincere
Unanimous Mediocrity?
Rest therefore, free from all despite,
Snugged in the arms of comfortable night.

Pontoosuce

Crowning a bluff where gleams the lake below,
Some pillared pines in well-spaced order stand
And like an open temple show,
And here in best of seasons bland,
Autumnal noon-tide, I look out
From dusk arcades on sunshine all about.

Beyond the Lake, in upland cheer
Fields, pastoral fields, and barns appear,
They skirt the hills where lonely roads
Revealed in links thro' tiers of woods
Wind up to indistinct abodes
And faery-peopled neighborhoods;
While further fainter mountains keep
Hazed in romance impenetrably deep.

Look, corn in stacks, on many a farm,
And orchards ripe in languorous charm,
As dreamy Nature, feeling sure
Of all her genial labor done,
And the last mellow fruitage won,
Would idle out her term mature;
Reposing like a thing reclined
In kinship with man's meditative mind.

For me, within the brown arcade—
Rich life, methought; sweet here in shade
And pleasant abroad in air!—But, nay,
A counter thought intrusive played,
A thought as old as thought itself,

And who shall lay it on the shelf!—
I felt the beauty bless the day
In opulence of autumn's dower;
But evanescence will not stay!
A year ago was such an hour,
As this, which but foreruns the blast
Shall sweep these live leaves to the dead leaves
past.

All dies!—
I stood in revery long.
Then, to forget death's ancient wrong,
I turned me in the brown arcade,
And there by chance in lateral glade
I saw low tawny mounds in lines
Relics of trunks of stately pines
Ranked erst in colonnades where, lo!
Erect succeeding pillars show!

All dies! and not alone
The aspiring trees and men and grass;
The poet's forms of beauty pass,
And noblest deeds they are undone,
Even truth itself decays, and lo,
From truth's sad ashes fraud and falsehood grow.

All dies!
The workman dies, and after him, the work;
Like to these pines whose graves I trace,
Statue and statuary fall upon their face:
In very amaranths the worm doth lurk,
Even stars, Chaldæans say, have left their place.
Andes and Apalachee tell
Of havoc ere our Adam fell,
And present Nature as a moss doth show
On the ruins of the Nature of the æons of long
ago.

But look—and hark!
                                        Adown the glade,
Where light and shadow sport at will,
Who cometh vocal, and arrayed
As in the first pale tints of morn—
So pure, rose-clear, and fresh and chill!
Some ground-pine sprigs her brow adorn,
The earthy rootlets tangled clinging.
Over tufts of moss which dead things made,
Under vital twigs which danced or swayed,
Along she floats, and lightly singing:

"Dies, all dies!
The grass it dies, but in vernal rain
Up it springs and it lives again;
Over and over, again and again
It lives, it dies and it lives again.
Who sighs that all dies?
Summer and winter, and pleasure and pain
And everything everywhere in God's reign,
They end, and anon they begin again:
Wane and wax, wax and wane:
Over and over and over amain
End, ever end, and begin again—
End, ever end, and forever and ever begin
        again!"

She ceased, and nearer slid, and hung
In dewy guise; then softlier sung:
"Since light and shade are equal set
And all revolves, nor more ye know;
Ah, why should tears the pale cheek fret
For aught that waneth here below.
Let go, let go!"

With that, her warm lips thrilled me through,
She kissed me, while her chaplet cold
Its rootlets brushed against my brow
With all their humid clinging mould.
She vanished, leaving fragrant breath
And warmth and chill of wedded life and death.

FROM *Moby Dick*

Jonah's Song

The ribs and terrors in the whale,
    Arched over me a dismal gloom,
While all God's sun-lit waves rolled by,
    And lift me deepening down to doom.

I saw the opening maw of hell,
    With endless pains and sorrows there;
Which none but they that feel can tell—
    Oh, I was plunging to despair.

In black distress, I called my God,
    When I could scarce believe him mine,
He bowed his ear to my complaints—
    No more the whale did me confine.

With speed he flew to my relief,
    As on a radiant dolphin borne;
Awful, yet bright, as lightning shone
    The face of my Deliverer God.

My song for ever shall record
    That terrible, that joyful hour;
I give the glory to my God,
    His all the mercy and the power.

FROM *Billy Budd*

Billy in the Darbies

Good of the Chaplain to enter Lone Bay
And down on his marrow-bones here and pray
For the likes just o' me, Billy Budd.—But, look:
Through the port comes the moon-shine astray!
It tips the guard's cutlass and silvers this nook;
But 'twill die in the dawning of Billy's last day.
A jewel-block they'll make of me tomorrow,
Pendant pearl from the yard-arm-end
Like the ear-drop I gave to Bristol Molly—
O, 'tis me, not the sentence they'll suspend.
Ay, Ay, all is up; and I must up too
Early in the morning, aloft from alow.
On an empty stomach, now, never it would do.
They'll give me a nibble—bit o' biscuit ere I go.
Sure, a messmate will reach me the last parting
 cup;
But, turning heads away from the hoist and the
 belay,
Heaven knows who will have the running of me
 up!
No pipe to those halyards.—But aren't it all
 sham?
A blur's in my eyes; it is dreaming that I am.
A hatchet to my hawser? All adrift to go?
The drum roll to grog, and Billy never know?
But Donald he has promised to stand by the
 plank;
So I'll shake a friendly hand ere I sink.
But—no! It is dead then I'll be, come to think.—
I remember Taff the Welshman when he sank.

And his cheek it was like the budding pink.
But me they'll lash me in hammock, drop me deep
Fathoms down, fathoms down, how I'll dream fast asleep.
I feel it stealing now. Sentry, are you there?
Just ease these darbies at the wrist,
And roll me over fair,
I am sleepy, and the oozy weeds about me twist.

Notes on the Text

The Portent

On October 16, 1859, John Brown, with a band of eighteen men, attacked the United States Arsenal at Harpers Ferry (then Virginia, now West Virginia), to get weapons to arm slaves whom he intended to rouse to an insurrection. At Charlestown, in the rich and peaceful Shenandoah Valley, he was tried on a charge of treason and inciting a slave rising, convicted and, on December 2, hanged. This was the single most provocative episode in the long series of frictions leading up to the Civil War. The fact that John Brown had been financed by a group of prominent Northern citizens was generally taken in the South as evidence that there was a deep-seated conspiracy, and played into the hands of the Southern "fire-eaters," the extremists who had no hope of, or desire for, a peaceful solution. The Southern reaction, and the hanging of Brown, exacerbated, in turn, the radical abolitionists, and even won them new converts. Though Lincoln and Whittier might agree with Hawthorne that "no man was ever more justly hanged," it was the rhetoric of Emerson, who declared that John Brown had "made the gallows glorious as the cross," that caught the imagination.

But not only in this general sense was the episode of John Brown a "portent." Robert E. Lee, then a colonel, was in command of the regiment of Marines that captured Brown; J. E. B. Stuart, then a lieutenant, was also present and treated with Brown at the door of the engine house where he had holed up with his surviving men for a last stand; and Professor Thomas J. Jackson, later "Stonewall," was commanding cadets of the Virginia Military Institute at the execution at Charlestown: and it was easy for Melville, looking back on the event, to see it as a sort of dress rehearsal for the bloodbath to come.

13 "Weird" has the sense of possessing the power of directing fate and that of suggesting the unearthly and supernatural; and the old man with the beard streaming like the trail of a meteor appears as an omen, and in his complex relation to the course of events is "weird" in the same way as the Weird Sisters in *Macbeth.*

Misgivings

In this poem, the image of the autumn storm repeats and develops the idea of "The Portent." We may even take "brown" in the second line as a kind of pun, linking this poem to that about John Brown. This would be consistent with Melville's practice elsewhere.

12 Here "shouts" is more than a casual descriptive metaphor. In its most obvious sense, it identifies the literal storms with the human violence feared in the future; but, as is developed further in the last two lines of the poem, it also relates the impending human violence to the blind forces of nature, suggesting the idea that historical process may be beyond rational and ethical considerations, may be a kind of "fate." Among the many references elsewhere to this tension between the rational-ethical interpretations of history and one of "necessity," see "The Conflict of Convictions," line 64.

The Conflict of Convictions

Melville's note gives the general background of the poem:

> The gloomy lull of the early part of the winter of 1860–1, seeming big with final disaster to our institutions, affected some minds that believed them to constitute one of the great hopes of mankind, much as the eclipse which came over the promise of the first French Revolution affected kindred natures, throwing them for the time into doubts and misgivings universal.

6 The reference to the "latter fall" is one of the several which set the poem in relation to *Paradise Lost,* and in contrast to it, in the sense that Milton promises a redemption whereas Melville leaves the issue with no final resolution, certainly with none at a supernatural level.

11 Revision: "at which" to "whereat."

35 "Apoplex" is used here in the sense of apoplexy. The

archaic form was used by the Elizabethans, and occurs as late as Coleridge. Here Melville's metaphor has something of the quality of an Elizabethan conceit, and will stand rigorous investigation, one sense of the several being the notion of history as the result of natural cycles of forces, another sense being a questioning of the rational and ethical assumptions of democracy. See Ungar's speeches in *Clarel,* Part IV, Cantos xx ("Derwent and Ungar") and xxi "Ungar and Rolfe"); also III, v ("The High Desert"), lines 117–23.

44 The "Iron Dome" is the new dome of the Capitol. According to the design of Dr. William Thornton, submitted in 1798, the dome was to be of wood, 150 feet in height. Under the supervision of Charles Bulfinch, this dome was completed in 1819. Thomas Ustick Walter, architect of the Capitol (1851–1865), was responsible for the dome of cast and wrought iron, of two shells, one enclosing the other, superimposed on the original, with a height of 287 feet from the base line of the east front to the top of the statue of Freedom. This statue, by Thomas Crawford, was set in place December 2, 1863, in the middle of the Civil War. But "The Conflict of Convictions," with its "dramatic" date of 1860–61, was composed, of course, much later, when the various symbolic implications of the new dome of iron were emerging for Melville.

52 Revision: *"blinking light"* to *"taper dim."*

54 *"A meagre wight"* to *"Which foldeth him."*

64 See "Misgivings," lines 12–14. In the brilliant metaphor here, we have one of the ideas, and ironies, which dominate *Battle-Pieces*—the idea that there may "be a strong necessity" which underlies history. The same idea appears in *Clarel* (II, iv, 106–8). Observe that the word "adore" appears here in the same connection as in "The Fall of Richmond." See note to line 12 of "Dupont's Round Fight." For the human stance in relation to such an irony, see "An Uninscribed Monument," "On a Natural Monument," and "Commemorative of a Naval Victory."

74–79 This passage develops, of course, the irony in the metaphor of the wind in line 64. The war is being fought for freedom, but even in the victory "unanointed" power may come to work against the very assumptions of the old republic, first, by "Dominion" over foreign lands (or over the states that have seceded?), and second, by a diminution of the responsible relation of the individual citizen to the central government—the new Iron Dome becoming, in other words, the image of the new "power state," created in the process of defending the old Union, but in actuality working to destroy the very principles on which the old Union had been established. Many men became very acutely aware of this irony in the period after the Civil War, for instance, Brooks and Henry Adams, James Russell Lowell, and William James. Melville's notion is similar to the more general one of James that might be called the principle of "historic costs." Melville's speculations here are also similar to those of Hawthorne's "Chiefly About War Matters," published in the *Atlantic Monthly,* July 1862. See also "The House-top."

The March into Virginia

In July 1861, General Irvin McDowell with an army of 35,000 men moved from Washington to engage General P. G. T. Beauregard, who commanded a force of 20,000 (to be increased to 30,000, by the arrival of Joseph E. Johnston). The Federal army had total confidence, and the march resembled a picnic more than a military operation. In fact, politicians and other sightseers, with their ladies, came out in carriages, with baskets of food and bottles of champagne, to admire the victory. At Bull Run, near Manassas Junction, after many shifts of advantage and much confusion among the green troops of both sides, Brigadier Thomas J. Jackson's command held "like a stonewall," the Federal attack was crushed, and McDowell's army, with the spectators, fled back to Washington. This was the first significant engagement of the war.

1 The meaning of "let" is hindrance or impediment, archaic and now common only in the phrase "let or hindrance."

6 One of the many polarities in Melville's poetry is that of youth and age. In its "ignorance," youth can commit itself to fate and be capable of action, action which, though sometimes tragic in its consequences, may be also redemptive, if in no other way than by instruction in the nature of manhood and man's role.

9 The verb "abate" is here intransitive. The construction here, as often elsewhere in Melville, is compact and gnarled. The turbid ardors and vain joys (of youth) do not barrenly (without consequences) abate (lessen, or end), but act as

stimulants for mature action, and prepare fate (which is what comes, shall we say, beyond will or knowledge).

13 As with "foreclosure" below, "precedent" is a metaphor based on the law, an echo in all likelihood, of Melville's reading of the Elizabethans.

18 A concealed pun. See Introduction, p. 14.

23 Children sacrificed to Moloch were cast into fire.

27 The "rapture" here ironically repeats the idea in lines 8–11. The relation of "act" and "legend" is a theme that occurs often in Melville, for instance, most effectively in "Battle of Stone River, Tennessee." This is an idea found also in Yeats, as in "Two Songs from a Play." But this also is related to the polarity between individual values and ideology—legend giving us the human stance as contrasted with the principled urgencies of action.

33 See Introduction, p. 14. The whole question of "experience" and knowledge is a constantly recurring theme in Melville, and the Battle of First Manassas is only one image of it.

35 Revision: "shame" to "some."

36 Melville made several attempts to revise this line:

(1) Thy after shock, Manassas, share.
(2) Manassas's second throe and deadlier share.
(3) Thy second shock, Manassas, share.

Numbers (1) and (2) are canceled, but he did not definitely settle on (3), for there is a question mark in the margin.

Ball's Bluff

On October 20, 1861, four regiments of Federal troops were ferried across the Potomac at two points on what was a reconnaissance in force. The next day they were pinned against the river at Ball's Bluff, with a hundred-foot drop behind them. When the green troops broke in rout, the battle became little better than a massacre. In the first volume of *Rebellion Record,* which Melville used for background information and suggestions for *Battle-Pieces* (see Introduction, p. 73), General Stone's report of the engagement, which somewhat modified the picture of panic, was reprinted:

> The enemy pursued to the edge of the bluff over the landing place, and poured in a heavy fire as our men were endeavoring to cross to the island [Harrison's

> Island]. . . . The men formed near the river, maintaining nearly half an hour the hopeless contest rather than surrender. The smaller boats had disappeared, no one knew where. The largest boat, rapidly and too heavily loaded, swamped some fifteen feet from the shore, and nothing was left to our soldiers but to swim, surrender, or die.

The Federal loss was some 1,000 men and the shock was similar to that of First Manassas. Lincoln burst into unashamed tears at the news; his good friend Colonel Edward D. Baker, who though on active service still held his seat in the Senate, was among those killed.

The poem is closely related to "The March into Virginia," but here the emphasis is, objectively, on the pathos of youth "marching lustily," and not on the subjective nature and value of the experience.

8 *Juny* is one of Melville's coined words. See Introduction, p. 15.

16 Behind this last stanza stand the last three stanzas of Keats's "Ode to a Nightingale," specifically evoked by the phrases "easeful sleep," which echoes Keats's "easeful Death," and "Wakeful I mused," which echoes his "Darkling I listen." Though the evocation of the "Ode" occurs merely by the verbal echoes, a mass of ironic counterpoints enter. Was it "rich" for the young soldiers to die? Does the muser envy such "richness"? How does the "ecstasy" in which the bird pours forth its soul "with no pain" relate to the death of the young in their "rapture sharp though transitory" (of "The March into Virginia")? Were the young soldiers "born for death" or are they "immortal" like the bird? Will the dead young soldiers (or their memory) escape being trodden down by the "hungry generations?" The question of the degree of consciousness, or the explicitness with which Melville may have analyzed the body of references, is not, in any final sense, relevant here. He did have the verbal echoes, and verbal echoes cannot be detached from the burden of the passage from which they come—no more in Melville's mind than in ours.

15–21 The stanza is not entirely clear. The following reading might be possible:

> *At my window, at night, I mused on the young soldiers I had seen marching to the battle, thinking that some of*

> *those marching feet had "found pause at last"* (in death) *by the cliffs which the Potomac had made. While I was thus musing, the imagined footfalls of the marching troops faded away.*

But it would seem more likely that the passage would end with this reading:

> *While I was thus musing I heard the literal footfalls of some night-walker, which fused with the recollection, the dying away of the literal footfalls suggesting the now ghostly tread of the troops.*

This reading would seem to make a more active play of the imagination, and would further enrich the poem in that it gives some sense of the loneliness of each soldier as he moves toward his individual fate, the word "footfall" not suggesting, for one thing, the marked rhythm of marching troops.

Dupont's Round Fight

In one of the earliest attempts (November 7, 1861) to gain coastal control and make the blockade effective, a Federal amphibious force of 12,000 men, commanded by Samuel F. Dupont, attacked Fort Royal, South Carolina. Only three river steamers were available for defense on water, but two forts, Fort Walker and Fort Beauregard, protected the port, one on each side of the Broad River, at this point some two and a half miles wide. In the *Rebellion Record,* Melville found a careful map of the battle, with a chart of the operation and a reprint of the report of the New York *Tribune,* summarizing the plan of attack:

> The plan of the attack was simple and effective, being for the ships to steam in a circle, or ellipse, running close to one shore as they came *down* the river, drifting or steaming as slowly as possible past the batteries there, and paying their fiery respects, then making the turn to go back, and as they went *up* the river, favoring the other batteries with a similar compliment.

Under this crushing attack, the defense held out only four hours.

In the *Record,* too, was a longish poem on the battle called "The Bombardment of Forts Walker and Beauregard," by Isaac M'Clellan. One stanza, emphasizing the plan of battle, which is the key to Melville's poem, is of some interest:

> Three times that triple dance he led;
> Three times that circuit, that ellipse so dread,
> Three times 'mid splintering spar and falling dead,
> He led the merciless path.

A detail of the episode which Melville did not use, but which might well have provided him with another poem on a congenial theme, was the fact that Percival Drayton, who was in command of one of the ships making the attack, was the brother of the Confederate General Thomas F. Drayton, of the defending garrison. See note on lines 135–61 of "Bridegroom Dick."

12 The idea of law—or with a different and less moralized implication, necessity—is recurrent in Melville's poetry, one of the poles in an opposition of law and will. In this connection, we may refer to the Supplement in which "destiny" and "fate" appear:

> It is enough . . . if the South have been taught by the terrors of civil war to feel that Secession, like Slavery, is against Destiny; that both now lie buried in one grave; that her fate is linked with ours; and that together we comprise the Nation.

"The Fall of Richmond" (not included in this selection) ends with the lines:

> And Right through might is Law—
> *God's way adore.*

The phrasing here and, indeed, the theme of the poem suggest the view of Justice Holmes on right, might, and law. While recovering from the wound received at Ball's Bluff, the twenty-year-old Holmes had decided that "good" and "general law" were "synonymous terms in the universe," and thus laid the basis for his pragmatic notion that law (and the right) in a society are what has been established by the might of the victorious faction—that, in other words, as he later put it to

Sir Frederick Pollock, "every society rests on the death of men." So we may adore "God's way" by simply equating it with "general law"—that is, with what happens to happen.

In the comparison of the American Civil War with the War of the Roses, in "Battle of Stone River, Tennessee," Melville gives an even more specific statement, here in the mouth of the Oxford don:

> The rival Roses warred for Sway—
> For Sway, but named the name of Right;
> And Passion, scorning pain and death,
> Lent sacred fervor to the fight.

Though the don's interpretation can be taken as only one aspect of Melville's thought, it is very close to the considered view of Holmes, as stated above; and with lines 3 and 4, very close to the notion of Holmes (and of Melville, too) that human virtue and valor, rather than ideological correctness, redeem history. As Holmes put it, in "The Soldier's Faith":

> I do not know the meaning of the universe. But in the midst of doubt, in the collapse of creeds, there is one thing I do not doubt, that no man who lives in the same world with most of us can doubt, and that is that the faith is true and adorable which leads a soldier to throw away his life in obedience to a blindly accepted duty, in a cause which he little understands, in a plan of campaign of which he has no notion, under tactics of which he does not see the use.

To change our subject somewhat, it can be argued that the Civil War is what gave the cutting edge to the rise of pragmatism in America, and here both Melville and Holmes may well be adduced as evidence.

Notice the word "adorable" here. See note on line 64 of "The Conflict of Convictions."

It is also worth remembering that Melville is very close to the doctrine of "necessity" held by his hero Lincoln. Lincoln had read Darwin and Spencer, and according to Herndon, held the belief in a "universal law, evolution, and from this he never deviated." He believed "in laws that imperiously ruled both matter and mind. With him there could be no miracles outside of law . . . There were no accidents in his philosophy . . . Everything to him was the result of the forces of Nature, playing on matter and mind from the beginning of time . . ."

See also "Venice" and note (pp. 439–41).

The Stone Fleet

Melville's note quotes a current report:

> "The terrible Stone Fleet, on a mission as pitiless as the granite that freights it, sailed this morning from Port Royal, and before two days are past will have made Charleston an inland city. The ships are all old whalers, and cost the government from $2500 to $5000 each. Some of them were once famous ships."—(From Newspaper Correspondence of the day.)
>
> Sixteen vessels were accordingly sunk on the bar at the river entrance. Their names were as follows:
>
> Amazon,
America,
American,
Archer,
Courier,
Fortune,
Herald,
Kensington,
Leonidas,
Maria Theresa,
Potomac,
Rebecca Simms,
L. C. Richmond,
Robin Hood,
Tenedos,
William Lee.
>
> All accounts seem to agree that the object proposed was not accomplished. The channel is even said to have become ultimately benefited by the means employed to obstruct it.

The first sentence of Melville's note is drawn from an elaborate account, published in *Rebellion Record* (Vol. II), by the correspondent of the New York *Tribune*, written aboard the *Catawba*, December 17 to December 29, 1861. Along with a map of the harbor approaches, there was a detailed description of the method to be used, the ships being placed "checkerwise." In the "Poetry and Incidents" section of the *Record* Melville would have found one piece of verse on the episode, by P. Remsen Strong, entitled "The Rat-Hole Squadron." Though the poem ends with piety and patriotism, the body of it emphasizes, as does Melville, the pathos of the old ships, the "Shattered wrecks of Time," with "Canvas sere and straining cordage."

17 Another of Melville's metaphors drawn from the law, with an echo of Elizabethan style, is found in "escheat."
33 "Nature is nobody's ally." This theme of the doubleness of nature, or the neutrality of nature, is a recurring one in Melville's poetry.

Donelson

The bitter siege of Fort Donelson, on the Cumberland River, in Tennessee, after the capture of Fort Henry on the Tennessee, lasted from February 13 to February 16, when Simon Bolivar Buckner surrendered unconditionally to Grant. The victory had great strategic importance, opening West Tennessee for the thrust southward that was to lead to Shiloh; but the symbolic importance was, in a sense, greater, for the victory laid the basis of Grant's reputation and began, as Melville puts it (line 416), the "habit of victory."

The relation of Grant and Buckner, though apparently unknown to Melville, bears on his sense of the War. Grant and Buckner had been friends at West Point, and when Grant came back from California, his career ruined, Buckner had given him money, and after the surrender of Fort Donelson, Grant offered him the benefit of his purse. Later, when Grant was dying of cancer of the throat, Buckner called on him, at his house on 66th Street in New York. For them, all had now become "legend." Grant died on July 23, 1885.

In *Rebellion Record,* Melville found, as well as the official reports of General Grant and of Commander Foote of the fleet of gunboats, a very full account from *The New York Times.* Foote's report gave him some details of the *Louisville,* and the *Times* account was very useful, especially with reference to the freezing weather and the sharpshooters of "Birge's celebrated regiment of riflemen," who were like hunters "waylaying deer at a salt-lick." This becomes, in the poem,

Our fellows lurk
Like Indians that waylay the deer
By the wild salt-spring.

Grant's report insisted on the significance of the victory: "Fort Donelson will hereafter be marked in capitals on the map of our united country . . . ."

Melville's use of the bulletins of the battle as a frame for the poem is effective, not only as a device to foreshorten the action but as a means of dramatizing the effect of the battle on the civilian North, after the disasters of First Manassas and Ball's Bluff.

"Donelson," though scarcely a success, is one of Melville's boldest experiments, an attempt to make poetry out of a style based on realistic, documentary prose. A comparison of this poem with some of Browning's work and with Hardy's *Dynasts*, as well as with Hardy's style in general, is fruitful.

28 "Perplex" represents the kind of diction and metaphor, in the context of realistic material, which Hardy might have used.
160 A Copperhead was a Southern sympathizer. There were a significant number in the North, as suppression of newspapers and the suspending of habeas corpus would indicate. The most famous was Clement Laird Vallandigham, Congressman from Ohio.
258–261 This quatrain gives one of the central ideas of *Battle-Pieces*, the polarity of ideology and human values. At the political level, this is argued in the Supplement. See also "The Swamp Angel," "Battle of Stone River, Tennessee," and "On the Slain Collegians."
284 This line suggests Hardy, again.
443 Revision: "deep" to "cross."
446–452 The image of the "death list" flowing down the sheet (superimposed, as it were, on the shadowy image of the real Tennessee River) to meet the "whelming waters" of the unspecified tears of the bereaved, is bold, original, and strong. What other American poet of the period would have risked it?

The Temeraire

Melville's note:

> The *Temeraire*, that storied ship of the old English fleet, and the subject of the well-known painting by Turner, commends itself to the mind seeking for some one craft to stand for the poetic ideal of those great historic wooden warships, whose gradual displacement is lamented by none more than by regularly educated navy officers, and of all nations.

Originally French, the *Temeraire* was a line-of-battle ship of 98 guns, captured by Nelson at the Battle of the Nile, in 1798. In 1805, at Trafalgar, under the command of Captain Hardy (claimed by Thomas Hardy as a kinsman), the *Temeraire*, placed next to Nelson's *Victory*, was involved in the famous episode referred to in lines 21–46. In 1838, she was broken up, and in the following year, Turner's "The Fighting Temeraire" showed her being towed away for this purpose. In London, in 1857, Melville had seen Turner's painting in the National Gallery, as reported in his *Journal Up the Straits*.

Very soon after the battle of the *Monitor* and the *Virginia*, Hawthorne visited Hampton Roads, and reported his impressions in an article "Chiefly About War Matters," in the *Atlantic Monthly*, in July 1862. It is safe to assume that Melville would have read this work of his old friend, which includes the following passage:

> That last gun from the Cumberland, when the deck was half submerged, sounded the requiem of many sinking ships. Then went down all the navies of Europe, and our own, Old Ironsides and all, and Trafalgar and a thousand other fights became only a memory, never to be acted over again: and thus our brave countrymen come last in the long procession of heroic sailors that includes Blake and Nelson, and so many mariners of England, and other mariners as brave as they, whose renown is our native inheritance. There will be other battles, but no more such tests of seamanship and manhood as the battles of the past; and moreover, the Millennium is certainly approaching, because human strife is to be transferred from the heart and personality of man into cunning contrivances of machinery, which by and by will fight out our wars with only the clank and smash of iron, strewing the field with broken engines, but damaging nobody's little finger except by accident.

17 The revision of "fair" to "rare" here is presumably not definite, for "fair" is not canceled, merely underlined.
20 Melville explains "armorial" in a note:

> Some of the cannon of old times, especially the brass ones, unlike the more effective ordnance of the present day, were cast in shapes which Cellini might have designed, were gracefully enchased, generally with the

arms of the country. A few of them—field-pieces—captured in our earlier wars, are preserved in arsenals and navy-yards.

A Utilitarian View of the Monitor's Fight

When the Federal forces, in April 1861, withdrew from Norfolk, they were compelled to abandon and burn the *Merrimac*, one of the five first-class modern vessels of the Navy, a frigate of sail and steam, then decommissioned for repairs. Following the example of the French, who had developed ironclads (really floating batteries rather than ships) and used them effectively against Russian land installations in the Crimean War, the Confederates raised the *Merrimac*, which had burned only to the water's edge and sunk in shallow water, and rebuilt her as an ironclad vessel, this under the supervision of Franklin Buchanan and Catesby ap Roger Jones.

On March 8, 1862, the *Merrimac*, now rechristened the *Virginia*, under the command of Flag Officer Buchanan, with Lieutenant Jones as Executive Officer, entered Hampton Roads, where the Federal blockading fleet lay. Sinking the *Cumberland* and burning the *Congress*, the *Virginia*, in the first naval battle between an ironclad and wooden warships, completely demonstrated her superiority. The next day, March 9, the *Virginia*, now commanded by Jones, Buchanan having been wounded in the first battle, returned to finish off the Federal fleet. She was challenged by the *Monitor*, the first Federal ironclad, just completed in New York by the Swedish inventor John Ericsson, a craft of a more radical conception, armed with two guns mounted in the first revolving turret, of shallower draft and much greater maneuverability than the *Virginia*. The *Monitor*, under the command of Lieutenant L. J. Worden, and the *Virginia* slugged it out for some three hours, to a tactical draw, in the first battle between ironclads. On April 11, the *Virginia* returned but was not challenged, and did not press her own attack.

The battles of March 8 and 9 were recognized by the world as a revolutionary development, and the events deeply affected Melville's imagination. He was to write five poems on the subject, "The Cumberland," "The Temeraire," "In the Turret," "A Utilitarian View of the Monitor's Fight," and, some twenty years later, "Bridegroom Dick." For Hawthorne's comment on the battle, see the general note on "The Temeraire."

Franklin Buchanan, the original commander of the *Virginia,* appears peripherally, and not by name, three times more in connection with Melville's work, with reference to the *Somers* case (see Introduction, p. 58), to "The Battle for the Bay" (not included here), and to "Bridegroom Dick." Buchanan had distinguished himself in the Navy long before the *Somers* case, and when, as a result of that scandal, it was decided to change the method of training officers, he was selected to plan and organize a Naval Academy; he did so, and served as the first commandant at Annapolis. Before the Civil War, he commanded the flagship of Perry's squadron that opened Japan, and was the first officer to step ashore on Japanese soil. Some time after commanding the *Virginia,* he was promoted to admiral (the only admiral in the Confederate Navy); and on the ram *Tennessee,* he fought a gallant single-handed action against the fleet of Farragut at Mobile (see "Bridegroom Dick," line 188), where he was again wounded, and was taken prisoner.

4 Here "orient" is underlined in Melville's copy, but not canceled, and the possible revision "painted" is in the margin.
25 Revision: "shall yet" to "yet shall."
27 Another transposition, as in line 25.

Shiloh

On April 6, 1862, the Confederates, under the command of Albert Sidney Johnston, surprised the Federal army at Shiloh Church, in wooded country near Savannah, Tennessee, and drove it nearly into the Tennessee River. Because of the death of Johnston, the Confederates did not fully exploit their advantage, and with the arrival of Federal reinforcements on April 7, there followed another day of violent and indecisive action; then the Confederates withdrew. It was a battle of enormous losses, the Federals losing 13,000 men, the Confederates 10,000. Grant had managed, by the slimmest margin, to hold the field, and the reputation earned at Donelson weathered the savage attacks on his generalship.

"The structure of the poem," as Hennig Cohen points out in his edition of Melville's poems, "is circular, a counterpart of the wheeling swallows at the beginning and end of what is grammatically a single sentence"—a structure which can be taken as appropriate for the sense of absorption of the human struggle into the cycle of Nature.

16 This brilliant line is, of course, related to the enlightenment that comes, in "The March into Virginia," from the "vollied glare," but here the nature of the enlightenment is somewhat different and simpler: at morning, men were deluded in thinking themselves foes, in accepting certain political and ideological views, in being concerned for fame or patriotism. Now, with the undeceiving of the bullet, they are reconciled in the natural lot of men and, shall we say, returning by implication to another idea of Melville's, in the sense that history, too, is a "natural" process.

Malvern Hill

On July 1, 1862, General George B. McClellan fought Malvern Hill, which did something to retrieve his situation after the failure of his Peninsula Campaign against Richmond. In mood and theme, "Malvern Hill' is a companion piece to "Shiloh." See Introduction, pp. 15–16.

Battle of Stone River, Tennessee

The battle, fought some twenty miles southeast of Nashville, Tennessee, lasted four days, December 30, 1862 to January 2, 1863, with General William Rosecrans in command of the Federal army and General John Breckinridge and General Braxton Bragg in command of the Confederate. The battle was, in itself, indecisive, but the Confederates failed in their objective of clearing Middle Tennessee. See Introduction, pp. 21–22. An entry in Melville's journal on his visit to England in 1857 describes the setting of Oxford as outside of "all the violences of revolutions"—the place, as it were, where "legend" is set against "action." The poem is closely related to the feeling in the Supplement.

1 Tewk[e]sbury and Barnet were two battles of the Wars of the Roses, Barnet in April 1471 and Tewkesbury the next month. In these battles, the House of York definitely established its claim over the Lancastrians and Edward IV ascended the throne.

The House-top

In his note Melville sets the tone of this poem:

> "I dare not write the horrible and inconceivable atrocities committed," says Froissart, in alluding to the remarkable sedition in France during his time. The like may be hinted of some proceedings of the draft-rioters.

Following the enactment of the Conscription Act of 1863, rioting, amounting almost to revolutionary action, broke out in New York City on July 13. There was a considerable pro-Southern sentiment in the city, but the motive of the riots was one of class resentment rather than sectional sympathy, the immediate provocation being the provision in the Act allowing the purchase of immunity from the draft on payment of $300, which, of course, made it "a rich man's war and a poor man's fight." The most obvious targets for resentment were Negroes. A number were tortured and lynched in the streets, and a Negro orphanage was burned. But several parts of the city were occupied by the rioters, and there was widespread property damage with large-scale looting and arson. Order was not restored until troops fresh from the Battle of Gettysburg, including the famous New York 7th regiment, were brought back to the city, and cannon, hub to hub and charged with grape, were turned on the mobs. The disturbance ended on July 16.

18 In the margin of Melville's copy "jars" is a possible revision for "shakes," which is not canceled, only underlined.
19 Draco was an Athenian statesman of the 7th century, B.C., whose code of laws made his name synonymous with severity.
21 John Calvin (Jean Chauvin), a French Protestant theologian, author of the *Institutes* and founder of the religious system bearing his name, was notable for his emphasis on hu-

man depravity, predestination, and salvation by divine grace without reference to works or deserts.

27 In Chapter XXXIV of *White-Jacket,* after a discussion of the evils of flogging, we find the passage:

> Is it lawful for you to scourge a man that is a Roman? asks the intrepid Apostle, well knowing, as a Roman citizen, that it was not. And now, eighteen hundred years after, is it lawful for you, my countrymen, to scourge a man that is an American?

The Armies of the Wilderness

The Wilderness was the name of a large section of almost trackless second-growth timber and tangled underbrush and vine, along the south side of the Rapidan, in Spotsylvania County, Virginia. The spread of time indicated by the dates Melville attaches would include the three major engagements fought on that blind terrain. The first was Chancellorsville, where Lee, after Jackson's famous march to attack the Federal rear, on the evening of May 2, 1863, won a crashing victory, ended Fighting Joe Hooker's drive to Richmond, and cleared the way for Lee's movement into Pennsylvania, which led to Gettysburg. (Jackson was killed by one of his own men at the moment of his greatest coup.) The second battle occurred on May 5, 1864, when Grant, who had recently taken command of the Army of the Potomac, and now moved to his first encounter with Lee, boldly chose the route through the Wilderness. Lee, inferior in numbers and equipment, struck Grant in the Wilderness rather than let him emerge into open country, and precipitated a battle notable for ferocity and valor, and for special horror when the woods caught fire and burned the wounded to death. The Battle of the Wilderness, which was indecisive (Grant losing 17,500 men to Lee's loss of less than 8,000), really merged into the Battle of Spotsylvania which began on May 9. The most interesting and original part of the poem deals, however, with the period of waiting in the winter of 1863–64, when the Federal army, under General George Gordon Meade until Grant took command in March, lay north of the Rapidan, and the Confederates lay just across, both waiting for what promised to be the decisive summer. In plan and style, this poem is very similar to "Donelson," but the temper of some of the lyric interpolations and of the conclusion reminds one of "Shiloh" and "Malvern Hill," as well. See Introduction, p. 16.

8 In the margin of Melville's copy "bravos" appears as a possible revision for "zealots," which is not canceled.
14 Melville tentatively altered "base-ball" to "football" in his copy, "base-ball" not being canceled. Since the scene is one viewed at a great distance through a spy-glass, the football would be more easily discerned.
25 "Gray-back" was slang in the Federal army for a Confederate—like Blue-belly among the Confederates for a Northern soldier.
66 The Wilderness of Paran in the Sinai Peninsula (see Genesis 21: 21).
76 At Chancellorsville Stonewall Jackson's attack did not begin until nearly sunset, and continued for some hours after the full moon had risen.
102 Thomas Fairfax, the sixth baron (1693–1781), inherited from his maternal grandfather, the second baron Culpeper, a colonial governor of Virginia, the land between the Rappahannock and the Potomac, known as the Northern Neck.
125 Grant had a basic distaste for military life and war, and was squeamish about bloodshed.
141 For Mosby, see "The Scout toward Aldie."
161 The Federal army was based on Culpeper (not Culpepper) Court House.
177 The surprise attack at Chancellorsville, when Jackson's command burst out of the woods just at evening.
220 Saba is the biblical Sheba, and Sabæan, a south Arabic language, is known only from a few inscriptions. The traces of the battle are, metaphorically, like such "lore."

On the Photograph of a Corps Commander

This poem is linked with "The Armies of the Wilderness." The hero of the poem is General Winfield Scott Hancock (1824–1886), commander of the II Corps, who, at dawn on the last day of the Battle of Spotsylvania, May 12, led a massive attack on a narrow front (a favorite tactic of Grant's), at the Mule Shoe Salient in the center of Lee's line. Hancock broke through, captured two general officers and several thousand men and would, no doubt, have converted Spotsylvania into a decisive battle, had not General John B. Gordon's savage counterattack flung him back to the first line of trenches, where he was contained at the famous Bloody Angle until past midnight, by which time Lee had consolidated a new line. In 1880, Hancock was candidate for President on the Democratic ticket. The poem, in celebrating the manliness of the Federal officer, hints at the theme of manliness which creates a brotherhood beyond particular side or commitment. See Introduction, pp. 19–20.

5 The spelling "Spottsylvania" is Melville's. Spotsylvania Courthouse was a tiny settlement where the main roads crossed to the southeast of the Wilderness.

9 The idea of "spirit" molding the "form" is probably an echo of the Neo-Platonism which is common in Elizabethan poetry.

The Swamp Angel

Melville's note identifies the "Angel":

> The great Parrott gun, planted in the marshes of James Island, and employed in the prolonged, though at times intermitted bombardment of Charleston, was known among our soldiers as the Swamp Angel.

The text of the note is very similar to the note at the head of a poem by the same title (signed "T. N. J.") in *Rebellion Record:* "The large Parrott gun used in bombarding Charleston from the marshes of James Island is called the Swamp Angel. *Soldier's Letter.*" The poem ends:

> Hear truth by Gospel trumpet blown—
> Shall ye not reap as ye have sown?
> Thistles for thistles, tares for tares,
> The whirlwind's breath—a rain of snares!
>
> The Avenging Angel rides the blast—
> You fired the first gun—we'll fire the last.

It would seem possible that the suggestion for Melville's poem came from the *Record,* but the final meaning of his poem is, of course, very different from that in the poem here quoted from.

3 Here the "hunted and harried" are slaves, for the swamps were famous as a refuge for runaways.

40–45 St. Michael's, characterized by its venerable tower, was the historic and aristocratic church of the town. Michael is, as Melville says in "The Conflict of Convictions" (line 48), the "warrior one." The phrase "our guilty kind" would seem to have a double meaning. First, the idea of the guilt of the white race, as oppressors of the black; second, the idea of the guilt in the human condition, in which case the racial guilt becomes an aspect of the more general guilt. But who is the "Angel over the sea" to whom Michael has fled? The gun, of course; but earlier in the poem (lines 1–2), the gun is identified with the black race, in one dimension of its meaning. Is the passage, then, to be taken as meaning that Michael, the "warrior one" whom the white men of Charleston, in their pride, had assumed to be their protector, has actually, in justice, now become the protector of the black? In which case the Angel to whom Michael has fled is the "coal-black Angel"—i.e., the cannon in the swamp which executes God's justice. The phrase "over the sea" then must refer to the fact that the gun was on James Island, separated from the city by some four and one half miles of water.

The College Colonel

The hero is William Francis Bartlett, who, as a student at Harvard, enlisted and was commissioned a captain in the 20th Massachusetts. Having been wounded and lost a leg in the Peninsula Campaign, he was invalided out; raised and commanded a regiment from West Massachusetts; was wounded three times, at Port Hudson, and in the Wilderness; and was captured in July 1864 at Petersburg, Virginia. Melville had seen Colonel Bartlett on August 22, 1863, when he led his men on a parade in Pittsfield. By this time Bartlett had, of course, lost the leg, and one arm was in splints from a wound received at Port Hudson; but other wounds and the imprisonment were to come. Melville transfers the date of the event.

14 With "lones," we find one of Melville's happier wrenchings of language. The same usage occurs in *Clarel* (I, xiii) in the line: "What isolation lones thy state."

26 The Seven Days, really a continuing battle over 20 miles, ending in Malvern Hill on July 1, 1862, marked the failure of McClellan's thrust at Richmond known as the Peninsula Campaign.

29 In the siege of Petersburg, in the summer of 1864, a Pennsylvania regiment with a number of miners in its ranks, ran a tunnel under the Confederate lines and laid a charge of four tons of powder. A Negro division, trained for the assault, was withdrawn for political reasons, and at the last minute white troops, unprepared and uncommanded (two commanders of divisions were drunk in a dugout), made the abortive attack. The explosion had taken place at dawn on July 30th. By afternoon, a heavy counterattack and concentrated artillery fire had controlled the break. Grant described the "Crater" as a "stupendous failure."

30 Libby Prison, in Richmond, a former tobacco warehouse, held some 1,000 captured Federal officers in cramped quarters and, as the war progressed, with inadequate diet. A system for exchange of prisoners broke down; Grant opposed it on the grounds that because the shortage of manpower was acute in the South, exchanges benefited the Confederacy.

31 The "truth" can be equated with the enlightenment from the "vollied glare" in "The March into Virginia." But in neither poem is the content of the "truth" specified: the reader must sense it from the context in the individual poem and the general context. This "open-endedness" is one of the features of Melville's method. For another example, see "Ball's Bluff."

"The Coming Storm"

Melville was a lover of art and, in the modest way which his means permitted, a collector of pictures. The artist here referred to is Robert Swain Gifford, a native of Massachusetts (1840–1905), a well-known painter and a teacher at Cooper Union. The picture was shown at the fortieth annual exhibit of the National Academy of Design, where Melville saw it, presumably a little after the assassination of Lincoln. The "E. B." who owned the picture was Edwin Booth, the brother of John Wilkes Booth, who had been playing *Hamlet* in Boston at the time of the death of Lincoln. These facts indicate the set of associations from which the theme of the poem grew.

"Shakespeare's pensive child" (Edwin Booth) "who felt this picture" as some "presage dim," could have had no "utter surprise" at the act of his brother, because having studied the lines of Shakespeare, "steeped in fable, steeped in fate," he knew that the human heart, like the heart of Hamlet and the world Hamlet discovered, was one in which good and evil are inextricably and tragically mixed. This poem echoes the "presage dim" which is the subject of "Misgivings."

"The Coming Storm," however, echoes something more than another poem. It echoes the winter of 1849 when Melville began his serious reading of Shakespeare and was overwhelmed and buffeted by the experience—by, as F. O. Matthiessen would have it (*American Renaissance* pp. 412–459), the discovery of Shakespeare's "blackness," which made him the "profoundest of thinkers." Melville seems to have found the same release of his powers through the immersion in Shakespeare that he was shortly to find in the acquaintance with Hawthorne's *Mosses from an Old Manse* and the discovery of his "blackness." See *The Trying Out of Moby Dick*, by Howard P. Vincent, pp. 36–37.

11–12 These two lines show a not uncharacteristic crabbedness and obscurity. Perhaps it can be read as follows: The Hamlet in Edwin Booth's heart would be aware that such hearts (as that of E. B. himself) could anticipate (this is one of the several senses of "antedate"). such an act as his brother's.

"Formerly a Slave"

Elihu Vedder, like Melville of Dutch background (born in New York 1836, died in Rome 1923), is best known for the five symbolic murals in the Library of Congress: "Good and Bad Government," and for his illustrations of the *Rubáiyát of Omar Khayyám,* but is also represented in several leading museums. Melville was particularly taken by his work, presumably because of its symbolic quality, and in 1891, though he was not acquainted with him, dedicated *Timoleon* to him; but Melville was dead before Vedder's grateful note reached him.

This particular picture described in the catalogue of the National Academy of Design in 1865 as "Jane Jackson, formerly a slave . . . drawing in oil-color," had as a model an old Negro woman who sold peanuts on Broadway and whom Vedder often encountered. In his autobiographical *Digressions,* he writes of her: "Her meekly bowed head and a look of patient endurance touched my heart and we became friends. She had been a slave down South, and had, at that time, a son, a fine tall fellow, she said, fighting in the Union Army."

9–12 The whole of the last stanza is a rather subtly developed metaphor. As the slave woman has been an outsider looking in at the "revel" of the privileged whites, so now, as she looks into the future, she is still an outsider—though a benign one—to the imagined revel of her own descendants. The phrase "sober light" may be taken in a double sense: first, there is the inner light of her own "sober" happiness; second, there is the reflected gleam on the dark face peering from shadow.

12 "Sibylline" raises a question. In his *Digressions,* Vedder says: "Time went on [after the picture of Jane Jackson] and I found myself in a mood. As I always try to embody my moods in some picture, this mood found its resting place in the picture of 'The Cumean Sybil.' Thus, this fly—or rather this bee from my bonnet—was finally preserved in amber-varnish and, thus, Jane Jackson became the Cumean Sibyl." But the date of the picture of the Sibyl is 1876 and *Battle-Pieces* had appeared in 1866. Had Melville's impression of Jane Jackson as "Sibylline" provided the germ of Vedder's inspiration?

On the Slain Collegians

Melville's note gives the background of the poem:

> The records of Northern colleges attest what numbers of our noblest youth went from them to the battle-field. Southern members of the same classes arrayed themselves on the side of Secession; while Southern seminaries contributed large quotas. Of all these, what numbers marched who never returned except on the shield.

Melville's attitude here is very close to that of Charles Francis Adams, who, in an address at Washington and Lee University (where Lee had been president after the War), on the centennial of Lee's birth, declared that, under the same circumstances, he would have done the same as Lee. "It may have been treason," he continued, ". . . but he awaits sentence at the bar of history in very respectable company. Associated with him are, for instance, . . . John Hampden, the original *Pater Patriae,* Oliver Cromwell, the Protector of the English Commonwealth, Sir Harry Vane, once a governor of Massachusetts, and George Washington, a Virginian of note." See Introduction, pp. 19, 27.

44 As a tentative revision in Melville's copy, "all" is in the margin for "both," which is not canceled.
46 In the margin, "be" is revised to "put," with "be" canceled.

America

This is the last, and summarizing, item of the main body of *Battle-Pieces,* the vision of reconciliation. Thematically, as such a vision, it follows "On the Slain Collegians," which, as the celebration of the virtues of the combatants of both sides and of the shared pathos, lays a basis for such a reunification of the country. As for the virtues of "America" as a poem, the less said the better. See Introduction, p. 31.

1 The phrase "sunny Dome" echoes both "Kubla Khan" and "The Conflict of Convictions." The "sunny Dome" had been first seen, the poem says, in the happy days before the Civil War. Then it had been, as it were, a "pleasure dome," but there had been the dire associations, as in Kubla's mystic demesne, with "Ancestral voices prophesying war." Thus, in "The Conflict of Convictions," the "sunny Dome" becomes the "Iron Dome"—which, presumably, it remains, even in victory. Though this is not to be taken as the whole account of Melville's attitude toward victory, its presence here is further documented by the lines describing the figure of America when she rises from her foul dream. Though she now carries

> Law on her brow and empire in her eyes,

it must be observed that she stands with "graver eye." In other words, things will never be quite the innocent same.
3 Berenice II, of Cyrene, Egyptian princess, wife of Ptolemy III, of 3rd century B.C., dedicated her locks in the temple of Aphrodite to insure the safe return of her husband from a mili-

tary campaign. It was reported by the astronomer Conon of Samos that her locks had become a constellation—the *Coma Berenices.*

29 With the phrase "earth's foundations bare" we have another echo from "The Conflict of Convictions," line 65.

42 See Introduction, pp. 19–20, and Supplement.

45 See "Dupont's Round Fight" for another use of the notion of "law."

The Fortitude of the North

At the second battle of Manassas, on August 29–30, 1862, Lee decisively defeated General John Pope, repeating the victory of a little over a year before. The theme, of course, is the same as that of "The March into Virginia," but the application here is to the North and not to individual soldiers.

1 "They take no shame" is transposed in Melville's copy to "No shame they take."

5 With the "Cape of Storms," we find Melville's favorite image for the crisis that makes possible the recognition of truth.

Inscription

On December 11, 1862, General Ambrose Burnside, with 122,000 men, forced passage of the Rappahannock River to attack Fredericksburg, which Lee, with 78,000 men, held. After other assaults failed, the attack was ordered on December 13 on Marye's Heights, at the base of which Longstreet's I Corps held the stone wall along a sunken road. Some 9,000 men were lost in the assault, to some 1,500 for the Confederates. Burnside withdrew. "It can hardly be in human nature," one observer said, "for men to show more valor, or generals manifest less judgment."

An Uninscribed Monument

See "The Armies of the Wilderness," "On the Photograph of a Corps Commander," "The College Colonel," and Introduction, pp. 19–21.

A Requiem

This poem is a counterpoint in theme to "An Uninscribed Monument on one of the Battle-fields of the Wilderness." See also "Shiloh" and "Malvern Hill."

The general structure of the poem is simple, falling into three distinct divisions:

(1) When, after storms, comes dawn, all earthly creatures rejoice.

(2) So, after gales, when dawn comes, do all ocean creatures—

(3) Except those "forever from joyance torn . . ."

But within these units, particularly in the first and second, the progression is by accretion rather than logic. We may note, too, that from line 9 to the end, that is, through sections 2 and 3, we have only one sentence, a sentence peculiarly loose in syntax. In the same spirit in which Hennig Cohen suggests that the structure of "Shiloh" (which, too, consists of one sentence) "is circular, a counterpart of the wheeling swallows" (see note on "Shiloh"), so we may surmise that Melville was here trying (consciously or unconsciously) to give a "counterpart" appropriate to the swaying, fluent motion of the "pale streams" that wash the bodies away. By Melville's own statement in "A Utilitarian View of the Monitor's Fight," he was there trying to adapt a technique to the subject; but we should also remember that in certain other poems we find examples of the same kind of loose syntax with no hint that they have any relation to decorum of style.

15 Here "Frolic" is an adjective, a form derived from Melville's reading in seventeenth-century poetry (as in Herrick's "Out-did the meat, out-did the frolic wine"). As it stands, the word cannot be a verb, for if "he" (line 13) is taken as the subject, the form should be "frolics," and if "things" (line 14) are doing the frolicking, then we need a relative pronoun as subject. But, of course, Melville could leave messes, as in lines 33–34 in "Pontoosuce."

19–24 Here is another echo of "Lycidas."

On a Natural Monument

The background of this poem is found in Melville's note:

> Written prior to the founding of the National Cemetery at Andersonville, where 15,000 of the reinterred captives now sleep, each beneath his personal head-board, inscribed from records found in the prison-hospital. Some hundreds rest apart and without name. A glance at the published pamphlet containing the list of the buried at Andersonville conveys a feeling mournfully impressive. Seventy-four large double-columned pages in fine print. Looking through them is like getting lost among the old turbaned head-stones and cypresses in the interminable Black Forest of Scutari, over against Constantinople.

This completes the little cluster of three poems dealing with the death of the "nameless."

Commemorative of a Naval Victory

This poem is set in contrast to the preceding three, in that the poet is here dealing, not with the nameless dead, but with the hero who survives to feast on his "festal fame."

4 With the "wave" we have an implied pun: the sea, which tempers human courage, and the lines in the Damascus blade left by the process of tempering with water.
8 Titian's picture is supposed to be "The Man with a Falcon."
24–27 Here the contrast between the living hero and the nameless dead is specified, and related to Melville's characteristic theme of the "elate" man. See Introduction, p. 4. See also the thematic role of other sharks in "In a Bye-Canal" and "The Maldive Shark."

The Scout toward Aldie

In April 1864, Melville, with a pass procured through Senator Sumner, visited "Mosby's Confederacy," the section known as the Wilderness, which was overrun by Mosby's command. Here

Melville accompanied a scouting party, under the command of Major William H. Forbes, of the Massachusetts Second Cavalry. In camp, Melville had heard of the young bride of Colonel Charles Russell Lowell, who had spent a period in the Wilderness, and this episode, coupled with the death of Colonel Lowell shortly thereafter, gave him the germ of the poem.

Melville's note reads as follows:

> Certain of Mosby's followers, on the charge of being unlicensed foragers or fighters, being hung by order of a Union cavalry commander, the Partisan promptly retaliated in the woods. In turn, this also was retaliated, it is said. To what extent such deplorable proceedings were carried, it is not easy to learn.
>
> South of the Potomac in Virginia and within a gallop of the Long Bridge at Washington, is the confine of a country, in some places wild, which throughout the war it was unsafe for a Union man to traverse except with an armed escort. This was the chase of Mosby, the scene of many of his exploits or those of his men. In the heart of this region at least one fortified camp was maintained by our cavalry, and from time to time expeditions were made therefrom. Owing to the nature of the country and the embittered feeling of its inhabitants, many of these expeditions ended disastrously. Such results were helped by the exceeding cunning of the enemy, born of his wood-craft, and, in some instances, by undue confidence on the part of our men. A body of cavalry, starting from camp with the view of breaking up a nest of rangers, and absent say three days, would return with a number of their own forces killed and wounded (ambushed), without being able to retaliate further than by foraging on the country, destroying a house or two reported to be haunts of the guerrillas, or capturing noncombatants accused of being secretly active in their behalf.
>
> In the verse the name of Mosby is invested with some of those associations with which the popular mind is familiar. But facts do not warrant the belief that every clandestine attack of men who passed for Mosby's was made under his eye, or even by his knowledge.
>
> In partisan warfare he proved himself shrewd, able, and enterprising, and always a wary fighter. He stood

> well in the confidence of his superior officers, and was employed by them at times in furtherance of important movements. To our wounded on more than one occasion he showed considerate kindness. Officers and civilians captured by forces under his immediate command were, so long as remaining under his orders, treated with civility. These things are well known to those personally familiar with the irregular fighting in Virginia.

There were many guerrilla bands roving the South, Unionist or Confederate in sympathy, or simply outlaws and deserters from either side, acting under the cover of principle. But Mosby's rangers were actually the 43rd Virginia Cavalry, and in his reminiscences he asserts: "I always wore the Confederate uniform, with the insignia of my rank." In the last few weeks, just before Appomattox, he was officially in command of Northern Virginia. He was anything but a ruffian, a young man of breeding and education, with a wide range of reading in classical literatures, and a training in the law. In politics, he had been opposed to secession and to slavery, but he went with his state and section. He had dash, humor, total courage, and a genius for the tactics of irregular warfare. His success was so great that his presence in the section north of the Rappahannock was an important factor in tying Grant's operations to the Tidewater, and the section he controlled, or at least rendered highly unhealthy, was known as "Mosby's Confederacy." On one occasion, he almost captured General Grant himself. In 1864, Grant had ordered that any of Mosby's men should, if captured, be hanged without trial, an order somewhat blunted by Mosby's retaliation in kind. But a strange friendship sprang up between Mosby and Grant at the end of the war, and Grant overrode Stanton, who after Appomattox had excluded Mosby from parole. After the war, Mosby wrote two notable books, *Mosby's War Reminiscences and Stuart's Cavalry Campaigns* and *Stuart's Cavalry in the Gettysburg Campaign.* In Grant's second campaign for the Presidency, Mosby voted for him, and was entertained at the White House.

Edmund Wilson, in *Patriotic Gore,* says that "The Scout toward Aldie" should be placed among Melville's stories like *Benito Cereno* and *Billy Budd.* He develops this idea as follows:

> What we recognize, of course, in this story is Melville's familiar theme: the pursuit or the persecution by one being of another, with an ambivalent relation between them which mingles repulsion and attraction but which binds them inescapably together: *Captain Ahab* and *Moby Dick*, *Claggart* and *Billy Budd*, *Babo* and *Don Benito*. For though the death of the young colonel is a tragedy and though Mosby plays the role of menace, the whole poem, in a way characteristic of Melville, involves a glorification of Mosby. We are made to feel that the colonel has a kind of fatal rendezvous with the sinister ranger, that he is drawn to his opponent by a kind of spell that is somehow a good deal more powerful than the attraction which had drawn him to his bride.
>
> Yet the story, though so personal a product of Melville's imagination, has also its historical significance in its insight into one aspect of the Civil War. What Melville has revealed in the fanciful tale inspired by his visit to his cousin is a mutual fascination of each of the two camps with the other, the intimate essence of a conflict which, though fratricidal, was also incestuous . . . . This peculiar entanglement with one another of the American North and South was, after the war, to give rise to a formula of romantic fiction which continued to be popular for decades and which produced all those novels and plays in which two lovers, one Northern, one Southern, though destined for one another, are divided by their loyalties to their different flags.

Wilson also suggests that the "central North-South relationship" may have in it a latent homosexual component which may appear in "The Scout toward Aldie."

13 See the shark in "Commemorative of a Naval Victory."

35 In this line there is a thematic relation to "The Conflict of Convictions" and to "The House-top." In the first, the Dome, as the sign of the virtues of the Union and democracy, is set against its shadow which may possibly become contrary to its original meaning; and here the Dome is set against Mosby, an opposing force, a "shark" figure. In the second poem, another inner tension of democracy is presented.

36 In the margin of his copy of *Battle-Pieces*, Melville cor-

rected "scout" to "ride" but did not cancel the original, presumably indicating the tentative nature of the revision.
53 The word "elate" ties the situation thematically to "Commemorative of a Naval Victory."
73 Here is an echo, verbal and thematic, of "The March into Virginia."
100 In the margin of the volume, Melville revises "lonesome" to "dreary," but does not cancel the original word.
115 Melville's note on this runs:

> In one of Kilpatrick's earlier cavalry fights near Aldie, a Colonel who, being under arrest, had been temporarily deprived of his sword, nevertheless, unarmed, insisted upon charging at the head of his men, which he did, and the onset proved victorious.

146 Again in the margin, Melville makes the tentative revision of "spell-bound land" for "strange lone land."
162 Melville revised "They leave the road" to "The road they leave."
200 Marginal revision: "deemed" for "thought."
206 "They skirt the pool" is reversed.
219–220 Here the youth-age contrast links this poem again to "The March into Virginia."
266 In the margin: "to think is brief" is revised to "for thought is brief," and the original is canceled.
540 Tentative revision: "Comrades" for "My blue-birds," which is not canceled.
644 Tentative revision: "This gold lace gleams" for "One's buttons shine," not canceled.
684 Tentative revision: "astray" for "lone and lost," not canceled.

Lee

This poem is closely related to "America" and the Supplement. Melville's note reads as follows:

> Among those summoned during the spring just passed to appear before the Reconstruction Committee of Congress was Robert E. Lee. His testimony is deeply interesting, both in itself and as coming from him. After

various questions had been put and briefly answered, these words were addressed to him:

"If there be any other matter about which you wish to speak on this occasion, do so freely." Waiving this invitation, he responded by a short personal explanation of some point in a previous answer, and, after a few more brief questions and replies, the interview closed.

In the verse a poetical liberty has been ventured. Lee is not only represented as responding to the invitation, but also as at last renouncing his cold reserve, doubtless the cloak to feelings more or less poignant. If for such freedom warrant be necessary, the speeches in ancient histories, not to speak of those in Shakespeare's historic plays, may not unfitly perhaps be cited.

The character of the original measures proposed about this time in the National Legislature for the treatment of the (as yet) Congressionally excluded South, and the spirit in which those measures were advocated —these are circumstances which it is fairly supposable would have deeply influenced the thoughts, whether spoken or withheld, of a Southerner placed in the position of Lee before the Reconstruction Committee.

27 Arlington was the estate of Lee's wife. See note to line 70.

37 John Pope (1822–1892) was the Federal general defeated by Lee at the second battle of Manassas (August 29–30, 1862).

70 Robert E. Lee belonged to the section and class that produced Washington, and the Lee family was closely identified with the Revolution. Henry Lee, his father (1756–1818), famous as a leader of cavalry, was known as Light-Horse Harry. After the Revolution, he served in the Virginia House of Delegates and in the Continental Congress, was a member of the Virginia Convention that ratified the United States Constitution, and later sat in Congress. He was the author of the epitaph of George Washington, "First in war, first in peace, and first in the hearts of his countrymen." Two other kinsmen of Robert E. Lee link the name to the Revolution. Francis Lightfoot Lee (1734–1797) and his brother Richard Henry Lee (1732–1794) were both active in the Revolutionary movement and both members of the Continental Congress, the latter on June 7, 1776, introducing the resolution that "these united colonies are and of right ought to be free . . ."—the resolution, of course, that led to the Declaration of Independence a month later. A further link with Washington and the Revolution was Lee's marriage to Mary Ann Randolph Custis, Martha Washington's great-granddaughter. One son was named for George Washington.

133 In the margin of Melville's copy of *Battle-Pieces*, "these" is changed to "those," and the original is canceled.

152 Tentative revision: "or" for "and," not canceled.

187 Lucius Cornelius Sulla, general in the civil war (88–82 B.C.) against the followers of Marius, was the first Roman to lead an army against Rome. Upon victory, he instituted sweeping and bloody proscriptions of the Marians and became an all-powerful dictator.

200 In his copy of *Battle-Pieces* Melville wrote a revision of this line:

> Forbear to wreak the ill you reprobate.

But the original line is not canceled.

A Meditation

The report of the correspondent of the Cincinnati *Commercial* on the surrender of Vicksburg, in *Rebellion Record* (Vol. VII) seems to have suggested the end of this poem:

> As melancholy a sight as ever one witnessed, for brave men conquered and humbled, no matter how vile the cause for which they fight, present always a sorrowful spectacle, and these foes of ours, traitors and enemies of liberty and civilization though they be, are brave, as many a hard-fought field can attest. They marched out of their entrenchments by regiments upon the grassy declivity outside their fort; they stacked their arms, hung their colors upon the centre, laid off their knapsacks, belts, cartridge-boxes, and cap-pouches, and thus shorn of the accoutrements of the soldier returned inside their works, and thence down the Jackson road into the city. The men went through the ceremony with that downcast look so touching on a soldier's face; not a word was spoken; there was none of that gay badinage we are so much accustomed to hear from the ranks of regiments marching through our streets; the

few words of command necessary were given by their own officers in that low tone of voice we hear used at funerals.

Note on *Clarel*

(*Clarel* is divided into four parts: Jerusalem, The Wilderness, Mar Saba, and Bethlehem. Each part contains a large number of cantos, of varying length. Reference in the notes is to part and canto—for example, the canto "Nathan," in Part I, would be referred to as I, xvii.)

The Hostel

10 The Epiphany, January 6, is the festival of the coming of the Magi. The poem is pegged, as it were, to the Christian calendar.

24 Siloh is the Pool of Siloam (see note to line 147). See John 9: 1–7, for the miracle of the healing of the blind man, as contrasted with the "naturalistic knell."

38 The plain of Sharon, in Israel, stretching along the coast from Jaffa (Tel Aviv) to Mount Carmel, was famous for fertility.

58 Louis IX was canonized in 1297. Walter Bezanson, in his edition of *Clarel,* quotes from Chateaubriand's account in *Travels in Greece, Palestine, Egypt, and Barbary,* how the pagans used machines to raise the burning sands of the desert against the Christians. This occurred during the second crusade undertaken by Louis (the Eighth Crusade), this against Tunis, where he died in 1270.

64 Salem is the ancient name for Jerusalem. The actual dreariness of Jerusalem as contrasted with romantic expectations repeats a fundamental theme in Melville's poetry; another version of the "Cape" theme.

139 Mount of Olives, with the Garden of Gethsemane at the base, just east of the walled city of Jerusalem.

147 Hezekiah, in the late 8th century B.C., was a purifier of religion and an enemy of idolatry; was victorious over the Philistines; and when Jerusalem was besieged by the Assyrians under Sennacherib, held the city. The biblical account (II Kings 19:35) is that the Angel of the Lord visited the Assyrian encampment and in one night slew 185,000 men. For a time it was assumed that the literal explanation of the miracle was a sudden outbreak of a plague, but now it is generally held that the Assyrians simply gave up and bit by bit withdrew.

The threat of an Assyrian attack, long anticipated by Hezekiah, had led to one of his great achievements, the building of the pool of Hezekiah. Fearing that Jerusalem might be reduced by cutting off the water supply, he had sealed off the cave of Gihon, which was outside the walls, and had dug a tunnel of 600 yards to lead the water into the city (II Kings 20:20, II Chronicles 32:30), thus not only guaranteeing the water to the city but depriving any besiegers. It is possible that thirst, not a plague, lifted the siege. The reservoir created by Hezekiah was known as the Pool of Siloam.

161 The Copts are the native Christians of Egypt, descendants of the ancient Egyptians, who in the fifth century separated from the Orthodox Church, and have maintained their own succession of patriarchs.

Of the Crusaders

7 Gibbon, in describing how the Crusaders, after the massacre performed at the capture of Jerusalem, were taken by a fit of tearful piety, says: "This union of the fiercest and most tender passions has been variously considered by two philosophers: by the one as easy and natural; by the other, as absurd and incredible" (Ch. lxviii). The philosophers are Hume and Voltaire: "So inconsistent is human nature with itself!" (Hume, *History of England,* Ch. vi); "Mais cette tendresse qui se manifesta par des pleurs n'est guère compatible avec cet esprit de vertige, de fureur, de débauche, et d'emportement." (Voltaire, *Essai sur les moeurs et l'esprit des nations,* Ch. liv). Melville finds an example here of one of his basic themes, the contrast between the "abysm" and the "star." The placing of the theme at this point in the poem is given, as it were, by the facts of history, but it is also demanded dramatically. The poem is concerned not only with the doubleness of human nature, but with the doubleness of "truth" in the working out of history: is history a meaningful progress or a meaningless process, all being, as Margoth will put it, "chemistry"?

14 The "Calabrian steep" is an echo of Melville's visit to Italy.

23 Tancred is the Norman hero of the First Crusade (1096–1099), famous in the battle of Ascalon and at the taking of Jerusalem, and celebrated in Tasso's *Gerusalemme liberata.* According to Gibbon, Tancred was the only Crusader who showed human pity (Ch. lviii).

Nathan

In Melville's *Journal* we find two figures encountered during his own journey that have a bearing on Nathan. One is a certain Warder Crisson, of Philadelphia, who had become a convert to Judaism, and who had a Jewish wife. The other is a native of Groton, Massachusetts, Devin Dickson, who had brought wife and children to Palestine to help prepare the way for the return of the Jews to Zion. In general, Nathan is an example of the religious ferment of nineteenth-century America, with its proliferation of sects and fanatical pieties. But more particularly, Nathan is one of the projections of Melville—or rather, of one aspect of Melville's nature—in the poem. See lines 194–199, which might well be taken to describe Melville's own motive in writing *Clarel:* the world of Nathan has all the elements encountered by Melville (or Clarel) in the debates, and in the background of the debates, in the Holy Land.

18 "Esdraleon" is a typographical error for "Esdraelon," the great plain extending west from Mount Gilboa to Mount Carmel on the coast.
22–23 "Pantherine" means spotted like a panther. The libbard-lily is the leopard-lily (*lilium pardalinum*). Libbard is an archaic variant of leopard. The lilies on the prairie appear again in the prose headnote to "John Marr" (p. 281). The scene here and that in the headnote are echoes of Melville's trip to the Middle West, in 1840, when he was turning twenty-one, to visit his uncle Thomas Melville, in Galena, Illinois, and seek his fortune. The feckless uncle was in no position to help his nephew, or even his own sons, and Melville's venture came to nothing except in the references mentioned here, and in *The Confidence Man.*
27 The Sporades are islands in the Aegean, including Melos, Thera, and Kos. This is also echoed in the headnote to "John Marr."

39 The Saco is a river rising in the White Mountains and flowing into the Atlantic near Portland, Maine.
84 The Ammonoosuc is a river rising near the source of the Saco and flowing west into the Connecticut River.
89 This is a reference to the slide that on August 28, 1836, at Crawford Notch in the White Mountains, overwhelmed a certain Willey, his wife, five children, and two hired men as they fled from the cabin, which had seemed to be in the path of the avalanche. The cabin, however, was spared, the slide being divided by a ledge on the slope above. Melville knew the region, and the story, with its overtones symbolic of the irrationalities and ironies of human fate. See also Hawthorne's "The Ambitious Guest," which has the same setting. As for the place of the episode in Nathan's philosophical development, it echoes an idea very important to Melville himself, most succinctly stated in "The Stone Fleet" in the line, "Nature is nobody's ally."
104 The "dusty book" is Thomas Paine's *The Age of Reason,* which was famous throughout the nineteenth century and into the twentieth as the prime document of infidelity. In some rural communities it is even now referred to with pious horror.
125 The Scot is well chosen for his role here, for the reputation of the breed in back-country America was a double one —on one hand that of the grim Presbyterian, and on the other, that of the hard-bitten "rationalist," perhaps a reader of David Hume, who, among the more literate of the faithful, shared the infamy of Paine.
166 Favonius is identified with Zephyrus in Roman mythology, the warm west wind bringing spring.
205 The name Nerea does not appear in classical dictionaries. It is possible that Melville derived it from Nereus and the Nereids, setting the pagan and poetic charm of a sea-nymph against the sibylline truth of Miriam, the sister of Moses. But it would seem more likely that the name may be a misprint, or a mis-remembering, of Neaera, in "Lycidas," in which case the "tangles of Neaera's hair" give us Nerea's "amorous net."
210 Rephaim is, in biblical geography, a valley southwest of Jerusalem. By Rama[h], Melville presumably means the home of Samuel, some ten miles north of Jerusalem; it is not a plain but a "high place."

Of Mortmain

7 The Black Jew is Abdon, the host of the inn where Clarel stops in Jerusalem. According to Bezanson, he is of the Cochin Jews who had wandered to India before the destruction of Jerusalem. Abdon, after living in Europe, has come back to be buried here with his forefathers.

24–25 Mortmain is the revolutionary humanist who, seeking the "uncreated Good" (line 49), is open to disillusionment because he expects that "faith" to take the place of religious certitude as well as that of the human warmth he has been deprived of. In this situation he is parallel to Clarel, who expects human love to serve as the surrogate of Divine love. Implicit in the name Mortmain is the suggestion that mere humanism is death. (See the discussion of the dog in *The Waste Land* in Cleanth Brooks's *Modern Poetry and the Tradition.*) But another suggestion may also lurk in the name. The meaning of the legal term *mortmain* is that the dead hand of the past controls the present. Here Mortmain has been committed to the enterprise of bringing forth the "uncreated Good"—that is, he would redeem the world from the evils of the past. But the dead hand of the past has prevailed. The doom of history, and all that it signifies, including the nature of man, has prevailed. And we may add that Mortmain's personal doom, springing from his parents and involving the "unrenderable thing" (line 133), has prevailed over his effort to free himself.

29 Psalmanazer is the pseudonym of a French adventurer whose *Memoirs* were published in 1764.

40 The period of 1840–1850 was the "decade dim"—dim in that the reasons for the violent social disturbances were not understood. The passage gives one pole of Melville's discussion of the problem of history. See "Misgivings" and "The Conflict of Convictions."

99 "Forty-eight" was the year of revolutionary ferment all over Europe. In France, in the face of rioting, Louis Philippe was forced to abdicate, and a republic was proclaimed; but the change could not deal with the economic problems, and the worst street fighting in the history of Paris ensued. When order had been restored, Louis Napoleon was elected President, but shortly thereafter assumed the title of Emperor. In Vienna, in

the same year, Metternich was overthrown; and revolution broke out in Germany, Bohemia, Hungary, and Italy, and the Chartist Movement occurred in England. A new element in the revolutionary unrest was the doctrine of a systematic socialism. Karl Marx and Friedrich Engels issued the *Communist Manifesto* on the eve of the revolutions of 1848. In III, i, lines 148–172, Mortmain again refers to 1848, saying that God may as well manifest himself in the destructive violence of revolution as in the brimstone that fell on the cities of the plain.

100–105 Conservative forces consolidated power after 1848. The German Empire was established. Italy was unified. Napoleon III entered on his career as Emperor.

108 The same idea occurs in *Battle-Pieces.*

124 Micah, the prophet, was a contemporary of Isaiah, at the end of the 8th century B.C., under Hezekiah. He proclaimed the fall of Israel and Judah, but offered hope of redemption through the Messiah. See Micah 6:8: "What doth the Lord require of thee, but to do justly, and to love mercy, and to walk humbly with thy God?"

128–145 The passage connects Mortmain's politics and philosophy with his unspecified sexual history, "some unrenderable thing" beyond even the "bale Medean" of his mother, who had rejected him. The "Syren" here is reminiscent, in another tonality, of the "Sirens" of "In a Bye-Canal."

Concerning Hebrews

The discussion in this canto is provoked by Margoth, the Jewish geologist. Margoth, who first appears at the Dung Gate of Jerusalem, is the spokesman for an extreme version of scientific materialism and the avowed enemy of all spiritual concerns, not merely religious ones. In person, he is squat and powerful, with the characteristic hammer in his hand (the hammer of professional investigation and, symbolically, of destruction); though not to be equated with Aminidab of Hawthorne's story "The Birthmark," he is reminiscent of that figure, as Clarel is of the hero of that story.

To return to Margoth as the provocation of the discussion here, the fact that he is a Jew is significant. From the Jews sprang the religious heritage of the Western world, and as Derwent puts it (line 17), it seems, at first glance, more odd that a Jew should profess Margoth's views than that a Gentile should. The burden of the discussion turns out to be that the impulses, bad and good, that have led to modernism are to be found among Jews as well as Gentiles—are part of the human fate.

What makes Margoth offensive, it should be observed, is not so much the fact that he is a scientific materialist as that the tone and interpretation he gives his doctrine deny sympathy for aspiration or feeling. He is arrogant and vain, as we shall see in the Cross episode. He shows no emotion at the death of Nehemiah. He is reductive: all is "chymestry." In contrast, we may take Melville's poem "Venice," in which a monistic relation is implied between the coral worm's work and the "reefs of palaces" which are Venice; but this implication does not, for Melville, reduce man to worm.

20 Aaron, the brother of Moses, wore, as high priest, an ornate jeweled breastplate. Exodus 28.

22 Horeb is Mount Sinai, in the Sinai Peninsula, in northeast Africa, where Moses received the Tablets.

52 "Genevan cloth," in contrast with Aaron's vest, is the drab of Protestantism, particularly of Calvinism, Geneva being the city of Calvin. Calvinism was the creed on which Melville had been raised.

67 Uriel Acosta (or da Costa), born Catholic as Gabriel da Costa, was a Portuguese philosopher and skeptic. After moving to Amsterdam, he was converted to Judaism, and changed his name to Uriel, but he was twice excommunicated by the synagogue for his skepticism. He died a suicide in 1647.

70–78 Heinrich Heine, the poet, was an apostate Jew, whose gay life and witty poetry were shockingly irreverent. For years before he died, in 1856, he suffered from an agonizing and incurable spinal disease, and during this period he was "reconverted"; but the paradoxes of his poetry and personality—the "dirge and castanet"—continued.

81–83 This passage refers to the attempt of Neo-Platonism to synthesize Greek philosophy and Judeo-Christian beliefs.

88 Moses Mendelssohn was a Jewish philosopher and theologian (1729–1786), called the German Socrates. He was greatly admired by Lessing and other scholars and literary men, and was the model for the hero of Lessing's play *Nathan* *the Wise.* Mendelssohn gave a revolutionary shift to Jewish thought, toward rationalism, after the superstitious bent developed in the deprivations of the ghetto, and urged that the Jews try to grasp the developments of modernity. His translations into German of the Pentateuch and the Psalms, on the other hand, attracted German attention to Jewish culture. He was also famous as a writer on aesthetics.

100 Johann August Wilhelm Neander, born David Mendel (1789–1850), the son of a Jewish peddler, became a Protestant convert and eminent theologian and historian, professor of theology at Berlin. His most famous work is *Das Leben Jesu* (1837). The relation suggested here between Mendel and Moses Mendelssohn is an error.

115 Baruch (or Benedict de) Spinoza (1632–1677), the philosopher, author of the *Ethics,* was a Jew who, like Acosta, was excommunicated.

122 Mamre lies just north of Hebron in biblical geography. The "mysterious three" referred to here are the angels who foretold to Abraham the birth of Isaac, even though both he and Sarah, his wife, "were old and well stricken in age." Genesis 18:1–15.

Vine and Clarel

Rolfe and Vine are the two most influential characters in the poem; with the Druse guide, they seem best to embody a truth by which Clarel may come to live. The general portrait of the mysterious Vine occurs in I, xxix:

> His home to tell—kin, tribe, estate—
> Would naught avail. Alighting grow,
> As on the tree the mistletoe,
> All gifts unique.

Vine's shyness might imply

> A lack of parlor-wont. But grace
> Which is in substance deep and grain
> May, peradventure, well pass by
> The polish of veneer.

He shows no trace of "passion's soil or lucre's stain." Should "Apollo slave in Mammon's mine?" He sheds a "subtle virtue" but is no saint, for he has "blood like swart Vesuvian wine." With such warmth there is, however, "austere control of self," not so much by "moral sway" as by the "doubt if happiness through clay" can be attained. His reserve is such that his "virgin soul" communes with others like a nun, only "through the wicket," and to him "thronged streets" are "but ampler cloisters." In I, xxxvii, he exhibits "deep human interest," and in II, i, it is said that he seemed characteristically to be poring over "some deep moral fantasy." In III, xxvi, after musing whether he deserts others or others desert him, Vine says of himself:

> For my part, I but love the past—
> The further back the better; yes,
> In the past is the true blessedness. . . .

The withdrawnness of Vine is mysterious, but there is the hint that it is based on fear or "an apprehensive sense—the sense of a secret that must be guarded." (I, xxix) In III, xiv, at the revels of Mar Saba, when Vine, "beset by such a Bacchic throng," would escape the pressure to give a song or tale, we find:

> "Ambushed in leaves we spy your grape,"
> Cried Derwent; "black but juicy one—
> A song!"

This, of course, is an echo of "Monody," Melville's poem on the death of Hawthorne. In III, vii, there occurs the famous scene in which Clarel stumbles upon Vine in a moment of ambiguous and discreditable weakness:

> Could it be Vine, and quivering so?
> 'Twas Vine. He wore that nameless look
> About the mouth—so hard to brook—
> Which in the Cenci portrait shows,
> Lost in each copy, oil or print;
> Lost, or else slurred, as 'twere a hint
> Which if received, few might sustain:
> A trembling over of small throes
> In weak swoll'n lips, which to restrain
> Desire is none, nor any rein.

In his edition of *Clarel* Bezanson gives a long and provocative note on the Cenci reference:

> Guido Reni's famous portrait of Beatrice Cenci, who was executed for incest with her father, and for murdering him; yet she seemed the very type of innocence. . . . In *Pierre* (Bk. XXVI) the picture is called "that sweetest, most touching, but most awful of all feminine heads" because of her blonde beauty and black crimes—"the two most horrible crimes (of one of which she is the object, and of the other the agent) possible to civilized humanity—incest and parricide." The *Journal* . . . indicates . . . that he went expressly to the Palazzo Barberini to see the original: "Expression of suffering about the mouth—(appealing look of innocence) not caught in any copy or engraving." Melville owned an engraving. . . . . Hawthorne's fascination with the picture if anything exceeded Melville's, and the *Passages from the French and Italian Notebooks,* which Melville acquired and marked in 1872 . . . indicates at least 4 visits to see it; Hawthorne thought it 'the most profoundly wrought picture in the world,' a picture 'resolved not to betray its secret of grief or guilt. . . .' He ended up 'perplexed and troubled . . . not to be able to get hold of its secret.' Drawing on these entries (Passages, pp. 89, 137, 504–505) Hawthorne made the picture central to *The Marble Faun* (1860) and the subject of Chap. 7; Melville acquired that novel in 1860 and read and marked it on his *Meteor* voyage that year. . . . In summary, Melville and Hawthorne shared equal fascination with the picture and agreed strikingly that its major attributes were femininity, weakness, suffering, inaccessibility, and *either* betrayed innocence or dark criminality.

The fact that now both the authorship of the portrait and the identity of the subject are held to be highly uncertain would suggest that the response of Hawthorne and Melville tells more about them than it does about the painting.

In any case, this episode when Clarel stumbles upon Vine, makes him slip aside:

> Ill hour (thought he), an evil sign:
> No more need dream of winning Vine
> Or coming at his mystery.

But Vine retains his importance to the end; this glimpse of his secret does little to diminish his charismatic quality.

As for the relation of Melville and Hawthorne, the objective facts are well known. They had first met on August 5, 1850, and saw each other for the last time when Melville, on his return from the trip to the Holy Land, took ship in Liverpool, on May 4, 1857. In his review of Hawthorne's *Mosses from an Old Manse,* at about the time of their first meeting, Melville hailed the older man's work with passionate (and astutely comprehending) admiration, and at the same time saw that the work gave some new power to him: "But already I feel that this Hawthorne has dropped germinous seeds into my soul. He expands and deepens down, the more I contemplate him; and further and further, shoots his strong New England roots into the hot soil of my Southern soul." Melville dedicated *Moby Dick,* on which he had been working at the time of the first meeting, to Hawthorne; and in thanking Hawthorne for his own letter of thanks for the book, Melville says: "your heart beats in my ribs and mine in yours, and both in God's." But such quotations are merely samples of the extravagance of feeling and rhetoric which Melville indulged in—feeling and rhetoric equally remote from Hawthorne's temperament and his cool eighteenth-century style. After Hawthorne died, in 1864, Melville's "Monody" refers to what he still felt to have been an inability to make communication. And in the poem we find, of course, the grape and vine image. In the light of the record, there seems little doubt that Vine is a projection of Hawthorne.

In *Pierre,* too, there is a projection of Hawthorne in the character of Plinlimmon, the author of the pamphlet "Chronometricals and Horologicals." Here, of course, the aspect of Hawthorne which is emphasized is quite different from that in *Clarel*—here the cool detached spectator of life, the "Paul Pry," as Hawthorne once referred to himself, the rebuker of enthusiasts and reformers, the advocate of practical morality in contrast to that preached by Christ. In the figure of Plinlimmon, Hawthorne is set in contrast to Pierre, who is actually equated with Christ—and in contrast to Melville. Plinlimmon and Vine—the two figures may be taken to indicate Melville's ambivalent relation to Hawthorne.

To what degree Melville intended Clarel as a projection of himself is not clear. Clarel would be, at the most, only one aspect of Melville, for Rolfe is certainly a deliberate, though deliberately idealized, self-image—a lover of history and letters, a man with a skeptical bent of mind but a deeply religious spirit, with a sense of the tragedy of life but with the courage to live it. He resembles the Druse in his air of self-fulfillment, and in I, xxxii, he is compared to Rama, of Hindu mythology, who was a god, "but knew it not," and is one of those who are

> Familiar with strange things that dwell
> Repressed in mortals; and they tell
> Of riddles in the prosiest lot.

This "self," even more than Vine, dominates the "self" which may be taken as Clarel, and serves as a guide and model for him. See Introduction, pp. 39–41, and the note on "After the Pleasure Party," pp. 430–37.

11 The "Venetian slats" echo the scene of "In a Bye-Canal," with the same atmosphere of a sexual threat.
44 Hagar, the handmaiden of Sarai (later Sarah), who is given by her mistress to Abram (later Abraham), and who, when got with child by him, is driven forth into the wilderness by the jealous mistress. The child is Ishmael.
49 This is in reference to the "mighty hunter," Nimrod. Genesis 10:8–12.
82 Lydda, a village between Jaffa and Jerusalem, site of a ruined church of the Crusaders which Melville had visited.
87 The Arabs, like Sir Philip Sidney, were capable of chivalric generosity.
92 The Ark of Noah came to rest "upon the mountains of Ararat." Genesis 8:4.
110 See "The Hostel," lines 15–17, for a description of Clarel. See also the encounter of Clarel with the Lyonese (IV, xxvi, 249–264).
125 The implicit admonition of Vine, "Go, live it out," foreshadows the only wisdom Clarel is to learn: in the basic pattern of human life reverently lived, is the wisdom of life.
126–130 See notes on "After the Pleasure Party," lines 79–100.
141 A "dizzard" is an idiot.

The Inscription

12 Nehemiah—The company has reached the Siddim Plain on the Dead Sea, while Rolfe (II, xxx, 40–45) has been speaking of the ruins of Petra:

". . . and Petra's there,
Down in her cleft. Mid such a scene
Of Nature's terror, how serene
That ordered form. Nor less 'tis cut
Out of that terror—does abut
Thereon: there's Art."

In this context of a landscape of terror out of which Art has sprung, they come upon a slanted Cross, and at the foot of the Cross, Nehemiah, the innocent, in sound sleep—by the Dead Sea. The arrangement of the scene demands no exegesis. In relation to Nehemiah's sleep under the Cross, see *Pierre* (Bk. VII), where the hero sleeps beneath the Memnon Stone.

13 Lot was, of course, the one righteous man of Sodom (there not being the ten for whom the Lord had promised Abraham the city would be spared); he was led forth, with his family, when the cities of the plain were to be consumed by the rain of "brimstone and fire from the Lord out of Heaven" (Genesis 19:24). The Dead Sea was to occupy the spot.

In the next canto (40–46) we find the topic again:

Ranging higher
Where vague glens pierced the steeps of fire,
Imagination time repealed—
Restored there, and in fear revealed
Lot and his daughters twain in flight,
Three shadows flung on reflex light
Of Sodom in her funeral pyre.

Three shadows only, for the wife, disobeying the command not to look back, had been turned into a pillar of salt.

In III, i, 131–139, the biblical account is paraphrased, and in II, xx, 50–59, we find Margoth's scientific comment.

29 After Clarel makes this comparison, Rolfe pursues it, pointing out that as the mariner approaches the Horn, the Southern Cross appears "brightly higher" until off the Horn it is at full height. Bezanson cites the "hell-landscape" in Melville's journal of his trip on the *Meteor* in 1860; ". . . in a squall, the mist lifted and showed, within 12 or fifteen miles the horrid sight of Cape Horn . . . a black, bare steep cliff, the face of it facing the South Pole . . . awful islands and rocks—an infernal group."

69 Orion, slain by Artemis, was transformed into a constellation. The subject of the passage is the possibility that Christianity may fade into mere mythology, at the level of all other mythologies. See Margoth's hammer (line 100) compared to Thor's, in relation to this—perhaps implying that the scientific beliefs of any one period, too, may enter mythology of a later period, having in the end no position more privileged that that of Christianity.

102–103 Margoth's arrogant positivism is directed primarily at religious belief. But he, as the spokesman for a reductive scientific view, is also the spokesman for utility: science as a tool (see IV, xxi, 15 and Margoth's suggestion for a railroad station at Gethsemane, II, xx, 94–96).

104–105 But nature cancels the blasphemy of Margoth's boast. In other words, even at the level of natural experience, there may be a logic of which Margoth is unaware—"evidence" which he does not take into account. See the Epilogue. The canto, thematically, has a triangular structure, as it were: Margoth's inscription is one point; Nehemiah asleep at the foot of the Cross another; the world of nature as the third.

Mortmain Reappears

Mortmain had lingered behind at Elisha's Fountain, on the edge of the desert of Christ's temptation, and now rejoins the group. He has, we may say, succumbed to his temptation.

10 Hekla is a volcano in southern Iceland, known for the violence and frequency of its eruption.

20 The Brook Cherith, in the Valley of the Jordan, where Elijah had been condemned to begin his prophecy—when the brook dried up (I Kings 17).

30–38 To read the passage: The pause of the artillery's boom would presumably be the end of the Franco-Prussian War (May 1871). But this is not a peace, merely a "pause" in violence, full of dire portents. "Hell's hot kingdom" would be the Commune of 1871, the fulfillment of the revolutionary upheavals of the past period—the moment when "Anti-Christ" and "Atheist," while the light in the Tomb flickers low, crown Anarchy with a "red" coronet, the red being in a double sense, that of blood and that of communism. To what kind of repentance does Mortmain call? Is this to be taken as merely theological? Or is there a social aspect too? See "The House-top" with its use of "Atheist" and "cynic kings."

40 The relevant passage here is John 1:21–23, the Vulgate version, the questioning of John the Baptist (here the "Mad John" who is Mortmain):

> Elias est tu? Et dixit: Non sum. Propheta es tu? Et respondit: Non. Dixerunt ergo ei: Quis es ut responsum demus his qui miserunt nos? Quid dicis de teipse? Ait: Ego vox clamantis in deserto "Dirigite viam Domini."

In what sense are we to take the "dire Vox Clamans of our day?" The new order proclaimed by the new John the Baptist is one of a new social arrangement. Rolfe takes the voice seriously. But Derwent, in his simple-minded optimism and faith in automatic progress, asks, "Why heed him?"

46 Djalea, the guide of the troop of pilgrims is a Druse of noble bearing, perhaps the son of an emir, an image of self-knowledge, self-control, dignity, and power; he is to be taken, perhaps, as a summation of those virtues to which the poem points. In III, xxiv, 15–24, Clarel comes upon him taking his repose and smoking, reclining

> . . . along the crag serene,
> As under Spain's San Pedro dome
> The long-sword Cid upon his tomb;
> And with an unobtrusive eye
> Yet apprehending, and mild mien,
> Regarded him as he went by
> Tossed in his trouble. 'Twas a glance
> Clarel did many a time recall,
> Though its unmeant significance—
> That was the last thing learned of all.

This scene may be put in contrast with the two scenes when Clarel comes upon Vine, the one (II, xxvii, 104–117) when Clarel's approach to Vine is rebuffed, and the other (III, vii, 17–39) when Clarel comes upon Vine in a moment of weakness and spiritual disorder. And it points, of course, to the end of the poem—even to a point beyond the formal end when Clarel finds his own terms of peace. Djalea is a variant of the Rolfe-self, another idealization.

The Druses are a religious sect, primarily of the mountains

of Lebanon and Syria, with a faith drawing elements from Judaism, Mohammedanism, and Christianity. Melville may have given the Druse his role as an unconscious embodiment of the highest human values because the sect, believing in the transmigration of souls, held out the hope of realizing human perfection. It may even be suggested that the course of the soul, according to the belief of the Druses, would be a parallel to the course of the soul through stages of belief and experience to wisdom, as indicated in the poem.

50–54 If Christ, crucified, was given to drink of the "Sodom waters," the water now covering Siddim, the valley in which Sodom and Gomorrah had been located, the unredeemable cities, then the meaning might be that Christ was, by that token, given to know that his suffering was in vain. As for the relevance to Mortmain, he, too, in his suffering, finds mankind unredeemable by the gospel of revolution which he had offered. But he is not merely a "Christ"; he is also the "sinner" who would sup the waters to make his own soul appropriately bitter. Do we have here another reference to Mortmain's "unrenderable" story, of II, iv, 128–145?

63 The word Marah in Hebrew means bitter, or bitterness. It is a place name in Exodus 15:23. The wells of Marah were found by the Israelites after three days in the wilderness without water, but could not be drunk from because of the bitterness.

Sodom

23 For the star called Wormwood, see Revelations 8:10–11:

> And the third angel sounded, and there fell a great star from heaven, burning as it were a lamp, and it fell upon the third part of the rivers, and upon the fountains of waters;
>
> And the name of the star is called Wormwood, and the third part of the waters became wormwood; and many men died of the waters, because they were made bitter.

The wormwood that John would have known was probably *artemesia absinthium,* known to the Greeks. It is bitter but not poisonous. There is no star called Wormwood.

31 For the following fifty lines the idea is elaborated that the really unredeemable crimes of this Sodom are those of cold respectability, crimes not punishable by any statute—"sins refined," "crimes of the spirit."

36–37 This paradox appears over and over in *Battle-Pieces*, most specifically in "The Conflict of Convictions."

56–85 There are numerous touches in this powerful passage that suggest Dante.

64 William Burke was the partner of William Hare in the killing of wayfarers and indigents to get bodies to sell for dissection. His crimes, for which he was executed in 1829, gave the verb "to burke," meaning to strangle or suffocate.

72–85 This passage might be taken as a perspective on American history before the Civil War and for a decade after it: American energy and cunning assume "holy forms" but, in the service of Mammon, condone slavery and general social injustice. See the end of the Supplement.

91–117 Bezanson reads "Tofana brew" as probably the wine from Tophanna outside Constantinople, which Melville had visited. But I do not know the relevance. As for the whole passage, here is a return to the theme of II, iv, 128–145, the "unrenderable thing." Medea—the "soft man-eater," who murdered her brother, children, and rival for the love of Jason, appears again, with Jael (who appears in "In a Bye-Canal," associated with the luring female eyes behind the lattice), and with Leah, the wife given Jacob by deception. The female is here the creator-bearer of evil—"Events are all in them begun"—the incarnation of the Fall. The various perspectives in the passage need no belaboring—but it is worth mentioning here how "thick" Melville conceives such a characterization as that of Mortmain, with history, anthropology, the social context, philosophy, theology, and psychology in one package. The withdrawal in pudeur of the companions at the opening of the "inmost" view is significant, and an index to the degree of Melville's consciousness of his method.

99 Chyle is the milky fluid produced by the action of pancreatic juice and bile in the small intestine on chyme, the pulpy mass into which food is converted in the stomach before it is passed into the small intestine.

Obsequies

This canto is closely tied to canto xxxviii, which concerns the death of Nehemiah, the carrier of simple evangelical faith, with an open Bible always in his hand. One night a vision of the New Jerusalem leads him, sleep-walking, into the Dead Sea, where he perishes. This episode is one of the best examples of the defect in the poem caused by the lack of a basic action drawn from life which Melville might develop and enrich. Here the event of the death is clearly determined by the symbolic structure and not by a logic of plot. This canto, at the end of Part II, the mathematical center of the poem, shows the pilgrims, and the Druse who is their guide, around the dead body of the innocent believer, each expressing a characteristic attitude. The episode, one of the several deaths in the poem (each having its own significance), is set against that of Ruth, at the end, which for Clarel is the death of another kind of faith, that in natural love.

1 The skull of the camel, which had already served one purpose as the seat for Mortmain as he gives his tirade, and the corpse of the human being are set side by side on the margin of the Dead Sea. Innocence, perfect faith, and vision, in the person of Nehemiah, end by the animal's skull.
38 For the "Assyrian low," see the note on line 147 of "The Hostel."
55 Vine, the projection of Hawthorne, understands and sympathetically broods over the experiences of his companions.
68 "All's chymestry" is the key statement of Margoth's position.
78 In Roman mythology Orcus is a god of the underworld, first identified with the Greek god of oaths and the punisher of perjury, Horcus, and later with Hades, the name of the god gradually becoming the name of the place.
92 Belex is a European Turk, a seasoned soldier, a stoical fatalist, who leads the guard of Arab Bethlehemites who accompany Clarel's party. He has his own courage and calm, and represents a stage toward the self-fulfillment of Djalea.
132–162 As the Bible is put in the hands of the dead ("And better guide who knoweth?"), there comes, by thematic counterpoint, the roar of the avalanche. The image of the

irrational and destructive power of nature recalls the symbolic significance of Willey's Slide in Nathan's spiritual development (I, xvii). The "fog-bow" (line 155) appears as a "counter object"—over the Dead Sea, of course—and we have the presentation in this general collocation of the old theme of the doubleness of nature and experience.

148 El Ghor, the Arabic name for the valley from Lebanon to the Gulf of Akaba. The passage from line 132 to this point is one of the most effectively developed in the whole poem.

The High Desert

8 The Convent of Saint Catherine, on Mount Sinai (Horeb). Bezanson, in his edition of *Clarel,* points out that the description of the annual penetration of the ray into the chapel, which gives Melville his extended simile, comes from *Sinai and Palestine in Connection with Their History,* by Arthur Penrhyn Stanley.

16 An incidental character whom the company have just met (III, iv) as they climb from the Dead Sea toward Mar Saba, where there will be the "revel." The youth, wearing a "Phrygian cap in scarlet pride" and gaily singing, bears a shroud, which, according to Greek practice as explained by Rolfe, would be dipped in the River Jordan and laid aside until needed—not morbidly, as Rolfe adds, but "with gay Hellene lightheartedness." The Cypriote is carrying this to his "good mother" (not his beloved, as Bezanson would seem to have it) as a surprise "present" which she, he says, will "value more than juicy pheasant." The Cypriote's Epicurean attitude toward life, and his gay acceptance of death, are in contrast with the preoccupation of the pilgrims, who have just buried Nehemiah by the Dead Sea. The Cypriote's view, with a different tonality, reappears in the person of the Lyonese, the handsome young Frenchman, who (IV, xxvi) descants to Clarel on the charms and sexual appeal of Jewesses (this in contrast to the substitute for religious and metaphysical certainty which Clarel seeks in Ruth), and whose own feminine good looks, like a Polynesian girl's, and with "much of dubious at the heart," seem to unsettle Clarel. See "Vine and Clarel," especially lines 65–140 with the general note, lines 15–17 of "The Hostel," Introduction pp. 39–41, and the notes on "After the Pleasure Party," pp. 430–37.

26 Ibrahim Pasha (1789–1848) was the Egyptian general who defeated the Turks, and captured Acre.
32 The ambiguity of nature, again.
36 In the dual system of Zoroaster, the good spirit Ormond, sometimes known as Ahara Mazda, is in conflict with Ahriman.
40 The Gnostics were a group of rationalistic sects arising in the 1st century B.C. and lasting until the 6th century A.D., which held that knowledge, not faith, leads to salvation, but that God is unknowable and that from him emanate various subsidiary deities, or principles. The Gnostics drew on various Greek and Oriental religions and philosophies and, by and large, held with the dualism of Zoroaster.
75 See Hawthorne's "The Man of Adamant."
89 St. Denis is the patron saint of France, beheaded in Paris, according to legend, about 250 A.D. The Capetian dynasty, the third of France, began with Hugh Capet, in 987, and ended with Charles IV, in 1328.
117–123 These lines repeat the idea in "The Conflict of Convictions" (lines 33–35).

Derwent and Ungar

Now that Mortmain is dead (in a last moment of reconciliation, III, xxviii), Ungar emerges as the carrier, with important variations, of Mortmain's repudiation of modernity and as the antagonist of the optimistic Derwent. Ungar is of a Maryland family, "sprung from Romish race" with a "Latin mind," and has Indian blood. He has been a Confederate soldier, and after the defeat has become, as a number of Confederate officers did, a wanderer and a soldier of fortune—a "wandering Ishmael from the West" (IV, x).

The character Don Hannibal, who appears in this canto, has just been introduced in canto xix as a "New-Comer." Don Hannibal Rohon Del Aquaviva, a Mexican revolutionist, is another variant on the Mortmain-Ungar line. He has lost an arm and leg fighting for freedom, and describes himself:

> "A cripple, yet contrive to hop
> Far off from Mexic liberty,
> Thank God! I lost these limbs for that;
> And would that they were mine again,

And all were back to former state—
I, Mexico, and poor old Spain."

In other words he, like Mortmain, is disillusioned with revolution and reform—a "*reformado* reformed," he calls himself. But where Mortmain, with some secret canker, rejects life, Don Hannibal (as his name Aquaviva indicates) gaily affirms it. If man is only a scoundrel and must live by "penalties" to maintain order, yet life in itself, and the courage and humor to live it, are compensations. Don Hannibal resembles Ungar in his distrust of "cursed *Progress*" and Democracy, but when Ungar, with his characteristic seriousness, picks up this theme in conversation, Don Hannibal gracefully excuses himself and hobbles off singing a "wild ranchero lay." Thus Don Hannibal, the gay and cynical "*reformado* reformed," introduces the debate which follows.

1 God spoke to Elijah in a "still small voice" (I Kings 19:11–12).

13 Derwent, whose views are stated a little more fully further on, cannot take his friend at his self-proclaimed value as a "*reformado* reformed," himself being committed to an unquenchable optimism about human nature and the course of history. He shares a bond with the Mexican, however—a physical life-belief, one might say, good spirits based on perfect digestion. But there is one crucial difference between them: Don Hannibal maintains his life-belief *in spite of* his personal experience, disappointment, and maiming, while for Derwent all remains untested and therefore of uncertain value.

There is an oblique but instructive relation between Derwent and Captain Brierly of Conrad's *Lord Jim,* whose "heroism" and success are based merely on good digestion and healthy nerves, but who, knowing this, cannot bear the fear of what may happen to him if tested in a moment when his "natural" heroism (as distinct from commitment to an "idea") will not be up to scratch. In apprehension of such a test (as exemplified in the fate of Lord Jim himself) he commits suicide. For Derwent the test does not come, and he must face the more or less amiable contempt of men like Mortmain, Ungar, and even Rolfe, whose views, for better or worse, have been derived from, and subjected to, experience. The attitudes of Mortmain and Ungar, though obsessive and distorted, correspond to some reality, as the "sanity" of Derwent does not. To return to Conrad, he and Melville are very close philosophically. In this connection, we may point out the transference of marine imagery to the desert setting.

24–27 The historical process which Ungar calls "reform" is here spoken of as a force in nature (as Margoth says "All's chymestry"), as though a chemistry of history.

28–32 A succinct statement of Derwent's attitude toward history and life: no mystery, no significance in struggle, automatic progress—"plain sailing." Ultimately Derwent is one of the respectable monsters of "Sodom" (II, xxxvi), who despite his good intentions and personal decency is doing little more than denying the nature of the world by "varnishing" it, and in so doing trades upon the "coast of crime." For his own comfort, as it were, he refuses to engage reality. The perfect example of this occurs in the long canto called "In Confidence" (III, xxi) when the troubled Clarel, on a tower overlooking the "Glare riven by gloom" of the desert of Saba, exposes his personal problem to Derwent. When Clarel presses for certainties and absolutes (as was in Melville's temper to do, a trait Hawthorne commented upon), Derwent replies,

> Less light
> Than warmth needs earthly wight.

In the end Clarel from his anguish, cries out (298–99):

> Own, own with me, and spare to feign
> Doubt bleeds, nor Faith is free from pain.

All Derwent can do is to refuse the challenge and answer:

> Alas, too deep you dive.

48 Marcus Aurelius was the philosopher and emperor of Rome, who wrote the *Meditations.*

90 Southern apologists for slavery, being bound by no need to justify the new industrialism of England and the North and having little confidence in "progress," were sometimes astute critics of the problem of poverty and the inner contradictions of the new capitalistic system. Ungar, a Confederate, does not develop this line here, but it was associated in Southern apologetics with the line he does pursue. See George Fitzhugh, *Cannibals All, or Slaves without Masters,* and C. Vann Woodward, "A Southern Critique of the Gilded Age" in *The Burden of Southern History,* where he discusses Ungar.

But this line of thought was not confined to Southern apologists, or to the period before the Civil War. Tolstoy, in his *What to Do?* (written ten years after the publication of *Clarel*), points out the resemblances between Russia and the United States. Slavery had been officially ended in both countries, but "only the word, not the thing, has been put down." And he goes on to say:

> Money is a new and terrible form of slavery . . . equally demoralizing . . . for both the slave and slave-owner; only much worse, because it frees the slave and the slave-owner from their personal, humane relations.

William Dean Howells, who was deeply affected by *What to Do?*, looked back on the Civil War and declared that the "war for the dollar" was consequent upon the "war for the union"—and the Negro remained a slave.

107 See this theme in "The Conflict of Convictions."

120 The episode here is contrasted with that referred to in the "new uprising of the Red" of 1871, when the Tuileries was burned, an illustration for Ungar of the inner logic of secular "reform." In this general connection see "The House-top."

Ungar and Rolfe

10 Notice here that after Derwent has broken off the "hot discussion," it is Rolfe who insists on pursuing it. The question he puts is a crucial one: does scientific progress provide a civilization with a means for defining and evaluating ends?

38 Ajalon: "Then spake Joshua to the Lord in the day when the Lord delivered up the Amorites before the children of Israel, and he said in the sight of Israel, Sun, stand thou still upon Gibeon; and thou Moon, in the valley of Ajalon." (Joshua 10:12)

160 Rolfe, Vine, and Clarel recognize a logic in Ungar's position—a logic easy to recognize in the Gilded Age and at the time of the Commune.

167 Terminus, the Roman god presiding over boundaries, was represented with human head but without hands or feet, this lack indicating that his position was fixed.

168 See "A Utilitarian View of the Monitor's Fight."

169 For Ungar, in the New World, with the Southern defeat, there had been a second Fall. The same idea of a second Fall, though differently interpreted, appears in "The Conflict of Convictions," line 6.

The Valley of Decision

The title comes from Joel 3:14: "Multitudes, multitudes in the valley of decision: for the day of the Lord is near in the valley of decision." The verses just after may also have some relevance for the poem:

> The sun and the moon shall be darkened, and the stars shall withdraw their shining.
>
> The Lord also shall roar out of Zion, and utter his voice from Jerusalem: and the heavens and the earth shall shake: but the Lord will be the hope of his people, and the strength of the children of Israel.

10 Coquimbo is a province in northern Chile, bounded on the west by the Pacific, and on the east by Argentina. The image of the tremor at Coquimbo forerunning the shock, etc., may be associated with the verses from Joel just quoted, in which the heavens and the earth shake and the only hope is in the Lord.

116 Korah was the leader of a rebellion against the leadership of Moses in the desert (Numbers 16): "Ye take too much upon you seeing all the congregation are holy, every one of them, and the Lord is among them. . . ." On the command of the Lord, Moses drew the faithful away from all that "appertained unto Korah" and then the earth opened and swallowed the rebels up.

138 This little struggle at the grave—indeed, the whole scene—is no doubt suggested by the burial of Ophelia, in *Hamlet*. But, alas for both dramatic and thematic intensity, there is no Laertes here; here, as elsewhere, Clarel has only abstractions, or figures who carry labels, for his antagonists. Incidentally, we have in this wrenched phrase "in hiss" an example of the slovenly composition often found in the poem, the easy surrender of sense or naturalness to the demands of meter or rhyme.

151 Kedron (Kidron) is, in biblical geography, a brook southeast of Jerusalem, flowing into the Dead Sea.

153 Symbolically, Clarel has come to his own suffering, his martyrdom. There is a double meaning in "port": literally the Gate of St. Stephen, but also the haven. In this sense of haven, it would be implied that through pain, when hope ("natural" hope) is withdrawn, man can approach wisdom. In this connection notice the use of "won," with the idea that the martyrdom is something, however unconsciously, striven for.
156 The poem is pegged to the Christian calendar, with the possible implication that the natural pattern of life corresponds to the pattern in that calendar.

Dirge

11 In both Judaic and Islamic lore, Azrael is the angel that waits for the instant of death to separate the soul from the body.

Passion Week

11–12 Vine is here given, in one sense at least, as the most significant figure for Clarel—as Hawthorne, despite the final failure in communication, was for Melville. The phrase "fate's pertinence" is not entirely clear. Perhaps it could be read as follows: Now the quality of Vine gives Clarel a sense of how the inevitable pattern of individual fate (i.e., loss, isolation, suffering) may lead to wisdom and strength, in selfhood—the sort of selfhood exemplified by Rolfe and the Druse, but not interpreted by them. Now the friends, "Blameless," must leave—for this is the pattern of life, a pattern enacted in the Passion Week. This is, appropriately, the period when Clarel, in isolation, must come to terms with the fact of death and his own fate.
105 The "Comforter" echoes John 14:16: "And I will pray the Father, and he shall give you another Comforter, that he may abide with you for ever." The Comforter is the Holy Ghost. Erebus is the son of Chaos and brother of Night, and her husband. The word is also used to refer to a place, the part of the underworld through which a soul must pass to come to Hades. Or it is even used to mean darkness itself.

Easter

6 The *Stabat* is a sequence concerning the sorrows of the Virgin, ascribed to Jacopone da Todi, with the opening words "Stabat mater dolorosa." Originally it was not liturgical and had no music, but by the end of the thirteenth cenutry it was very popular. Among the early settings was one by Palestrina.
7 The *Tenebrae* is an office sung in the afternoon or evening of Wednesday, Thursday, and Friday of Holy Week. The candles are extinguished in memory of the darkness that fell at the Crucifixion.
57 Thammuz (also Tammuz) was the Babylonian god of agriculture, etc., personifying the power of spring. His festival was held at the new moon of the summer month of Tammuz. In the Hebrew year the month of Tammuz is the fourth ecclesiastical and the tenth civil month, part of June and July.
65 "He is not here: for he is risen, as he said." Matthew 28:6.

Via Crucis

22 Whitsunday is Pentecost, the fiftieth day after Easter, the last holy day of the cycle celebrating the life of Christ. It commemorates the descent of tongues, as described in Acts 2:1–4. The name is from the white worn by those being baptized on this special day for baptism.
34 Edom, in biblical geography, is a region in the lowland south of the Dead Sea, rugged and infertile.
51–53 The Atlantic cable had been first used on August 5, 1858, in an exchange of greetings between Queen Victoria and President Buchanan. The cable failed later that year, but in 1868 a new cable was laid. The image here is, of course, that of the failure of science to solve ultimate mysteries.
55 Obsolete or dialectal, "wynd" means a passage or narrow street.

John Marr

The volume *John Marr and Other Sailors* was privately printed by Melville in 1888 in an edition of twenty-five copies, for personal distribution. The book was dedicated to W.C.R.—William

Clark Russell. Russell, though born in New York City, had been educated in England and had made his career there, as a novelist of the sea. He greatly admired Melville and had dedicated a book to him, *An Ocean Tragedy.* In a long "Inscription Epistolary," Melville expresses special admiration for *The Wreck of the Grosvenor*, which, he declares, "entitles the author to the naval crown in current literature."

The figure of John Marr, far from the sea and among people who could not understand him or his interest in his past, is a touching image of Melville's own situation in the Gilded Age.

12 In the margin "hold" is corrected to "held."
36 In *Billy Budd* (Ch. 24), in the scene of the Chaplain's visit, the condemned sailor appears as a "barbarian": "a barbarian Billy radically was," standing near to "unadulterate Nature," being of "essential innocence." At the end of the interview with the "barbarian," the Chaplain "felt that innocence was even a better thing than religion wherewith to go to Judgment." Billy as "barbarian" is, in one sense, an echo of the primitive Eden world of Melville's early work—one of the poles of his thought. See Introduction, p. 16.
37 The general idea of such "unworldly servers" is not uncommon in Kipling, for instance, in "The Merchantmen," "The Galley-Slave," "Sons of Martha," and "Song of the Galley-Slaves."
50–55 The sea burial here affords another link to *Billy Budd* and to "Billy in the Darbies."

Bridegroom Dick

Melville had experience of the Navy, having been on the *United States* from August 1843 to the fall of 1844, and that period provides the background for *White-Jacket,* which preceded *Moby Dick.* In "Bridegroom Dick," some thirty-five years after that book, Melville returns to the same experience. Though the date on the printed poem is 1876, according to the date on the manuscript, it was finished December 4, 1887.

15 The word "fig" means dress, array, or costume.
52 It is sometimes suggested that Dainty Dave is Guert Gansevoort, Melville's cousin. But see note on lines 217 ff.

55 To "twig" is to watch or inspect.
68 Thomas ap Catesby Jones (1790–1858) was appointed midshipman in 1805 and early served under Hull, Decatur, and Oliver Hazard Perry. Promoted to lieutenant in 1812, he saw distinguished service against the British. After becoming a captain in 1829, he served in the Pacific, being three times commander of the Pacific Squadron, including the period when Melville was on the *United States;* he was also commander of the South Sea Surveying and Exploring Expedition. His nephew, Catesby ap Roger Jones, commanded the *Virginia* (the *Merrimac*) in the fight with the *Monitor.*
75 Stephen Decatur (1779–1820) won fame in the war against Tripoli, and confirmed it in the War of 1812. He was killed in a duel with James Barron, the cashiered captain of the *Chesapeake,* on whose court-martial he had sat.
76 Oliver Hazard Perry (1785–1819), appointed midshipman in 1799, served in the war against Tripoli, but his reputation rests on his victory over the British on Lake Erie, on September 10, 1813. One of his dispatches contained the often quoted statement: "We have met the enemy and they are ours."

Isaac Hull (1773–1843) commanded his first ship at the age of 21. He saw action in the war against Tripoli, and in the War of 1812 commanded his frigate *Constitution* ("Old Ironsides") in the famous defeat of the *Guerrière.*

David Dixon Porter (1813–1891), the son of a naval officer, saw service in the Mexican War, and in the Civil War commanded the mortar fleet on the Mississippi, under Farragut.
82 Guert Gansevoort; see note on lines 215 ff.
91 Winfield Scott (1786–1866) became a brigadier general in the War of 1812, and in 1847 was appointed as chief commander in the Mexican War. This line falls at the end of a page in *John Marr,* but in the manuscript this is marked for a section break, with a blue bracket at the beginning of line 92, the indication throughout for a new section.
95–96 In the manuscript line these lines read:

> But how to speak of the lamentable days—
> Hawsers parted, and started stays;

In the proofs the lines were revised to the present version.
101 See note on lines 135 ff.
117 The Uzzite is Job, who, when he suffered from boils, "took him a potsherd to scrape himself withal." Job 2:8.

122 In the margin, "either" is written as a revision for "one," which is canceled.

125 The term "keelson" applies to various interior structural elements parallel to, and above, the keel of a vessel. The image seems rather forced: the thrills and throes felt deep in a ship? In the manuscript this line reads:

Of all these throbs at the kelson, and throes.

126 In the North the making of "shoddy" for uniforms was a public scandal. Here the term shoddyites applies to profiteers in general.

135–161 The descriptions of the *Cumberland* are not in general agreement. She is called a frigate by Melville, by the *Rebellion Record,* by numerous historians, and by the *Dictionary of American Fighting Ships* (issued by the Navy Department). But she is called a sloop-of-war by other historians, and by some reports in the *Official Records* (Series I, vol. vii). The difference is to be accounted for by the fact that she had been launched, in 1842, as a frigate, but in 1856 was cut down ("razeed") to a sloop-of-war, or corvette, and as such fought the *Virginia.*

The conversion to a sloop accounts, no doubt, for some, though not all, of the very great confusion about the armament of the *Cumberland,* with descriptions ranging from the 50 guns of the *Dictionary* down to 24. An account of the armament as both frigate and sloop is given by Howard I. Chapelle in his *History of the American Sailing Navy,* and by Thomas O. Selfridge, Jr., who, as lieutenant, commanded the gun deck of the *Cumberland* during the battle, and later as a rear admiral was to write two narratives of the event (*Memoirs,* and "The Story of the Cumberland," in *Papers* of the Military Historical Society of Massachusetts, vol. xii). Chapelle is in substantial agreement about the armament with Selfridge, who gives the sloop a battery of 22 9-inch shell guns (supplied with solid shot for the *Virginia*) and with two pivot guns, fore and aft, the former a 10-inch smooth-bore, the latter the only rifled gun in the armament, a 70-pound Dahlgren.

The fear of rifled guns was the reason, as we are told by H. Ashton Ramsay, Chief Engineer of the *Virginia* (in *The Monitor and the Merrimac*), that Buchanan had determined, before the battle, to ram the *Cumberland* and get her out of action. But the Dahlgren could not be brought to bear, because of the tide, and for 15 minutes Buchanan lay off at some 300 yards, with the solid shot of the smooth-bores ricocheting off his tallow-smeared armor, and performed great slaughter before he closed. The *Virginia* struck her victim on the starboard bow; but she took considerable punishment before being able to disengage, and then left her 1500-pound cast-iron beak in the side of the now sinking *Cumberland.*

In their official reports Buchanan and Jones, of the *Virginia,* and George U. Morris, of the *Cumberland,* mention only one ramming. But Selfridge reports two rammings, and his view is independently corroborated by two other eyewitnesses, an infantry captain who was on the *Congress,* moored close to the *Cumberland* (*O. R.,* p. 36), and the commander of the French frigate *Gassendi,* anchored in the Roads (*O. R.,* p. 66). As for the call for surrender, Buchanan, Jones, and Morris do not mention it, but Ramsay does, and records Morris' reply, placing this before the ramming (as do *Rebellion Record* and Melville). Selfridge, however, places it after a first ramming.

Whether or not Melville is inaccurate about the hailing, he is in the names of the commanders. If the "Will" referred to is supposed to be William Radford, commander of the *Cumberland,* Melville was apparently unaware that at the time of the battle he was on horseback, dashing along the shore to get back to his post, having been on board the *Roanoke,* on a court of inquiry. It was Lieutenant George U. Morris, his executive officer, who was in charge and would have replied to a hail.

As for Buchanan, there is no basis, in so far as I can determine, for calling him "Hal"; later, and perhaps already, he was sometimes referred to as "Old Buck." He may, however, have been well acquainted with William Radford, for most officers of the then miniscule United States Navy did know one another. If there was no intimacy between Buchanan and Radford, there was for Buchanan, in the attack on the *Congress,* which followed the sinking of the *Cumberland,* an even more poignant wrenching of ties.

William Smith, commanding the *Congress,* seeing the fate of the *Cumberland,* sought refuge in shoal water; but after a raking fire from the *Virginia,* he ran up the white flag—two, in fact. The *Beaufort,* an escort of the *Virginia,* approached the *Congress* and received the surrender of her flag and of the side arms of Smith and his second in command, who delivered themselves as prisoners, but who were permitted to return aboard the vessel to assist in removing the wounded. Meanwhile Federal shore batteries, disregarding the surrender, opened fire. Buchanan, considering this a breach of the truce declared by the white flags of the *Congress,* recalled the *Beaufort,* and ordered that shot be heated to set the *Congress* afire. The *Congress* burned with great loss of life. When this final attack took place, Buchanan knew that his brother was on the *Congress* as an officer; and the brother, already wounded by Federal fire from the shore, died in the flames.

Melville may have known of this division of loyalties and adapted it for the episode of the *Cumberland;* or it may have come to him in a garbled version. It does not appear in the prose accounts of the battle in the *Rebellion Record.* Melville did, however, find there four poems on the *Cumberland.* The first, "On Board the *Cumberland,*" by the poet, dramatist, and diplomat George H. Boker ("Bokker" in the *Record*), does present, as does Melville, the version that the *Virginia* does not fire before the ramming, and no second ramming is referred to; the *Cumberland* simply fights on till her powder is gone and she is foundering. No reference is made to a demand for surrender, and hence none to the reply by Morris. Melville, in line 152, has the phrase "the *Merrimac*'s tusk," which conceivably could have been suggested by Boker's phrase "tusk of that sea-boar." The other poems in the *Record* are without interest, except for an explanatory prose note introducing "The Frigate Cumberland," by Elizabeth T. Porter Beach, which gives the version that the crew of the *Cumberland* "bravely fired a broadside, even while sinking, in response to the call of their commanding officer, Lieut. Morris: 'Shall we give them a broadside as she goes?' "

As a peripheral matter, we may add that the father of the young lieutenant who so gallantly fought the guns of the *Cumberland* to the last, had a somewhat more immediate connection with Melville than did his son. In 1850, Rear Admiral Thomas O. Selfridge, Sr., infuriated by the attacks in *White-Jacket* on naval discipline and practice, had written a blistering rejoinder to the man who "would have laws, democratic in all respects, for the rule of our Navy." And added: "What absurdity!" Melville could not have known of the important hackles he had caused to rise, for the manuscript was not published until 1935, when it appeared in *American Literature* (Vol. VII) in an article by Charles Anderson entitled "A Reply to Herman

Melville's *White-Jacket* by Rear Admiral Thomas O. Selfridge, Sr."

135–152 In the manuscript this section read:

> Listen.—A trump from the iron-clad calls
> Summoning the battle-ship with wooden walls:
> "Surrender that frigate, Will! Surrender!
> Or I will *ram*, and that will end her."
> 'Twas Hal. And Will, from the unclad oak,
> Will, the old messmate trumpet, spoke
> Very impolitely, "Sink her, and be d——d!"
> No more. But gathering way Hal rammed,
> And O the havock wreck—the wrack:
> The *Cumberland* sunk by the *Merrimac!*

147 Historic (Melville's note).

153–155 At the ramming the 1500-pound iron "tusk" of the *Virginia* was broken off and left in the wound in the starboard bow of the victim. This fact may have saved the *Monitor* when she was rammed the next day.

160–161 Actually the *Cumberland* sank "canted to port," as Morris said in his official report, and though the masts were visible, they were at an angle of 45 degrees, sunk with "the American flag at the peak." But when, a few weeks after the battle, Hawthorne visited the spot, he saw, as he reports in his essay "Chiefly About War Matters" (in the *Atlantic Monthly,* July 1862), only "a tattered rag of a pennant" fluttering from one of the masts. He continues:

> The hull of the latter ship [the *Cumberland*] seems to be careened over, so that the three masts stand slantwise; the rigging looks quite unimpaired, except that a few ropes dangle loosely from the yards. The flag (which never was struck, thank Heaven!) is entirely hidden under the waters of the bay, but is still doubtless waving in its old place, although it floats to and fro with the swell and reflex of the tide instead of rustling on the breeze. A remnant of the dead crew still man the sunken ship, and sometimes a drowned body floats up to the surface.

167 The misprint "jamb" is corrected to "jam."

185 At 2 A.M. April 24, 1862, Rear Admiral David G. Farragut, with a squadron of warships and 19 mortar schooners, ran Fort St. Philip and Fort Jackson, below New Orleans, and by dawn had the city under his guns. In the operation, however, Farragut's flagship was for a time aground, and ablaze from a fire-raft.

David Glasgow Farragut (1801–1870) was a Tennessean, but from boyhood was bred up in the Navy, being adopted, in 1810, by Captain David Porter, the father of David Dixon Porter (see note on line 76), who was to serve under Farragut on the Mississippi. Farragut was the outstanding naval commander in the Civil War, and his achievements were recognized in 1866, when the grade of full admiral was created for him.

188 The Battle for the Bay refers to Farragut's capture of Mobile, on August 5, 1864. The "one aloft" is, of course, Farragut, who, when warned of the danger of pressing his attack, said: "Damn the torpedoes. Full steam ahead!" There is a poem entitled "The Battle for the Bay" in *Battle-Pieces*.

212 Tom Tight is another image of Guert Gansevoort. Guert (1812–1868) was the grandson of a Revolutionary hero, General Peter Gansevoort, and the first cousin of Herman Melville. He became a midshipman in 1823, upon the recommendation of his uncle Peter Gansevoort (who was Melville's benefactor and, in fact, paid for the publication of *Clarel*) and of several of his influential friends, including the grandfather of Philip Spencer, in whose execution he was to be involved. Guert, already a lieutenant, was attached to the *Somers* in May 1842. In 1862 he was promoted to captain.

Guert was second in command on the *Somers* at the time of the execution of Philip Spencer, and presided at the council of officers (not a court-martial) which Captain Alexander Slidell Mackenzie had convened. Apparently, he served as a sort of go-between for Mackenzie in enforcing his opinion of the guilt of Spencer and the two seamen accused with him. None of the three men was summoned to appear in his own defense, and as soon as the council had adjourned, they were hanged. In fact, even while the council was sitting, Mackenzie was making preparation for the execution. At the subsequent Court of Inquiry into the incident, and at the later Court-Martial of Mackenzie, Guert also played a prominent part as a witness for the defense.

This is not the place to analyze the case, but it would seem that Spencer, a cross-eyed, lonely, rebellious, day-dreaming, and highly neurotic youth, with a taste for drink, probably indulged himself in a fantasy of mutiny and as part of the game tried to frighten the purser's steward, who turned informer. As for Mackenzie, the most generous construction to be put on his behavior may well be that offered by James Gordon Bennett, editor of the New York *Herald*, who wrote that the Captain "acted under a species of insanity, produced by panic, lively imagination, and the spirit of the age." In any case, Mackenzie pressured the council for a verdict of guilty, and hanged Spencer, Cromwell, and Small without having given any of them a hearing in their own defense. And even if they had been clearly guilty, Mackenzie was obligated, if possible, to hold them until a proper court-martial could be convened; he clearly failed to do this, and his critics offered bad judgment, funk, or self-interest, or a combination of all three, as the disreputable explanation. The voluminous reports and statements which Mackenzie (he was by way of being a writer, with books of travel and naval history to his credit) wrote before and during the court-martial provided the ferocious James Fenimore Cooper (see Introduction, pp. 38–39) and various succeeding critics of his conduct with some of the most damaging items in their arsenal.

It is hard for a reader—at least for this one—to escape the impression that the author of the remarkable documents was as vain, illogical, self-serving and self-deluding a Bible-thumper as ever set shoe leather to quarterdeck. He seems, too, to have been as accomplished a fantasist as young Spencer, and the tragedy may be supposed to have resulted only because Spencer's fantasy played into that of Mackenzie. In the midst of his rhetoric and cunning Mackenzie was also stupid enough to report, in writing, such things as the statement he made to Spencer in the last few minutes of his life: "I told him that . . . it was not in nature that his father should not have interfered to save him—that for those who have friends and money in America there was no punishment for the worst of crimes. . . ." In other words, this burst of idiotic candor scarcely tallies with the official justification, the certainty that without the hangings the ship was in dire and immediate danger. But this is only one of a number of slips and contradictions, and with judges who shrewdly scrutinized such literary compositions Mackenzie might well have written himself out of the service and perhaps into a halter.

There may be ground for the suspicion that the court-martial was a device to save Mackenzie from trial in a civil court. Certainly, some aspects of the procedure were greatly to the benefit of the accused. Legally, the accused had the privilege of defending himself by presenting written statements not subject to the cross-examination, and without cross-examination there was no wind to break the massive fog of words. Again, quite legally, the court, whether by design or ineptitude, appointed as Judge Advocate, a man "little known to his profession," as a Commodore not associated with the court-martial complained to Cooper, and one who showed little astuteness or stamina in the prosecution. Another matter that not legally but illegally worked in favor of the accused was the fact that, in spite of a written injunction from the Secretary of the Navy that all witnesses (i.e., the officers and crew of the *Somers*) should be held safe and protected from intermeddling, the exact opposite was done. Could comedy go further than to entrust the crew (except eleven men arrested by Mackenzie and still held in jail awaiting trial as mutineers) to the protection of the very officers of the *Somers*, who, if Mackenzie was convicted, would automatically be branded as accomplices? (In fact, both the widow of Cromwell and the father of Spencer tried to get Guert indicted for murder, along with Mackenzie, and might well have succeeded except for the protecting arm of, first, the investigative hearings, and then, the court-martial.) The officers, with Guert as the responsible commander, allowed the crew to be taken off ship and coached by the lawyers for the defense, and were in general slack enough to let several members of the crew simply walk away bearing whatever knowledge or sympathies they had.

In the end Mackenzie was acquitted on the key charges, but not unanimously. On the charge of murder, the judges divided 9 to 3; on that of "oppression," 8 to 4. Only on the technical charge of illegality in his procedure did Mackenzie elicit unanimity. The acquittal was, however, not "honorable." The vote again split, with 9 of the 12 judges holding for the less comforting verdict.

An ambiguous footnote to the case is to be found in the suicide of Passed Assistant Surgeon R. W. Leecock, who had been a member of Mackenzie's "council," and who stands out as the only member to offer the damaging testimony that Mackenzie had sent an order by Guert to hurry up the verdict, an order amply explained by the fact, stupidly admitted by

Mackenzie in the course of his documents, that he had long since determined to hang Spencer, *et al.*, and had made preparations, council or no council. Another footnote, somewhat less ambiguous, is the fact that Mackenzie, in a report to the Navy Department, dated December 19, 1842, 18 days after the execution, hastened to urge the promotion of ten persons on the *Somers*, including his nephew O. H. Perry, who was especially recommended for the place "left vacant by the treason of Mr. Spencer," and crowned his eulogy of Guert (who, however, is not specifically recommended for promotion) with a comment on the "perfect harmony of our opinions," further cementing, by intent or happy accident, the united front against the dead.

As a final footnote, with no ambiguity, the eleven members of the crew who had been arrested by Mackenzie as parties to the conspiracy and were still held, were quietly released—a fact that obviously restricted the conspiracy, if there had been one at all, and not merely a fantasy of Spencer's, to the three dead men, and would certainly imply that in urging the safety of the brig as the overriding reason for the executions, Captain Mackenzie had been, to say the least, overzealous. Mackenzie would have had, as a matter of fact, only three more days to hold the ship; he put in at Charlotte Amalie on December 4, before proceeding to New York.

214 In the margin "bowsing" replaces "boozing," which is canceled.

215 Before "voyage" "last" is inserted. This hint that Guert died, or was lost, on a voyage to China is fiction; Melville would of course have known the facts of Guert's career. Some ten years after the *Somers* episode, he became commander, and in 1862, captain. He retired in 1867, and died the following year. The politician Thurlow Weed, who knew the family well, claims in his *Autobiography* to have had, from Hunn Gansevoort, a cousin of Guert with whom Guert had presumably discussed the case immediately after the *Somers* reached New York, some damaging testimony about Mackenzie's pressuring the council, through Guert, for a conviction. Weed describes Guert's behavior when he told him that he and Hunn had sat "gossiping" over hot whiskey punch into the small hours:

> The lieutenant (Guert), with evident surprise, asked, with emphasis, "Did he tell you that I passed the previous night with him?" I answered in the affirmative. He

> said, "What else did he tell you?" I replied, with equal emphasis, "He told me all that you said to him about the trial of Spencer." Whereupon he looked thoughtfully a moment, then drank off his champagne, seized or raised the bottle, again filled his glass and emptied it, and, without further remark, left the table.
>
> I did not see him again for seven years,—seven years which had told fearfully upon his health and habits. In the last years of his life he was stationed at the Brooklyn Navy Yard, then a sad wreck of his former self. He came frequently to see me, but was always moody, taciturn, and restless. In my conversation with him I never again referred to this affair, nor do I know that he ever spoke of it to others. But I do know that a bright, intelligent, high principled, and sensitive gentleman, and a most promising officer of the navy spent the best part of his life a prey to unavailing remorse for an act the responsibility of which belonged to a superior officer.

The name Tom Tight may be taken to suggest not only that Guert was tight-lipped, but was apt to get "tight" from drink. Tom is presented in the poem as drinking.

219 The Captain of the *Somers* was acquitted in the court-martial, but the acquittal, as we have said, was not "honorable."

227 A garboard strake (or streak) is the first range of planks laid on a ship's bottom, next to the keel.

230–233 The anomalous role of a chaplain on a man-of-war more than once occupied Melville. See *White-Jacket* (Ch. XXVIII) and *Billy Budd* (Ch. 24).

233 In *John Marr* this line falls at the end of a page, but in the manuscript a section division is marked here.

234 A horse block is a grating or platform for the officer of the deck to stand on.

247 Captain Turret, the "Kentuckian colossal," was Captain James Armstrong of the *United States*.

255 The episode of the flogging of the Finn comes from the flogging of one William Hoff, in 1843. In connection with this episode, see *White-Jacket*, Chapter XXXIII, from which some details are drawn. The toughness of the Finn finds a model in John, who, waiting for the scourge, is drenched by icy spray (here sleet) and does not even shudder, and who takes the lash with no sound. But the punishment of Peter, the mizzen-top lad (who is a sort of "handsome sailor" like Billy Budd), gives another detail used here: "the shuddering and creeping of his dazzling white back. . . ."

261 Og, King of Bashan, a giant, was defeated by the Jews. Deuteronomy 3:11.

288 In the margin "shows" is corrected to "lours."

295 The angel of the brig is the master-at-arms.

308 "And there we saw the giants, the sons of Anak . . ." (Numbers 13:33).

316 "Threap" means to bicker, quarrel, complain.

335 A scrutineer is one charged with the duty of examining or overseeing, especially at an election.

367 For Jack Genteel, see "Jack Roy" (pp. 305–06), and the connection with Jack Chase.

402–425 See, in *Battle-Pieces,* "The Cumberland," "The Temeraire," "In the Turret," and especially, "A Utilitarian View of the Monitor's Fight."

410 Castle Tantallon, in East Lothian, Scotland, is the old seat of the Douglas clan, long since in ruins.

414 In the margin "armed" is revised to "in armor."

435 In the margin "booze" is corrected to "bowse."

Tom Deadlight

This poem, giving the last musings of a tough old sailor facing death, is very much akin to the original notion of "Billy in the Darbies," already commented on in the Introduction (pp. 56–57). In fact, one may speculate that one impulse behind the change in the conception of Billy may have been the sense of mere repetition. But even so, in the tone and the hints of double reference, and in the scene of farewell and sea-burial, this poem is related to the final version of "Billy in the Darbies," though in the later poem there is much greater subtlety and emotional force.

1–2 The "famous old sea-ditty" referred to in the prose headnote is "Spanish Ladies," of which this poem is a close adaptation. The original poem records a passage up the English Channel.

3 The Deadman is Dedman Point, near Plymouth.

5 In the manuscript this line reads:

> I have hove my ship to, with the wind at sou'west, boys.

This early version is much closer to the original, which is:

> We hove our ship to with the wind from sou'west, boys.

17–20 This scene is very similar to that in *Billy Budd* when the Chaplain visits the condemned boy and decides that the natural goodness of the "barbarian" Billy is as good a thing as religion with which to meet the Judgment. This is the view of old Tom, another "barbarian," who must trust in "dead reckoning" rather than the "light" (of revelation) which the Chaplain would insist on.

23 The blue-blazes refer to a blue pyrotechnic torch, called Bengal light, used to signal at night. A shank-painter is a short rope or chain, used to fix an anchor to a ship's side.

Jack Roy

Jack Roy is the image of Jack Chase, captain of the maintop on the frigate *Neversink* in Melville's *White-Jacket*, which is derived from his own experience on the frigate *United States*, on which he served from August 1843 to October of the next year. The germ of the poem is in Chapter IV of *White-Jacket:*

> There was such an abounding air of good sense and good feeling about the man, that he who could not love him, would thereby pronounce himself a knave. I thanked my sweet stars, that kind fortune had placed me near him, though under him, in the frigate; and from the outset, Jack and I were fast friends.
>
> Wherever you may be now rolling over the blue billows, dear Jack! take my best love along with you; and God bless you, wherever you go!
>
> Jack was a gentleman. What though his hand was hard, so was not his heart, too often the case with soft palms. His manners were easy and free; none of the boisterousness, so common to tars; and he had a polite courteous way of saluting you, if it were only to borrow your knife. Jack had read all the verses of Byron, and all the romances of Scott. He talked of Rob Roy, Don Juan, and Pelham; Macbeth and Ulysses; but, above all things, was an ardent admirer of Camoens. Parts of the Lusiad, he could recite in the original. Where he had obtained his wonderful accomplishments, it is not for me,

his humble subordinate, to say. Enough, that those accomplishments were so various; the languages he could converse in, so numerous; that he more than furnished an example of that saying of Charles the Fifth—*he who speaks five languages is as good as five men.* But Jack, he was better than a hundred common mortals; Jack was a whole phalanx, an entire army; Jack was a thousand strong; Jack would have done honour to the Queen of England's drawing room; Jack must have been a by-blow of some British Admiral of the Blue. A finer specimen of the island race of Englishmen could not have been picked out of Westminster Abbey of a coronation day."

The name Rob Roy appears, as will be noted, in the foregoing passage and may have suggested Roy as the last name of Jack in the poem. But Roy, of course, means king, and Jack is a king among men—though, as the poem puts it, "not overmuch the king." But the king-knave opposition appears, too, in the poem, and so we have here the implication of a deck of cards, and incidentally the game aspect of life to the gay-hearted sailor. As Roy may have been suggested by Rob Roy in the original passage of *White-Jacket,* so the use of knave there may be the germ of the king-knave opposition in the poem, etc. The impression made upon Melville by the real Jack Chase is best indicated by the fact that *Billy Budd* is dedicated to him.

1–2 See the end of *Clarel* and of "Pontoosuce" for other and fuller presentations of the theme of nature's constant self-renewal and the sense of individual fulfillment by absorption in the general process. With a different emotional emphasis, see also the end of "The Haglets."

26 See Jack Genteel in "Bridegroom Dick" as the same figure of the sailor who is one of Nature's gentlemen, "in escapade."

The Haglets

This is one of the many poems which echo Melville's personal disaster, the theme of the "elate" man whom ruin overtakes. The key of the particular poem is in Melville's *Journal up the Straits,* in the entry of December 7, 1856, which reports how the captain of his ship "told a story about the heat of arms affecting the compass." See also *Clarel*, the Timoneer's story (III, xii, 57–130).

On May 17, 1885, there appeared in the New York *Daily Tribune* and the Boston *Herald*, a poem entitled "The Admiral of the White, by the author of 'Omoo,' 'Typee,' 'Moby Dick,' Etc.," the first version of which, according to Leon Howard's biography, had been composed on the *Meteor*, during Melville's voyage to San Francisco in 1860. Among Melville's manuscripts there is a poem of the same title, with a note on it in Elizabeth Melville's hand: "Herman gave this to Tom"—Tom being, of course, his brother, who was master of the *Meteor*. The poem follows:

The Admiral of the White

Proud, O proud in his oaken hall
The Admiral walks to-day,
From the top of his turreted citadel
French colors 'neath English play.

Why skips the needle so frolic about,
Why danceth the ship so today?
Is it to think of the French Captain's rout
Surrendered when ended the fray?
O well may you skip, and well may you dance
You dance on your homeward way;
O well may you skip and well may you dance
With homeward-bound victors today.

Like a baron bold from his mountain-hold,
At night looks the Admiral forth:
Heavy the clouds, and thick and dun,
They slant from the sullen North.

Catching at each little opening for life,
The moon in her wane swims forlorn;
Fades, fades mid the clouds her pinched paled face
Like the foeman's in seas sinking down.

Tack off from the land! And the watch below
Old England the oak-crowned to drink:—
Knock, knock, knock, the loud billows go,
Rapping, "Bravo, my boys!" ere they sink—

Knock, knock, knock on the windward bow;
    The Anvil-Head Whale you would think.

Tis Saturday night,—the last of the week,
    The last of the week, month and year—
On deck! shout it out, you forecastle men,
    Shout 'Sail ho, Sail ho—the New Year!'

Drink, messmates, drink; tis sweet to think
    Tis the last of the week, month, and year,
When perils are past and old England at last,
    Though now shunned, in the morn we will near;
We've beaten the foe, their ship blown below,
    Their flags on St. Paul's Church we'll rear.

Knock, knock, knock, the loud billows go—
    God! what's that shouting and roar?
Breakers!—close, close ahead and abeam:
    She strikes—knock, knock—we're ashore!

Why went the needle so trembling about,
    Why shook you and trembled today?
Was it, perchance, that those French Captains' swords
    In the arms-chest too near you lay?
Was it to think that those French Captains' swords,
    Surrendered, might yet win the day?
O woe for the brave no courage can save,
    Woe, woe for the ship led astray.

Nigh-beetling the rocks below which she shocks,
    Her boats they are there by her side,
Forked seas lick her round, as in flames she were bound,
    Roars, roars like a furnace the tide.

O jagged the rocks, repeated she knocks,
    Splits the hull like a cracked filbert there,
Her boats are torn, and ground-up are thrown,
    Float the small chips like filbert-bits there.

    Pale, pale, but proud, 'neath the billows loud,
The Admiral sleeps tonight;
    Pale, pale, but proud, in his sea-weed shroud,—

The Admiral of the White;
    And by their guns the dutiful ones,
Who had fought, bravely fought the good fight.

(Melville's handwriting is at times almost impenetrable, and some of the readings here are conjectural. For instance, "shocks" and "Forked" in stanza 10. But "Forked" is supported by a line in "The Haglets": "In dance of breakers forked or peaked.")

The version of "The Admiral of the White" which appeared in the newspapers some twenty-five years later is a very different poem, and "The Haglets" is a further development from that. The manuscript from which the poem in *John Marr* was set is composed of clips of a newspaper printing with the addition of new material. The following lines of "The Haglets" are the sections from the clips: 1–19, 31–54, 67–78, 115–126, 133–255.

A haglet is the same as a kittiwake or hacklet, a small species of gull. The origin of the word is unknown. Here Melville is punning, with the word taken as meaning "little hags," the Fates being "hags."

12 In the proofs, a bar comes after this line to mark the end of a prologue, and Melville wrote in a note to the printer: "The stanza of eighteen lines here begins." But in *John Marr*, line 12 falls at the bottom of a page and there is no bar or any other device to indicate a break. Counting from this point on, however, the poem is divided into stanzas of eighteen lines, each in three sections of six lines, as indicated here, up through line 228.

228 In neither *John Marr* nor the proofs is there extra space after this line to correspond to the break after line 12. But in the paste-up text of the setting copy there is a note: "Widen the space between these two lines." This is obviously to set off the epilogue.

240 This is an echo of "Sir Patrick Spens," but the fact cannot be taken to mean an identity of theme, except in a most general sense.

242 If the haglets are the Fates, now the Admiral, by the very fact of his disaster, has escaped their power and has, like the little pilot-fish in "The Maldive Shark," found "asylum in the jaws of the Fates."

250 In "The abysm and the star" we find the theme, common in Melville's poetry, of the doubleness of nature in relation to men's strivings and aspirations. There is some hint, too, of the doubleness of man's own nature, capable of heights and depths: courage and grandeur are in the Admiral, but at the same time he is a figure of rapacity. Such a line of thought is prepared for in lines 229–232, where it is said that the flags and arms seized by the Admiral, as his "trophy" and as the "victor's voucher," will now never hang in the Abbey to "take Time's dust with holier palms"—that is, with signs of man's nobler or more spiritual part.

The Man-of-War Hawk

4–5 Here the hawk is beyond the vicissitudes of human fate, but the image is bound to evoke that of the "sky-hawk" that, at the end of *Moby Dick,* "with archangelic shrieks, and his imperial beak thrust upwards, and his whole captive form folded in the flag of Ahab, went down with his ship, which, like Satan, would not sink to hell till she had dragged a living part of heaven along with her, and helmeted herself with it."

The Maldive Shark

The Maldive Sea and Maldive Islands are southwest of India. The shark appears in *Mardi:* "There is a fish in the sea that ever more, like a surly lord, only goes abroad attended by his suite. It is the Shovel-nosed Shark. A clumsy lethargic monster, unshapely as is his name, and the last species of his kind, one would think, to be so bravely waited upon as he is. His suite is composed of those dainty little creatures called Pilot Fish by sailors." (Chapter xviii)

12 Here is an example of the carelessness and ineptitude that haunted Melville in even some of his best poems. Logically, "Fates" should be singular. The common saying, "in the jaws of fate," is singular. In the poem the Maldive Shark himself, in whose jaws the fish hide, is singular. When the word is plural we get the preposterous image of something hidden in the jaws of each of the three hags, Parcae, or Norns, like a nut in a squirrel's or a wad of chewing gum in a child's. The problem

was simply that Melville felt himself stuck with the rhyme on "gates" and did not have the stamina to fight the thing out.

To Ned

Ned Bunn of the poem is Richard Tobias Greene, who is also the Toby of *Typee*, Melville's companion in those adventures, who came forward in later years to vouch for the accuracy of Melville's account.

18 Would the "Syrian pilgrimage" be Melville's journey to the Holy Land? The contrast here between the Eden found by the "Typee-truants" and the land visited on the "Syrian pilgrimage" might imply the polarity I have discussed earlier. See Introduction, p. 6.

Crossing the Tropics

The Saya-y-Manto, of which this poem, according to the title, is a part, does not exist. Presumably Melville never undertook it and may never have even intended to. The word is the name of a day dress of the ladies of Lima.

10 Vasco da Gama, the Portuguese navigator (c. 1460–1524) who discovered the sea route to India.
14 This line fell at the end of a sheet in the manuscript, and therefore the stanza break was omitted in *John Marr*. But obviously, by the regular structure of the poem, lines 13–14 are a separate couplet.

The Berg

See Introduction, pp. 52–53.

15 In *John Marr* this falls at the bottom of a page, and so there is no indication of a section break. But in the manuscript such a break is indicated. But the division here suggests a speculation. Lines 5, 15, and 27 form a kind of refrain, each ending with the phrase "went down." Lines 15 and 27 mark the

end of sections, and it is very hard to see why Melville did not make a break after line 5, and close the break after 9. This arrangement would more effectively point up the intrinsic structure of the poem.

17 In the manuscript "Around" appears in the place of "Circling."

37 In the book "dead indifference" is disastrously corrected to "dense stolidity."

FROM *Pebbles*

1–2 In the manuscript, line 1 ends with a dash instead of a colon, and line 2 ends with a comma instead of a dash.

5 In Revelations 7:1–3 there are "four angels standing on the four corners of the earth, holding the four winds of the earth, that the wind should not blow on the earth, nor on the sea, nor on any tree." The poet can bless the Angels for the peace of his reconciliation, but at the same time can bless them for the "pitiless breath" which had taught him the inner meaning of experience, had "enlightened" him, or "undeceived" him.

7 Rosmarine is rosemary, the botanical name of which is Rosmarinus—sea dew. Rosemary traditionally was supposed to have curative properties. Here Melville echoes Ben Jonson's *Masque of Queenes:*

> . . . steep
> Your bodies in that purer brine,
> And wholesome dew call'd Ros-marine.

After the Pleasure Party

Lewis Mumford, in his *Herman Melville: A Study of His Life and Vision,* uses this poem as evidence for a crisis in Melville's sexual life, on his visit to Italy after the trip to the Holy Land (1857):

> The pilgrim, dusty with travel in barren lands, revels in the sensuous peace of the terraces down to the sea; he is not so completely the pilgrim, so thoroughly the hermit, that his heart is entirely his own: on the contrary, it is out of a desperate dryness and loneliness of

soul that Melville is suddenly beset by such temptations as the hermits of Thebaid found in the desert. We have no image of the woman who walked with Melville through these green walks, under the star-bright sky: he himself tried, in the years that followed, to forget "the glade wherein Fate spun Love's ambuscade," tempting him to flout pale years of cloistral life and "flush himself in sensuous strife." We do not know if it was she who repulsed him, as the shore repulses the hungry billows, tired of the homeless deep, or whether it was a resistance within himself that wrecked and scattered the impulses that were driving him toward the warm object of his desire; but we know that, flushed perhaps by wine, and stirred by the fragrant Spring night, sex asserted itself again in Melville: the "dear desire through love to sway" came over him, and when he found himself baffled, attempting to rule his own passion, yet not able to reign, neither conquering the woman herself nor the passion she had awakened, he was aware of a dreary shame of frustration. Blocked in his highest powers of thought, in his career as a writer, Melville found himself equally defeated . . . and perhaps by the same cluster of images . . . in that other citadel of personality. Bitterly he cries: "And kept I long heaven's watch for this, contenting love, for this, even this?"

It has been pointed out, of course, that the poem cannot, in any literal sense, bear the reading Mumford puts on it. The poem is divided into several sections. The first section (in italics as a kind of prologue, with a separate title) is spoken, as it were, by "Amor threatening," to serve as a text which the poem proper is to illustrate; the second section (lines 7–17) is, presumably (see note below), spoken by the poet; the third section (lines 18–110) is spoken, as indicated by quotation marks in the manuscript, by the woman Urania, the astronomer who has forfeited love for learning; the fourth section (lines 111–130) is spoken by the author; the fifth section (lines 131–147) is again by the heroine Urania; and the last section (lines 148–157) is spoken by the author, commenting on the meaning of the reported experience of Urania. It is clear that it is the woman Urania who is bitterly torn between human love and intellectual aspirations—not Melville.

There are other tangles in Mumford's discussion. For instance, in addition to attributing Urania's speech to Melville himself, Mumford changes the pretty peasant girl with the "blossoming rod," who in the poem is the object of Urania's jealousy, into an object of sexual attraction for Melville: "he [Melville] remembered and magnified other incidents of his journey; the barefoot peasant girl in Naples who had climbed up the hills near the wheels of his carriage. . . ." And Mumford, too, attributes to Melville himself the impulse to resolve the issue of the poem in Catholicism—an impulse which belongs to Urania—and says that Melville was withheld from such a resolution by "something reflected in the mighty statuary and art of the Roman and the Greek" (this being Mumford's interpretation of Urania's appeal to the Virgin Athena against the Virgin Mary), and adds that "no institution or activity could share Melville's burden," for "at bottom, he feels hopeless of either Church or of [*sic*] Art."

Richard Chase, in his provocative *Herman Melville,* agrees with Mumford in taking the poem at an overtly autobiographical level. He says that the party "had been held, apparently, in Italy," and that "Melville seems to be recalling an incident of his 1856–57 travels." Chase then proceeds to take Urania as the "poet's muse," and not as a real woman, but, in a somewhat confusing fashion, says that Urania "recalls the sudden upswelling of sexual desire she had experienced at the pleasure party," and discovers that the "invasion of sexual desire" has destroyed her "dream world" of "myth and art." Urania next recalls the peasant girl beside a carriage in which the "poet rode" (presumably taking this as an actual incident, as does Mumford), and how "Amor's 'glance' fell 'moistly' " on her—not the glance of the "he" of the poem. This leads the "muse" to demand of Amor whether he supposes that because she is not "roseate . . . she had felt 'no sun' nor thrilled 'with Spring,' " and complains that his arm—Amor's—is always about "some radiant ninny flung." The poet then says "that he does not know the final fate of Urania, but he confronts her with three different visions of life as possible sources of renewed art and fantasy": the pagan, which could "set free her 'sex' and her 'self-hood,' " the Christian, to which, disturbed by the first possibility, she has the impulse to flee, and the "armed Athena" to free her from the "sexual feud." The last, Chase says, would be no solution but a "spiritual disaster," for the "celibate muse" will never transcend the demands of sex; and this last statement would seem to be a fair summary of the poem.

It is hard to know exactly how Chase wishes us to take Urania as Melville's muse, but in any case, in ignoring the literal fiction of the poem, he adds to the reader's difficulties. The literal fiction concerns, of course, the sudden assault of passion on the intellectual woman who has not known her deeper self, and now finds herself in love with the unnamed "he" of the poem, who, unfortunately, prefers any radiant and more obviously feminine "ninny." Both Mumford and Chase are right in wanting to interpret the fiction, but one cannot interpret it by ignoring or distorting it.

Both Mumford and Chase would argue that the subject of thwarted sexuality in the poem involves a struggle on Melville's part with a more or less latent homosexual impulse. Mumford refers to Melville's "burden" that no "institution or activity could share," and Chase finds the cause of Urania's "surged emotion" at the Villa Albani in the bas-relief of Antinoüs, the beautiful male favorite of the Emperor Hadrian, which Melville twice comments on in his journal. See also Chase, pp. 220–229, 294–295, and *Clarel,* II, xxvii, 58–132.

Whatever validity one may accept for Chase's theory that Urania is Melville's muse, there seems to have been a quite literal suggestion for at least a part of her. On July 7, 1852, a few months after finishing *Pierre*, Melville was on Nantucket, where he spent the evening with William Mitchell, the astronomer, and his daughter Maria, who was following the same vocation in the same remote spot, and who had already earned a considerable reputation. This encounter presumably provides the germ of Urania as a lady astronomer, and there is apparently little way of knowing if Maria provided more. Dr. Murray, in a letter, toys with the idea that the poem may have had for its primary model Augusta, Melville's favorite sister, who was never married, and who, in her last illness, refused to let the attending physician perform a complete physical examination. But he adds that Augusta had neither astronomy nor any association with Italy to qualify her for the post.

Beyond the sexual aspects of the poem, there is a more general theme, that of the struggle between the commitment to life and the commitment to art, between the values of life and those of art. In this connection, Chase suggests that the poem may be a development from Matthew Arnold's sonnet "Austerity of Poetry," which Melville read in 1871, and of which he underscored some lines. Arnold had, in fact, a great influence on Melville, especially on *Clarel* and, to a lesser degree, on *Battle-Pieces*. See Walter Bezanson's "Melville's Reading of Arnold's Poetry," in *PMLA*, 1954. For the more general question of art and life, see "The Ravaged Villa," "Art," and "Venice."

It is clear from Melville's working manuscript, as from the setting manuscript prepared by his wife, that he considered several different titles. They are "Urania," "A Boy's Revenge," "After the Pleasure Party," and "A Boy's Revenge, or After the Pleasure Party." The last, according to his manuscript, appears early as a possibility, and it is the choice in his wife's manuscript. But in *Timoleon,* the title definitively becomes the present one.

The location of the poem in the collection is also of some interest. In both manuscripts the poem comes ninth, but by the time the book was finally set it had been promoted to the second place, just after *Timoleon.* Presumably Melville was coming to attach greater significance to it.

There is a peculiar parallelism between "In a Bye-Canal" and "After the Pleasure Party." To begin with, both are associated with Melville's Italian visit, "In a Bye-Canal" dating back to that "Travel long ago," and "After the Pleasure Party" being composed in recollection of it, in so far, at least, as background is concerned. Both poems, too, deal with sexual dislocation and ambivalence, the former with man's fear of woman, and the latter with woman's failure to accept man. There are, of course, considerable differences between the two poems. Except for the eloquent, and unexpected, passage lines 14–22, "In a Bye-Canal" is much lighter and wittier in tone, while Urania's utterance is a tortured self-examination and *cri de coeur*. But with line 148 the poet interrupts Urania's lament to give his own clinical analysis of her plight, and then, by the witty turn of the last two lines, detaches himself further from the whole unpleasant business. These devices of detachment, however, and the fact of the dramatic objectification of the theme in Urania, would seem to invite scrutiny, and we might even wonder at the apparently trivial detail of the omission of the quotation marks that had appeared in the manuscript (see below). In any case, "After the Pleasure Party" gives the impression of being a more serious and probing development of the earlier poem.

1–6 This is clearly a separate section, spoken by Amor, and has its own separate title. In *Timoleon* it is printed in italics on a separate page.

18 In Melville's manuscript, though not in the copy prepared by his wife, quotation marks appear at the beginning of each stanza up to, but not including, line 79. This fact provokes several questions.

(1) What about lines 7–17? Are they from the point of view of the poet, or are they spoken by Urania? Conceivably they could be spoken by Urania, but the fact that lines 111–130 and lines 148–157 are clearly by the poet would strongly imply that the poet's own words set a frame for the utterances of Urania. The fact that Melville, however careless he was in such matters, begins the quotation marks here strongly supports this theory.

(2) Does the fact that we find no quotation marks to begin line 79 mean that the speech of Urania is now ended? The evidence strongly indicates that the speech continues. First, there is no closing quotation mark at the end of the previous stanza. Second, and more positively, in the three stanzas that begin with lines 79, 86, and 101 (which are without quotation marks), there appear the first-person pronouns used by Urania in speaking of her plight. The fact that her first speech is concluded with line 110 is, by the same token, clear from the fact that now she is referred to in the third person by the poet, as well as by the fact that in the manuscript Melville instructed the printer to use a double space here (and was obeyed). The resumption of her speech in line 131 is clear from the colon at the end of line 130, and, more positively, from the return in line 131 to the first-person pronoun, which appears, for the last time, in the climactic line 147, which ends her speech for good.

(3) Why do we not find quotation marks after line 79? The answer, as far as his manuscript is concerned, may lie in his characteristic carelessness about punctuation in his working drafts. Or it may well be that by this point he had decided to follow the course indicated in his wife's setting copy, and trust context to clarify the shifts in point of view.

51 Cassiopeia, the wife of the mythical king Cepheus of

Ethiopia, and the mother of Andromeda, was placed among the stars, as the constellation of that name. Cassiopeia is called "sister" by the heroine of the poem: the crime of Cassiopeia was pride, which had brought the vengeance of the sea-nymphs in the form of the sea-monster to whom her daughter would have been sacrificed but for the timely arrival of Perseus; and the crime of Urania is pride, too, for she would see herself queenly in a "Golden Chair," until she discovers that she more nearly resembles the lunatic locked in a cell, and she, too, in her pride, by withdrawing from natural life, sacrificed her child; that is, the hope of children. Furthermore, in the sky, Cassiopeia, being situated near the pole, is upside down part of every night, to teach her humility; and the heroine of the poem, who has sinned pridefully against Amor, is punished in a parallel fashion: she must look *down* and envy the lowliest peasant girl in her natural life, and not *up* at the stars.

56 The words "enlightened" and "undeceived" recall the end of "The March into Virginia" and "Shiloh," for Urania, like the uninstructed young soldiers marching into battle with their delusions and ideologies, finds herself confronting a new dimension of truth in experience.

79–100 The imagery here of Urania's sexual release (the "lunge piercing," etc.) is male, not female. This may be unconscious on the part of Melville, but unconscious or not, it is meaningful in relation to Urania. Just before this passage she has spoken contemptuously of "some radiant ninny" who would attract the man she yearns for. Next, Urania reverses her feelings and says she would exchange her "starry lore" (for the lack of which the natural woman whom she envies is a "ninny") for the "wanton's rose" wherein the "bee" might repose. She longs, in other words, to be the rose which will accept the bee—longs, that is, for the natural female role. Then she cries out, "Could I remake me." But in what sense? Following on the rose-bee image, the sense would seem to be to *make me more fully woman.* But the next lines might be interpreted as follows: *or if I can't be remade more fully woman, let me be made into a man, for the man doesn't have to wait passively, he can go and do what he likes; he can go get a "radiant ninny" or a "wanton."* This is not to say that Urania is consciously saying this; the imagery is saying it for her.

86–88 In the manuscript Melville wrote:

Could I remake me! could I be
Pure sexless intellect, and plunge
Alone into Pan's wide mystery . . .

92–100 This is an echo of Plato's Symposium where Aristophanes relates how originally there had been a third "Androgynous" sex which sprung from the moon, and which partook of the nature of both male and female, including "double genitals," and which had been so full of strength, energy, and arrogance that its members had attempted to scale heaven and set upon the gods. In punishment and for protection, Zeus had simply split each creature into two halves, a male and a female, and, after the work was done, each half, with a desperate yearning, sought the missing half "to reintegrate our former nature, to make two into one, and to bridge the gulf between one human being and another." Merlin Bowen, in *The Long Encounter*, relates Urania's complaint that single sex is a "Cosmic jest or Anarch blunder" with Melville's more general theory of the need for completed "Self-hood." See pp. 27 ff. The theme of the yearning "to bridge the gulf' is not uncommon in Melville.
100 The image here, and the phrase "life's gate"—in fact, the temper of the passage and even the presence of the unresponsive woman—is related to Marvell's "To His Coy Mistress."
111 Urania, the daughter of Zeus and Mnemosyne, or Memory, was one of the nine Muses, that of Astronomy.
121 The Villa Albani, now the Villa Torlonia, was built in 1760 for the Cardinal Alessandro Albani, for whom Winckelmann there assembled an extraordinary collection of classical sculpture. The collection, looted by Napoleon and not wholly recovered, was subsequently added to. There are a large number of pieces in the portico, including the colossal masks, but there is no way to identify what Melville had particularly in mind, if anything.
138 The armed Virgin is Athena.

The Ravaged Villa

In his journal, Melville comments on the ruins of villas seen in his travels in Italy, particularly on the massive ruin of the Villa of Hadrian, at Tivoli. The poem itself owes something in both style and content to Landor, as do a few other pieces of Melville's.

8 In the Middle Ages, it was the practice in Rome to burn the marble of buildings and statuary merely to get lime for plaster. This may, perhaps, be taken as another appearance, in metaphor, of the conflict between the demands of life and the demands of art, which appears also in "After the Pleasure Party."

Monody

The word "Monody" undoubtedly echoes Milton's use of the term in the subtitles of "Lycidas."

Melville had met Hawthorne, whose death provoked this poem, on August 5, 1850, at Stockbridge, Massachusetts, during the period when Melville was living at Arrowhead Farm, and Hawthorne in Lenox. Melville was just about to write an admiring review of *Mosses from an Old Manse*, the most deeply perceptive comment Hawthorne's work had at that time received, and the meeting with the older man (Hawthorne was now 46, some fifteen years older than Melville) was dramatically important for him. He wrote: "It is that blackness in Hawthorne . . . that so fixes and fascinates me." And again, "Already I feel that this Hawthorne has dropped germinous seeds into my soul." The ambiguous depth of Hawthorne's work was, for all the differences, a sort of mirror to his own and gave him the sense of companionship in the working out of a new literature for America; and then in the throes of composing *Moby Dick*, which he was to dedicate to Hawthorne, he could write in a letter to him that "the Godhead is broken up like bread at the Supper, and that we are the pieces."

Hawthorne died on May 19, 1864. The poem was inscribed in Melville's copy of Hawthorne's last book, *Our Old Home*, but the poem was not published until the *Timoleon* volume of 1891.

3 In one sense it could hardly be said that Melville and Hawthorne were "estranged." Hawthorne was, simply, far too reserved and enigmatic to respond to Melville's need for communion and, as far as is known, there was never any rupture between them, merely a dwindling in communication. See Introduction, p. 5, for Hawthorne's account of their conversation among the dunes near Liverpool. Melville called on Hawthorne once more, on his return journey, before taking ship.

11 The metaphor of the "cloistral vine" can be crudely paraphrased by saying that Hawthorne's "cloistral" qualities (his reserve and detachment from the world) produced and concealed something rich, ripe, and intoxicating. The word "cloistral" echoes "hermit-mound" above, in the winter scene; and the chill, "houseless" quality of the scene, even the glaze of ice, has an echo of Melville's sense of Hawthorne's detachment. In this connection, we may remember that in *Clarel* the name of the character supposed to be modeled on Hawthorne is Vine, and that Derwent, addressing Vine at the revels of Mar Saba, says, "Ambushed in leaves we spy your grape." See notes on "Vine and Clarel."

Art

In Melville's manuscript there is a very tangled work sheet, but in spite of the struggle which this indicates, he did not achieve the kind of sharp, epigrammatic economy and clarity at which the poem aims.

10 Jacob (Genesis 32:24–32) wrestled all night with the angel, and though he received the wound in the thigh, extorted the blessing he craved, and could say that he had "seen God face to face." The wound, however, carries us back to the idea of the life-cost in art, and that of the opposition between life and art. See "Venice," "In a Church of Padua," "After the Pleasure Party." In *Pierre* (Book XXII, Ch. i), the image of the wrestling also appears: "If a man must wrestle . . . it is well that it should be on the nakedest possible plain."

Venice

Pantheistic energy, the divine creative force, works in all nature, from the coral worm to man. In one perspective then, the Venetian palaces are as natural—as much the work of blind Necessity—as the coral reef. The issue appears in various forms in Melville's work, for instance, in *Pierre,* in the passage of the exploration of the self and the exploration of a pyramid (see "In a Church of Padua" and note, pp. 443–45). Here the explorer, when he finally comes to the inner chamber and the sarcophagus of the king, finds the king gone. Which I take to be saying that at the center of the "soul" there is emptiness, and we have no god-king but merely natural explanation. The whole question was, of course, a vital one for the time. Henry Adams, in 1863, could write of it: "But my philosophy teaches me, and I firmly believe it, that the laws that govern animated beings will be ultimately found to be at bottom the same with those which rule inanimate nature, and . . . I am quite ready to receive with pleasure any basis for a systematic conception of it all." The formulation of such an idea is even closer to Melville in Santayana's remark on "material functions spiritually realized" in *The Genteel Tradition at Bay* (1931): "No true appreciation of anything is possible without a sense of its *naturalness,* of the innocent necessity by which it has assumed its special and perhaps extraordinary form." Such bland acceptance was never Meville's, but there was a certain change of attitude with *Clarel* and, more significantly, with *Billy Budd.*

In *Pierre* (Book XXI, Ch. i), Melville also uses the image of the coral in much the same sense, saying that "grand productions of the best human intellects ever are built round a circle, as atolls (i.e., the primitive coral islets which, raising themselves in the depth of profoundest seas, rise funnel-like to the surface, and present there a hoop of white rock, which though on the outside everywhere lashed by the ocean, yet excludes all tempests from the quiet lagoon within), digestively including the whole range of all that can be known or dreamed."

In *Pierre* the point of the image is, however, somewhat different from that in the poem. The circle (art, shall we say), though "digestively including the whole range" of experience, "excludes all tempests"; so here we have another version of the "action-legend" polarity. Merlin Bowen, in *The Long Encounter* (pp. 39 ff.), aptly relates this passage to Melville's theory of artistic creation—the artist's search for the still center of being where his vision comes and his work is, after effort, suddenly effortless and fulfilling. In *Moby Dick* (Ch. lxxxvii), Melville describes that charmed spot and moment, "surrounded by circle upon circle of consternations and affrights," saying that "amid the tornadoed Atlantic of my being, do I myself still for ever centrally disport in mute calm; and while ponderous planets of unwaning woe revolve round me, deep down and deep inland there I still bathe me in eternal mildness of joy."

There is a letter sometimes ascribed to Mozart but now generally taken to be a forgery, that gives an account of his experience in composing. Even if a forgery, this letter, as some authorities suggest, may well be true in spirit and may be drawn from various pieces of testimony by the master (Jean-Victor Hocquard: *La Pensée de Mozart,* pp. 315–323). In any case, the letter is very close to Melville's testimony, and is the best statement I know of the experience of composition by at least some writers:

> My ideas come as they will, I don't know how, all in a stream. If I like them I keep them in my head, and people say that I often hum them over to myself. Well, if I can hold on to them, they begin to join on to one another, as if they were bits that a pastry-cook should join together in his pantry. And now my soul gets heated, and if nothing disturbs me the piece grows larger and brighter until, however long it is, it is all finished together in my mind, so that I can see it at a glance, as if it were a pretty picture or a pleasing person. Then I don't hear the notes one after another, as they are hereafter to be played, but it is as if in my fancy they were all at once. And that *is* a revel. While I'm inventing, it all seems to me like a fine vivid dream; but that hearing it all at once (when the invention is done), that's the best. [Quoted by Josiah Royce, *The Spirit of Modern Philosophy,* p. 457.]

In a Bye-Canal

Melville's work sheets of the poem indicate that, as in the case of "Art" and "Venice," he struggled desperately with this poem. See Introduction, pp. 7–8.

1–5 Strangely enough, this poem seems to have had its inspiration from Melville's visit to Cairo rather than to Venice. In the entry of his journal dated Saturday, January 3, 1857, we find:

> Lattice-work of the projecting windows. With little square hole, just large enough to contain the head. Curious aspect of women's faces peeping out . . . . Some of

> the streets of private houses are like tunnels from meeting overhead of projecting windows, etc. Like night at noon.

Melville does, of course, change the setting to the canal, but the feel is that of the Cairo entry, with the germ of line 5 in "Like night at noon."

6 Jael is the slayer of Sisera (Judges 4:12–23). After Sisera had been defeated by the Jews under the command of Barak (who had been inspired and urged on by Deborah), Sisera "fled away on his feet to the tent of Jael the wife of Heber the Kenite," who met him with hospitable promises of protection but who, when he slept, drove a tent-pin into his temple so that it pierced through into the ground. (Jael is celebrated by Deborah's song of victory in Judges 5.) The "wiled one" is, of course, Sisera and the word *wiled* may be a pun—the one who is deceived by wiles, but who also is "wild," outside of the ordinary world, is strong and dangerous, and is hunted like a beast. Melville, of course, corresponds to Sisera, Melville, too, having been defeated and being in flight; an outcast and, as proclaimed in *Moby Dick*, an Ishmael. But Melville, unlike Sisera, does not succumb. See "After the Pleasure Party," lines 67–69, where it is said that "strong man's a novice weak" to the "wiles" of the young peasant girl; also, "Vine and Clarel," line 11 and note.

In *Timoleon*, line 6 falls at the end of a page, but in both Melville's manuscript and that of his wife, a section break is indicated.

13–14, 30–34 As has been said in the Introduction, we have here, with the wit of *vers de société*, a version of the Petrarchan theme of the "cruel fair." The poem, however, may provoke a second thought beyond such matters. How seriously, for instance, are we to take the couplet about the "loveliest eyes" that, beyond the slats of the lattice, here a "basilisk glance"? After all, it is this combination of promise and threat that, strangely, precipitates the sudden shift of tone in the lines that follow. And in that powerful passage, how much of the seminal reference is to Melville's defeat and fear of madness, and how much to other and deeper questions? And how seriously, under the wit, are we to take the conclusion of the poem? See *Clarel* (II, lv, 143–145), where we find "The Syren's kiss—the Fury's thong!" See also notes on "After the Pleasure Party."

In a Church of Padua

This poem repeats one of Melville's most fundamental and obsessive themes, the problem of knowing the self, or as it is put in *Clarel* (II, xxxv), "The heart, with labyrinths replete." In one perspective, we can say that the central theme of *Pierre* is the problem of the hero's attempt to know himself, and it is an attempt that, in its very heroism, comes to nothing: "It is ambiguous still," he cries. (Book XXVI, ch. vi) But in the course of the novel, Melville more and more tortures the theme: "For surely no mere mortal who has at all gone down into himself will ever pretend that his slightest thought or act solely originated in his own defined identity." (Book X, Ch. i) And: "Deep, deep, and still deep and deeper must we go, if we would find out the heart of a man; descending into which is as descending a spiral stair in a shaft, without any end, and where that endlessness is only concealed by the spiralness of the stair, and the blackness of the shaft." But the theme appears in many places. As Ishmael puts it: "The subterranean miner that works in us all, how can one tell whither leads his shaft by the ever shifting muffled sound of his pick?" (*Moby Dick*, Ch. xli) In this poem Melville is treating the question of knowledge of the self (and of the self of another) in its general reference. But the theme is very close to his notion of artistic creation, which he saw, primarily, as a process of self-exploration (*Mardi*, Vol. II, lxxvi):

> When Lombardo set about his work, he knew not what it would become. He did not build himself in with plans; he wrote right on; and so doing, got deeper and deeper into himself; and like a resolute traveler, plunging through baffling woods, at last was rewarded for his toils. . . .

Melville's journal, in a long entry for Saturday, January 3, 1857, concerning his visit to Cairo, discusses the pyramids and describes how an old man: "Tried to go into the interior—fainted—brought out—leaned against the pyramid by the entrance—pale as death . . . Too much for him; oppressed by the massiveness & mystery of the pyramids. I myself too. A feeling of awe & terror came over me." Melville had used the idea of the descent into a pyramid in *Pierre* (Bk. XXI, Ch. i):

> Not yet had he dropped his angle into the well of his childhood, to find what fish might be there; for who dreams to find fish in a well? the running stream of the outer world, there doubtless swim the golden perch and the pickerel! Ten million things were as yet uncovered to Pierre. The old mummy lies buried in cloth on cloth; it takes time to unwrap this Egyptian king . . . . By vast pains we mine into the pyramid; by horrible gropings we come to the central room; with joy we espy the sarcophagus; but we lift the lid—and no body is there! —appallingly vacant as vast is the soul of a man!

In the poem "The Great Pyramid" (not reprinted here) it is said that he who braves the innermost labyrinths may not penetrate to the central chamber but

Comes out afar on deserts dead
And, dying, raves.

A more elaborate development of the same general theme, and image, appears in the sketch "I and My Chimney." In this the narrator is trying to defend the great central chimney of his old house against his wife's efforts to have it removed. The architect "Scribe" is called in by the wife. Inspection of the shaft of the chimney leads into the vast cellerage "whose numerous vaulted passages, and far glens of gloom, resemble the dark, damp depths of primeval woods." Scribe says that he "would not have inferred the magnitude of this foundation," and in the end gives a certificate of the soundness of the structure to the narrator, who hangs it above his fireplace.

In a very important paper (*American Literature*, XIII, 1941) Merton M. Sealts, Jr., interprets this sketch in relation to Melville's state of mind after the failure of *Moby Dick* and *Pierre*. When the family (primarily Melville's mother, who was living with them, and who here is in the role of the wife—significantly, in a psychological sense, as Newton Arvin and other critics would have it) calls in medical opinion (perhaps Dr. Oliver Wendell Holmes, a "scribe"), Scribe gives the "certificate" to the narrator to guard his chimney (his identity, his center of warmth, his source of creativity). But, further, Sealts relates the sketch to *Pierre* and the theme there of the exploration of the dark self as a source of creative power. There are various parallels between *Pierre* and "I and My Chimney" (as with other works of Melville), including the pyramid image and the notion of the "sacredness" of the dark self. The word "sacred" is used in *Pierre,* and in the sketch we are told that the ancestral builder of the house and chimney was named Dacres—an anagram for "sacred."

Though the point is not more than hinted at in the sketch, it is clear elsewhere that Melville regarded the creative force rooted in the depth of being as a source of terror as well as of joy; and here we are close to the idea of the *poète maudit* of the Romantics, and later.

The whole question of "I and My Chimney" has been more recently reviewed by Sealts, in "Melville's Chimney, Reexamined" (*Themes and Directions in American Literature,* ed. R. B. Brown and D. Pizer. Purdue, 1969).

17 The question is: found by whom? The first impulse is to answer that the father-confessor does not find the truth because there is duplicity in the penitent, or simply because it is difficult to explore the self of another. As a matter of fact, much is made by Melville of the difficulty of knowing another. But the great problem is to know one's own nature. The penitent cannot be sure of finding the "truth," however sincere he is.

The Parthenon

This poem is the first of two on the Parthenon, the second being entitled "Nearer Viewed." Like "Art" and "After the Pleasure Party," this has for its theme the relation of art and life. As given here, there is a parallel between this idea and the idea of the relation of "action" and "legend" in such poems as "The March into Virginia" and "Battle of Stone River, Tennessee."

6 There may be an echo here of Landor's "Past Ruined Ilion."

Immolated

The burning of the poems implied here would probably have occurred when Melville left his farm, Arrowhead, and moved back to New York. But in a letter to his brother, Thomas, dated May 25, 1862, he had reported that he had sold his "doggeral" to a trunk maker for lining, at ten cents a pound.

1 In the manuscript "happier prime" had originally been "Tempe prime."

4 Manuscript: "mother" had been "dame."
6 Manuscript: "flowers and light" had been "daisies light."
7 Manuscript: "morning meadows" had been "meads auroral."
15 Manuscript: "Unanimous" had been "Elect of."
16–17 These lines are very Elizabethan in tone, but I have found nothing of which they might be a specific echo. The lines—and in fact the last eight lines of the poem—suggest Ben Jonson's "Ode to Himself" and Marston's "To Everlasting Oblivion." It is not known, however, that Melville knew Marston's poem.

Pontoosuce

The lake Pontoosuc is north of Pittsfield, Massachusetts, in the section where Melville lived from 1850 to 1863. The manuscript shows that Melville's first title was spelled as is the lake. His next title was "The Lake," and his final choice was "Pontoosuce," with the final "e."

The poem has a close relation to the notion of the polarities of life as we find it in *Battle-Pieces,* but the temper is vastly different, acceptance taking the place of tension. In this sense, it resembles "John Marr," "Bridegroom Dick," *Clarel,* and *Billy Budd.*

The poem was unpublished in Melville's lifetime; the manuscript is, in fact, a set of work sheets, not a finished version. The poem first appeared in the collected edition of Melville's works, edited by Raymond Weaver, and published in London by Constable in 1924.

5–6 In the manuscript these lines earlier read:

> Autumnal noon-tide, I look forth
> From dusk arcades upon a sunlit North.

13–15 These lines earlier read:

> While far the faint blue mountains sleep
> In hazed repose of trances deep.

The second line was then revised to the intermediate version:

> Hazed in romance of more than trances deep.

The space between the original versions of lines 14 and 15 is great enough to indicate a stanza break, but it is now occupied by the third version of line 14. At the beginning of line 15 we find a bracket, the sign Melville uses elsewhere to indicate to the printer a new stanza.

30 This line stands in the manuscript as follows:

~~marked felt And Felt au~~

~~saw~~
~~I knew the opulence of autumn's dower~~,
In opulence of autumn's dower

32–34 In the manuscript these lines stand:

~~blest~~
A year ago was such an hour,~~bland hour~~
As this, which but foreruns the blast
Shall sweep these live leaves to the
~~leaves~~
dead ~~ones~~ past.

Presumably Melville, having canceled "bland hour" and then having canceled the revision of "blest" [hour], was persuaded to maintain the four-beat movement of the passage. This would have given him: "A year ago was such an hour, / As this, . . ." But he neglected to remove the comma after "an hour" and retained the comma after "As this," with the consequent confusion. A greater confusion is caused, of course, by the lack of any subject for the word "shall" in the last line—a deficiency that might reasonably be repaired by a relative pronoun with "blast" as the antecedent. But this would give a very awkward construction and a limping meter:

As this which but foreruns the blast
Which shall sweep these live leaves . . .

We may hazard that this awkwardness made him pass on with the intention of coming back later to clear up the mess. Before going on, however, he did puzzle over the next to the last word, "ones," and changed it to "leaves," canceled that, and then, upon reflection, restored that revision, as is indicated by the broken line underscoring the canceled word.

35 In the manuscript "All dies!" is printed as a single line, but the metrical line of four feet is completed by "I stood in reverie long." No stanza break is indicated here, nor after lines 50 and 60.

38 This line is ordinarily printed with "deep arcade," but the manuscript runs as follows:

~~brown~~ brown
I turned me in the ~~deep~~ arcade

I surmise that Melville first struck out *deep* and revised it to *brown;* then, being dissatisfied with *brown* he struck it out and restored *deep,* indicating this by putting broken lines under the canceled word; then he wrote *brown* again and this time did not cancel it. Alas—for this destroys the sense of perspective in the scene.

43 After line 42 there is, in the manuscript, a space, then a new stanza is begun. But Melville cancels the first two lines and one foot of the third. This leaves "All dies! and not alone," which would have completed the metrical line. This, of course, does not begin at the left margin. Some editors print it indented. But it would seem logical that, with the deletion before it, the line should be drawn back to left margin, where began the metrical line to which it had originally belonged.

48–49 These lines do not appear in the manuscript of the poem, but come from an extra sheet. All the printings of the poem up through Howard P. Vincent's *Collected Poems of Herman Melville* (in which there is, in a textual note, a description of the extra sheet) have these lines. The sheet from which they come disappeared, however, at sometime between Vincent's edition (1947) and Hennig Cohen's *Selected Poems of Herman Melville* (1964), which does not give the lines; but it has recently been found, stuck in the manuscript of the rather long poem "To M. de Grandvin." Melville had, in fact, taken a sheet from that manuscript on which to scribble down, on the verso, the new lines—probably seizing, on impulse, the handiest sheet of paper. The lines, in pencil, run as follows:

And truth lo truth, ~~decays~~ it may not las[t]
~~at last~~
And noblest deeds ^ they are undone
Even
~~And~~ truth itself decays, ~~in end~~ and lo,
~~And from its ashes fraud aspires~~

> ~~Fraud aspires rising from~~
> From truth's sad ashes fraud and falsehood grow.

I am not certain about "lo truth" in the first line, which is in handwriting even worse than usual and which seems to have been flung down in such a hurry that the *t* did not even get on "last." I am also uncertain about "rising" in the next to the last line.

55 In the manuscript the line stands as follows:

> Even ~~fade from the starry space~~
> ~~And~~ stars, Chaldeans say, ~~have left their place~~.

This would indicate that "Even" is a definite revision, but that the status of the other and more important revision is uncertain. In general, but not invariably, when Melville wished to restore a cancellation, he underscored the word or phrase with a broken line (as we have seen with the word "leaves" in line 34). It is possible here that Melville was rejecting both readings, with expectation of hitting on a third. But under the present circumstances, with the rejection of the revision, it seems logical to accept, *faute de mieux*, the original reading.

90–91 We cannot be absolutely sure of the space between these two lines. There is a page end in the manuscript after line 90, but the space left at the bottom is not enough to certify beyond the shadow of a doubt the gap. It does, however, seem to be justified.

96 As in line 55, here Melville struggled over a revision:

> ~~wedded~~
> And warmth and chill of ~~mingled~~ life and death.

The phrase "wedded life" is, in fact, slightly disturbing: there is the shadow of the ordinary meaning—like "married life." Even so, it is better than "mingled," and since, after being canceled, it is restored, it apparently represents a final choice.

Jonah's Song

The poem is the hymn Father Mapple conducts in Chapter ix of *Moby Dick*. It is Melville's adaptation of the first part of Psalm 18 in the hymnal of the Reformed Protestant Dutch Church. The first quatrain of the original reads:

Death, and the terrors of the grave
  Spread over me their dismal shade;
While floods of high temptations rose
  And made my sinking soul afraid.

Billy in the Darbies

Darbies are handcuffs. For a general discussion of the poem, see Introduction, pp. 64–71. According to the date on the manuscript, the poem was finished April 19, 1891.

7 A jewel-block is the pulley at the end of the main and fore topsail yards. In the first version of the poem, the old, tough Billy is referred to as a "jewel" for his ability at his calling, and we have a witty pun he makes on his name. But with the gentle young Billy, the temper of the pun is changed.

The wordplay about jewelry in "Billy in the Darbies" may echo, however remotely, the wordplay Melville gives in *White-Jacket* (Ch. LXX) in discussing the barbarity of the Articles of War: ". . . here am I, liable at any time to be run up at the yard-arm, with a necklace, made by no jeweler, round my neck!" It is, in fact, in this long discussion that Melville's first reference to the *Somers* case occurs (Ch. LXXII).

10 In the manuscript this line at one time read:

O 'tis Billy, not the sentence they'll suspend

13 Originally:

On an empty stomach, no, never it would do

16 "To belay" is to coil a running rope around a cleat or pin to make it fast.

22 Originally not Donald, but "a chum." See Introduction, note 29.

30–32 The manuscript of the poem is clearly not a final copy, but only in the last three lines is there a serious difficulty:

    darbies ~~shackles~~
Just ease this ∧ iron at the wrist,
~~Ease it~~, and roll me over fair,
        sleepy
I am drowzy, and the oozy weeds about me twist.

Shackles has been written in as a revision of *iron,* and then canceled. As a second thought, we have *darbies.* Even though *iron* is not canceled, *darbies,* since it appears in the title, would seem to be the logical choice. In the next line, after striking out *Ease it,* Melville does not capitalize *and,* but since there is no replacement of *Ease it* indicated, presumably *and* capitalized would begin the line. I can see no justification for moving this up to become a part of the previous line, as some editors do. Here the matter of rhyme strikes me as decisive. In the last line the choice between *drowzy* and *sleepy* cannot be finally made, but provisionally we may take *sleepy.* The difference here would not substantially affect the discussion of the technical aspects of the passage.

Chronology

1819 Born, August 1, in New York City, son of Allan Melvill, a prosperous importer of good family, and Maria Gansevoort, of the rich and distinguished Gansevoort family of Albany. The *e* was added to the name to indicate kinship with the aristocratic Scottish family of that name.

1830 Move to Albany after failure of father's business. Two years in Albany Academy.

1832 Death of father, mad. Melville in various odd jobs; period in Albany Classical School, and as schoolteacher.

1838 Move to Lansingburgh, N.Y. Melville studies surveying.

1839 First writing published in *Democratic Press and Lansingburgh Advertiser*, "Fragments from a Writing Desk." First voyage, in crew of packet *St. Lawrence*, New York to Liverpool.

1841 Ships as seaman on whaler *Acushnet*, New Bedford to South Seas.

1842 Deserted July 9, in Marquesas Islands, with Richard Greene. Period in the Taipi Valley, with cannibals, and escape on another whaler. At Tahiti among group accused of mutiny.

1843 Enlists in American Navy, at Honolulu.

1844 October, mustered out of Navy.

1846 *Typee* published.

1847 *Omoo* published; also enlarged edition of *Typee*. Marries Elizabeth Shaw, daughter of Chief Justice Lemuel Shaw, of Boston, August 4. Home in New York; literary acquaintances.

1849 Birth of Malcolm. *Mardi* and *Redburn* published.

1850 *White-Jacket* published. Farm "Arrowhead" bought, near Pittsfield, Massachusetts. Beginning of intimacy with Hawthorne.

1851 *Moby Dick* published; relative failure. Birth of Stanwix.

1852 *Pierre; or, The Ambiguities* published; failure.

1853 Elizabeth born. Unsuccessful attempt to get consular appointment.

1855 *Israel Potter* published. Frances born.

1856 *The Piazza Tales* published. Trip to Holy Land, with visit to Hawthorne at Liverpool, where he is consul.

1857 *The Confidence Man* published. Return from abroad. First of three seasons as lecturer.

1860 Voyage for health to San Francisco on clipper *Meteor*, commanded by brother Thomas.

1861 Beginning of Civil War; interest in the war.

1863 Sale of "Arrowhead," and move to New York City.

1866 *Battle-Pieces and Aspects of the War* published; another failure. Becomes Customs Inspector.

1867 Death of Malcolm, possibly suicide. *Clarel* possibly begun.

1876 *Clarel* published, underwritten by his uncle Peter Gansevoort; failure.

1885 Resigns post at Customs House. Probably begins *Billy Budd*; renewed interest in writing.

1886 Death of Stanwix in San Francisco. Period of developing *Billy Budd*.

1888 *John Marr and Other Sailors* published privately, in edition of twenty-five copies.

1891 *Timoleon* published privately, in edition of twenty-five copies. Death, September 28. *Billy Budd* left but not in a final version.

1924 *Billy Budd* published.

Index of Titles and First Lines

A swoon of noon, a trance of tide, 337
About the Shark, phlegmatical one, 318
Admiral of the White, The, 425
After the Pleasure Party, 327
All dripping in tangles green, 317
All feeling hearts must feel for him, 141
America, 145
Armies of the Wilderness, The, 128
Art, 335
As by the wood drifts thistle-down, 223
Ay, man is manly. Here you see, 136

Ball's Bluff, 98
Battle of Stone River, Tennessee, 125
Berg, The, 322
Billy in the Darbies (FROM *Billy Budd*), 349
Bridegroom Dick, 285
But on the third day Christ arose, 268
By chapel bare, with walls sea-beat, 307

Children of my happier prime, 343
College Colonel, The, 139
Come out of the Golden Gate, 316
"Coming Storm, The," 141
Commemorative of a Naval Victory, 152
Concerning Hebrews (*Clarel*, II, xxii), 223
Conflict of Convictions, The, 93
Crossing the Tropics, 321
Crowning a bluff where gleams the lake below, 344

Day passed; and passed a second one, 265
Delay!—Shall flute from forth the Gate, 259
Derwent and Ungar (*Clarel*, IV, xx), 251
Did all the lets and bars appear, 96
Dirge (*Clarel*, IV, xxxi), 264
Donelson, 102
Dupont's Round Fight, 99

Easter (*Clarel*, IV, xxxiii), 268
Epilogue (*Clarel*, IV, xxxv), 272
Estranged in site, 340
Farewell and adieu to you noble hearties, 302
Fear me, virgin whosoever, 327
"Formerly a Slave," 142
Fortitude of the North, The, 147
Full night. The moon has yet to rise, 237

Good of the Chaplain to enter Lone Bay, 349

Haglets, The, 307
Hanging from the beam, 91
Hard pressed by numbers in his strait, 180

He rides at their head, 139
High Desert, The (*Clarel*, III, v), 246
Hostel, The (*Clarel*, I, i), 203
House-top, The, 127
How often in the years that close, 187

I have a feeling for those ships, 100
I saw a ship of martial build, 322
If Luther's day expand to Darwin's year, 272
Immolated, 343
Implacable I, the old implacable Sea, 324
In a Bye-Canal, 337
In a Church of Padua, 339
In chamber low and scored by time, 203
In placid hours well-pleased we dream, 335
In shards the sylvan vases lie, 333
In time and measure perfect moves, 99
In vaulted place where shadows flit, 339
Inscription, 148
Inscription, The (*Clarel*, II, xxxi), 232

Jack Roy, 305
John Marr, 277
Jonah's Song (from *Moby Dick*), 348

Kept up by relays of generations young, 305

Lee in the Capitol, 180
Like snows the camps on Southern hills, 128

Maldive Shark, The, 318
Malvern Hill, 123
Man-of-War Hawk, The, 315
March into Virginia, The, 96
Meditation, A, 187
Misgivings, 92
Monody, 334
Mortmain Reappears (*Clarel*, II, xxxiv), 235

Nathan (*Clarel*, I, xvii), 209
Nathan had sprung from worthy stock, 209
No sleep. The sultriness pervades the air, 127
No trophy this—a Stone unhewn, 151
"Not thou com'st in the still small voice," 251

Obsequies (*Clarel*, II, xxxix), 241
Of Mortmain (*Clarel*, II, iv), 219
Of the Crusaders (*Clarel*, I, iv), 208
Old Counsel, 316
On a Natural Monument, 151
On starry heights, 93
On the Photograph of a Corps Commander, 136
On the Slain Collegians, 143
One noonday, at my window in the town, 98
"Our friend there—he's a little queer," 219

Parthenon, The, from, 340
Passion Week (*Clarel*, IV, xxxii), 265
Pebbles, from, 324
Plain be the phrase, yet apt the verse, 120
Pontoosuce, 344
Portent, The, 91
Proud, O proud in his oaken hall, 425

Ravaged Villa, The, 333
Requiem, A, 150

Sailors there are of gentlest breed, 152
Scout toward Aldie, The, 153
Shiloh, 122
Silence and Solitude may hint, 149
Since as in night's deck-watch
ye show, 282
Skimming lightly, wheeling still, 122
Sodom (*Clarel*, II, xxxvi), 237
Some leading thoroughfares
of man, 270
Stay, Death. Not mine the
Christus-wand, 264
Stone Fleet, The, 100
"Such earnestness! such wear
and tear," 255
Sunning ourselves in October on
a day, 285
Swamp Angel, The, 137

Temeraire, The, 117
The bitter cup, 102
The camel's skull upon the beach, 241
The cavalry-camp lies on
the slope, 153
The gloomy hulls, in armor grim, 117
The ribs and terrors in the whale, 348
The sufferance of her race
is shown, 142
There is a coal-black angel, 137
They take no shame for dark
defeat, 147
To have known him, to have loved
him, 334
To Ned, 319
To them who crossed the flood, 148
Tom Deadlight, 302
Tuft of Kelp, The, 317

Ungar and Rolfe (*Clarel*, IV, xxi), 255
Uninscribed Monument, An, 149
*Utilitarian View of the Monitor's
Fight, A*, 120

Valley of Decision, The (*Clarel*, IV, xxx),
259
Venice, 336
Via Crucis (*Clarel*, IV, xxxiv), 270
Vine and Clarel (*Clarel*, II, xxvii), 228

When, after storms that woodlands
rue, 150
When ocean-clouds over inland
hills, 92
When sighting first the towers
afar, 208
Where is the world we roved,
Ned Bunn? 319
Where silence and the legend
dwell, 246
Where the wings of a sunny Dome
expand, 145
While now at poise the wings of
shade, 235
While now the Pole Star sinks from
sight, 321
While now, to serve the pilgrim
train, 228
While yet Rolfe's foot in stirrup
stood, 232
With Pantheist energy of will, 336
With Tewksbury and Barnet
heath, 125

Ye elms that wave on Malvern Hill, 123
Yon black man-of-war hawk that
wheels in the light, 315
Youth is the time when hearts are
large, 143

General Index

Note: Where a poem is reprinted in its entirety, page numbers are in **BOLD**.

Adams, Brooks, 44, 354
Adams, Charles Francis, 374–375
Adams, Henry, 44, 354, 440
Agar (in *Clarel*), 40
Age of Reason, The (Paine), 388
"Ambitious Guest, The" (Hawthorne), 388
American Renaissance (Matthiessen), 373
"Ancient Mariner, The" (Coleridge), 64
Anderson, Charles, 415–416
Andersonville, 378
Arnold, Matthew, 44, 434
Ash Wednesday (Eliot), 44
"Austerity of Poetry" (Arnold), 434

Baker, Col. Edward D., 35
Bartlett, Col. William Francis, 371
Bartlett, William P., 10
Beauregard, Gen. P. G. T., 354
Bennett, James Gordon, 418
Bezanson, Walter E., 45, 72, 393–394, 401, 403
Billson, Charles James, 78
Billy Budd, Sailor: An Inside Narrative (Hayford and Sealts), 59, 79, 87
"Birthmark, The" (Hawthorne), 61, 390
"Bombardment of Forts Walker and Beauregard, The" (M'Clellan), 358
Booth, Edwin, 372, 373
Bowen, Merlin, 437, 440
Brodtkorb, Paul, Jr., 87
Brooks, Cleanth, ix, 389
Brown, John, 10, 351, 352
Browning, Robert, 362
Bryant, William Cullen, 33
Buchanan, Franklin, 365, 414–415
Buckner, Simon Bolivar, 361
Bulfinch, Charles, 353
Bull Run, Battle of, 354
Burnside, Gen. Ambrose, 376
Byron, Lord, 44

Calvin, John, 367–368, 391
Cannibals All, or Slaves without Masters (Fitzhugh), 406
Cantos, The (Pound), 44
Celio (in *Clarel*), 37, 38
Cenci, Beatrice, 393, 394
Chancellorsville, Battle of, 368, 369
Chase, Jack, 79, 423–424
Chase, Richard, 432–434
Chatterton, Thomas, 64
Childe Harold (Byron), 44
"Chiefly About War Matters" (Hawthorne), 354, 363, 416
Claggart (in *Billy Budd*), 59, 62, 84
Cohen, Hennig, 66, 68, 69, 377, 448
Coleridge, Samuel Taylor, 64, 375
"Come up from the Fields, Father" (Whitman), 27
Congress (ship), 414–415

Conrad, Joseph, 74, 405–406
"Convergence of the Twain, The" (Hardy), 53
Cooper, James Fenimore, 83, 84–85, 418
Crawford, Thomas, 353
Crews, Frederick C., 75
Crisson, Walter, 387
Cumberland (ship), 73, 413–416

Das Leben Jesu (Neander), 392
Decatur, Stephen, 412
"Definitive *Billy Budd*, The: 'But aren't it all sham?'" (Brodtkorb), 87
Democratic Vistas (Whitman), 29, 44
Derwent (in *Clarel*), 37, 40, 405, 406
Dibdin, Charles, 88
Dickson, David, 387
Digressions (Vedder), 374
Don Hannibal (in *Clarel*), 404–405
"Dover Beach" (Arnold), 44
Draft riots of 1863, 367
Drayton, Percival, 358
Drayton, Gen. Thomas F., 358
Druses, 399–400
Dupont, Samuel F., 357
Dynasts, The (Hardy), 44, 362

Eliot, T. S., 36, 44, 389
Ellis, Havelock, 78
Erskine, Albert, x
Ethics (Spinoza), 392

Fairfax, Sir William George, 72
Fairfax, Thomas, 369
Farragut, David Glasgow, 416–417
Feidelson, Charles, ix, 73, 74
Fitzhugh, George, 406
Fort Donelson, 361
Four Quartets (Eliot), 44
"Frigate Cumberland, The" (Beach), 415
"From Paumanok Starting I Fly Like a Bird" (Whitman), 28

Gallup, Donald, x
Gansevoort, Guert, 58–59, 62, 82–83, 412, 417, 419, 420–421
Gansevoort, Peter, 47, 78
"Genesis of *Billy Budd*, The" (Anderson), 72
Genteel Tradition at Bay, The (Santayana), 440
Gibbon, Edward, 386, 387
Gifford, Robert Swain, 372
Glaucon (in *Clarel*), 37
Gnostics, 404
"Good and Bad Government" (Vedder), 373
Gordon, Gen. John B., 370
Grant, Ulysses S., 10, 361, 368, 380
Greene, Richard Tobias, 429
Greene, Robert, 81

Hamilton, Gail, 82
Hancock, Gen. Winfield Scott, 369–370
Hardy, Thomas, 53, 79, 362, 363
Hawthorne, Nathaniel, 5, 9, 61, 75, 78, 351, 354, 363, 373, 388, 390, 393–395, 404, 416, 438–439
"Hawthorne's Unfinished Work" (Lamont), 75
Hayford, Harrison, 59, 79, 87
Heine, Heinrich, 391
Herman Melville (Chase), 432–434

Herman Melville: A Study of His Life and Vision (Mumford), 430–432
Herman Melville, marin, métaphysicien, et poète (Simon), 72
Herrick, Robert, 377
History of the American Sailing Navy (Chapelle), 413
Hollander, John, x
Holmes, Oliver Wendell, 358, 359, 444
Holy Land, 5–6, 35–36, 43–44
Horsford, Howard C., 72
Houghton Library (Harvard), viii, x, 78
Howard, Leon, 73
Howells, William Dean, 407
Huckleberry Finn (Twain), 85
Hull, Isaac, 412
Hume, David, 386, 388

In Memoriam (Tennyson), 44
Isabel (in *Pierre*), 75

Jack Genteel (in "Bridegroom Dick"), 424
Jackson, Jane, 373, 374
Jackson, Thomas J. "Stonewall," 19, 351, 354, 368, 369
James, William, 20, 30, 32, 44, 354
Jarrell, Randall, vii
Johnston, Albert Sydney, 365
Johnston, Joseph E., 354
Jones, Catesby ap Roger, 412
Jones, Thomas ap Catesby, 412
Jonson, Ben, 49, 430, 446

Keats, John, 64, 356
Kipling, Rudyard, 411
"Kubla Khan" (Coleridge), 375

"La Belle Dame Sans Merci" (Keats), 64
Lamont, John H., 75
Landor, Walter Savage, 445
Lanier, Sidney, 31
Leaves of Grass (Whitman), 47
Lee, Francis Lightfoot, 383
Lee, Henry, 383
Lee, Richard Henry, 383–384
Lee, Robert E., 19, 351, 368, 374–375, 383–384
Leecock, R. W., 419
Lewis, R. W. B., ix
Libby Prison (Richmond), 372
Lincoln, Abraham, 32, 351, 359
Long Encounter, The (Bowen), 437, 440
"Long, Too Long, America" (Whitman), 28
Longfellow, Henry Wadsworth, 31, 74
Lord Jim (Conrad), 74, 405
Lot, 397
Lowell, Col. Charles Russell, 379
Lowell, James Russell, 31, 74, 354
Lucy (in *Pierre*), 75
"Lycidas" (Milton), 377, 388, 438
Machiavelli, 35
Mackenzie, Capt. Alexander Slidell, 58, 61, 62, 82–83, 417–420
"Man of Adamant, The" (Hawthorne), 404
Manassas, Battles of, 354, 376
Marble Faun, The (Hawthorne), 394
Margoth (in *Clarel*), 37, 390–391, 398
Marston, John, 49, 446
Marvell, Andrew, 8, 72, 437
Marx, Leo, 75
Masque of Queenes (Jonson), 430
Matthiessen, F. O., 373
McClellan, Gen. George B., 366
McDowell, Gen. Irvin, 354

M'Clellan, Isaac, 358
"Meditation of Columbia, The" (Lanier), 31
Melville, Elizabeth ("Bessie") (daughter), 81, 82
Melville, Elizabeth (Shaw) (wife), 6, 10, 46–47, 425
Melville, Frances ("Fanny") (daughter), 81, 82
MELVILLE, HERMAN (1819–1891)
Life: chronology, 452–455; *Moby Dick* appears, 3; lectures for three seasons, 3–4; travels to Holy Land, 5–6, 35–36; travels to San Francisco on *Meteor*, 6, 394, 397, 425; burns poems, 78–79, 445; inspector at Customs House, 33–34; *Battle-Pieces* published, 8; Son Malcolm dies, 34, 79; *Clarel* published, 46–47; retires from Customs House, 48; Son Stanwix dies, 60, 79–82; *John Marr* published, 48; *Timoleon* published, 48; dies, 71
Poetry: "Admiral of the White, The," *425–427* (*see also* "The Haglets"); "After the Pleasure Party," ix, **327–332**, 403, 430–437, 438, 442, 445; "America," 31, 145–146, 375–376, 382; "Apparition, The," 23; "Armies of the Wilderness, The," 16–17, 30, **128–135**, 368–369, 376; "Art," **335**, 434, 439, 441, 445; "Ball's Bluff," **98**, 355–357, 372; "Battle for the Bay, The," 365, 417; "Battle of Stone River, Tennessee," 21–22, 48, **125–126**, 359, 362, 366–367, 445; *Battle-Pieces and Aspects of the War*, vii–ix, 8–35, 48, 69, 72–74, 76, 78, 87, 91–199; "Berg, The," 15, 52–54, 79, **322–323**, 429–430; "Billy in the Darbies," ix, 55–56, 58, 63, 64–71, 85–88, **349–350**, 411, 422, 450–451 (*see also* Novels and Tales: *Billy Budd*); "Bridegroom Dick," 50–51, 55, 59, 61, 83, **285–301**, 365, 411–422, 424, 446; "Chattanooga," 73;
Clarel, 6, 35–47, 69, 72–78, 87–88, 201–273, 385–410, 440, 446; "Concerning Hebrews" (II, xxii), **223–228**, 390–392; "Derwent and Ungar" (IV, xx), **251–254**, 353, 404–407; "Dirge" (IV, xxxi), **264–265**, 409; "Easter" (IV, xxxiii), **268–270**, 410; "Epilogue" (IV, xxxv), 41–42, 44, 71, 76, **272–273**; "High Desert, The" (III, v), **246–250**, 353, 403–404; "Hostel, The" (I, i), **203–208**, 385–386; "Inscription, The" (II, xxxi), **232–235**, 396–398; "Mortmain Reappears" (II, xxxiv), **235–237**, 398–400; "Nathan" (I, xvii), **209–218**, 387–388; "Obsequies" (II, xxxix), **241–245**, 402–403; "Of Mortmain" (II, iv), **219–223**, 353, 389–390; "Of the Crusaders" (I, iv), **208–209**, 386–387; "Passion Week" (IV, xxxii), **265–268**, 409; "Sodom" (II, xxxvi), **237–241**, 400–401; "Ungar and Rolfe" (IV, xxi), **255–259**, 353, 407–408; "Valley of Decision, The" (IV, xxx), **259–264**, 408–409; "Via Crucis" (IV, xxxiv), 40, **270–272**, 410;

Poetry (*continued*)
"Vine and Clarel" (II, xxvii), **228–232**, 392–396, 433; "College Colonel, The," 10, 22–23, 30, 55, **139–140**, 371–372, 376; " 'Coming Storm, The,' " 23, **141**, 372–373; "Commemorative of a Naval Victory," 23, 55, **152**, 353, 378, 381, 382; "Conflict of Convictions, The," 18, 30, 31, 34, **93–95**, 352–354, 359, 371, 375, 376, 381, 389, 401, 408; "Crossing the Tropics," **321**, 429; "Cumberland, The," 73, 364, 422; "Donelson," 19, **102–116**, 361–362; "Dupont's Round Fight," **99**, 353, 357–360; "Fall of Richmond, The," 353, 358; " 'Formerly a Slave,' " **142**, 373–374; "Fortitude of the North, The," 74, **147**, 376; "Fruit of Travel Long Ago," 6, 7, 48; "Gettysburg," 73; "Great Pyramid, The," 444; "Haglets, The," 53, 54, 70, 71, 88, **307–314**, 424–428; "House-top, The," 29–30, **127**, 354, 367–368, 381, 399, 407; "Immolated," 49, **343**, 445–446; "In a Bye-Canal," 7–8, 13, 76, **337–338**, 378, 390, 434, 441–442; "In a Church of Padua," 7, **339**, 439, 443–445; "In the Turret," 364, 422; "Inscription," **148**, 376; "Jack Roy," 55, **305–306**, 422, 423–424; "John Marr," 51–52, 55, **282–284**, 387, 410–411, 446; *John Marr and Other Sailors with Some Sea-Pieces*, 48–49, 55, 275–324, 410–424; "Jonah's Song," 7, **348**, 449–450 (*see also* Novels and Tales: *Moby Dick*); "Lee in the Capitol," **180–186**, 382–384; "Like the Fish," 6; "Magnanimity Baffled," 20; "Maldive Shark, The," 52, **316**, 378, 427, 428–429; "Malvern Hill," 15–16, 20, **123–124**, 366, 377; "Man-of-War Hawk, The," 52, 315, 428; "March Into Virginia, The," 12–15, 55, 73, 74, **96–97**, 354–355, 366, 372, 382, 436; "March to the Sea, The," 73; "Meditation, A," 20, 30, 73, **187–189**, 384–385; "Misgivings," 18, **92**, 353, 389; "Monody," 48, **334**, 393, 395, 438–439; "Nearer Viewed," 445; "Old Counsel of the Young Master of a Wrecked California Clipper," **4**, 53, **316**; "On a Natural Monument," 21, **151**, 353, 378; "On the Photograph of a Corps Commander," 19, **136**, 369–370, 376; "On the Slain Collegians," 19, 27, 30, **143–144**, 362, 374–375; "Parthenon, The," 7, 340, 445; "Pebbles," 53, 324, 430; "Philip," 73 (*see also* "Sheridan at Cedar Creek"); "Pontoosuce," 49–50, 70–71, 79, **344–347**, 424, 446–449; "Portent, The," **91**, 351–352; "Ravaged Villa, The," **333**, 434, 437–438; "Requiem, A," **150**, 377; "Running the Batteries," 17; "Scout toward Aldie, The," 10, **153–179**, 369, 378–382; "Sheridan at Cedar Creek," 20, 33, 73; "Shiloh," 14, 17, **122**, 365–366, 377, 436; "Stone Fleet, The," 18,

Poetry (*continued*)
53, **100–101**, 360–361, 388; "Swamp Angel, The," 19, 30, 73, **137–138**, 362, 370–371; "Temeraire, The," 17, **117–119**, 362–364, 422; *Timoleon, Etc.*, 6, 48–49, 325–340; "To Ned," **317–320**, 429; "Tom Deadlight," 51, 55, **302–304**, 422–423; "Tuft of Kelp, The," 52, 53, **317**; *Uncollected Poems*, 341–350; "Uninscribed Monument, An," 21, 80, **149**, 353, 376, 377; "Utilitarian View of the Monitor's Fight, A," 17–18, **120–121**, 364–365, 377, 407, 422; "Venice," 69, **336**, 360, 391, 434, 439–441; *Weeds and Wildings Chiefly: with a Rose or Two*, 49;

Novels and Tales: "Bartleby the Scrivener," 3, 25, 75, 79; "Bell Tower, The," 78; "Benito Cereno," 3; *Billy Budd, Sailor*, 4, 41, 56–63, 72, 79–88, 411, 421, 440, 446 (*see also* Poetry: "Billy in the Darbies"); *Confidence Man, The*, 3, 78, 79, 387; "Encantadas, The," 3, 36; "I and My Chimney," 444–445; *Israel Potter*, 3; "Lightning Rod Man, The," 78; *Mardi*, 6, 443; *Moby Dick*, 3, 34, 56, 395, 428, 440, 443 (*see also* Poetry: "Jonah's Song"); *Pierre; or, The Ambiguities*, 3, 24–25, 75–77, 394, 395, 439, 440, 443, 444–445; *Redburn*, 33–34; *White-Jacket*, 4, 59, 82–83, 368, 411, 415–416, 421, 423–424, 450

Other Writings: *Journal of a Visit to Europe and the Levant*, 72, 387, 394; *Journal up the Straits*, 363, 424; "Roman Statuary," 5; Review of Hawthorne's *Mosses from an Old Manse*, 395, 438; Supplement to *Battle-Pieces*, 32, **191–199**, 366, 382; "Traveling, Its Pleasures, Pains, and Profits," 5; *Typee*, 429

Melville, Malcolm (son), 34, 79, 81–82
Melville, Stanwix (son), 60, 79–80, 81, 83–84
Melville, Thomas (brother), 6
"Melville's Chimney Reexamined" (Sealts), 445
"Melville's Parable of the Walls" (Marx), 75
Melville's Quarrel with God (Thompson), 85–86
Mendelssohn, Moses, 391–392
Merrimac (ship), 364
Michael (saint), 371
Milton, John, 352, 377, 388, 438
Modern Poetry and the Tradition (Brooks), 389
Monitor (ship), 363
Monitor and the Merrimac, The (Ramsay), 413
Morris, Lt. George U., 414
Mortmain (in *Clarel*), 37, 45, 75, 389, 390, 398
Mosby, John S., 378–381
Mosby's War Reminiscences and Stuart's Cavalry Campaigns (Mosby), 380
Mosses from an Old Manse (Hawthorne), 373, 395, 438
Mozart, W. A., 441
Mumford, Lewis, 430–434

"Murder of Philip Spencer, The" (Hamilton), 82
Murray, Henry Alexander, x, 24–25, 75, 76
"Mutiny on the Somers" (Smith), 82

Nathan (in *Clarel*), 74, 387
Nathan the Wise (Lessing), 391–392
Neander, Johann August Wilhelm, 392
Nehemiah (in *Clarel*), 37, 397, 402
New York Evening Post, 33
Nore mutiny (in *Billy Budd*), 83–84

Ocean Tragedy, An (Russell), 411
"Ode: To Himself" (Jonson), 49, 446
"Ode to a Nightingale" (Keats), 356
"On Board the *Cumberland*" (Boker), 415
Our Old Home (Hawthorne), 438
"Over the Carnage Rose a Prophetic Voice" (Whitman), 28

Paine, Thomas, 84, 388
Paradise Lost (Milton), 352
Pasha, Ibrahim, 404
Passages from the French and Italian Notebooks (Hawthorne), 394
Patriotic Gore (Wilson), vii, 43–44, 380–381
Perry, Oliver Hazard, 412
Petersburg, siege of, 372
Pioneers, The (Cooper), 84–85
Plato, 437
Plinlimmon (in *Pierre*), 395
"Poetry of Barbarism, The" (Santayana), 28
Pope, Gen. John, 383
Porter, Capt. David, 417
Porter, David Dixon, 412
Pound, Ezra, 44
"Pragmatism and Religion" (James), 20
Prince (Machiavelli), 35

Radford, William, 414
"Rat-Hole Squadron, The" (Strong), 360
Rebellion Record (Moore, ed.), ix, 10, 73, 355, 357, 358, 360, 361, 370, 384, 415
"Reply to Herman Melville's *White-Jacket* by Rear Admiral Thomas O. Selfridge, Sr.," 415–416
Rolfe (in *Clarel*), 36, 37, 39, 40, 41, 45, 395–396, 407
Rothenberg, Dr. Albert, x
Russell, William Clark, 410–411
Ruth (in *Clarel*), 37, 38, 39, 40, 43, 74
Ryan, Robert, ix

Sanborn, F. B., 33
Santayana, George, 28, 30, 440
Scott, Winfield, 412
"Scholar Gipsy, The" (Arnold), 44
Sealts, Merton M., Jr., ix, 59, 79, 87, 444–445
Sedwick, William Ellery, 34
Selected Poems of Herman Melville (Cohen, ed.), 448
Selfridge, Thomas O., Jr., 413
Selfridge, Thomas O., Sr., 415–416
Shakespeare, William, 352, 373, 408
Shaw, Robert Gould, 30
Siloam, Pool of, 385, 386
Simon, Jean, 72
Sinai and Palestine in Connection with Their History (Stanley), 403
Sins of the Fathers, The (Crews), 75

Smith, Lt. H. D., 82
Smith, William, 414–415
Snow-Bound (Whittier), 74
"Soldier's Faith, The" (Holmes), 359
"Some Lines from Whitman" (Jarrell), vii
Somers (brig) mutiny, 58–59, 63, 82–83, 417–421
"Song of Myself" (Whitman), 26
"Song of the Banner at Daybreak" (Whitman), 28
"Southern Critique of the Gilded Age, A" (Woodward), 406
Spencer, Philip, 58, 61, 62, 82, 417–418
Spinoza, Benedict de, 392
Stanley, Arthur Penrhyn, 403
Strong, P. Remsen, 360
Stuart, J. E. B., 351
Stuart's Cavalry in the Gettysburg Campaign (Mosby), 380
Sumner, Sen. Charles, 10
"Swamp Angel, The" (T. N. J.), 370
Symposium (Plato), 437

Tate, Allen, vii, x
Thompson, Lawrence, 85
Thornton, Dr. William, 353
Thorp, Willard, ix
"To His Coy Mistress" (Marvell), 8, 437
"To [Everlasting] Oblivion" (Marston), 49, 446
Tolstoy, Leo, 407
"Tom Bowling" (Dibdin), 88
Tom Tight (in "Bridegroom Dick"), 59, 417, 421
Trying Out of Moby Dick, The (Vincent), 373
Turner, J. M. W., 363

Ungar (in *Clarel*), 37, 404–405, 406
"Upon Appleton House" (Marvell), 72
Urania (in "After the Pleasure Party"), 431–434, 435–436

Veblen, Thorstein, 45
Vedder, Elihu, 373–374
Vere (in *Billy Budd*), 59, 60, 72, 82, 83, 84–85
Vicksburg, Battle of, 384
Vincent, Howard P., 373, 448
Vine (in *Clarel*), 37, 39, 45, 392–396, 399, 409, 439
Virginia (ship), 363, 365, 413–415
Voltaire, 386

Walter, Thomas Ustick, 353
Wars of the Roses, 359, 367
Washington, George, 383–384
Waste Land, The (Eliot), 36, 44, 389
Weaver, Raymond, 446
Wellek, René, x
What to Do? (Tolstoy), 407
Whitman, Walt, 25–30
Whittier, John Greenleaf, 74, 82, 351
Wilderness, Battle of the, 368
Willey's Slide, 388, 403
Wilson, Edmund, vii, 45, 380–381
Woodward, C. Vann, 406
Wormwood, 400
Wreck of the Grosvenor, The (Russell), 411

Robert Penn Warren

was born in Guthrie, Kentucky, in 1905. After graduating *summa cum laude* from Vanderbilt University (1925), he received a master's degree from the University of California (1927) and did graduate work at Yale University (1927–28) and at Oxford as a Rhodes Scholar (B. Litt., 1930).

In a career spanning six decades, Warren published many books, including ten novels, sixteen volumes of poetry, and a volume of short stories; also a play, two collections of critical essays, three historical essays, a biography of John Brown, studies of Dreiser, Melville, and Whittier, and two essays in race relations in America. During this entire period, Warren also had an active career as a professor of English.

All the King's Men (1946) was awarded the Pulitzer Prize for Fiction. The Shelley Memorial Award recognized Mr. Warren's early poems. *Promises* (1957) won the Pulitzer Prize for Poetry, the Edna St. Vincent Millay Prize of the Poetry Society of America, and the National Book Award. In 1944–45 Warren was the second occupant of the Chair of Poetry at the Library of Congress. In 1952 he was elected to the American Philosophical Society, in 1959 to the American Academy of Arts and Letters, and in 1975 to the American Academy of Arts and Sciences. In 1967 he received the Bollingen Prize in Poetry for *Selected Poems: New and Old 1923–1966*, and in 1970 the National Medal for Literature and the Van Wyck Brooks Award for the book-length poem *Audubon: A Vision*. In 1974 he was chosen by the National Endowment for the Humanities to deliver the third annual Jefferson Lecture in the Humanities. In 1975 he received the Emerson-Thoreau Award of the American Academy of Arts and Sciences. In 1976 he received the Copernicus Award from the Academy of American Poets, in recognition of his career but with special notice of *Or Else—Poem/Poems 1968–1974*. In 1977 he received the Harriet Monroe Prize for Poetry and the Wilma and Roswell Messing Jr. Award. In 1979, for *Now and Then*, a book of new poems, he received his third Pulitzer Prize. In 1980 he received the Award of the Connecticut Arts Council, the Presidential Medal of Freedom, the Common Wealth Award for Literature, and the Hubbell Memorial Award (The Modern Language Association). In 1981 he was a recipient of a MacArthur Fellowship. In 1986 he was designated as this country's first official Poet Laureate.

For most of his adult life, Robert Penn Warren lived in Connecticut and summered in Vermont. He was married to Eleanor Clark (the author of *Rome and a Villa*, *The Oysters of Locmariaquer*, and other books), with whom he had two children, Gabriel and Rosanna. He died in 1989.